Learning DOS

Learning DOS

Dan Derrick

SAMS
A Division of Macmillan Computer Publishing
11711 North College, Carmel, Indiana 46032 USA

FIRST EDITION
FIRST PRINTING—1991

International Standard Book Number: 0-672-30042-7
Library of Congress Catalog Card Number: 91-62812

Publisher: Richard K. Swadley
Publishing Manager: Joseph Wikert
Development Editor: Ella Davis
Managing Editor: Neweleen Trebnik
Production Editors: Virginia Noble and Rebecca Whitney
Editorial Assistant: San Dee Phillips
Technical Reviewer: Rob Caserotti
Book Design: Scott Cook and Michele Laseau
Cover Design: Macmillan Computer Publishing
Index: Jeanne Clark
Production: Sandy Grieshop, Phil Kitchel, Sarah Leatherman, Laurie Lee, Anne Owen, Howard Peirce, Johnna VanHoose, and Christine Young

---

Composed in Garamond and Macmillan Digital by Macmillan Computer Publishing
Printed in the United States of America

Screen reproductions in this book were created by means of the program Collage Plus from Inner Media, Inc., Hollis, NH.

Dedicated to my family — Cathy, T.J., and Rachael

Contents

Part III Guide to Using the Disk, 405

Acknowledgments

The creation of a book is a wondrous thing. It starts with one idea and ends with hundreds of pages of ideas. The author was just the beginning of the process. After these ideas were committed to disk files, the book was developed by Ella Davis, edited by Ginny Noble, and tech-edited by Rob Caserotti. Thank you all for enhancing and smoothing my rough start.

But even before the material entered the rapids of editing, friends read and commented on those ideas. They were "beta" readers. They offered suggestions on the first pass and even complained about my neglecting to spell-check the pages. Special thanks go to Jan Strohl, Jo Spangler, and my father, Jim Derrick

Many software tools were used to help create this book. For their contributions, thanks to Susan Wilson at Corel, Patricia Parker at ZSoft, Christy Gersich at Microsoft, Dee Dee Walsh at ButtonWare, Nan Borreson at Borland, and Gloria Pfeif at Fox Software.

And, as always, a special thanks goes to my wife, Cathy, and children, T.J. and Rachael. They provided the encouragement and support for this book—my first as a full-time author.

D

Trademarks

All terms mentioned in this book that are known to be trademarks or service marks are listed below. In addition, terms suspected of being trademarks or service marks have been appropriately capitalized. SAMS cannot attest to the accuracy of this information. Use of a term in this book should not be regarded as affecting the validity of any trademark or service mark.

Apple and Macintosh are registered trademarks of Apple Computer, Inc.

Commodore 64 is a registered trademark of Commodore Electronics Limited.

CompuServe Information Services, dBASE, and MultiMate are registered trademarks of Ashton-Tate Corporation.

Delphi is a trademark of General Videotext Corporation.

DR-DOS is a trademark of Digital Research, Inc.

Epson is a registered trademark of Epson America, Inc.

Fastback Plus is a registered trademark of Fifth Generation Systems, Inc.

FoxPro is a trademark of Fox Software, Inc.

GEnie is a trademark of General Electric Company.

HP is a registered trademark of Hewlett-Packard Co. LaserJet is a trademark of Hewlett-Packard Co.

IBM, PC XT, and PS/2 Models 25 and 30 are registered trademarks of International Business Machines Corporation. OS/2 and PS/2 are trademarks of International Business Machines Corporation.

Intel is a registered trademark of Intel Corporation.

Lotus, 1-2-3, and VisiCalc are registered trademarks of Lotus Development Corporation.

Mace Utilities is a trademark of Paul Mace Software.

Microsoft, MS-DOS, Microsoft QuickBASIC, and Microsoft Excel are registered trademarks of Microsoft Corporation. Windows is a trademark of Microsoft Corporation.

Norton Utilities is a trademark of Symantec Corporation.

PC-File is a trademark of ButtonWare, Inc.

PC Paintbrush is a registered trademark of ZSoft Corporation.

PC Tools is a trademark of Central Point Software.

ProComm Plus is a registered trademark of Datastorm Technologies.

Quattro is a registered trademark of Borland International, Inc.

Rolodex is a registered trademark of Rolodex Corporation.

Spinrite II is a trademark of Gibson Research Corporation.

UNIX is a registered trademark of AT&T.

Introduction

The personal computer is a powerful tool for information management. With that power comes complexity. This book is designed to help you use your computer's power and flexibility as quickly and efficiently as possible. The book will help you use the Disk Operating System (DOS), which will, in turn, help you use your computer as an information management tool.

Notice that most of the pages look like those of a dictionary or an encyclopedia. Topics are organized in alphabetical order, and each topic discussion presents the most helpful information first. These topics include the most useful DOS commands and programs as well as essential concepts about DOS. They are selected for the user who

- just wants to get computerized tasks done as quickly as possible,
- does not feel the urge to read a computer book from cover to cover to become reasonably proficient,
- has already used the computer to write letters or create spreadsheets or make lists,
- runs into problems and error messages and does not know what to do, or
- is, in short, a reluctant DOS user.

This book focuses on the problems frequently encountered by DOS users. Although each DOS command is intended to accomplish a specific task, each command also represents many ways to make a mistake. Most problems can be solved in one of several ways. It is not the successful use of DOS that causes frustration, but the mistakes made in finding the solution. So, above all, this book is designed to help you solve the problems frequently encountered when you use your DOS computer.

Who Needs This Book?

Millions of people use DOS every day. In many cases, they don't even realize that DOS is necessary to accomplish their tasks, whether creating a report or calculating the bottom line. Most people just want to get one task done and move on to the next. All the while, DOS runs the software and hardware needed to accomplish those tasks.

Learning DOS is not the starting place for first-time computer users. The book may be helpful for someone first trying to get a computer to work. It certainly provides a reference for terms and problems that occur with that process. But it really is geared toward someone who has been using a computer for at least a few weeks.

Getting accustomed to your computer is important. Learning DOS first is not the way to do that. Once a software package is on your machine, learn to use it first. Learn how to enter and print a letter. Or learn how to add numbers in a spreadsheet program. Learn to accomplish the main task for which you purchased the computer. Only then are you ready for DOS.

The person most likely to benefit from this book

- uses a computer system with a hard disk,
- has used the computer successfully for at least one task,
- may have had minimal training on the computer and DOS,
- may have few resources for help, and
- wants to learn enough DOS to get the job done.

With the exception of a few computer power users who can speak in hexadecimal, anyone who uses a DOS computer can benefit from *Learning DOS*.

A Quick Tour

This book is divided into three parts. Part I, "Orientation," provides an orientation to all the material covered. Because the organization of *Learning DOS* is different from that of most books, Part I also suggests several ways in which you can use the book. Read Part I to learn best how to use the rest of the book.

Part II, "Topic Reference," contains an alphabetical list of 100 DOS topics and dozens of cross-references for these topics. The organization of the topics is explained in Part I. Finally, Part III, "Guide to Using the Disk," provides installation instructions for the disk included with this book, as well as information about the disk's contents.

The few minutes you spend in Part I will pay off every time you use Part II for learning and reference. If you have already used DOS and just want to improve your DOS skills, you will be especially interested in the Learning Guide program provided on the accompanying disk. That program helps you zoom in on the topics you should know.

Part I

Orientation

Part I

Orientation

Every sentence of this book is written to help you learn how to solve problems with DOS. The entire book, as well as the accompanying program disk, is structured to save you time in this effort. This orientation (Part I), like each topic in Part II, is presented with the most critical information first. For example, understanding type conventions (what the different type styles mean) is extremely important when you use this book. How the book is structured is also helpful but not quite as important. The other subjects presented here are not as important as the type conventions and book structure.

Each of the 100 topics, as well as this orientation, is presented with this "top-down" method. When you have enough information on a topic to satisfy yourself, you can move to another topic or return to solving the problem at hand.

Type Conventions Used in This Book

The variety of type styles presented in computer books can be confusing. *Learning DOS* contains just one style to signify what you type and a second style to show the computer's response. Note the following conventions used in this book:

- The keys you are to type are in **`bold monospace text`**. If a sentence states, "When you type **`FB`**, the system responds in one of several ways," the letters **`FB`** are exactly what you are to type to get the response. Because you will always press the Enter key after any DOS command, that action is assumed as the end of the instruction. Reminders are provided from time to time.

- The response from the computer is in `monospace text`. In some cases, this screen output (the characters that appear on the computer screen) will be reproduced in a figure. In other cases, the response from the computer will be provided in a line or two of monospace text.

- In the topic exercises, special keys on the keyboard appear in bold monospace and are designated with angle brackets. The Enter (or Return) key is shown as **<Enter>**. The Backspace key, which moves the cursor back one character and removes that character, appears as **<Backspace>**. And the F6 function key is shown as **<F6>**.

  In regular text, the names of special keys are just shown as the Enter key, the Backspace key, the F6 key, and so on. Occasionally you may be instructed to press a special key after typing a DOS command or other characters. The name of the key you are to press is in bold monospace and angle brackets. For example, the sentence "Now type **BATCH <Enter>** at the system response" instructsyou to type the letters B A T C H and then press the Enter key. All DOS commands are shown in uppercase in this book, but you can type these commands in either upper- or lowercase.

- In some instances, the way you press the keys makes a difference. A *key sequence* will be the rule more often than not. You just press and release the keys in the order they appear. In a few instances, you are to press two or three keys in *combination*. In other words, you are to press and hold down the first key while you press the second key. Or, in the case of three keys, you are to press and hold down the first two keys while you then press the third key.

  In the topic exercises, the special keys you are to press in combination appear in angle brackets and with no space between the names of the keys. Example are **<Ctrl><Alt><Del>** and **<Ctrl>C**. In regular text, however, this special way to type the keys is shown with a hyphen (-) between the key names. For instance, "pressing Ctrl-C together will stop some programs from running." Remember not to press the hyphen key. In most cases, if you just try to press the keys in sequence (in this example, press and release the Ctrl key and then press the C key), nothing will happen. More information about key sequences and combinations is included in the topic Keyboard (39).

Disk Contents

The disk included with this book is a 360K 5 1/4-inch floppy. It contains a number of different programs and exercise material, some requiring the book and others not. One of the first tasks you should do with the accompanying disk is to make a copy of it or install the programs on your hard disk. Although the programs on the disk can be used as they are, making a copy of the disk first is an excellent idea. The last page in this book (facing the inside back cover with the disk attached) provides a quick outline of that process. Part III, "Guide to Using the Disk," contains detailed information about the contents of the accompanying disk and how to make a backup copy.

Because the book contains so much material, an overview may help you decide where to start. The disk contains one program, the Learning Guide, which you'll want to use immediately for this purpose. You can use the utilities after reading about them in this book. And you'll use the practice area on the disk only if you want to complete some of the exercises in this book.

The Learning Guide

The Learning Guide, a computer program written specifically for this book, provides an assessment of your current DOS skills and suggests topics you might want to cover in the book. The program asks a series of multiple-choice questions about using DOS and how you use your computer.

Some of the questions have no right or wrong answers—for example, "How long have you been using your computer?" Others do, such as "The DOS prompt looks like which of the following?" The good part is that there is no grade, no ranking of your current skill level. No one likes to remember getting a C– on a science test. The answers are just recorded for the report that is provided.

The report becomes your guide to learning more about DOS. If you are interested, you can tackle the topics mentioned in the report so that you can advance your DOS skills. If you are satisfied with the results, you may not want to use the Learning Guide program again. However, you may want to read the topics, do the exercises, and return to the Learning Guide to try again. Because the program has recorded your answers from the last time, it will ask only the questions you missed and then move on to new topics. From that new report, you'll get a list of the next few topics to cover.

Part III contains a thorough description of the Learning Guide program. Keep in mind that the Learning Guide is a tool like any other computer program. You do not need to use this program to get value from *Learning DOS*. But if you want guidance about learning DOS, the program is available for you to use.

Utility Programs

Also available on the disk are several DOS utility programs. Each of these programs has been provided because it performs a task or solves a problem that cannot be easily solved with standard DOS programs. The utilities were selected because they are helpful. In some cases, the author of the program provided a version of it specifically for the disk that accompanies this book. In other cases, the program has been generally available, author unknown.

Hundreds, if not thousands, of these utility programs are available to DOS users. But, like diamonds in a large mine, the best of the best are hard to locate. The utilities included on the disk are some of the best and most useful. Detailed instructions for these programs are provided. As is true for the Learning Guide program, you do not need to use the utility programs in order to use this book. But if you spend a few moments reading Part III, you'll soon find at least a couple of programs that will make you wonder how you ever did without them.

Exercise Material

Many of the topic areas in this book contain exercises to help you learn more about the commands. The sample files and subdirectories for these exercises are on the accompanying disk. Instructions such as "Type **CD\WORDPROC <Enter>**" lead you directly through the examples.

Using This Book

Isn't it enough that you have to read instructions to use your computer? Why should you read a section titled "Using This Book"? Read it and find out all the different ways in which this book can help you use your computer.

Solving Problems

Because the main part of this book is an alphabetical reference, you can just turn to the closest word or phrase that describes your current problem. If that entry does not have the information, it will "point" to, or cross-reference, a topic. When you have found the relevant topic, the most important information is provided first in the topic's discussion. You may need to read only two paragraphs to solve your problem. The immediate need is met.

If you want to learn more about the topic, you can continue to read the rest of the discussion. You can do the exercises related to the topic and pursue related topics that are cross-referenced. After thoroughly studying the topic, you will have saved time and aggravation both by eliminating the problem and by knowing immediately how to accomplish the task the next time.

Picking up this book only when you are unsure about what to do suggests that you are a reluctant DOS user. That's OK. If you keep *Learning DOS* next to your computer and use the book just once a week, it will still save you time and reduce frustration. The book will have done its job.

Using the Learning Guide

Learning DOS provides a learning smorgasbord, enabling you to pick and choose what you want to learn about DOS. After running the Learning Guide program, you'll have a clear understanding of what you know, and you'll see what else you might want to learn, based on the report summary provided by that program. You need not start with the first page of the book and read all the material until you find something you should know. Instead, you can go immediately to the material you must learn.

This approach to learning DOS is more structured, more like returning to school. If you decide to run the Learning Guide program every two weeks, doing your "homework" between those sessions, you'll be taking an aggressive approach to mastering your computer. Just remember that this school is tailored to your learning pace and there are *no* grades!

Browsing DOS Topics

Perhaps you just have some questions about DOS. You use your system every day to gather information and produce reports. You know a few DOS commands, enough to make sure that you don't lose your work and that you can find files when you need them. But you have wondered whether there is a better way to organize your hard disk. Or you want to print five long reports without having to wait for each one to finish printing before going on to the next.

You may decide to browse through *Learning DOS*. Because each topic is self-contained, you can pause on topics of interest and see what there is to learn. Ask yourself a question and see whether *Learning DOS* can help you answer it. This way, you will become a curious user of DOS.

Helping Other DOS Users

Becoming more comfortable with the computer can certainly be satisfying. You have more time to devote to the task at hand. You know immediately how to copy a file or create a batch file. But with this knowledge comes a new burden: you may be asked to help other computer users working around you, but not quite as experienced as you, learn the ways of DOS. All the time you saved by using *Learning DOS* may be expended in teaching others what you have learned.

Save yourself additional time by handing the seekers of DOS knowledge a copy of this book, with specific suggestions for the topics they need to cover in answering their own questions. In this role, you will be serving as a learning guide and can then be available to answer the questions of other users *after* they cover the material. The time they spend reading about topics will be time you don't have to spend explaining them.

Traditional Reading

If you do want to cover all the topics in this book in a progressive sequence (from simple topics to complex topics), you can still do so even if you can't start on page 1 and read through to the end. (Topics are alphabetical, not sequential.) Each topic is numbered in the approximate order of complexity. You may start reading topic 1 and read through to topic 100. Listed at the end of each topic are additional references if you want to wander off the "path." The topic name (and number) next in sequence is also included so that you can turn quickly to that alphabetical location. A list of topics, in order, is provided at the end of this orientation.

Learning DOS can become a tool for occasional reference, learning, or browsing—depending on your needs and interests. Most likely, you will use this book in all these ways.

Topic Structure

Each of the 100 topics included in this book has a specific structure. As mentioned, the most critical information is presented first. Additional information then covers some of the finer points about the topic, and exercises are provided when appropriate.

Besides providing complete information on 100 topics, the alphabetical list in Part II, "Topic Reference," contains dozens of cross-references to many of those topics. For example, if you know that you need to do something to a new floppy disk before you can use it, you might look under *New disk* or *Blank disk*. These entries in Part II of the book point to the topic FORMAT — Disks (12).

Or perhaps you have a file somewhere on your hard disk, but you've forgotten where. So you look under *Finding a file*. This reference points you to Lost Data Files (77). In this particular example, DOS provides a number of ways to find a lost file.

Each of the 100 topics contains some or all of the following sections:

Topic name and number	A word or phrase that identifies the topic, followed by the topic number
Topic icon	A "quick glance" icon
Summary	A short paragraph that summarizes the topic
Before You Begin	What you need to know to understand the topic
Syntax	Examples of command lines or program lines
Problems	Command problems with solutions
Explanation	More information on the topic
Exercises	Specific exercises to learn more about the topic
References	Related topics and the next topic (in numerical order)

Most of the topics that are either DOS commands or DOS programs contain all the sections listed here. Discussions of DOS concepts and error messages contain only some of these sections because they do not lend themselves to exercises. In all cases, a number of cross-references are provided so that you can continue the learning path if you're interested. The rest of this discussion explains in more detail what these topic sections contain.

Topic Name and Number

The first line of the topic contains the name of the topic (a word or phrase) covered or cross-referenced. Following the name is a number. This topic number is used in several places, including cross-references and the Learning Guide program. Whenever one of the 100 topics is mentioned, the topic number is included also.

Topic Icon

Located beneath the topic line and beside the summary paragraph is a topic icon, or "quick glance" icon. This icon contains two sets of buttons. One set (the top three buttons) indicates the version of DOS covered. The other set (the bottom four buttons) indicates the type of topic. Figure I-1 shows an example of a topic icon.

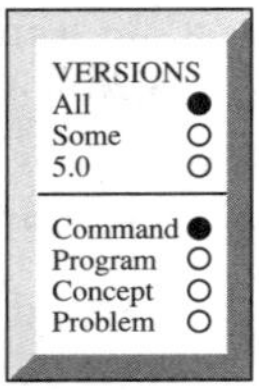

Figure I-1. A topic icon that identifies a command relevant to all versions of DOS.

As you can see from the figure, the first button in the top portion of the icon indicates that a topic is relevant to all versions of DOS. Most of the concepts and many of the commands show this top button darkened. If the middle button of the top three is darkened, the topic relates to some versions of DOS but not others. The middle button is necessary because MS-DOS versions 3.3 and 4.01 have some commands not available in older versions. In most cases, you can just try out the program or command. If it does not work, your version of DOS does not have it.

Because MS-DOS 5.0 has been introduced with a number of new commands, the third button of the top three is darkened when a topic is relevant to *only* that version of DOS. If you do not have DOS version 5.0, you won't be able to use that command. You may want to look quickly at the command to see if you are interested in upgrading to MS-DOS 5.0. (For your version number, type **VER** at the DOS prompt.)

If this discussion about DOS versions is a bit confusing, check the topic History of DOS (88). By the way, this is a topic cross-reference. If you like, you can jump to that topic now, take a look at it, and then return to continue reading.

The bottom four buttons of the topic icon indicate the type of topic: command, program, concept, or problem. *Commands* and *programs* are specific actions you can invoke at the DOS command prompt. *Concepts* are topics that provide background for commands or programs, or are just general ideas you may want to know about DOS and computers. *Problems* relates to specific DOS error messages or to problems that DOS users frequently encounter.

Summary

Below the topic line is a brief summary of the topic. This short paragraph lets you know quickly if you are looking at the topic you want to cover. As you glance through the alphabetical list in Part II, keep in mind that many entries (words or phrases) are not discussed topics at all but are cross-referenced to one or more topics. As noted earlier, the entry *New disk* refers you to the DOS program topic FORMAT — Disks (12), as well as to the concept of Floppy Disks (19).

Before You Begin

Before using many of the DOS commands and programs, you may need some essential information about your computer, or you may need to know how to do certain tasks. Because these "before you begin" entries also contain the topic numbers, you can drop back to another topic, cover it, and then return to this topic. If you understand the topic (or topics) recommended in this section, you will be able to proceed, confident that you are ready to cover the current topic.

Syntax

Almost all DOS commands and programs have a specific *syntax*—the way you type them or use them to achieve the results you want. In many cases, this is as basic as typing the command and a parameter. For example, you type **FORMAT A:** to tell DOS to use the FORMAT program to format the disk in drive A:. If the topic is a concept or problem, this section is not included.

This section contains the *most common* uses and variations of a command or program. Additional parts of the command or program are covered later in the topic's discussion, if necessary. If the syntax provided is not what you need, look in later sections of the topic.

Problems

Problems you may encounter when you try to use a command are listed here. Some of the problems cited will apply generally to all commands, and others will be specific to the command. Each problem is briefly described, with possible solutions given. The "Explanation" section may also provide ideas to solve the listed problems. Most of the problems are included in the alphabetical list, with references to the topic where each problem is explained.

Explanation

If you want to know more about the topic, this section provides more information, as well as additional uses for the command or program. If the topic is a problem or concept, this section will be the largest in the topic's coverage. Remember that for all topics the most important information is provided first, and this section is similarly organized. The most important points to understand are presented first. Once you are satisfied with that information, you may want to skip to the next section, move on to another topic, or just put the book down and see what you can accomplish.

Exercises

This section leads you through a series of steps to learn more about DOS commands and programs. Some of the exercises use files on the accompanying disk. These exercises include demonstrations on how to use a command as well as how the command *may not work!* You learn, by example, the kinds of errors you can make and how to recover from them. In all cases, the proper precautions are given before you begin a part of an exercise.

The exercises are presented in two columns, labeled TRY and NOTE. The left column shows the exact keys you are to press. The right column explains why you should take that action or what you should observe as the result of it. Remember how special keys are designated; for example, the Enter key is shown as **<Enter>**, the space bar appears as **<space bar>**, and the Backspace key is shown as **<Backspace>**. Here is an example of an exercise for the topic Boot/Startup (1):

TRY	NOTE
C:\>**<Ctrl><Alt><Del>**	When you press and hold down the Ctrl and Alt keys and then press the Delete key, the system restarts. Watch the screen as it returns to the menu or DOS prompt.

References

At the end of each topic are additional references, including the next topic in numerical order. Use these references to explore similar concepts or areas covered in the alphabetical list.

Margin Icons

In addition to the quick-glance icon provided at the beginning of each topic, several other margin icons highlight portions of the material. The most important of these icons is the *caution* icon. The information tagged with a caution icon often appears in a box.

> Critical information about a command or concept appears in a box like this. Examples are warnings about the possible loss of data or damage to the computer.

Although several topics relate only to DOS 5.0, some commands and programs have additional features in that version of DOS. These features are highlighted with a margin icon that displays the number 5.

The utilities provided on the accompanying disk either can save you time or are more convenient to use than DOS commands. When a topic relates to a utility on the disk, the *utility* icon appears beside a paragraph that gives a brief description of the utility and notes how the utility can help. More information on the utility is provided in Part III, "Guide to Using the Disk."

Some of the exercises at the end of the topic refer specifically to files on the disk provided with this book. When the disk is needed to work on an exercise, the *disk* icon appears in the margin.

List of 100 Topics

The topics are listed alphabetically in this book. Topic numbers are included with each topic for reference. Table I-1 lists, in topic order, all 100 topics in Part II. These topics have been arranged in order of importance and complexity. Between the need to understand a topic and its complexity, the need to know is considered more important.

Table I-1. The 100 topics listed in topic (numerical) order.

Order	Topic
1	Boot/Startup
2	Files
3	Default Drive
4	File Names
5	CLS — Clear Screen
6	`Bad command or file name`
7	A: B: C: — Drive Designation
8	DIR — Directory
9	CD, MD, and RD — Working with Directories

continues

Table I-1. continued

Order	Topic
10	COPY — Files
11	Wild Cards * and ?
12	FORMAT — Disks
13	Backing Up Dat
14	Solving Problems
15	Printers
16	`Strike a key when ready...`
17	File Organization
18	Software
19	Floppy Disks
20	CHKDSK — CHecK DiSK
21	AUTOEXEC.BAT
22	CONFIG.SYS
23	DATE
24	TIME
25	DOSKEY
26	PROMPT — Command Line Information
27	Interfaces
28	Learning More
29	PATH — Program Search
30	DEL — DELete Files
31	UNDELETE
32	Floppy Drive Failure
33	Hard Drive Failure
34	Command and Program Parameters
35	Disk Full
36	Disk Damaged
37	XCOPY — Files
38	Hardware
39	Keyboard
40	Ports
41	BACKUP — Files

Order	Topic
42	RESTORE — Files
43	Word Processing
44	DOSSHELL — DOS 5.0 Menu
45	PRINT — Spooler
46	Application Software
47	Program Versions
48	Spreadsheets
49	Databases
50	Utility Software
51	Copyright
52	Data File Formats
53	Manuals and Documentation
54	Product Registration
55	Communications
56	Modems
57	SHARE
58	SUBST
59	No One to Help
60	Installing Programs
61	Monitor
62	ATTRIB — Protecting Files
63	DISKCOPY — Duplicating Disks
64	Redirection < > ¦
65	Upgrading Your Software
66	GRAPHICS — Printing Screens
67	Bytes and Computer Math
68	Paper in Printer
69	Labels in Printer
70	FASTOPEN — Speeding Up Disks
71	New Programs on Old Computers
72	Hardware and Software Compatibility
73	Memory
74	ASCII — Character Codes

continues

Table I-1. continued

Order	Topic
75	Operating Systems
76	REN — REName Files
77	Lost Data Files
78	COMMAND.COM/EXIT
79	Networks
80	Compressed Files
81	TYPE — Looking at Files
82	FIND — Searching Files
83	MODE — Configuring System Devices
84	MORE — Pausing Screen Display
85	Workspace — User Comfort
86	UNFORMAT
87	TREE — Directory Map
88	History of DOS
89	FAT — File Allocation Table
90	MEM
91	MIRROR
92	Virus
93	Sharing Devices
94	System Maintenance
95	Security
96	Microprocessors
97	Partitions — FDISK
98	EDIT — DOS 5.0 Text Editor
99	EDLIN — Line Editor
100	Batch Files — Write Your Own

Final Notes

The term DOS is commonly used to refer to the disk operating system in the generic sense. The references to DOS in this book are based on MS-DOS, the Microsoft version of DOS. Another version of DOS, PC DOS, is distributed by IBM but written by Microsoft. In this book, unless otherwise noted, all references to the generic term DOS are to the brand-specific name of MS-DOS, especially references to version 5.0.

Some readers have a special reverence for books. Dating back to early grade school, the admonishment "never write in a book" still echoes clearly. The reasons are numerous:

1. Others will use the book after you.
2. Margin notes look messy.
3. Adding your comments detracts from the meaning.
4. Making notes slows you down.
5. Crayons smudge the other page.

Cast out those reminders of days past. This is your book. Do with it what you will. To those objections, you can give these responses:

1. It is my book. I can do what I want.
2. Margin notes help me find the information I need quickly.
3. Adding notes enhances my use of the book. They provide the information I need.
4. I want to take my time reading this material. It is not a novel. There is no plot. The slower I go when reading computer books, the more I am likely to understand.
5. So who says I have to use a crayon?

D

Part II

Topic Reference

Part II

Topic Reference

A: B: C: — Drive Designation (7)

VERSIONS	
All	●
Some	○
5.0	○
Command	●
Program	○
Concept	●
Problem	○

These letters designate the disk drives for DOS. When you type one of the letters and then a colon (:), the default drive changes to the letter of the drive you typed. The default drive is the drive that DOS attempts to use for any command typed at the prompt. Systems, especially networks, can have drives ranging from A: to Z:.

Before You Begin

Default Drive (3)

Syntax

C:\>**A: <Enter>** A:\>	The DOS prompt and the default drive change to A:.

Problems

Forgetting the colon. Users frequently forget to type the colon after the drive letter. If you type just **A** and then press Enter, you get the error message Bad command or file name. To change the drive to A:, you must type **A:** and press Enter.

Forgetting to use the Shift key. Pressing the colon key without first pressing the Shift key results in a semicolon after the drive letter. Whenever this happens, DOS provides `Bad command or file name`. You must retype the letter followed by a colon.

`Invalid drive specification`. Typing a drive letter for a physical drive that does not exist results in this message. As for the preceding errors, you must retype a valid drive letter. DOS then moves the default to that drive.

```
Not ready reading drive B:
Abort, Retry, Fail?
```

This message, which differs slightly among DOS versions, occurs when you type a drive designation for a floppy drive but no disk is in that drive. DOS attempts to move to the drive and issues this message if there is no disk, or if the disk drive door is not closed or latched. Whenever you get this message, insert the disk and type **R** for Retry. If the letter you typed was a mistake, type **F** for Fail. This may take several tries. The prompt returns with the message `Current drive no longer valid>`. Type another drive letter, such as **C:**.

Explanation

You can think of drive designations as the names of buildings. First you move into the building you want to work in, and then you go to work. (Subdirectories may be thought of as rooms within these buildings. For more information on changing directories, see topic 9.) By typing **A:**, you tell DOS that you want to use drive A: as the main drive for your next command. The formal term for the building you are working in is the *default drive*. This default drive is so important that even the most basic DOS prompt (`C>`) shows the drive. Most DOS prompts show at least the subdirectory also (`C:\>`). For more about the DOS prompt, refer to the topic PROMPT — Command Line Information (26).

All DOS systems have an A: drive. This is typically the top floppy drive or the only floppy drive. Many systems have a C: drive, which is a hard drive located inside the computer.

With newer versions of DOS and with networks, the drive letter may not represent a physical drive on your system. The DOS SUBST command enables you to substitute a drive letter for a path. You can set up your system so that M: is really C:\WORDPROC\MONEY>. Typing **M:** is the same as typing

```
C: <Enter>
CD \WORDPROC\MONEY <Enter>
```

This point is important if, in Exercise 2, you discover some drive letters with files that also appear in subdirectories on the hard drive. Check your DOS manual under SUBST and read topic 58 for more about that command.

Exercises

Moving the default drive from C: to A: requires that you type **A**, type a colon, and press the Enter key. As just noted, several problems are possible, none of them major. In these exercises, you explore your system by first switching drives and then finding out how many drives you have (starting with the first drive, A:).

Exercise 1 of 2

If you are not looking at the DOS prompt, use whatever commands are necessary to leave your menu system. Refer to the topic Interfaces (27) if you need help. In the following steps, the TRY column shows the information on the screen in `monospace` and your input (what you are to type) in **`bold monospace`**. The NOTE column contains comments about the process. Additional instructions appear in italic in the TRY column. If your DOS prompt does not match the one shown, type **`PROMPT $p$g`** to change the prompt.

TRY	NOTE
Make sure that you have a disk in drive A:.	The disk included with this book will do fine. You won't change anything. Watch the computer drive lights as you try these steps. You'll see the lights turn on briefly each time you switch drives.
C:\>**A: <Enter>**	If your prompt is already A:\>, just skip this step. Be sure to press the Enter key after you've typed each command. (Note that **<Enter>** is provided only as an occasional reminder.)
A:\>**C:**	This puts you back in C: drive.
Remove the disk in A:.	Here you are getting ready to create a DOS error message.
C:\>**A:**	When you type this, you get this next message.
Not ready reading drive A: Abort, Retry, Fail? **F**	Type **F** for Fail here. You might need to do it several times.
Current drive no longer valid> **C:** C:\>	The prompt returns to C:\>. DOS, once again, knows which drive is the default drive.

Older versions of DOS may not be quite as forgiving about the drive designation. You'll have to try these steps to see what happens. Remember that you are not causing any damage with this exercise, just discovering and solving a common DOS problem.

Some systems have a second floppy drive (B:). In some cases, the size of B: will be different from that of A:. That is, if you have a 5 1/4-inch floppy drive as A:, you are likely to have a 3 1/2-inch floppy drive as B:. Then again, you might have two drives of the same size. The key is to make sure that you know which physical drive is represented by which letter. You may want to label the drives with embossed tape (the kind with raised letters) to remember the size of each drive.

Exercise 2 of 2

This exercise applies to systems with hard drives and to networks. No specific steps are provided, just a goal: make sure that you know all the drives available on the system. If you like, put notes in the margin of this book to remind yourself of the types of drives in your system.

Start in drive C: and type **`D:`** to see whether you get a `D:\>` prompt. If you get the message `Invalid drive specification`, you don't have a D: drive. Some hard drives, though, are set up as C: and D: drives, and there can be even more. Continue to try other letters in alphabetical order. Unless you have a network, you probably won't have a drive beyond F:.

If you have a network, keep going all the way through Z:. Several popular networks use drives X:, Y:, and Z: as network drives. When you type **`Z:`** in this case, you are actually "talking" to the network host. For more information about networks, read the topic Networks (79).

References

CD, MD, and RD — Working with Directories (9), Networks (79)

NEXT TOPIC: DIR — Directory (8)

Abort, Retry or Fail?

See Default Drive (3)

Access denied

See ATTRIB — Protecting Files (62)

Accidental format

See UNFORMAT (86)

Accidentally deleted file(s)

See DEL — DELete Files (30)

Added extension in file name

See File Names (4)

Added file directory

See File Names (4)

Application Software (46)

VERSIONS	
All	●
Some	○
5.0	○
Command	○
Program	○
Concept	●
Problem	○

The category of programs known as *application software* helps you accomplish specific tasks. Other categories are utility software and system software.

Before You Begin

Files (2)
Software (18)
Word Processing (43)

Problem

What software to buy or use? This may be a catch-22. If you don't understand how the software works, how can you decide what to do with it? If you can't decide what you want to do with the software, how can you buy the software?

Explanation

The term *application* may come from "applying" the software to the task at hand. You need application software to accomplish certain tasks with the computer. Other kinds of software include utility software to manage the computer system, and operating system software to control the hardware and run the application software.

When you are considering which software to use, start at the end. You know that you have a goal. The goal may be as specific as "print office phone numbers in alphabetical order" or as general as "use the computer to keep track of expenses." The better you define your goal, the easier is the task of choosing the right application software.

Use the next section to examine your application software needs. The time you spend now in planning will be invaluable, and you are likely to save time in the long run.

Specific examples of application software are word processing, spreadsheets, and databases. Each type of program applies to a specific type of task. If you want to create and change reports efficiently, you can use a word processing program. If you want to determine the best price for your product, a spreadsheet program can help. Keeping track of hundreds or thousands of items can be done with a database program.

Exercise

This is not a test. All you need are a pencil, paper, and your thinking cap. You have some questions to consider and some answers to think about, in no particular order. There are no right or wrong answers.

1. *What do you want to do?* Develop a list of tasks that lead to the final product (output) or goal.
2. *What will the result look like?* Sketch what you want the output to look like, or use a copy of the current form. In this step, you may develop a number of ideas worth exploring.
3. *How often will you do it?* Determine whether the result is required daily, weekly, monthly, or only as needed.
4. *How much time can you spend in learning the software?* Budget this time just as you budget the amount of money you can afford to pay for the software.
5. *How will using the software improve your output?* This is a hard question because using the software to do a task may take longer than doing the task manually. If, however, the results are more accurate and look much better, the time is well invested.

6. *Who receives the output?* The more critical the information and the more influential the recipients, the more effort you want to expend on the result.
7. *What is your general attitude about computers?* Do you think computers are challenging and helpful? Or do you think computers mostly cause problems and are more trouble than they are worth?
8. *Who can provide help if you need it?* The more popular the software, the more likely someone can help with it. Don't let this be the deciding factor, though. There are enough popular packages available for you to find one that suits your needs and provides other accessible users.

With your answers to these questions, you have a better idea of what you want and how much time you can devote to getting it. Use the answers to ask questions about the software you are considering. If, for example, you don't want to spend more than a few hours learning the software, you can immediately eliminate a package that proclaims proficiency in "as little as a week." If the output goes to five people, none of whom is your boss, you won't want to spend hours making the report look perfect. As with any project, weigh the investment of time against the expected results.

References

Spreadsheets (48), Databases (49), Utility Software (50), Copyright (51), Manuals and Documentation (53), Product Registration (54)

NEXT TOPIC: Program Versions (47)

Archiving disks

See Floppy Disks (19)

Are you sure (Y/N)?

See DEL — DELete files (30)

Ask someone about the problem

See Solving Problems (14)

ASCII — Character Codes (74)

VERSIONS	
All	●
Some	○
5.0	○
Command	○
Program	○
Concept	●
Problem	○

The ASCII character set refers to the 255 standard characters used in DOS systems. The commonly used characters available from the keyboard range from ASCII 32, which is a space, to ASCII 126, which is a tilde (~). Characters below 32 are used as control characters. Those above 126 provide various line drawings and unique characters.

Before You Begin

Files (2)
Data File Formats (52)

Explanation

The ASCII character set is the lowest common denominator for data. Almost all programs can read and use an ASCII file, and most programs can produce output in an ASCII format. Because the lower 126 characters are common to almost all computers, ASCII files can be used to exchange data between different systems. Special formatting codes kept by a program in its normal file format are usually lost within an ASCII file.

A program stores its program and data files in a format unique to that program. Some files, such as batch files (see topic 100) use the ASCII format. Many times, files with the extension TXT or ASC are also in ASCII format and can be viewed on the screen with the DOS TYPE command (topic 81).

You can produce the *extended* ASCII characters (above 126) by using the Alt key and the number keys on the *right side* of the keyboard. The number keys across the top will not work in producing these extra ASCII characters. Most word processing programs support the use of these characters but, depending on the printer, the printed characters may not match those on the screen.

To create these special characters, press the Alt key and then type the number, usually three digits. When you release the Alt key, the character appears on the screen. Figure 74-1 shows some of these characters arranged in convenient forms, along with the ASCII code for each.

Several other extended ASCII characters can be used to create images on the screen or provide shadow effects. Figure 74-2 shows those characters and their codes, along with two sample boxes.

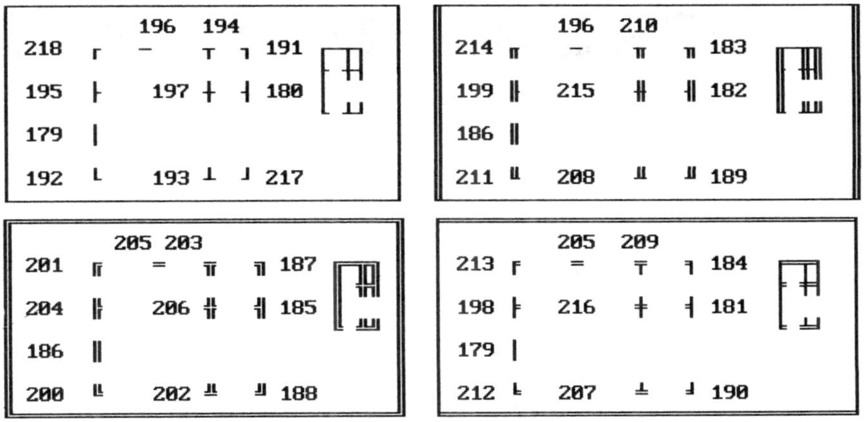

Figure 74-1. Some extended ASCII characters you can use to create line drawings.

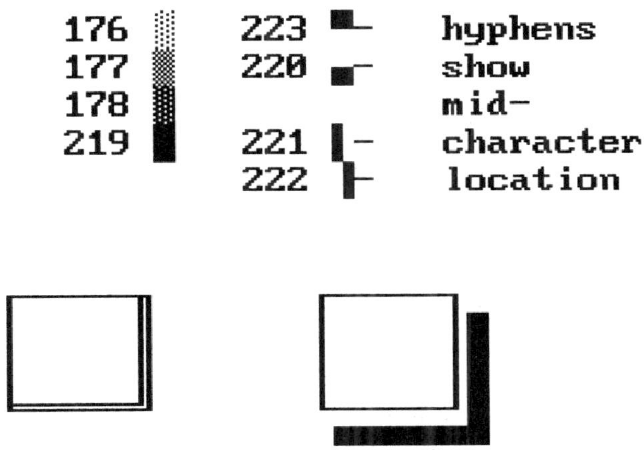

Figure 74-2. Additional extended ASCII codes.

Table 74-1 contains the entire ASCII code for the United States keyboard and code pages.

Table 74-1. ASCII code.

Char	Value	Char	Value
0	null	32	
1	☺	33	!
2	☻	34	"
3	♥	35	#
4	◆	36	$
5	♣	37	%
6	♠	38	&
7	●	39	'
8	■	40	(
9	○	41	)
10	■	42	*
11	♂	43	+
12	♀	44	,
13	♪	45	-
14	♪♪	46	.
15	☼	47	/
16	►	48	0
17	◄	49	1
18	↕	50	2
19	!!	51	3
20	¶	52	4
21	§	53	5
22	–	54	6
23	↨	55	7
24	↑	56	8
25	↓	57	9
26	→	58	:
27	←	59	;
28	∟	60	<
29	↔	61	=
30	▲	62	>
31	▼	63	?

Char	Value	Char	Value
64	@	98	b
65	A	99	c
66	B	100	d
67	C	101	e
68	D	102	f
69	E	103	g
70	F	104	h
71	G	105	i
72	H	106	j
73	I	107	k
74	J	108	l
75	K	109	m
76	L	110	n
77	M	111	o
78	N	112	p
79	O	113	q
80	P	114	r
81	Q	115	s
82	R	116	t
83	S	117	u
84	T	118	v
85	U	119	w
86	V	120	x
87	W	121	y
88	X	122	z
89	Y	123	{
90	Z	124	¦
91	[	125	}
92	\	126	~
93	]	127	Δ\
94	^	128	Ç
95	_	129	ü
96	‘	130	é
97	a	131	â

continues

Table 74-1. continued

Char	Value	Char	Value
132	ä	165	Ñ
133	à	166	a
134	á	167	o
135	ç	168	¿
136	ê	169	⌐
137	ë	170	┐
138	è	171	1/2
139	ï	172	1/4
140	î	173	¡
141	ì	174	«
142	Ä	175	»
143	Å	176	░
144	É	177	▒
145	æ	178	▓
146	Æ	179	│
147	ô	180	┤
148	ö	181	╡
149	ò	182	╢
150	û	183	╖
151	ù	184	╕
152	ÿ	185	╣
153	Ö	186	║
154	Ü	187	╗
155	¢	188	╝
156	£	189	╜
157	¥	190	╛
158	Pt	191	┐
159	ƒ	192	└
160	á	193	┴
161	í	194	┬
162	ó	195	├
163	ú	196	─
164	ñ	197	+

Char	Value	Char	Value
198	╞	227	π
199	╟	228	Σ
200	╚	229	σ
201	╔	230	µ
202	╩	231	t
203	╦	232	Φ
204	╠	233	u
205	═	234	Ω
206	╬	235	d
207	╧	236	∞
208	╨	237	ø
209	╤	238	∈
210	╥	239	∩
211	╙	240	≡
212	╘	241	±
213	╒	242	≥
214	╓	243	≤
215	╫	244	⌠
216		245	⌡
217	┘	246	÷
218	┌	247	≈
219	█	248	°
220	▄	249	•
221	▌	250	·
222	▐	251	√
223	▀	252	h
224	a	253	²
225	β	254	■
226	Γ	255	

ASCII stands for American Standard Code for Information Interchange.

References

PRINT — Spooler (45), Redirection — < > ¦ (64), TYPE — Looking at Files (81)

NEXT TOPIC: Operating Systems (75)

Attempting to print a file from another program while PRINT is running

See PRINT — Spooler (45)

ATTRIB — Protecting Files (62)

VERSIONS: All ○ Some ● 5.0 ○
Command ○ Program ● Concept ○ Problem ○

The DOS ATTRIB program enables you to prevent files from being accidentally erased. Other file attributes can also be changed with ATTRIB.

Before You Begin

File Names (4)
DEL — DELete Files (30)
Command and Program Parameters (34)

Syntax

`C:\>`**`ATTRIB`**	Shows the file attributes of the files in the root directory
`C:\>`**`ATTRIB +R AUTOEXEC.BAT`**	Read only (file cannot be deleted or modified)
`C:\>`**`ATTRIB -R AUTOEXEC.BAT`**	File can be deleted

Problems

Preventing accidental file deletions. You can easily erase any DOS file with the DEL command. Although there are ways to recover a deleted file, they may not be readily available to all DOS users. Some files must be in the root drive in order for the system to boot, so avoiding accidental deletion is a good preventative measure. You can apply the **ATTRIB +R** command to COMMAND.COM, AUTOEXEC.BAT, and CONFIG.SYS to keep these files from being erased. This same command can be applied to any critical files.

Finding and erasing hidden files. Sometimes the RD command does not work on a subdirectory because it contains hidden files. DOS 5.0 users can use +H to locate hidden files within a subdirectory. Since you do not know the name of the file, the command **ATTRIB +H *.*** will bring them out of hiding. If the files still cannot be deleted, use **ATTRIB -R *.*** to remove the read-only setting, and then use **DEL *.***.

Access denied. Trying to delete a file with the read-only attribute set on will result in this DOS message. Use **ATTRIB -R FILENAME.EXT** to reset the attribute. Then the DEL command will work.

Explanation

In addition to the name, extension, size, date, and time, DOS keeps file settings called *attributes*. These attributes, not usually visible with the DIR command, control several aspects of each file:

R The *read* status determines whether a file can be erased or written to. A file with read status is like a printed page. You can read information on the page, but you can't change the information or throw away the page.

A The *archive* status is used by a number of programs to determine whether a file has been changed since the last time it was backed up. Programs like BACKUP and XCOPY set the archive switch off, showing that the file has been copied elsewhere. As soon as any program makes a change to that file, the archive switch is set on. Imagine the file as holding its hand up and saying, "Copy me. Oh, please copy me!"

H DOS, as well as some programs, likes to *hide* files. This keeps them from being erased and generally tampered with. Your root directory has two hidden system files. Some programs copy and then hide files as a method of copy protection.

S Some files have a special status as *system* files. These include the two hidden files in the root directory.

You can view the attributes of one or more files with just ATTRIB and wild cards. For example, the command

```
C:\>ATTRIB *.*
```

produces

```
     SH      C:\IO.SYS
     SH      C:\MSDOS.SYS
  A          C:\CONFIG.SYS
  A          C:\AUTOEXEC.BAT
  A     R    C:\COMMAND.COM

        R    C:\WINA20.386
```

Notice the two hidden files, IO.SYS and MSDOS.SYS, which come out of hiding. They also have the S for the system file attribute set on. COMMAND.COM and WINA20.386 are protected because they have the R for the read-only attribute set on. The R attribute was manually set on for COMMAND.COM. An installation program sets the R attribute on as part of its operating procedure.

All DOS users can manually change both the read and archive attributes with the ATTRIB command. To turn an attribute on, you use the plus sign (+) with the letter R or A. The command

```
C:\>ATTRIB +R AUTOEXEC.BAT
```

keeps the AUTOEXEC.BAT file from being erased or changed. If you want to make changes, you'll have to turn the read-only bit off with the command

```
C:\>ATTRIB -R AUTOEXEC.BAT
```

Although some users rarely make changes to their AUTOEXEC.BAT or CONFIG.SYS files, other users make changes all the time. Setting the read-only attribute on for these files may not make much sense. However, the COMMAND.COM file in the root directory is a critical file that must be there when the system first boots. Typing the command

```
C:\>ATTRIB +R COMMAND.COM
```

keeps that critical file from being erased.

All DOS users can also change the archive setting with the –A or +A switches in ATTRIB. If you use the /M and /A switches in XCOPY and the /M in BACKUP, you may need to change the archive settings manually for these files.

DOS 5.0 users can change the H and S attributes of files. Although changing the S attribute can easily lead to trouble, the H attribute may be useful in a number of ways. To hide all the files within a subdirectory, use the command

```
C:\>ATTRIB +H *.*
```

The DIR command will not list any files in that subdirectory. But the command

```
C:\>ATTRIB *.*
```

or

```
C:\>ATTRIB
```

will list all the files and their attributes. These files, then, are not invisible to anyone who knows the ATTRIB command.

Exercise

Protecting the COMMAND.COM program in the root directory is a good idea. Therefore, most users should perform at least the first part of this exercise.

Exercise 1 of 1

In this exercise, you set the read-only attribute on for several important system files in the root directory. Before making any changes to these files, you should copy them into the DOS subdirectory as a precaution.

TRY	NOTE
`C:\>COPY COMMAND.COM \DOS` `C:\>COPY AUTOEXEC.BAT \DOS`	Now you have a second copy of each of these files in the DOS subdirectory.
`C:\>COPY CONFIG.SYS \DOS`	If your DOS subdirectory has a different name, substitute that directory name for \DOS. If you do not have an AUTOEXEC.BAT or a CONFIG.SYS file, you'll get the message `File not found`.
`C:\>ATTRIB +R COMMAND.COM`	This keeps the COMMAND.COM program file from being erased.
`C:\>ATTRIB +R AUTOEXEC.BAT` `C:\>ATTRIB +R CONFIG.SYS`	No noticeable changes are made to these files unless you use ATTRIB or you try to delete or change a file.
`C:\>ATTRIB *.*`	This shows the status of all the files in the root directory. If the listing is longer than the screen, add **¦ MORE** to the end of the command.

`C:\>DEL AUTOEXEC.BAT`
`Access Denied`
`C:\>`
	The read-only bit is set on. The file cannot be deleted.

If you plan to change your AUTOEXEC.BAT and CONFIG.SYS files regularly, you'll need to turn the read-only bit off with **ATTRIB -R AUTOEXEC.BAT**. Because some installation programs also make changes to these files, you may need to reset the R status before you install new programs.

References

COMMAND.COM/EXIT (78)

NEXT TOPIC: DISKCOPY — Duplicating Disks (63)

AUTOEXEC.BAT (21)

VERSIONS
All ●
Some ○
5.0 ○

Command ○
Program ●
Concept ○
Problem ○

DOS runs this batch file program first (AUTOmatic EXECution) when the system is booted. The AUTOEXEC.BAT file typically sets the PATH, may prompt for the DATE and TIME, and may run a menu or another program.

Before You Begin

Boot/Startup (1)
Files (2)
File Names (4)

Syntax

`C:\>`**`AUTOEXEC`**	Reruns the program that normally runs when the system is booted

Problems

AUTOEXEC.BAT missing. DOS looks for the AUTOEXEC.BAT file in the root directory. If the file does not exist, DOS prompts for the DATE and TIME and then provides the minimal `C>` or `A>` prompt. Because AUTOEXEC.BAT contains commands that can be issued one at a time from the DOS prompt, AUTOEXEC.BAT is a convenience, not a necessity.

AUTOEXEC.BAT changed. A number of programs change the AUTOEXEC.BAT file during installation to make sure that the settings conform to the program's needs so that it can run. Most of these programs create a backup copy of the old file in case the changes keep the system from working properly with the new file. If, after you install a new program, your system does not work the way it used to, the first place to check is in the AUTOEXEC.BAT file. Compare AUTOEXEC.BAT with AUTOEXEC.OLD for differences. Unfortunately, correcting the problem may take some time and experience. The first resource to use is the company that provided the new software.

AUTOEXEC.BAT out of control. Because the AUTOEXEC.BAT file begins automatically when the system first starts, it may be executing instructions you no longer want. For example, someone may have set up the system to go into a menu program automatically. You just want to "drop" to DOS. You need to stop the AUTOEXEC.BAT file. Pressing Ctrl-C (pressing and holding down Ctrl and then pressing C) will provide the message `Terminate batch file (Y/N)?` Reply with `Y`, and the program will stop. Then you will be looking at the DOS prompt.

Explanation

Almost all systems with hard drives have an AUTOEXEC.BAT file. This file can do several tasks automatically every time the system is started. Here is a typical AUTOEXEC.BAT file:

```
ECHO OFF
DATE
TIME
PATH C:\DOS;C:\WORD;C:\UTILS
MOUSE
PROMPT $P$G
CLS
```

The commands in this batch file are fully discussed as topics in this book. Once you have covered them, each command will make sense. For now, you need to understand the purpose of the AUTOEXEC.BAT file and to realize that the installation of other programs may affect this file.

5 DOS 5.0 users will discover that the SETUP program creates or modifies the AUTOEXEC.BAT file to optimize the system. As mentioned, MS-DOS does make a backup of the old file before making changes to AUTOEXEC.BAT.

Exercises

You may want to make a note to yourself to return to this topic after you have covered more of the DOS commands. If you really want to know more about AUTOEXEC.BAT now, use the first exercise to examine your AUTOEXEC.BAT file and discover everything it does. The second exercise shows a quick way to create a minimal AUTOEXEC.BAT file. For a thorough understanding of batch files, refer to Batch Files — Write Your Own (100).

Exercise 1 of 2

This exercise shows you how to examine your personal AUTOEXEC.BAT file. You won't change it or in any way affect how your system works.

TRY	NOTE
`C:\>`**`TYPE AUTOEXEC.BAT`**	Make sure that you are in the root directory of your drive. The TYPE command displays the file. If you get an error message, you don't have an AUTOEXEC.BAT file. In that case, move to the next exercise to create a "quicky."
Look at the screen.	How many DOS commands do you recognize? If you want to have a printed copy of this file, make sure that the printer is on; then type this next line.
`C:\>`**`TYPE AUTOEXEC.BAT > LPT1:`**	Now you can make notes on the sheet if you like.

If you need to understand all the commands in the AUTOEXEC.BAT file, you can now go through the alphabetical list and look up the first word on each line. These words represent DOS commands, programs, or batch commands. Many of the words are included in this book. You may have to refer to your DOS manual for some of them.

Exercise 2 of 2

Complete this exercise *only* if you do not have an AUTOEXEC.BAT file in your root directory. If, when you turn on the system, you are prompted for the DATE and TIME, you may not have an AUTOEXEC.BAT file. The first step provided here checks to make sure that you do not have that file.

TRY	NOTE
`C:\>`**`DIR AUTOEXEC.BAT`**	If you do not see `File not found`, stop now. You have an active AUTOEXEC.BAT file. If you proceed with this exercise, you will destroy that file.
`C:\>`**`COPY CON: AUTOEXEC.BAT`**	This is a quick way to create an ASCII (text) file. You will not see a cursor or prompt until you finish these steps.

TRY	NOTE
DATE **TIME**	If you have an XT, you want to include the DOS request for the current date and time. If you have an AT or a later system, this part of the file is not necessary.
PATH C:\;C:\DOS	This statement should include at least the subdirectory containing your DOS programs. It can include more subdirectories if you want. See PATH — Program Search (29) for more information.
PROMPT pg	This makes sure that the system prompt always shows the drive and current subdirectory. For more about PROMPT, see PROMPT — Command Line Information (26).
CLS	This clears the screen.
<F6>	Pressing the F6 key tells DOS that you are finished.
1 file(s) copied C:\>	DOS tells you that the file was copied from the console to the disk file.
C:\>**TYPE AUTOEXEC.BAT**	This command lists the file you have just created. If you need to make any changes, you can use an editor or just repeat these steps.
C:\>**AUTOEXEC**	The AUTOEXEC.BAT file now runs. If you included the DATE and TIME lines, you'll have to respond to those. If not, the screen just clears.

This little AUTOEXEC.BAT file sets your PATH to include your DOS subdirectory and creates a more informative prompt on the command line. For a more extensive explanation of batch files, see Batch Files — Write Your Own (100).

References

PROMPT — Command Line Information (26), PATH — Program Search (29), TYPE — Looking at Files (81), EDIT — DOS 5.0 Text Editor (98), EDLIN — Line Editor (99), Batch Files — Write Your Own (100)

NEXT TOPIC: CONFIG.SYS (22)

AUTOEXEC.BAT missing, changed, or out of control

See AUTOEXEC.BAT (21)

Backing Up Data (13)

VERSIONS	
All	●
Some	○
5.0	○
Command	○
Program	○
Concept	●
Problem	○

Data files are kept on floppy disks and hard disks. These disks fail occasionally, and the data is lost. Backing up the data minimizes data loss when the disk fails. The key is to have more than one copy of a file in more than one location.

Before You Begin

Files (2)
File Names (4)
COPY — Files (10)

Problems

No backups. The most common problem related to file and data loss is that users often have no duplicate copies of their files. Once a hard drive fails or a floppy disk is lost or destroyed, the data on the disk is gone. The only hope for a shortsighted user with no backups is to use a special recovery program such as Norton Disk Doctor or Mace Utilities.

Irregular backups. Backing up files occasionally is like paying your life insurance premium only when you feel sick. When data is lost, you need to know exactly how old the backup file is so that you can begin reconstructing the data you entered since the last backup. If you have not followed a clear backup schedule, figuring out what is missing from a file may take as much time as just reentering all the data. Maintain a regular schedule for backing up data and copy important files onto floppies between backup sessions.

Backing up too late. Backing up files is a preventative measure. If you are reading this topic after having lost files and are hoping for a solution, the only encouraging thought is that you are not likely to forget to back up files from now on.

Explanation

Permanent data is most commonly stored by the computer on disks. These disks use a magnetic medium similar to video and audio tapes. Although a loss of signal in video or audio is an inconvenience, the loss of the signal in a computer file will ruin the entire file. The question of data loss is not *if* but *when*.

Those data files represent all the time and effort in compiling and entering the data. In many cases, a data file is the only place where all the data has been gathered in one location. Consider the amount of time it would take to re-create the data files. In some cases, it just could not be done. Insurance can pay for a blackened computer, burned manuals, and melted program disks. But no amount of money can replace that data. If your business or job depends on the data, the best insurance is to maintain a regular backup schedule.

Planning for the eventual loss of data can take several forms. But the best approach to backing up data is to have at least two current copies of each file in different locations. Critical data files should have three copies, with one copy kept in a very safe pace, usually miles away from the computer. Depending on the data, a ***hard copy*** (printout) of all the data may be kept as a backup as well.

> Unfortunately, the first time that you seriously consider the process of backing up files may be right after you have lost a file and all of its data! Remember, it's not a question of *if* you lose data but *when*.

The easiest way to maintain two usable copies of data is to save a copy to a floppy disk right after you save a copy to the hard disk. You'll still use the data on the hard disk each time you need the data. Keep a floppy disk in the drive. After it fills up with the second copies of files you are working on, label the disk with the date(s) and put the floppy away. If you rotate the disks every 30 days, the cost of the disks will be minimized. Those floppy disks, labeled and put in a safe place, are the best insurance against the files being damaged or lost.

If you are not this careful about making second copies of all the files you use during the day, at least make copies of your critical files. These are likely to be the mailing list of 2,000 customers, the company budget spreadsheet, and the accounting data. Imagine what would happen to your company if such data were lost. You can see how important that second (and third) copy of the data file is.

On the accompanying disk is a utility called FILL. This program copies a number of files to floppy disks, selecting files as needed from the list to fill the disk. Files are in standard DOS format. More information on the FILL utility is provided in Part III, "Guide to Using the Disk."

Just copying a file to a floppy disk is not feasible if the file is larger than the capacity of the largest floppy disk in the system. A data file containing a 2,000-name mailing list may be larger than one 360K disk (double-density 5 1/4-inch) can hold. If this is the case, the special programs described here will be necessary to copy such a file to a series of floppy disks.

DOS includes programs to back up and restore data on a hard disk. These programs are covered in the topics BACKUP — Files (41) and RESTORE — Files (42). The BACKUP program makes a complete copy of all the files on the hard disk to floppy disks — typically dozens of disks, depending on the capacities of the hard drive and the floppy disks. Not only does the DOS BACKUP program require many disks, but a complete backup of a hard drive also can take hours. If your hard drive has never been backed up and DOS BACKUP is the only program available, use the program *now!*

Several commercially available programs can save you both time and disks. They copy files to floppies but compress the data as they make the copy. As with BACKUP, the files cannot be directly used from the floppy disk, but these programs do allow you to find a specific file within the entire set of disks. Two popular programs are PC Tools and Fastback Plus. They can reduce the number of required disks by half and the backup time by two-thirds.

Even if you do use DOS BACKUP or a commercial program, you do not have to copy the entire hard disk to floppies every time you make a backup. All these programs allow an *incremental* backup. This means that they can locate only those files that have changed since the last time the hard disk was backed up. With a biweekly schedule of backing up the entire hard drive, the daily incremental backup should take only a few minutes.

The actual schedule for backing up data files depends on how often and how much the data on the hard disk changes. If someone makes changes to the data every day for more than two hours, a backup should be made daily. If the system is used mostly for one-time word processing documents, a complete monthly backup may be adequate. The keys to the backup process are to perform the backups regularly and to make careful notes on the disks about the date and type of backup.

Other methods of backing up data from hard disks are available. Your system may have a tape drive or some other large-capacity disk system. These systems are typically quicker and easier to use because they are designed just for backing up files. In some cases, computers have a connection in the back. Someone travels around weekly with the tape drive and extra tapes in hand. After plugging into your system and making the backup, that person takes care of storing the backup tapes elsewhere in case your drive fails. Still, it is up to you to back up the files you've changed during the week.

In any event, find out when the system was last backed up. If it has not been backed up lately, arrange for a supply of disks. An estimate of the disks needed is provided in Table 13-1. Make a complete backup of your hard drive. If someone else has completed the backup, find out how often it is done and where the backup disks are kept. You may need to find them in a hurry. Table 13-1 shows the approximate number of floppy disks needed to back up hard disks of different sizes.

Table 13-1. Disks required for various sizes of hard disks.

	Hard Disk Size (in Megabytes)			
Disk Size	**20**	**40**	**80**	**120**
5 1/4-inch 360K	56	111	222	333
5 1/4-inch 1.2M HD	17	33	67	100
3 1/2-inch 720K	28	56	111	167
3 1/2-inch 1.44M HD	14	28	56	83

The backup software also requires a special process to restore the files, because the files do not have the normal DOS format when they are copied. With any luck, you won't have to learn how to use the restore process of the backup program. But without restoring the files, you cannot be sure that they have been copied properly. So the first time the hard disk is backed up, most programs will recommend that you "verify" the files. This involves reinserting each disk while the program reads the file on the floppy disk backup and compares that version to the file on the hard disk. This verification process is just additional insurance that the files on the floppy disks are accurate.

Figure 13-1 shows a sample screen from Central Point's PC Tools backup program. With this program, you can easily use either the mouse or the keyboard. The program compresses the files as it copies them to the floppy disk. Even before you begin backing up the files, PC Tools estimates the number of disks you'll need to complete the backup. The estimate is always the highest number of disks you'll need.

Exercise

Complete the following exercise because it is the right thing to do.

Exercise 1 of 1

This exercise does not require a computer or software. It falls under the "What's the plan?" category of learning. On a separate sheet of paper, answer the following questions:

1. What am I doing to make sure that I don't lose valuable data files?
2. What program or method do I use to back up these files?
3. Where are the backup disks located?

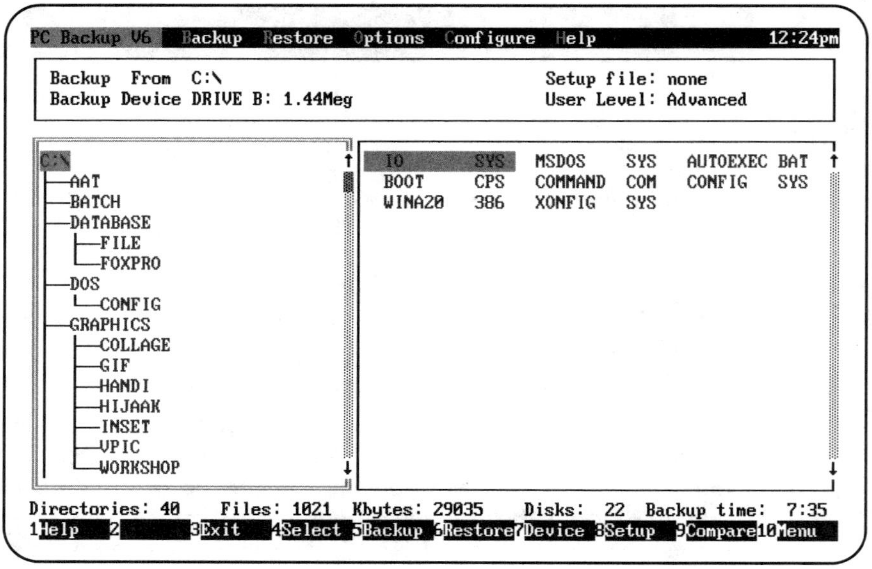

Figure 13-1. The PC Tools backup program.

4. How often are critical files backed up?
5. How do I restore the files if necessary?
6. Who do I contact for help?

If your answers to these questions are rather vague, answer the questions the way they should be answered and then begin backing up your data regularly. Here are some sample answers:

1. What am I doing to make sure that I don't lose valuable data files?

   I copy all files in the following subdirectories to high-density disks:

   C:\SHEETS
   C:\MAILLIST
   C:\ACCOUNT\GL
   C:\ACCOUNT\PAY
   C:\ACCOUNT\AR
   C:\ACCOUNT\AP

2. What program or method do I use to back up these files?

   I use the PC Tools PCBACKUP version 6.0. A copy of the PCBACKUP program is on a separate disk with this system's configuration and is located in the MIS department.

3. Where are the backup disks located?

   The most recent set is taken home by the department manager. She then brings back the set she has at home to be used as the third set.

   Set One <- At manager's home
   Set Two <- Next set to be used
   Set Three <- Just returned from manager's house

4. How often are critical files backed up?

   Incremental backups are performed daily and added to the current set. All critical files are backed up weekly and sent home with the manager on Friday night. MIS does a complete system backup once a month and keeps those disks.

5. How do we restore the files if necessary?

   Complete restoration of the disk:

   Contact MIS for the complete set.

   Restore that set, including programs, to the hard drive.

   Use the current backup set, beginning with the oldest disks. The newer files on later disks in the series will overwrite the older files.

   Selected restoration of files:

   PCBACKUP allows selective restoration.

6. Who do we contact for help?

   Call Jack N., support tech. in MIS at x 4534.

References

BACKUP — Files (41), RESTORE — Files (42), Utility Software (50), System Maintenance (94), Security (95)

NEXT TOPIC: Solving Problems (14)

Backing up too late

See Backing Up Data (13)

BACKUP — Files (41)

VERSIONS	
All	●
Some	○
5.0	○
Command	○
Program	●
Concept	○
Problem	○

The DOS BACKUP program copies files from a hard disk to many floppy disks with just one command. However, you cannot access the files on the backup floppies unless you use the RESTORE program. Backing up files regularly is the best way to prevent data loss in case your hard disk fails.

Before You Begin

Default Drive (3)
Backing Up Data (13)
Command and Program Parameters (34)

Syntax

`C:\>`**`BACKUP C:\ A: /S/F`**	This backs up all files, including subdirectories, from C: to A: and formats the floppy disks if needed.
`C:\>`**`BACKUP C:\ A: /S//F/M`**	The /M switch instructs BACKUP to back up only those files changed since the last backup.
`C:\>`**`BACKUP C:\ACCNT\*.* A: /F`**	This backs up files in just one specific subdirectory, /F (for FORMAT), as needed.

Problems

No backups. This problem has no solution. If your hard disk fails or your files become unreadable *and* you have not been backing up regularly, you are out of luck.

Backup disks out of order. All backup programs save files to disks *in order*. In most cases, you can recover from a disk out of sequence by inserting the proper disk. If you neglected to number the labels on the disks, you may have to abort the current restore and use **`DOS DIR`** on each disk so that you can read its sequence number.

Mixed disk capacities. Older versions of DOS BACKUP required the use of formatted disks. You had to format each disk to its proper capacity. DOS BACKUP 3.3 allowed BACKUP to format the disk but used the drive capacity. If you inserted double-density disks in a high-density drive, you had a problem with DOS 3.3. You had to use high-density disks in a high-density drive. With DOS 5.0, you can include a parameter after the /F switch to set the capacity of the disk format. For example, you can insert double-density disks in a high-density drive and use the /F:360 switch. The backup takes almost four times as many double-density disks, but you can still do this with DOS 5.O if you want.

Old version of RESTORE. DOS version 3.2 and earlier versions cannot restore files backed up with newer versions of BACKUP.

Explanation

BACKUP solves several problems related to keeping data files in more than one location (known as data redundancy). The command allows files larger than the capacity of the floppy to be copied across one or more disks. In addition, BACKUP allows incremental copies of files. It can use the archive bit to find and copy only those files created since the last backup session.

> Read RESTORE — Files (42) before using BACKUP.

The BACKUP program has changed with the versions of DOS. Probably the most significant change is BACKUP's capability to format disks before copying files to the disk. Older versions of DOS required disks that were previously formatted. Newer versions can include the /F switch to format floppy disks, if necessary.

The hardest part about using BACKUP is to set a schedule and keep it. Only when used regularly does BACKUP provide the insurance necessary to protect data files. See the topic Backing Up Data (13) for more information about the need for backups and how to schedule them.

Even though the file names of the backed-up files are visible with the DIR command, these files cannot be used as normal DOS files. Each file contains additional header information that is meaningless to any program other than RESTORE. With RESTORE, you can search the backup disks and restore individual files. This task is easier if you use the /L switch to keep a log file of the backup.

To perform the first complete backup of your hard drive, you should include the /S switch on the BACKUP command line so that all files in all subdirectories are included in the backup. With DOS versions 4.0 and 5.0, you can create and print a log file. Be sure to put the disks in a safe place. If the backup disks will be in drive A:, use this command line:

```
C:\>BACKUP C: A: /S/F/L:MAINBACK.LOG
```

If you want to print the MAINBACK.LOG file log to the printer, use this command:

```
C:\>TYPE \MAINBACK.LOG > LPT1:
```

With your weekly backup, include the /M switch with BACKUP so that only those files changed in the last week will be copied to the disk. You can use the /A switch to add the files to the last set of backup disks. This way, the disk set continues to be numbered in sequence. Without the /A switch, an additional set of disks is created with each backup.

The following command line with BACKUP 5.0 creates files on a new set of disks:

```
C:\>BACKUP C: A: /S/F/M/L:WEEK0826.LOG
C:\>PRINT \WEEK0826.LOG
```

Notice the log file name, which contains the word `WEEK`, `08` for the month, and `26` for the day.

You can also back up specific files based on the file date or time (or both) by using the /D switch for *d*ate or the /T switch for *t*ime. Table 41-1 shows all the BACKUP switches.

Table 41-1. The switches available in BACKUP 5.0.

Switch	Meaning
/S	Includes subdirectory files
/M	Backs up only those files changed since the last backup
/A	Adds backup files to existing backup disks
/F:*size*	Specifies the size of the disk to be formatted
/D:*date*	Backs up only those files changed on or after the specified date
/T:*time*	Backs up only those files changed at or after the specified time
/L:*logfile*	Creates a log file and entry to record the backup operation

The DOS BACKUP program is probably the least desirable of the programs for backing up files. A number of commercial programs can back up files more quickly. And the files take less space on the disk because the programs compress the data as the files are copied to the disk. PC Tools and Fastback Plus are highly rated backup programs. If you don't have one of these programs, using BACKUP is preferable to doing nothing at all.

A program included on the accompanying disk may provide an alternative to using BACKUP. The program, called FILL, copies files from the hard disk to floppies and instructs you to insert the next disk when the first one becomes full. FILL *cannot* copy a file larger than the disk capacity, though. For more information about FILL, see Part III, "Guide to Using the Disk."

The DOS 5.0 BACKUP program provides more information than previous versions of BACKUP. Figure 41-1 shows the progress of the backup of drive C:. Notice the use of the /S switch, which makes sure that the backup includes all the subdirectories below the root.

```
C:\>backup c: a: /s

Insert backup diskette 01 in drive A:

WARNING! Files in the target drive
A:\ root directory will be erased
Press any key to continue . . .

*** Backing up files to drive A: ***
Diskette Number: 01

\AUTOEXEC.BAT
\BOOT.CPS
\CONFIG.SYS
\MIRORSAV.FIL
\PCTRACKR.DEL
\WINA20.386
\XONFIG.SYS
\LD0013.PCX
\CONFIG.01
\LD0027.PCX
\AAT\AATEMP.OPT
\AAT\AATEMP.TXT
\AAT\AATEMP.FLX
```

Figure 41-1. The DOS 5.0 BACKUP program just after it begins to back up the files in the root directory of drive C:.

Exercise

To make sure that you are using BACKUP properly, you should run a test. In this exercise, you'll find a subdirectory on your disk and use BACKUP to copy the files to a disk. The next topic, RESTORE — Files (42), shows you how to restore the files back to the hard disk.

Exercise 1 of 1

Look around on your hard disk for a small subdirectory. It can contain 10 or 100 files, but the more files it contains, the longer the backup will take and the more disks you will need. For this exercise, that subdirectory is named TEST. Substitute your entire subdirectory path for the word TEST in the steps presented here. For example, if the command line is **BACKUP C:\TEST*.* A: /F**, you might type **BACKUP C:\WORD\DOCS*.* A: /F**.

Gather several blank disks. The DOS BACKUP program does not provide an estimate of the disks needed for a particular list of files. (Most commercial programs do.) The best approach may be to know where the new disk supply cabinet is. If you run out of disks in the middle of the backup, just let the system sit while you find more disks.

As mentioned, DOS versions 4.0 and 5.0 provide the /F switch for formatting the disk, if necessary, before BACKUP copies the files. If you are using an older version of DOS, you must first format your disks. These newer versions also include the /L switch for logging the backup process. Use of this switch is highly recommended. If you have DOS 4.0 or 5.0, you may want to use that switch on the command line as well.

TRY	NOTE
`C:\>`**`BACKUP C:\TEST\*.* A:`**	As with COPY, the first part of the command contains the location of the files to be copied. But the second part (in this case, A:) will always be just a drive letter. Additional switches can follow the A:.

Depending on the number of files, you may have to insert additional disks when prompted by BACKUP. You should label them in some way, making sure that you number and date every disk. You now know how to back up the files and label the disk(s). Be sure that you know how to use RESTORE (topic 42) to return the files to the hard disk.

References

Hard Drive Failure (33), Lost Data Files (77), Compressed Files (80), System Maintenance (94)

NEXT TOPIC: RESTORE — Files (42)

Backup disks out of order

See BACKUP — Files (41)

Bad command or file name (6)

VERSIONS
All ●
Some ○
5.0 ○

Command ○
Program ○
Concept ○
Problem ●

The error message `Bad command or file name` is displayed when you type a word that does not represent a DOS command or an available program. The system returns to the DOS prompt.

Problems

Mistyped command. Although DOS does not distinguish between upper- and lowercase words typed on the command line, the operating system does not know that **`DUR`** may be someone's effort to type **`DIR`**. Always check to make sure that you type your commands accurately.

Not an available program. After determining that the word typed is not a command, DOS searches the current directory and path for a program name that matches the word. If none is found, the error message is displayed. Possible solutions are presented in the next section.

Explanation

Some DOS messages are more serious that others. In the case of `Bad command or file name`, nothing happens after the message except that DOS returns to the prompt. (Some messages keep DOS from continuing.) Corrective action consists of retyping the command or program name.

Correcting the typed word is effective if that word is a DOS command. But what if the word represents a program you normally run and you are sure that you've typed the name correctly? There are several possibilities.

You may have forgotten to move into the appropriate subdirectory before issuing the command, even though you typed it correctly. In that case, DOS will not be able to run the program. Knowing where a program is located (in which subdirectory) is as important as knowing the file name of the program. Make sure that you are in the proper subdirectory and type the word again. If you need to know more about subdirectories, read the topic CD, MD, and RD — Working with Directories (9). If your prompt does not show which subdirectory you are in (that is, if it appears as `C>`), refer to the topic PROMPT — Command Line Information (26) or just type **`PROMPT $P$G`**.

Another possible reason for this error message is that the PATH setting in DOS has been changed or wiped out. In that case, DOS can no longer locate the program regardless of your location when you typed the name of the program. Type **PATH**. If the DOS response is `No path`, the PATH setting has been removed. The quick fix is to type **\AUTOEXEC**. If that doesn't fix the immediate problem, refer to the topic PATH — Program Search (29).

References

CD, MD, and RD — Working with Directories (9), Solving Problems (14), PROMPT — Command Line Information (26), AUTOEXEC.BAT (21)

NEXT TOPIC: A: B: C: — Drive Designation (7)

Bad or missing Command interpreter

See COMMAND.COM/EXIT (78)

Batch Files — Write Your Own (100)

VERSIONS	
All	●
Some	○
5.0	○
Command	○
Program	○
Concept	●
Problem	○

Batch files are one of the three types of program files (EXE, COM, and BAT) in DOS. These batch programs are typically used to run other programs and perform DOS operations.

Before You Begin

Default Drive (3)
File Names (4)
PATH — Program Search (29)
ASCII — Character Codes (74)
EDIT — DOS 5.0 Text Editor (98), EDLIN — Line Editor (99), or another word processor that can save files in ASCII format

In addition, you'll need to know most DOS commands and programs.

Syntax

`C:\>CLEAN`	You can run a batch file by simply typing its file name at the system prompt. The extension BAT is not necessary. Here a batch file named CLEAN.BAT is being called.

Problems

Unexpected batch file results. Be careful when you type batch file names just to see what the files accomplish. That could prove hazardous. To examine an unknown batch file before using it, use the TYPE method described later in this discussion.

Wrong directory for the batch file. Some batch files work correctly only in specific directories or with active paths. If the proper directory is not the default, the worst that can happen is that some DOS error messages will be generated and the batch file will not work as expected.

Time required to learn how to write batch files. Although batch files are small programs, they frequently do not work as you want them to the first or second time. Correcting them may require effective problem-solving skills and be time-consuming. In the long run, however, learning how to write batch files can save you a great deal of time.

Explanation

Batch files are actually program files written in the "batch" language. These files, along with COM and EXE files, are programs that control the computer. COM and EXE files are created by programming languages such as BASIC and PASCAL, whereas BAT files consist mostly of standard DOS commands, although additional batch commands do provide a fairly sophisticated language.

The term *batch* comes from the original use of these files. A "batch" process consists of a series of standard commands contained in one list. Within DOS, this list of commands is contained in an ASCII file with the BAT extension. Any DOS command or program that you can use at the standard system prompt can be included in a batch process.

The phrase *batch file* is typically used to designate the process of stringing together a series of DOS commands into a file that can be run like a program. You might think that "batch program" would be a more appropriate phrase. For consistency with standard terms, the phrase *batch file* is used in this book even though these files act like computer programs.

Writing batch files can be a very creative process. Although the batch language is fairly limited, batch files are typically used for the following operations:

- Running DOS programs more easily
- Performing routine housekeeping tasks
- Preventing the use of potentially damaging procedures
- Installing software
- Customizing DOS commands
- Setting up a complete menu system

Running DOS Programs

A common use for batch files is to start other DOS programs. A popular graphics program, PC Paintbrush IV Plus, must be started with the following series of commands and parameters:

```
FRIEZE HPLASER P1 0000 ACNQ 640 480 4
PBPLUS M ACNQ 640 480 4
FRIEZE
```

The first word on each line is the name of a program. The additional words and numbers represent information used by that program as it begins running. To start each program manually would require at least 70 keystrokes, assuming the user could remember and accurately type all those numbers. Fortunately PC Paintbrush IV Plus, when installed on the hard drive, asks several questions and then creates a batch file based on the responses to those questions. In this case, the program creates a batch file called PAINT.BAT, which contains the preceding lines. To run the PC Paintbrush IV Plus program, you just type **PAINT**. The batch file then issues each line as if it were a DOS command, and the program runs properly each time.

If you are somewhat familiar with batch files, you can see that the actual program which runs in this batch file is PBPLUS. Batch files can run other DOS programs or even other batch files and then return to continue processing. You'll explore this feature later when you create a batch menu system.

Routine Housekeeping

After using a hard disk for a few weeks or months and then examining various directories, you will probably see a fair amount of "clutter." Similar to the Sunday paper strewn around the living room at night, this clutter consists of old backup files and temporary files left behind by one program or another. These files take up disk space needlessly and fill up the directory. You can usually identify them by the extensions of BAK or TMP, or by such names as 098ABBCC.000. These are not files you knowingly created, so what do you do with them?

You can, of course, type **DEL 098ABBC.000** to delete that file. You can even use **DEL *.BAK** to erase all the backup files in the current subdirectory. But if you create a command that cleans out all the clutter in one step, you have gone from the broom to the vacuum cleaner of DOS batch file efficiency.

A series of DOS commands can provide you with a "clutter cleaner." Suppose that you notice many BAK and TMP extensions. A batch file can do all the work with just these two lines:

```
DEL *.BAK
DEL *.TMP
```

If you call the file CLEAN.BAT, you can simply type **CLEAN** every time you want to remove the files cluttering up your directory. When removing unknown files, you should be aware of some cautions. These are covered later when you create some sample batch files in the "Exercises" section.

Preventing Trouble

A few DOS programs can cause trouble. One of them is FORMAT. As you know, using FORMAT on a disk erases all the files on that disk. Even though DOS 5.0 users and a number of commercial programs can recover those files, you are still gambling that you can recover data accidentally lost when you weren't careful using FORMAT. Assume for a moment that you cannot recover the lost data and that other users are not as aware of the consequences of the FORMAT command.

If users have, for some reason, the misguided notion that they must type **FORMAT A:** before they use any disk, they could easily lose data on that disk. You can create a batch file to provide a warning about the consequences of that action. Then, when a user types **FORMAT A:**, a warning message like that shown in Figure 100-1 appears on the screen.

Renaming the original FORMAT program and placing the batch file in a subdirectory in the current PATH can also help prevent this accident as well as other DOS-related problems.

Installing Software

Installing software can be as simple as typing **COPY *.* C:** to get the program files onto the hard disk. But in many cases, the software has been compressed to fit on fewer disks, or may require special initialization procedures before it will run properly. Some of these programs use batch files to ensure that all the steps for installing the programs on the user's system are completed in the proper order.

Even though you don't create this kind of batch file in the "Exercises" section, it is helpful to know that frequently when you type **A:INSTALL** with a new program disk, you are executing a batch file.

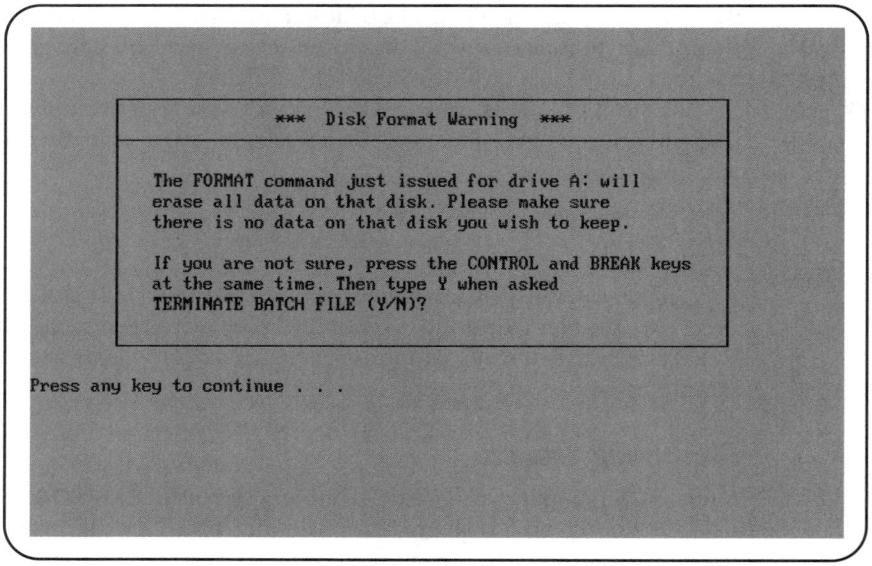

Figure 100-1. A batch-file warning message.

Customizing DOS Commands

If, as a typist, you are less than 100 percent accurate, you may occasionally type **DUR** when you mean to type `DIR`. Or you may prefer to use the /P switch with the DIR command. Perhaps you like to do as little typing as possible, and you therefore want to see your directory by typing **D**. You can solve all these problems by using batch files.

For the first fumble-fingered example, you can create a batch file named DUR.BAT that contains the single line `DIR`. Instead of the DOS message `Bad Command or file name` appearing on the screen, your DUR batch file will execute with the DIR command you intended. For both the second and third examples, you can name a batch file D.BAT and include in it one line with the command `DIR/P`. Type **D** and you will have a screenful of the directory listing, paused for you to `Press any key`.

DOS 5.0 users have a "cleaner" way to solve the fumble-fingered problem. See the topic DOSKEY (25) to make this even easier.

Setting Up a Batch Menu System

Plenty of menu systems are available for use with DOS. Some menu systems provide multiple levels and high security. Almost all of them cost more than the price of this book. If you need these features, by all means, find a menu system to meet those requirements.

If, however, you just want an easy-to-use menu that can be changed quickly, you can use batch files to create a simple menu system. With the DOS TYPE command and batch file names like 1.BAT and 2.BAT, you can get as fancy or stay as plain as you like. In the "Exercises" section, you learn how to create a menu system based on batch files.

Getting Ready

Anyone familiar with the uses for batch files mentioned in the "Explanation" section and with an interest in saving time can design, create, test, and use batch file programs. Although batch files eventually save you time, the initial cost is the time you spend learning how to create them.

The batch files you'll create in the "Exercises" section may be just the beginning of your batch programming efforts. Entire books are devoted to writing batch files, and you may become so interested in the topic that you'll want to do even more. For now, this discussion shows you how to build batch files by helping you build several that are useful.

Because the batch language is a "programming" tool, you need to apply standard programming methods to creating and using batch files. First you determine what you want to accomplish with the batch file. This phase is known as *design*. Then you physically create the program—in this case, a batch file. You test the newly created program, and if you are satisfied with the result, you put the batch file in a permanent location for easy use. If the batch file does not work as you expect, you must determine the problem, make corrections, and test again. This loop of testing and fixing is called *debugging*. Anyone who writes programs is all too familiar with the debugging process.

In the following discussion, a sample batch file is used to illustrate the four phases of creating a successful batch file: designing, creating, testing, and installing. You don't need to type any of the examples, although you may if you like. More specific instructions for creating batch files are included later in the "Exercises" section.

Designing

What is the program supposed to do? Preparing an answer to this question provides the framework for the design phase. In the case of batch files, the overriding answer is "to save time and effort." You need to be more specific, though, by deciding how you will save time. A helpful aspect of writing batch files is that you can try out each step in a batch file from the DOS prompt. More about the mechanics of creating batch files is included in Exercise 1.

Suppose that your specific goal is to restore the system prompt to your preferred form. You need a batch file to do this task because several batch programs installed from other applications keep changing the prompt to `C>`. Because you prefer `Mon 08-26-91 C:\>`, you want a quick way to fix the prompt when it has been corrupted by those other programs. (Actually, after you finish the exercises in this topic, you could find those "other" batch files and just fix them.)

If you are familiar with the DOS PROMPT command (topic 26), you know that $d provides the date, $p provides the current path, and $g provides the > character. To begin the design phase for the sample batch file, you type

```
PROMPT $d$p$g
```

at the DOS prompt, and you get the response

```
Mon 08-26-91C:\>
```

That's not exactly what you want. There is no space between the date and the C in the prompt. You try again by typing

```
prompt $d $p$g
```

and then you see

```
Mon 08-26-91 C:\>
```

Now that you know exactly what to put in the batch file, you need to decide what to name it. This sample file can be called CP.BAT for "clean prompt." Batch file names follow standard formats for DOS file names (topic 4). Note the following guidelines for naming a batch file and deciding where to keep it:

- Use a descriptive file name, long enough to be descriptive but short enough to be convenient.
- Don't try to use a DOS internal command, such as DIR or TYPE.
- Be careful about using DOS program names or names associated with other programs you use.
- A batch file's extension is always BAT.

The third guideline needs some explanation. Although you can use a DOS program name such as FORMAT, some additional work is necessary: you must rename the original DOS file. The FORMAT example presented earlier, in the section "Preventing Trouble," requires this approach. In that case, you can name the batch file FORMAT.BAT and rename FORMAT.COM (the original DOS file) as BFORMAT.COM. When you type **FORMAT**, the FORMAT.BAT batch file runs. Then BFORMAT runs after the warning message shown in Figure 100-1 is displayed.

Your final decision is where to put the batch file. The location of the file on the PATH statement can affect the use of the file name. If you create a batch file called WP.BAT but have a program on your hard disk called WP.EXE, your current location and the PATH variable will determine which of those two files runs when you type **WP**. Whichever of these two programs (WP.BAT or WP.EXE) is in the current directory is the program that will run. If DOS has to search the current PATH, the first subdirectory or drive in which DOS finds WP.BAT or WP.EXE determines which program runs.

Assume, for instance, that your current PATH is C:\;C:\DOS;C:\BATCH;C:\WORDPROC. WP.BAT is in \BATCH, and WP.EXE is in \WORDPROC. At the prompt `C:\GRAPHICS>`, you type **WP**. Which program runs—WP.BAT or WP.EXE? The answer is WP.BAT. In this case, DOS will always find WP.BAT first when searching for the program to run.

The design phase, then, is more than just deciding which DOS commands go in the batch file. This part of the process includes thinking about the file name and the final location of that file. Now you know exactly what you want to accomplish (for this example), the exact command to do it, and what you will name the file (CP.BAT).

Creating

You are now ready to create the batch file. The only requirement is that your word processor can save the file in ASCII format. All batch files are ASCII files. If you are not familiar with ASCII character codes, refer to topic 74. If you do not have a favorite word processing program, you can use EDLIN, which comes with all versions of DOS. Or you can use EDIT, which comes with MS-DOS 5.0. These two programs are covered in topics 99 and 98, respectively. The specific steps to create batch files are covered in more detail in the "Exercises" section of this topic.

Testing, Testing, Testing

Once you have created the actual file with a word processor, you should test it immediately by typing its file name. In this example, you type **CP** at the prompt `Mon 08-26-91 C:\>`. The batch file quickly runs, and the prompt `Mon 08-26-91 C:\>` appears again on the screen. How do you know that the batch file even worked?

Remember the reason for creating this batch file? Some programs that you use change the prompt to `C>`. You wanted to create a quick batch file to fix that. To test CP.BAT, then, you must create the condition you are attempting to resolve. In this case, you can just type **PROMPT**, and you'll have the plain vanilla prompt of `C>`. Then when you type **CP**, you should return to your preferred prompt of `Mon 08-26-91 C:\>`.

Testing this simple batch file is easy. Keep in mind that larger, more complicated batch files (and programs) take longer to test and may require more elaborate testing conditions before you can be sure that the batch files work. Most of the batch files that you create will be easy to test. Just remember that if you use destructive commands like DEL *.BAK in batch files, you'll want to test those files in a subdirectory where you won't lose anything important. For example, if you accidentally include the line DEL *. instead of DEL *.BAK, you'll lose all the files without an extension and without any warning!

Installing

Once you have designed, created, and tested the batch file, you should place it in a subdirectory specified in your PATH statement. A good subdirectory for this is \BATCH. If the PATH contains that subdirectory, you can use the batch file from anywhere in the system. Your PATH statement would look similar to `C:\DOS;C:\BATCH`. You should check your current PATH statement to make sure that placing your batch files within this subdirectory will work. For more information on the PATH command, see topic 29.

Exercises

As with many of the DOS commands, if you don't practice what you have learned about batch files, you'll soon forget most of it. The following exercises explore some of the reasons for writing batch files. From the four phases just described, you can see that the process is not automatic. But if you work through the seven exercises, you'll understand the process clearly, and you'll begin to create useful batch files of your own.

As mentioned earlier, complete books have been published about writing batch files. In these exercises, you just touch on the many ways to use batch files, and you sample only some of the commands available within batch files. If you are interested in batch programming, more advanced DOS books can provide all the commands and show you how to use them. Here is a summary of what each exercise covers:

Exercise 1	Running other programs with batch files and introducing the DOS command CLS and the batch commands ECHO and REM
Exercise 2	Making changes to a batch file
Exercise 3	Doing common chores and using the batch command PAUSE
Exercise 4	Providing user information and using the DOS command TYPE
Exercise 5	Creating a batch-file-based menu system
Exercise 6	Debugging batch files
Exercise 7	Using batch files with some more advanced batch commands and concepts

If you have problems with the first few exercises, jump ahead to Exercise 6, which provides hints on debugging batch files. Three helpful batch files are presented in Exercise 7.

For the first few exercises, use the disk supplied with this book. You'll branch out later to cover the specifics you can change to suit your batch file needs. If you do not already have that disk in drive A:, put it there now. Type **A:** to move to drive A:. The prompt should be A:\>. If the prompt is just A>, type **PROMPT pg**.

Exercise 1 of 7

Your first task is to create a batch file that runs a program called FIRSTBAT from anywhere within the system. You'll work out the design by typing each command at the DOS prompt. Once you know that the commands work as expected, you'll create the actual batch file, called FB.BAT for "first batch."

Remember that the instructions are in two columns. The left column shows you exactly what to type. The right column provides an explanation or indicates what you should see on the screen. **<Enter>** means that you are to press the Enter key.

TRY	NOTE
A:\>**CD\PROGTEST <Enter>**	You move into a specific subdirectory called PROGTEST on this disk.
A:\PROGTEST>**FIRSTBAT <Enter>**	Because FIRSTBAT is a program in this subdirectory, it runs now, like any EXE or COM program. (Silly message, huh?)
A:\PROGTEST>**CD\ <Enter>**	After FIRSTBAT is finished, the CD\ command returns you to the root directory.

These are the three commands you need for this batch file: PROGTEST, FIRSTBAT, and CD\. The first command moves you into the subdirectory containing the program you want to run. The second command runs the program. The last (and optional) command returns you to the root directory of your current disk. The actual batch file looks like this:

```
CD\PROGTEST
FIRSTBAT
CD\
```

With batch files under four or five lines, you'll use COPY CON in these exercises to create the files.

TRY	NOTE
C:\>**COPY CON:FB.BAT <Enter>**	Remember to press the Enter key at the end of each line. This command results in a promptless screen. Keep going.
CD\PROGTEST **FIRSTBAT** **CD**	These three lines make up the whole batch file.
<F6> <Enter>	Pressing the F6 key creates a Ctrl-Z character, which means "end of file." You've just copied the keystrokes from the CONsole to the file called FB.BAT.
C:\>**FB**	When you type **FB**, you run this newly created batch file, and the message should appear. Then, after you press any key, you will be left at the root directory (see Figure 100-2).

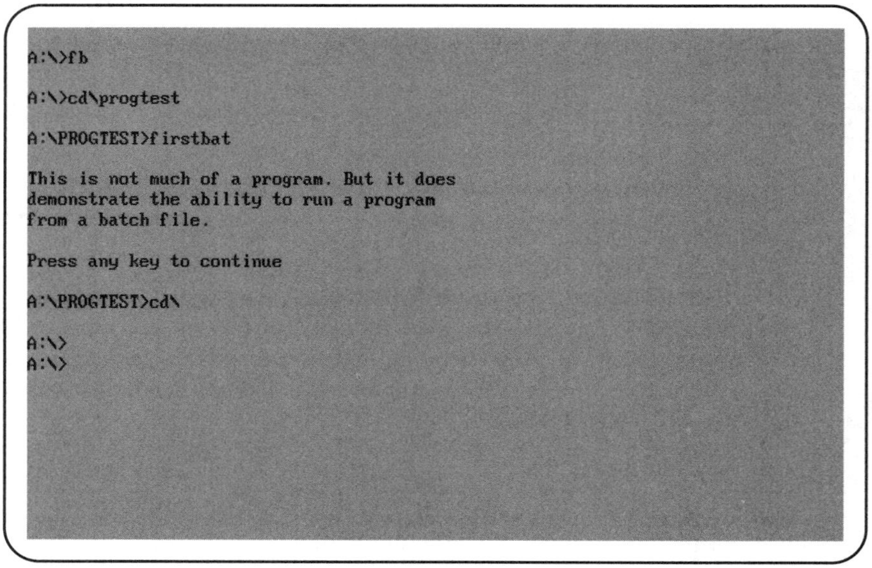

Figure 100-2. The result of running FB.BAT.

Notice in Figure 100-2 that the screen is a little cluttered. The message from the program remains on the screen, and the prompt showing the last subdirectory is still there. There is a DOS command that you can add to this batch file to make things look nicer when the program is completed. And there are several other specific batch commands to provide information to the user and to you.

The DOS command is CLS. Used on the DOS command line, CLS just clears the screen. Used in a batch file, CLS makes the screen look cleaner before, during, and after a batch file is running. More information on the CLS command is provided in topic 5.

Batch files also have their own command language. The commands will not work by themselves (or are of little use) on the command line. But within a batch file, the commands do have a purpose. The ECHO command prevents each line of the batch file from being displayed (echoed) on the screen. ECHO OFF keeps the lines from being displayed. ECHO ON restores the display of lines to the screen.

The other batch command, REM, is a noncommand. It does not do anything. It just allows you to document the purpose of your batch file. REM stands for REMark and tells DOS to ignore the rest of the line. You can then insert notes to yourself and anyone else who looks at the file. These notes can be as simple or as complete as you like. You'll provide some REMarks in the rest of these exercises.

As indicated earlier, the FB.BAT file contains the following three lines:

```
CD\PROGTEST
FIRSTBAT
CD\
```

Exercise 2 of 7

You are now ready to step through the DOS EDLIN program to make changes to this file. If you have another word processor or DOS 5.0 EDIT, just make the changes as shown in the steps. Before you begin, you need to know how to use EDLIN, EDIT, or your word processor so that you can create and change the ASCII file. When you are done, the file will look like this:

```
ECHO OFF
CLS
REM  FB.BAT
REM  Runs FIRSTBAT on the demo disk
REM  Jodi J. 08/26/91
CD\PROGTEST
FIRSTBAT
CD\
CLS
```

TRY	NOTE
`C:\>`**`EDLIN FB.BA <Enter>`**	You see *, which is the EDLIN asterisk prompt.
`1i <Enter>`	These characters are the number *1* and the letter *i*. You will be inserting five lines in front of the list of commands.
`ECHO OFF` **`CLS`** **`REM FB.BAT`** **`REM Runs FIRSTBAT on demo disk`** **`REM Jodi J. 08/26/91`**	Type each line exactly as shown. You may want to use your name and the current date, however. You'll see the EDLIN prompt (*) for each numbered line.
`<Ctrl>C`	Press and hold down the Ctrl key and then press the C key. EDLIN returns to the * prompt.
`9I <Enter>`	Begin inserting lines after line number 9.
`CLS` **`<Ctrl>C`**	Pressing Ctrl-C returns you to the EDLIN prompt (*).
`L <Enter>`	This lists the current file with line numbers 1 through 9. You don't have to do this step; it's just a way to make sure that things look right.
`E <Enter>`	This ends the EDLIN edit and saves the file.

The new version of FB.BAT is now on the disk. Test FB.BAT just as you did before, but notice the differences in Figure 100-3. The lines from the batch file don't appear on the screen (ECHO OFF), and the screen is cleared (CLS) before and after the program runs. Anyone who examines the file will know the purpose of the batch file and when you first created it.

The added REM, ECHO OFF, and CLS lines are not essential to running this batch file, but they do make things look better. A nine-line program may not seem to need three lines of REMarks. Consider that some batch files contain hundreds of lines. REMarks in those files are essential. Regardless of the size, a few REMark lines provide helpful information.

Now that you have designed, created, and tested a batch file, you would normally tuck it anywhere it can be useful (the installation process). A common location is a subdirectory called \BATCH. In this case, just leave FB.BAT on the disk included with this book.

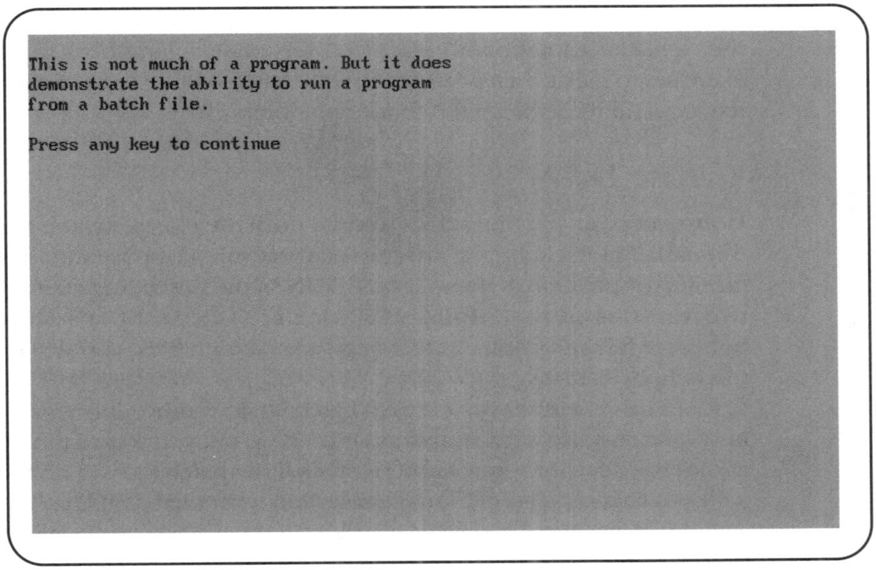

Figure 100-3. The result of running FB.BAT with REM, ECHO OFF, and CLS lines.

You can easily make changes to this batch file to suit your needs. Here is a generic version of FB.BAT:

```
ECHO OFF
CLS
REM  — Put the actual name of the file here
REM  — Explain the purpose of the batch file here
REM  — Give yourself credit and a date
CD\THE\FULL\PATH\NAME\GOES\HERE
PROGNAME
CD\
CLS
```

In your batch file, just change the italic text to whatever you like. Remember that you can provide additional parameters to the line with the program name, as for the PAINT.BAT file discussed earlier.

Go practice. Follow the steps in this exercise and create a batch file to run several of your most frequently used programs. Create, for example, a batch file named WP.BAT to start your word processing program. Use SHEET.BAT to start your spreadsheet program. COM.BAT might start your communications program. You've just learned about the most valuable batch file there is. It will save you dozens of keystrokes a day.

What if all your new batch file names are as hard to remember as the commands they replace? A solution is presented in Exercise 5. First work through the next two exercises to pick up a few more ideas for batch files. Exercise 5 then shows you how to gather all these batch files under one umbrella.

Exercise 3 of 7

Housekeeping. No one wants to do it until the closet, er, the hard disk is full. In this case, "housekeeping" means the removal of old backup files and temporary files left by programs. If you used EDLIN in the preceding exercise, you now have two versions of the FB file: FB.BAT and FB.BAK. EDLIN left the BAcKup file behind. After you create and change a few batch files, you will have on your disk many useless files.

In this exercise, you create a batch file to remove those extraneous files. You know that it could be as simple as DEL *.BAK, but you want a more utilitarian file. In addition, you want some warning of what the batch file will do before it does it, as well as a chance to stop it. In this case, you want the batch file to work in two parts. The first part shows you what the file will do. The second part does it if you don't stop the file. Of course, you need to be able to pause the batch file during execution.

A useful batch file command is PAUSE. A PAUSE line in the batch file stops the process and presents the user with the prompt `Press any key to continue...` (Older versions of DOS may say `Strike a key when ready...`) Once the user presses any key, the batch file continues. But since you can press Ctrl-C to stop a batch file, you have the chance to change your mind about letting the batch file continue with its—in this case, destructive—command.

Assume that you have BAK files you don't want. In addition, you have a program that creates backup files with the tilde (~) in the extension. Backup files from this program have names like THIS.~TX and THAT.~DO. You want to rid your directories of these files as well. You know that you need to type both **DEL *.BAK** and **DEL *.~??** to clean things up. Because you also want to see the files you are removing, you first need to type **DIR *.BAK** and **DIR *.~??** so that you can decide whether you really want to delete those files. If you have not done any house keeping for a while, you may have quite a few old files. For that reason, you want to include the /P switch on the DIR command line so that the screen pauses if it fills up with the BAK and ~?? directory listing. With those design decisions made, your batch file is beginning to take shape:

```
DIR *.BAK /P
DIR *.~?? /P
PAUSE
DEL *.BAK
DEL *.~??
```

This batch file will work. It just won't give you much information. You can add some information for anyone who uses the file:

```
ECHO OFF
CLS
REM CLEAN.BAT
REM Removes backup files after showing the
REM files that would be deleted.
REM Cheri C. 8/26/91.
DIR *.BAK /P
DIR *.~?? /P
ECHO  Press <CTRL>C now if you do not
ECHO  want to erase these files.
PAUSE
DEL *.BAK
DEL *.~??
CLS
```

The only thing left in the design phase is to decide what name to call the file. You already know that you'll call it CLEAN.BAT from the REMark in the third line. Now create the file with your favorite word processor and make sure that you save the file on the disk that comes with this book.

You should have on that disk several files that you are going to turn into "backup" files for testing. If you run this program and don't have any files with the extension BAK or ~??, there won't be anything to test. In that case, use the COPY command in the root directory of the accompanying disk to create these test backup files. Just type

```
COPY  *.* *.BAK
```

This copies all the files in the current directory to the same directory but renames all the files with the extension BAK. There is little reason to use this trick in everyday DOS. In this exercise, it helps you to test CLEAN.BAT. Now COPY some files so that they have the strange extension with the tilde. Use the FB.BAK and CLEAN.BAK files:

```
COPY FB.BAK FB.~BA
COPY CLEAN.BAK CLEAN.~BA
```

You should now have a directory listing that includes such file names as

```
FB.BAT
FB.BAK
FB.~BA
CLEAN.BAT
CLEAN.BAK
CLEAN.~BA
```

Other files are likely to be listed as well, depending on what else you have done on the disk that comes with this book.

Figure 100-4 shows the result of running CLEAN.BAT with this small list of files. (Your screen may list more files, of course.) If you have other file extensions that you know are leftover files, you can add two lines for each new extension, one line in the DIR part of the batch file and the second line in the DEL part of the file.

The only step left is to put (install) this batch file in your BATCH subdirectory. Just copy the file from A: to that subdirectory. Now, whenever you are in a subdirectory cluttered with BAK and ~?? files, just type **`CLEAN`**, make sure that the list represents files you want to delete, and `Press any key...`

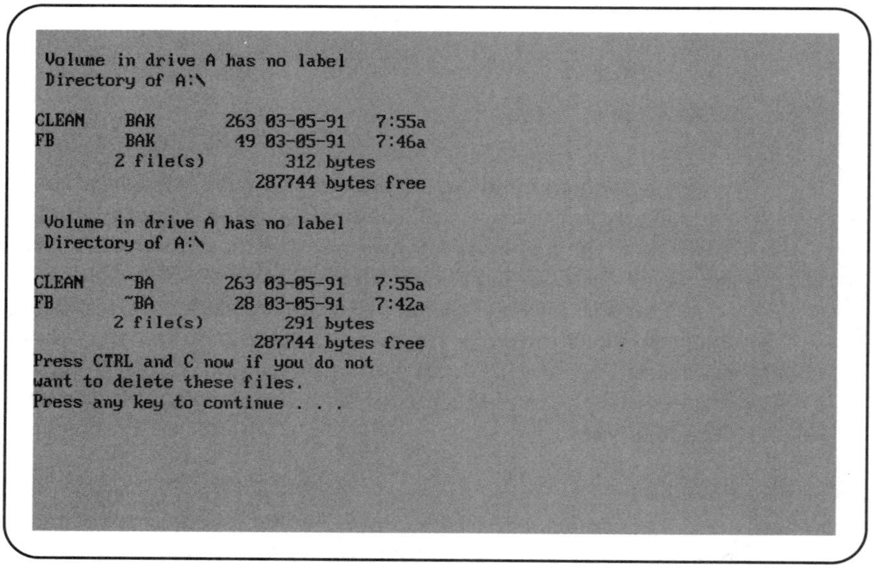

Figure 100-4. The result of running CLEAN.BAT.

Exercise 4 of 7

Many DOS programs and commands use switches, as explained in the topic Command and Program Parameters (34). Remembering those switches, even if you use them daily, can be difficult. The series of batch files presented in this exercise can help you format a variety of disks in the two types of floppy drives available in DOS machines: 5 1/4 inch and 3 1/2 inch. For more information, refer to Floppy Disks (19). Here you just build the batch files to make the process of formatting easier.

Assume that you have a high-density 5 1/4-inch drive as A: and a high-density 3 1/2-inch drive as B:. If you don't have one of these or a hard disk, at least follow along in this exercise. To learn why formatting with all these commands may be necessary, read the topic FORMAT — Disks (12). During the design phase, you should consider the following:

- Providing information to the user
- Allowing for the proper selection of disk and drive
- Performing the appropriate action for that disk and drive

First you create the information file for the user. This also helps you plan the actual choices for the user. With your favorite word processor, create the following file and save it as FORMINFO.SCR:

```
              *** Batch Format Choices ***

          1F)   Format a 1.2 meg (HD) disk in drive A:
          2F)   Format a 360 k (normal) disk in drive A:
          3F)   Format a 1.44 meg (HD) disk in drive B:
          4F)   Format a 720 k disk in drive B:
          5F)   Return to the main menu

Type the number of your choice, type the letter F, and then press <ENTER>
  Remember that any existing data is destroyed on the disk!
```

When a user types FORMAT (the name of the batch file), this message appears on the screen. Once you have saved FORMINFO.SCR, use the DOS TYPE command to look at that file:

TYPE FORMINFO.SCR

In fact, this is the only line necessary in the actual batch file. Here is what FORMAT.BAT looks like:

```
ECHO OFF
CLS
REM FORMAT.BAT
REM Replaces the DOS FORMAT program
REM Becky W. 08/26/91
TYPE FORMINFO.SCR
```

You could use a series of ECHO statements in the batch file to achieve the same effect. This file instead includes the TYPE command, which is the method you'll use in the next exercise as well. Before you can test this batch file, you must make a major change to the DOS program FORMAT.COM. You need to rename it as BFORMAT.COM. Return to your hard disk and the DOS subdirectory so that you can rename this file. The command lines will look something like this:

```
A:\>C:
C:\>CD\DOS
C:\DOS>REN FORMAT.COM BFORMAT.COM
```

Again, these particular lines may vary. Your hard disk may be D:, your DOS subdirectory may be named SYSTEM or BIN, and your FORMAT.COM may be FORMAT.EXE. Adapt as necessary.

Remember that renaming a program file does not change the function of the program in any way. It just means that you have to type **BFORMAT** instead of **FORMAT** in order to format a disk. If renaming a program file makes you a bit nervous, you may want to look at REN — REName Files (76). After you are done with this exercise, you'll type **FORMAT**, and this helpful series of batch files kicks into action.

Now when you test the file called FORMAT.BAT, you should get a screen that looks just like that in Figure 100-5.

Of course, all those menu choices don't mean anything yet. You have to create the batch files by those same names in order for this process to be useful. Each batch file looks almost the same. You create and test the first one, 1F.BAT, as described here. Then you'll see what lines to substitute in creating the additional files. Here is the first batch file:

```
ECHO OFF
CLS
REM 1F.BAT
REM Formats the default disk type in drive A:
REM Kathy E. 08/26/91
BFORMAT A:
FORMAT
```

This batch file is called when you type **1F**. It runs the newly renamed BFORMAT.COM, which performs the formatting process on the disk in drive A:. This batch file then redisplays the Batch Format Choices menu.

Each of the next three files is almost the same except for the line that calls BFORMAT (line 6). The REMark lines should also be changed but, as you have learned, they will not have any influence on the performance of the file. Table 100-1 contains the different lines for the three files. For more information on these FORMAT switches, read FORMAT — Disks (12).

```
                 *** Batch Format Choices ***

          1F)  Format a 1.2 meg (HD) disk in drive A:

          2F)  Format a 360 k (normal) disk in drive A:

          3F)  Format a 1.44 meg (HD) disk in drive B:

          4F)  Format a 720 k disk in drive B:

          5F)  Return to the main menu

 Type the number of your choice, type the letter F, and then press <ENTER>.

       Remember that any existing data is destroyed on the disk!
```

Figure 100-5. The opening screen for the helpful FORMAT batch files.

Table 100-1. The BFORMAT line in each of the three remaining batch files.

File Name	The BFORMAT Line
2F.BAT	`BFORMAT A: /4`
3F.BAT	`BFORMAT B:`
4F.BAT	`BFORMAT B: /t:80 /n:9`

Use your word processor, call up 1F.BAT, and make the appropriate change for the next file. Then save that changed file under a new name, such as 2F.BAT. Do this for 3F.BAT and 4F.BAT if you have a 3 1/2-inch drive B:.

The 5F.BAT program is completely different. This batch file needs to "return to the main menu." For now, just assume that you want to clear the screen and return to the root directory. Later you can add a line to this batch file to actually "return to the main menu." This batch file is very basic. The only real operations are CLS and CD\. But to be consistent, use the file name 5F.BAT for the novice user. Here is the file:

```
ECHO OFF
CLS
```

```
REM 5F.BAT
REM Return to the main menu
REM Kathy E. 08/26/91
CD\
```

As always, test this series of batch files carefully. When you are satisfied that they work, copy them to the appropriate subdirectory (such as BATCH). You have also renamed your FORMAT.COM program to BFORMAT. When you are through, you will have added the following files to that directory:

```
FORMAT.BAT
FORMINFO.SCR
1F.BAT
2F.BAT
3F.BAT
4F.BAT
5F.BAT
```

It looks as though the next time you type **FORMAT**, you'll get this helpful series of commands and will be able to handle a wide variety of formatting tasks with just three keystrokes and a minimum of brain drain. Well, not exactly. You have a condition you haven't tested yet.

Move into another subdirectory and type **FORMAT**. What happens? You get a `File not found` message and no Batch Format Choices menu. This slipup occurred because you tested the batch files within the same subdirectory. Because you want to issue the FORMAT command from any location on the disk, you need to modify the batch file slightly so that FORMAT.BAT knows exactly where to find the FORMINFO.SCR file, regardless of the default directory. Change the FORMAT.BAT file to include the final subdirectory containing FORMINFO.SCR. For example, you might change `TYPE FORMINFO.SCR` to `TYPE C:\BATCH\FORMINFO.SCR`. Now test the batch file again. This time, it should display the Batch Format Choices menu. Use each of the menu choices. If all of them work, the installation is complete.

Exercise 5 of 7

By now, you are familiar with the process of designing, creating, testing, and installing batch files. This exercise provides one of the easiest menu systems a DOS system can have. The menu system is a hypothetical one, based on commands and concepts described in the preceding exercises. You won't actually use the batch files as presented here, but you can build similar files to use on your own system. This batch file menu is easy to change and will not conflict with other programs.

The overall design for the menu system was laid out in Exercise 4, and the batch file format was introduced in Exercise 1. The batch file to display the menu screen is called MENU.BAT. The actual text on the screen is MENU.SCR. Each batch file is named with a number—1.BAT, 2.BAT, and so on.

The menu screen can be as simple or as fancy as you like. Just remember that a fancy screen is more difficult to change when you invariably need to add or delete parts of it. Figure 100-6 shows a screen designed with ASCII characters, including the extended characters for lines and corners. The menu in this exercise will not be as complicated. It will not include the lines.

Figure 100-7 shows the directory structure of the hypothetical disk used in constructing the menu system.

On this disk, you want to be able to run five programs quickly. Table 100-2 shows the programs, their paths, and their names.

Table 100-2. Five programs you can run with the batch menu system.

Program	File Name	Subdirectory
FOXPRO	FOXPRO	DATABASE\FOXPRO
PC-File	PCF	\DATABASE\PCFILE
Microsoft Word	WORD	\WORDPROC\WORD5
Power Basic	PB	\LANGUAGE\PBASIC
Batch format menu	FORMAT	\BATCH

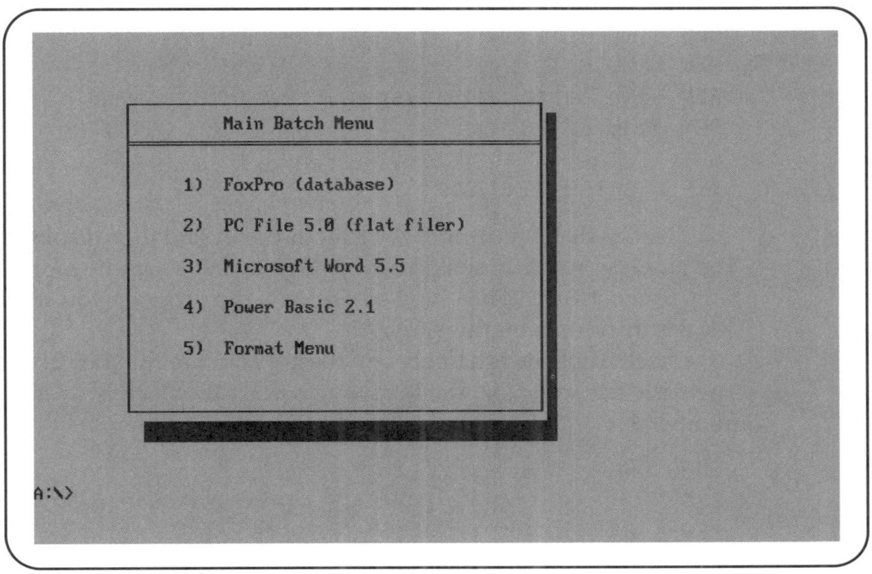

Figure 100-6. A batch file menu with extended ASCII lines.

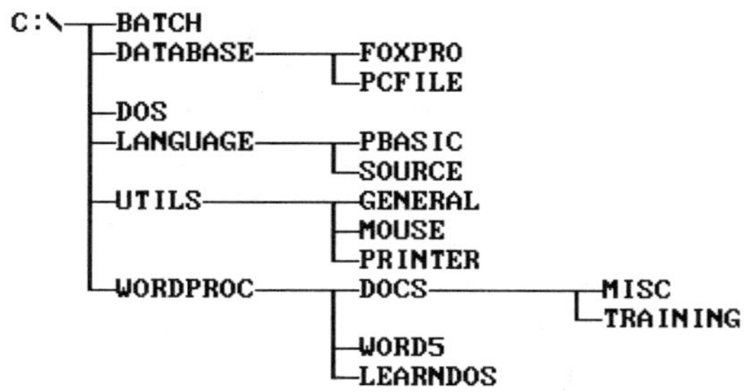

Figure 100-7. A sample directory structure.

The screen file just contains the menu text. When you create your menu screen, arrange the lines however you like. Here is a suggested arrangement:

```
     Main Batch Menu
1)   FoxPro (database)
2)   PC File 5.0 (flat filer)
3)   Microsoft Word 5.5
4)   Power Basic 2.1
5)   Format Menu
```

Now look at the main file, MENU.BAT:

```
ECHO OFF
CLS
REM MENU.BAT
REM Main batch menu system
REM Andy S. 08/26/91
CD\
TYPE \BATCH\MENU.SCR
```

Notice that it returns to the root directory and then displays the menu screen. The menu system is based on a loop. MENU.BAT starts the loop. The specific batch file (named 1.BAT, 2.BAT, and so on) calls the program you want to run and then restarts the loop with this program.

Each batch file is named with the appropriate number from the menu screen. The basic file looks like the following batch file, which is written for menu choice number 1:

```
ECHO OFF
CLS
REM 1.BAT
REM Runs FOXPRO database
REM Andy S. 08/26/91
CD\DATABASE\FOXPRO
FOXPRO
MENU
```

The information in Table 100-2 shows what you need to change in the other batch files. The fifth choice represents a batch file (5.BAT) calling a batch file (FORMAT.BAT). Although it is possible to have one batch file call another and then return to itself, it is easier just to make sure that the second batch file returns you to the start of the menu loop. As cautioned before, the 5.BAT program needs to be changed slightly to work with the entire menu system. Add the line MENU to the end of the FORMAT.BAT file, and it will work within this system.

Exercise 6 of 7

Debugging is the process of trying to figure out what is going wrong with your program—in this case, a batch file. The design phase should prevent any serious bugs. Remember to be extremely cautious when working with DOS commands like DEL and REName. Here are a few hints, in order of effectiveness, for ways to discover batch file bugs:

1. Edit the file by putting REM in front of ECHO OFF and CLS. Each line of the batch file will then be displayed on the screen. Take REM out of the line after you solve the problem.
2. Press Ctrl-Print Screen to echo all the lines to the printer. This enables you to keep track of messages that disappear too quickly on the screen. Remember to press Ctrl-Print Screen after working the problem out.
3. Insert a PAUSE line just before and after the suspected problem line in the batch file.
4. Check the spelling of all subdirectories and program names.
5. Make sure that the batch file changes to the proper drive before you change directories.
6. Be sure that the PATH statement includes the subdirectory with the batch files, such as C:\DOS;C:\BATCH.
7. Make sure that your current version of DOS supports the batch command you are trying to use. (The examples presented so far should work with all versions of DOS. Some of the examples in the next exercise may not.)
8. Be certain that no < and > characters are in any lines unless they are serving as redirects.
9. Check your design logic.
10. Check your test conditions.
11. Read the manual.

Exercise 7 of 7

Presented here are three batch files. They demonstrate new concepts, including the use of parameters and another way to use the ECHO command. These files are more powerful and dangerous. Develop and test them in a safe area of the disk.

Removing a Subdirectory and Its Files (NUKE.BAT)

Have you even wanted to rid your disk of a subdirectory and all its files? As you know, you cannot just RD the subdirectory if it contains something. This first batch file, called NUKE.BAT, performs the following tasks:

- Displays the contents of the targeted subdirectory and pauses for your approval
- DELetes those files and removes the subdirectory
- Uses a batch file's capability to read additional information from the program line, and inserts that data into the batch file process
- Provides a message, through the GOTO and IF commands, if you don't give the name of the subdirectory to NUKE.BAT

  Test this one carefully (it's hot):

```
ECHO OFF
CLS
REM NUKE.BAT - Displays files in a subdirectory and then removes
REM the files and that subdirectory.   Dan Derrick 08/26/91
REM
IF "%1"=="" GOTO HELP
DIR %1\*.* /P/W
ECHO ***** The subdirectory: %1 and
ERASE %1\*.*
RD %1
ECHO If there is another subdirectory under this one,
ECHO %1 will not be removed. Run NUKE within %1.
GOTO END
:HELP
ECHO You must supply the name of the subdirectory to
ECHO remove when running this batch file i.e. NUKE TEMP
:END
```

Backing Up Special Files (LEARNDOS.BAT)

Backing up files regularly is an important but often neglected task. The many ways to back up files, along with suggested schedules, are explained more completely in the topic Backing Up Data (13). You want a batch file that copies files from a particular directory to a specified disk drive and automatically erases the target floppy drive before the copy. This batch file, named LEARNDOS.BAT, is limited to files that will fit on one disk. The key is to run the batch file often, probably daily! Here is LEARNDOS.BAT:

```
@ECHO OFF
CLS
REM LEARNDOS.BAT
REM Copies critical data files to a floppy
REM Dan Derrick 08/26/91
REM
ECHO  Insert the target disk in B: All data will be erased.
PAUSE
ERASE B:*.* < C:\BATCH\Y.DTA
COPY D:\BOOKS\LEARNDOS\*.* B:
ECHO Remove the disk and put today's date on the label.
PAUSE
CLS
```

LEARNDOS.BAT has several new tricks. DOS users with version 3.3 or a later version can use the @ in front of a command to keep the command from echoing to the screen. The ERASE command also uses the redirect symbol (<). The Y.DTA file just contains the letter Y. This file provides the response to the prompt `All files in the directory will be erased. Are you sure (Y/N)?` More information on redirection is available in the topic Redirection < > ¦ (64).

You can readily adapt this file to your needs. Choose a name that is easy to remember, and include it in your batch file menu system. Use the appropriate drive, either A: or B:. Have the COPY line point specifically to the files you want to back up regularly. And keep in mind that the Y.DTA line must contain the complete path name to the batch file that uses Y.DTA —in this example, C:\BATCH\Y.DTA.

Reorganizing Your Hard Disk (MOVE.BAT)

After using a hard disk with multiple subdirectories for a while, most users see better ways to organize the data. Data files usually need to be moved from one subdirectory to another in the reorganization process. MOVE.BAT does this with one command. And with GOTO, the batch file also prompts for the required source and target (where the files come from and go to). MOVE.BAT looks like this:

```
@ECHO OFF
CLS
REM MOVE.BAT - Moves files in a subdirectory to another
REM and then deletes the files in the first subdirectory.
REM Dan Derrick 08/26/91
```

```
REM
IF "%1"=="" GOTO HELP
IF "%2"=="" GOTO HELP
COPY %1 %2
ERASE %1 < C:\BATCH\Y.DTA
GOTO END
:HELP
ECHO .
ECHO You must supply the name of the source and target
ECHO when running this batch file i.e.
ECHO "C:\WORDPROC> MOVE\WORDPROC\BOSS\WORDPROC\FIRED"
ECHO .
:END
```

This batch file uses two replaceable parameters, %1 and %2. If the file does not find two entries on the command line, the help screen appears, and the batch file quits. Also notice that two ECHO lines have only a period. Because the command ECHO (with nothing else on the line) presents the message `ECHO is ON` or `ECHO is OFF`, placing a period on the line provides a blank line. This feature is just cosmetic, but it does make the message more readable.

The accompanying disk contains a program called MV (MoVe) that does essentially the same thing as the MOVE.BAT program except that MV doesn't cross drives. See Part III, "Guide to Using the Disk," for more information about MV.

Reference

NEXT TOPIC: More about This Book (101)

Blank disk

See FORMAT — Disks (12)

Blurry screen

See Monitor (61)

Boot disk missing message on screen

See Boot/Startup (1)

Boot failure

See Boot/Startup (1)

Boot/Startup (1)

VERSIONS	
All	●
Some	○
5.0	○
Command	○
Program	○
Concept	●
Problem	○

Boot means to start the computer. Turning the computer on is a *cold boot*. Pressing Ctrl-Alt-Del (pressing and holding down Ctrl and Alt while you then press Del) restarts the computer with a *warm boot*. The operating system must be on a disk in drive A: or on the hard disk inside the computer in order for the boot to work properly.

Problems

Warning!

Warm booting when a program is running may result in the loss of some or all of your work.

Do not turn the computer off and immediately back on again. Wait at least 10 seconds.

You turn on the switch, but nothing happens. Very shortly after you flip the power switch, most computers start a fan. (Small laptops don't.) If there is no sound, check to see whether the computer is plugged into a power strip and the power strip is turned on. Check all connections, including the power cord connection in the back of the computer.

Nothing appears on the screen. As the computer starts, a series of numbers should appear on the screen. (Newer PCs may finish this memory check before the screen warms up, so it may not be numbers that appear.) If, after a minute, nothing appears on the monitor, check to make sure that the monitor is on. It has its own switch. Check the cable and connector between the monitor and the computer, as well as the monitor's power cord.

Nothing else happens. A blinking light (cursor) appears on the screen, and one or more drive lights come on, but that's all. Some older systems just stop if they cannot find the proper DOS files. Read the next problem for the solution.

The `BOOT disk missing` message is on the screen. Other messages may include `COMMAND.COM missing`, `System halted`, or `Boot failure`. In all cases, the reason is the same. The system files that contain DOS were not found when the computer looked for them on a disk in drive A: or on the internal hard disk. The immediate solution is to insert a system or boot disk and restart the system. See FORMAT — Disks (12) to create a system disk.

Explanation

When the computer is first turned on, the hardware inside the computer follows its own series of internal steps. The first step includes checking the power supply and memory. As the memory is being checked, numbers usually appear in the upper left corner of the monitor. The final internal step is to look for the operating system on a disk. Most systems look in drive A:, the main floppy drive on every computer, for the disk containing the operating system. If no disk is in drive A:, the system looks on the hard disk, drive C:.

Once the computer hardware finds the operating system (usually DOS) software on the disk, the computer turns operation over to that software. The first files located and started are the "boot" files. These files begin issuing commands to the computer to get it ready to run the application programs, which are the word processing or spreadsheet programs you want to use. Without these initial "bootstrap" programs, the computer stops working and may (or may not) issue an error message and additional instructions. For more information on what the operating system software does, read the topic Operating Systems (75).

If the computer does not respond in any way (it is locked up), pressing Ctrl-Alt-Del should warm boot (restart) the computer. DO THIS ONLY AS THE LAST RESORT. Any program that is running at the time may have data still in memory. That data is lost when the system restarts with a boot. For example, if you have not saved a letter to disk with a specific save command, the data will be lost. If you saved part of the work earlier, that part may be on the disk after the restart. The work you have done since the last file save will be lost if the system is rebooted.

If Ctrl-Alt-Del does not work, you may have to turn the computer off. Do *not* immediately turn it back on again. Wait at least 10 seconds. This allows the hard drive to stop spinning and various electronic parts to discharge. Powering off and back on immediately may not damage the system in the short run. Repeatedly doing this is likely to damage the computer.

Depending on the type of computer you have, you will see different screens as the system boots. The oldest PCs had just a flashing cursor in the upper left corner of the screen. The next generation, the XT systems, at least provided in the upper left corner a series of numbers that showed the progress of the internal memory check. The newer AT and 386 systems have much more. For information on these systems, see Microprocessors (96).

Typically the video card displays information, and then the system performs a memory check. Because some systems contain a lot of memory and this task can take a few moments, most systems suggest that you `Press <ESC> to bypass memory test`. If you are impatient and allow the memory test to run to completion some of the time, pressing Esc does not harm the system.

Once the memory test is completed, you will see the prompt `Press <DEL> if you want to run SETUP/EXTD-SET`. This allows you to make changes to the system time and date. But since you can also change the hard drive type, be careful if you do use the Delete key. You can easily make setting changes that prevent the system from working at all.

When the hardware has run through its steps, you may see information from various devices loaded from CONFIG.SYS and AUTOEXEC.BAT. These small programs (topics 21 and 22) set up the system to work the way that you or someone else wants it to work. Only in rare cases would you try to interrupt this process.

At some point, you will also hear one or more beeps. Most systems provide just one "OK" beep in the process of booting. The purpose of the beep is to signal trouble with the system. If the beep pattern is different—such as two beeps, or one short and one long beep—the system is warning you that something is wrong. In some cases, it may be that the keyboard has come loose. In any case, if the beep changes, solve the problem before continuing to use the system.

Exercise

The following exercise shows you how to warm-boot your computer system. If you normally turn your system on in the morning, this exercise should work. If your system remains on all the time, you may want to check with someone before performing this action.

Exercise 1 of 1

Make sure that you are not in a program. You may be looking at the DOS prompt (`C:\>`) or a menu system. Be sure to read through this exercise before trying it.

TRY	NOTE
`<Ctrl><Alt><Del>`	When you press and hold down the Ctrl and Alt keys and then press the Delete key, the system restarts. Watch the screen as it returns to the menu or DOS prompt.

Notice that you must press and hold down the first two keys while you then press the Delete key. Any other order will not work.

References

Solving Problems (14), AUTOEXEC.BAT (21), PROMPT — Command Line Information (26), Operating Systems (75), History of DOS (88)

NEXT TOPIC: Files (2)

Bytes and Computer Math (67)

VERSIONS	
All	●
Some	○
5.0	○
Command	○
Program	○
Concept	●
Problem	○

Computer measurements are based on a binary system of math. Binary numbers use 0 and 1 to count, which results in the rounding of numbers. The large numbers are abbreviated as K for kilobyte, M for megabyte, and G for gigabyte.

Problem

Confusing kilobytes and megabytes. One kilobyte equals approximately 1,000 (one thousand) bytes. One megabyte equals approximately 1,000,000 (one million) bytes. There are approximately 1,000 kilobytes in one megabyte. The approximation is the result of rounding binary numbers to decimal numbers. Later in the "Explanation" section, you'll see what the real values are and how they got that way.

Explanation

Computers really use only *on* and *off* to measure and record data. This is binary math, meaning the base of two, using 0 and 1. When these numbers are converted to decimal, they are rounded. And because these numbers tend to be large, they are also abbreviated. Knowing the abbreviations for these large numbers is useful. Knowing how to round the numbers and what the real numbers are is not quite as useful. Consider the abbreviations first.

A double-density 5 1/4-inch floppy can hold 360,000 bytes (characters). This number can also be expressed as 360 thousand characters. In computer terms, the number is usually expressed as 360 kilobytes. Because *kilo* means thousand, that phrase is the same as 360 thousand bytes. But computer people like to make things as short as possible, so they just use the expression 360K. The K in this case represents kilobytes. So 360K of disk space is the same as 360,000 characters of disk space.

A standard-sized hard disk can hold 20,000,000 bytes. This number can also be expressed as 20,000 kilobytes. Or, better yet, it can be expressed as 20 million bytes. In computer terms, that same number is expressed as 20 megabytes. Because *mega* means million, 20 megabytes is the same as 20 million bytes. If you have followed along so far, you are waiting for the abbreviation for megabyte, aren't you? It's M. The capacity of a standard hard disk is expressed as 20M.

Until recently, dealing with millions was sufficient. But hard disk capacities have increased enough that the next abbreviation is a billion bytes. This is a *gigabyte*. A very large hard drive would have one gigabyte of storage capacity. This one-gigabyte drive has the same space as five 20-megabyte hard drives. (1,000,000,000/20,000,000 = 5). Table 67-1 summarizes these hard disk capacities.

Table 67-1. Hard disk capacities.

Decimal Number	Abbreviation	Term
360,000	360K	Kilobyte
20,000,000	20M	Megabyte
1,000,000,000	1G	Gigabyte

These nice round decimal numbers have been a bit misleading. A double-density 5 1/4-inch floppy disk can actually hold 368,640 bytes of data. The extra 8,640 bytes not accounted for in the 360K abbreviation are the result of the binary base used in computer math. The human tendency to round numbers makes 368,640 bytes of data 360K bytes of data instead.

To understand this difference between what we say the number represents and the real number, remember that 0 and 1 are used by the computer to count. Because the computer can recognize only *off* and *on* (0 and 1, respectively), the number system must be based on those two conditions. The position is critical in binary math. Although decimal (10) can use 0 to 9 to count in the one's place, binary has either 0 or 1 in the first position. So the next position is doubled in value. What would be the ten's position in decimal is just 2 in binary. Table 67-2 shows the relationships of some decimal and binary values.

Table 67-2. The relationships of decimal and binary values.

Decimal	Binary
1	1
2	10
3	11
4	100
5	101
6	110
7	111
8	1000
9	1001
10	1010
11	1011
12	1100
13	1101
14	1110
15	1111

Notice in the table the different values for each position in the binary number. From right to left, if the column contains a 1, the values are 1, 2, 4, and 8. From left to right, the values are 8, 4, 2, and 1. The binary number 1001 is equal to decimal 8 + 0 + 0 + 1, or 9. The binary number 110 is equal to decimal 4 + 2 + 0, or 6. The columns actually continue on out in values, doubling each time. (There is a point to this, really.)

Because the computer designers decided that these binary numbers are easy to group by 8 columns, they are expressed as 0000 0000. Each number is a *bit* (on or off, remember?), and the group is a *byte*. A byte can represent up to 255 in decimal. From left to right, the 8 columns are

```
128, 64, 32, 16    8, 4, 2, 1
```

The binary number 1111 1111 represents 255. You can add those decimal numbers to find that total (128 + 64 + 32 + 16 + 8 + 4 + 2 + 1 = 255). From 0000 0000 to 1111 1111 is from 0 decimal to 255 decimal. Actually, 256 numbers are represented because the number 0 counts as a value in computer/binary math.

You do not need to know any of this to use a computer. But it does explain the differences in the real numbers and the numbers as they are expressed. Table 67-3 provides some examples of common capacities.

Table 67-3. Some common computer capacities.

Measurement	Example
64K	Memory of a Commodore C-64 computer
256K	Memory of an original IBM PC computer
360K	Capacity of a standard 5 1/4-inch disk
640K	Memory of a newer IBM PC/XT computer or clone
720K	Capacity of a standard 3 1/2-inch disk
1M	Memory of most AT computers or clones
1.2M	Capacity of a high-density 5 1/4-inch disk
1.44M	Capacity of a high-density 3 1/2-inch disk
4M	Typical memory of a 386 computer
10M	Old XT hard drive capacity
20M	Minimal hard drive on an AT
40M	Typical-sized hard drive on a system
80M	Good-sized hard drive on a personal computer system
330M	Common-sized hard drive on a network computer
1G	Good-sized hard drive on a network computer

The numbers in Table 67-3 measure both memory capacity and disk capacity. But they are not the same thing simply because the same number system is used to measure them. Both a lemon and a movie can be measured as good, very good, or excellent. They are still completely different items. See the topics Memory (73) and Floppy Disks (19) for more about how these measurements are different.

Exercises

The best part about reading a book like this is that you don't have to do the exercises if you don't want to. And when it comes to math, who wants to? Here are just a few ways to explore binary math, which you can ignore completely.

0001 Count to decimal 15 in binary, using just 4 fingers.

0010 Construct a table of the 4 common disk capacities, using the actual number of decimal bytes instead of the commonly used rounded numbers.

0011 Convert the following decimal numbers into binary:

64 ________

256 ________

1,000 ________

1,000,000 ________

0100 Convert the following binary numbers into decimal:

0000 1001 ________

1111 0001 ________

1010 0101 ________

0101 Add the binary numbers 0010 and 0011.

0110 Convert your age to binary and put it on a T-shirt.

References

Memory (73)

NEXT TOPIC: Paper in Printer (68)

Cable connections

See Ports (40)

CD, MD, and RD — Working with Directories (9)

VERSIONS
All ●
Some ○
5.0 ○

Command ●
Program ○
Concept ○
Problem ○

The DOS CD (Change Directory) command changes the current directory to a new directory. Related commands are MD (Make Directory) and RD (Remove Directory).

Before You Begin

Files (2)
A: B: C: — Drive Designation (7)
DIR — Directory (8)

Syntax

C:\>**CD SUBNAME**	Changes to the SUBNAME directory.
C:\SUBNAME> C:\SUBNAME>**CD ..** C:\>=	Moves the default directory back up one directory (in this case, to the parent directory).
C:\> C:\>**MD NEWSUB** C:\>**CD NEWSUB** C:\NEWSUB>	Makes a new subdirectory called NEWSUB and then changes to that subdirectory. The default is now NEWSUB.
C:\>**RD NEWSUB**	Removes (deletes) the NEWSUB subdirectory.

If you prefer, you can use the following forms for these commands:

CHDIR for CD

MKDIR for MD

RMDIR for RD

Problems

Invalid path, not directory, or directory not empty. DOS provides this three-part message for several problems related to the CD, MD, and RD commands. Some possible causes are presented here.

`Invalid path.` The name of the path was mistyped or did not include all the directories leading to it. This message usually results when you forget to begin the path with the backslash (\), which refers to the root. If the prompt is `C:\WORD>` and you type **`CD DATA`**, DOS looks for DATA under the current WORD directory (\WORD\DATA). If DATA is located off the root, you have to type **`CD \DATA`** to get there.

`Not directory.` You tried to move into a file instead of a directory. Use the DIR command to look for the `<DIR>` next to the names in the directory list.

`Directory not empty.` This part of the message applies when you use RD to try to remove a directory containing files or subdirectories. Without this error message to warn you, you could delete hundreds of files just by removing the directory! Because you're not allowed to do that, you must erase the files intentionally and remove any subdirectories before using RD on the directory.

Lost subdirectories. This problem relates to the organization of the hard disk. If the directory system is well organized, subdirectories will be in predictable locations. If someone else originally "designed" the directory system, use the DOS TREE program (see topic 87) to create a map of all the subdirectories.

Use of the root backslash (\). As noted for `Invalid path`, the use of the backslash (\) changes how DOS interprets the CD command. **`CD\WORD`** and **`CD WORD`** are different depending on the current directory. The first command says that the WORD directory is under the root. The second command assumes that the WORD directory is under the current directory. Confusion can occur if you are currently in the root directory, because both of these commands will work since both are true.

Sitting on the tree branch you are trying to remove. You can't type **`RD BRANCH`** while you are in the BRANCH directory. You'll have to move up one level to remove BRANCH.

Explanation

The three commands for working with directories allow movement (change), creation (make), and deletion (remove). With the exception of some programs that create their own directories when installed, how the disk is organized by subdirectory is up to you. An entire topic is devoted to File Organization (17). The CD, MD, and RD commands enable you to create this organization.

Note that the use of the words *directory* and *subdirectory* is determined by the position of the current directory (the default). A subdirectory is *under* the current directory. Once you change directories and move into that subdirectory, it becomes *the* directory under discussion. Anything under that directory is now a subdirectory.

CD is an abbreviation of CHDIR, MD is an abbreviation of MKDIR, and RD is an abbreviation of RMDIR. The commands in each of these sets work exactly the same.

The short version takes two keystrokes, and the long version takes five. Net savings: three keystokes each.

CD — Change Directory

Using CD to change the DOS directory is like moving from one cave to another to see (or use) the contents of that cave. Although it is possible to peer from one cave into another, it is easier to move into that cave, er, directory before you issue other DOS commands.

Creating an informative DOS prompt is critical for moving through subdirectories. The standard prompt of `C>` does not change except when other drives are selected. Use the command **`PROMPT $p$g <Enter>`** to provide constant information about the current directory location. For more information about the prompt, see the topic PROMPT — Command Line Information (26).

After the CD command, you type the subdirectory into which you want to move. For example, if you type

```
C:\>CD\WORDPROC\DOCS <Enter>
```

the DOS prompt changes to this:

```
C:\WORDPROC\DOCS>
```

You have moved into the DOCS subdirectory, which is under the WORDPROC directory. To move back up one level, type

```
C:\WORDPROC\DOCS>CD ..
```

The prompt then looks like this:

```
C:\WORDPROC>
```

To return to the root (top) directory, you can type

```
C:\WORDPROC>CD\
```

or

```
C:\WORDPROC>CD ..
```

Now the prompt shows that you are in the root directory:

```
C:\>
```

MD — Make Directory

Using MD to make a new DOS directory is like creating a new cave in which to store items or even more caves. The new cave leads away from the current cave. The new cave cannot have the same name as anything (another file or subdirectory) in the current cave.

For example, you can use the following commands to create and move into a new subdirectory under TARGET:

```
C:\>CD TARGET
C:\TARGET>MD SUBT2
C:\TARGET>CD SUBT2
C:\TARGET\SUBT2>
```

If you are creating a new subdirectory to copy files into, remember to use CD immediately after using MD. Making the directory does *not* move you into it. This is a common misconception. If you forget to type **CD** after creating the subdirectory, the next step of copying files into that directory will put them in the original directory instead, not the subdirectory. You must then delete the files from the original directory, move into the new subdirectory, and perform the COPY again (see topic 10).

Directory names have the same limitations as file names. Directories are actually files. Like file names, directory names can have extensions, but usually they don't. Remember to make directory names descriptive yet easy to type. Because the directory name represents a "doorway," which you'll use frequently with the CD command, use a word (or word combination) instead of a cryptic abbreviation. For example, QTR1 is easier to type than FSTQTR.

RD — Remove Directory

Using RD to remove a directory may take time. You must first delete the contents of all the subdirectories below the directory (see topic 30 on deleting files) *and* remove those subdirectories (**RD** *SUBNAME*) before you can delete the target directory. Look at the example in Figure 9-1. To RD the TARGET directory, you must first delete the files in SUBTARGET and SUBT2 and remove those subdirectories. You must then delete the files in TARGET. Finally, after moving back to MAIN, you can type **RD TARGET**.

```
MAIN────TARGET<DIR>────┬─SUBTARGET<DIR>
          FILE.EXT     │    SUBFILE.TXT
          FILE2.EXT    │    SUBFILE2.TXT
                       └─ SUBT2<DIR>
                            SUBFLE.TXT
                            SUBDUH.TXT
```

Figure 9-1. A sample directory tree that illustrates the complexity of removing the TARGET directory.

Assume that all the files in TARGET and its subdirectories are no longer needed. Here is one of several ways to remove the TARGET directory:

```
C:\>CD\TARGET\SUBT2
C:\TARGET\SUBT2>DEL *.*
Are you sure (Y/N)? Y
C:\TARGET\SUBT2>CD ..\SUBTARGET
C:\TARGET\SUBTARGET>DEL *.*
Are you sure (Y/N)? Y
C:\TARGET\SUBTARGET>CD ..
C:\TARGET>RD SUBT2
C:\TARGET>RD SUBTARGET
C:\TARGET>DEL *.*
Are you sure (Y/N)? Y
C:\TARGET>CD ..
C:\>RD TARGET
C:\>
```

The process of removing a directory is not easy. Some utilities exist to make the process quicker, even with the added risk of deleting valuable files and subdirectories without prior warning.

Exercises

Now that you know how to move from one drive to another (such as from A: to C:), how to use DIR to look at directories, and how to use CD to change from one directory to another, you can really begin to get around in your system. This first exercise does not present keystroke-by-keystroke instructions but instead provides a series of useful steps for discovering what your system looks like. The second exercise focuses on creating and removing subdirectories on a practice floppy disk.

Exercise 1 of 2

Unless you created the entire subdirectory system yourself, you may need some time to learn where everything is. As you work through this exercise, sketch out the directory tree as you discover the various branches. The DOS TREE program (topic 87) can help you in mapping out a system for the first time.

1. If your prompt does not display the full directory now, type **PROMPT pg**.
2. Use the **DIR /P** command to look at the root directory. Note the names with <DIR> next to them.
3. Use **CD** with one of those names to change into that subdirectory. Use **DIR /P** again to look at the files and subdirectories.

4. Use **CD** to move into one of the subdirectories (if there is one). Repeat this process, going as deeply into the subdirectories as possible.
5. Once you are at the bottom, use **CD ..** to move back up one step. Look for subdirectories again and repeat the process.
6. When you are ready to return to the surface (root directory), just use the **CD** command.

Exercise 2 of 2

In this exercise, you create and remove subdirectories on a *practice* floppy disk. Once you are comfortable using the floppy, you can move to the hard disk.

TRY	NOTE
C:\>**A:** A:\>**DIR**	Make sure that a disk is in A, move to that drive, and look at the directory.
A:\>**MD SUBTEST**	This creates a subdirectory called SUBTEST.
A:\>**DIR**	Notice that the new subdirectory has been added to the directory on the floppy disk.
A:\>**CD SUBTEST** A:\SUBTEST>	Now you have moved into the SUBTEST subdirectory.
A:\SUBTEST>**DIR**	Because SUBTEST is a new subdirectory, you see only two listings (. and ..). These represent the current directory and the parent directory.
A:\SUBTEST>**RD SUBTEST** Invalid path, not directory, or directory not empty. A:\SUBTEST>	Here you have tried to remove the current subdirectory, but you've failed because you are not in that subdirectory.
A:\SUBTEST>**CD ..** A:\>	This moves you back up one level to the root. In this case, you could also type **CD** to return to the root.
A:\>**RD SUBTEST** A:\>	Notice that DOS does not provide any confirmation that the subdirectory is removed. You'll have to use the DIR command if you want to check.

In this exercise, you created a subdirectory and then immediately removed it. That, understandably, is not the normal life span for a subdirectory. Usually you create and use them to keep specific files. The RD command is generally needed when housekeeping is required to recover unused space on the hard disk. The longer you wait, the more time you'll need to get everything cleaned up.

References

File Organization (17), XCOPY — Files (37), TREE — Directory Map (87)

NEXT TOPIC: COPY — Files (10)

Capturing program output to a file or printer

See Redirection < > ¦ (64)

Case-sensitive output

See Lost Data Files (77)

Changed AUTOEXEC.BAT

See AUTOEXEC.BAT (21)

Changing DOS commands

See DOSKEY (25)

CHKDSK — CHecK DiSK (20)

VERSIONS	
All	●
Some	○
5.0	○
Command	○
Program	●
Concept	○
Problem	○

CHKDSK is a DOS program that can locate and recover missing parts of damaged files. It also reports on the amount of conventional memory and the hard disk capacity.

Before You Begin

Floppy Disks (19)

Syntax

`C:\>CHKDSK C:`	Reports but does not recover lost clusters on drive C:
`C:\>CHKDSK D: /F`	Recovers any lost clusters on the D: drive

Problems

You run CHKDSK to attempt to recover lost parts of files. Several causes for these lost clusters are discussed here.

Power failure. A momentary loss of power to the computer automatically reboots the system. If a program is active and has an open file, DOS is unable to write the proper data to the disk to close the file. When a program next attempts to access the file, the correct file marker may be missing or misplaced. DOS or the application program may provide an error message, or the application program may just lock up. If any programs were running, the first action after a power failure should be to run CHKDSK with the /F option.

Intentional reboot or power down. Although power failures can be prevented with additional equipment (uninterruptable power sources, or *UPS*), you should not reboot or turn off the system just because you are finished with the current program. Every program closes files when it finishes. Always quit or exit from a program before turning the computer off. Either the DOS prompt (`C:\>`) or the main menu should be on the screen. The only exception to this rule occurs when the program has locked up and does not respond to any keyboard actions.

Hard disk size or remaining space unknown. CHKDSK provides information on both the size of the hard disk and the remaining space on that disk. You can use CHKDSK to find the total capacity of your hard drive(s).

Explanation

One of the many tasks that DOS performs is to keep track of all the files on a floppy disk or hard disk. The user simply needs to know the file name in order to use the file. DOS tracks all the locations on the disk and reads each location when necessary. As files grow in size and are deleted or added, they become fragmented across the disk. This fragmentation may result in a slightly slower response from the computer, yet the user is unaffected. But if DOS loses track of parts of a file, they become *lost clusters*, or unattached portions of files. The original file is missing data, and DOS does not know what to do with the "orphaned" clusters.

CHKDSK checks each part of the disk to make sure that every cluster is connected to a file name. If CHKDSK finds lost clusters, it reports how many there are. If you use the /F option, CHKDSK makes the lost clusters into files named FILE0001.CHK, FILE0002.CHK, and so on. The last four characters in the file name increase by one for each lost cluster recovered.

Once these lost clusters have been recovered, the resulting files are like scraps of leftover cloth at the tailor's. It takes a special skill to find out if and how these files can be used. Because many programs include formatting information at the beginning of the file and because these scraps are not likely to have that information, the files cannot be used by the program they came from originally. The best way to examine these files is to use the TYPE command (topic 81) to determine what the files contain. With a great deal of work, you might be able to save the data in ASCII format and incorporate the data into the original file.

As Listing 20-1 shows, CHKDSK (DOS 5.0) reports four different items of information. The first item indicates the volumn identification, the date of creation, and the unique volume serial number (with DOS 5.0 only).

Listing 20-1. Typical output from CHKDSK version 5.0.

```
Volume LEARN DOS   created 08-26-1991 11:17a
Volume Serial Number is 1681-A996

  33419264 bytes total disk space
     81920 bytes in 34 directories
  29655040 bytes in 1017 user files
   3682304 bytes available on disk

      2048 bytes in each allocation unit
     16318 total allocation units on disk
      1798 available allocation units on disk

    655360 total bytes memory

    165488 bytes free
```

The second item provides information on the total amount of disk space, the number of directories, the number of files, and the amount of disk space remaining. All this information is represented as bytes. To find the megabyte capacity of the drive, divide the number by 1,000,000. In the preceding example, 33419264 bytes equals a 33.4-megabyte hard drive.

A utility program called DMD (Disk Meter Deluxe), included on the disk that accompanies this book, provides a graphic representation of the remaining disk space. More information on DMD is available in Part III, "Guide to Using the Disk."

DOS versions 4.01 and 5.0 provide a section with technical information on allocation units. This information does not appear in earlier versions of CHKDSK.

CHKDSK reports also the amount of memory available and the amount of memory being used. If you run CHKDSK at the DOS prompt, the remaining memory represents what is being used by DOS and other active programs. If a program requires 512K of memory to run and CHKDSK reports an amount less than that, the program may not run. The DOS 5.0 command MEM (topic 90) provides more information about memory and memory usage.

Exercise

This exercise shows a sample CHKDSK report and explains what to do if CHKDSK reports lost clusters. The display will vary depending on your version of DOS.

Exercise 1 of 1

Because CHKDSK provides the status of lost clusters, you may not see anything except the standard display. If you do, use the next step in the exercise to recover the lost clusters.

TRY	NOTE
`C:\>`**`CHKDSK`**	This runs CHKDSK on the default drive—in this case, C:.
Look at the screen.	If the display reports that there are lost clusters on the disk, use the /F option.
`C:\>`**`CHKDSK /F`**	This recovers the lost clusters. You should next examine the root directory for the recovered clusters (with such names as FILE0001.CHK). In most cases, you'll just have to type this next command.
`C:\>`**`DEL *.CHK`**	This command deletes the extraneous files.

References

Hard Drive Failure (33), Lost Data Files (77), FAT — Fat Allocation Table (89)

NEXT TOPIC: AUTOEXEC.BAT (21)

CLS — Clear Screen (5)

VERSIONS	
All	●
Some	○
5.0	○
Command	●
Program	○
Concept	○
Problem	○

When you type the CLS command at the DOS command prompt, the screen is cleared of all images.

Before You Begin

Default Drive (3)

Syntax

`C:\>CLS`	Clears the screen (the prompt moves to the upper left corner)

Problem

Screen clears too soon. In some cases, a batch file may clear the screen before a user has had time to read the message. When a user types **CLS**, you can safely assume that the user has finished reading the screen.

Explanation

Although CLS is not a critical DOS command, it is a good one to start with in learning how to use commands and what happens when you make a mistake in DOS.

Exercise

CLS provides practice in getting started with basic DOS commands. Remember that the TRY column shows the keys you press, and the NOTE column provides an explanation of your action or a description of what appears on the screen.

Exercise 1 of 1

Before you begin this exercise, you must be at the DOS prompt. If you have a menu system, you'll have to exit to DOS. If you need help, refer to the topic Interfaces (27). The DOS prompt should look like one of the following: `A>`, `A:\>`, `C>`, or `C:\>`. If the prompt contains words, that's all right. For this exercise, the current subdirectory is not important.

TRY	NOTE
`C:\>`**`CLS <Enter>`**	The letters CLS can be in upper- or lowercase. As a reminder, **`<Enter>`** means that you are to press the Enter key.
Look at the screen.	After you type **`CLS`**, the screen becomes blank. Nothing else has been affected.

Using CLS is like moving all the papers off your desk to make it look neater. That's all CLS does. This exercise is probably the shortest one in this book: you type one command and view the result. But now consider what else might happen with this command.

TRY	NOTE
`C:\>`**`CSL <Enter>`**	This is not a DOS command and is guaranteed to produce the error message `Bad command or file name` (topic 6). Basically the message means that DOS has no idea what you want it do to.

So you made a mistake typing the command! Not much happens with DOS. It just issues an error message and then returns to the prompt. The point of presenting CLS and showing the DOS error message `Bad command or file name` is simply this: you attempt to use a DOS command, and then see what happens when you make a mistake.

Correcting this mistake requires only that you type the command correctly. Notice that nothing drastic happened when you made this mistake. With a few exceptions, you can just try the command again *without penalty*. If a mistake is serious, you will be warned and given advice about how to recover from the mistake.

References

Batch Files — Write Your Own (100)

NEXT TOPIC: `Bad command or file name` (6)

Cold boot

See Boot/Startup (1)

Color combinations

See Monitor (61)

Command and Program Parameters (34)

VERSIONS	
All	●
Some	○
5.0	○
Command	○
Program	○
Concept	●
Problem	○

Commands and programs typed at the DOS prompt can include additional instructions on the same line. These are called *command line parameters*, or *switches*. Each command or program may use different switches. Some are optional, and some are required.

Before You Begin

Files (2)
File Names (4)
Wild Cards * and ? (11)
Interfaces (27)

Problems

`Required parameter missing`, **`File name must be specified`**, or **`Invalid switch`**. Some DOS commands and programs require additional information on the command line before running. If that information is missing, the process generates one of these error messages and then returns to the DOS prompt. To correct the error, retype the command or program and include the additional information on the line.

Explanation

One advantage of a *command line interface* like DOS is speed. (For more information on interfaces, refer to topic 27.) Because the command or program accepts (or requires) the data on the same line, the entire process is begun quickly. This additional information can include a file to use, file(s) to act on, or specific instructions to the program.

The DOS program EDLIN, for example, is quick and small but still very effective. One way to make it smaller is to require the name of the data file on the same command line. The line **`EDLIN TEST.TXT`** starts the EDLIN program and opens the file `TEST.TXT` to be edited. If the file does not exist, EDLIN creates it. The program does not waste time with menus or a prompt for a file name. If a file name is not provided, EDLIN presents the error message `File name must be specified` and quits.

Another example is the COPY command. Usually COPY requires two additional bits of information: the file(s) to be copied (the *source*), and the location where they are to be copied (the *destination*). If only one of these is provided, the command terminates with the error `File cannot be copied onto itself` and stops. Because the purpose of COPY is to make duplicate files, this requirement makes sense. (NOTE: For those who know, there is a way to provide only one parameter with COPY. But typical use is with both source and destination on the command line.)

Switches provided on the command line tell the command or program how to operate. These switches usually include a slash (/) and one or more letters. Some programs use a hyphen (-) and a letter. Consider the DIR command. **`DIR /P`** pauses the list of files when the screen fills up. **`DIR /W`** produces a wide display of files. In most cases, a number of switches may be combined at the same time. **`DIR /P/W`** produces a wide listing and pauses when the screen becomes full.

5

The only way to know all the possibilities with a command or program is to read the documentation. In some cases, as with DOS 5.0, most commands and programs can be "switched" with /? to provide more information about that program. For example, **`DIR /?`** shows all the possible switches you can use with the DIR command. Just typing **`HELP`** in DOS 5.0 provides a list of available help topics.

References

Application Software (46), Manuals and Documentation (53), No One to Help (59)

NEXT TOPIC: Disk Full (35)

COMMAND.COM/EXIT (78)

VERSIONS	
All	●
Some	○
5.0	○
Command	○
Program	●
Concept	○
Problem	○

The COMMAND.COM program is the command processing program for DOS. In most cases, COMMAND.COM must be in the root directory of the boot disk in order for DOS to load. Some programs can suspend themselves and "drop" to DOS. Once you are finished with the DOS commands, you can return to the original program by typing **`EXIT`**.

Before You Begin

Boot/Startup (1)
AUTOEXEC.BAT (21)
CONFIG.SYS (22)

Syntax

`SHELL=COMMAND /E:320`	Doubles the environment space when placed in CONFIG.SYS
`C:\>`**`EXIT`**	Exits a second command processor
`C:\>`**`SET`**	Shows the contents of the environment

Problems

`Out of environment space.` This DOS message may appear when you add additional variables with the SET command. The default space is only 160 bytes. The /E switch can increase this to 32,768 bytes (32K).

Path suddenly not working. The environment space holds the entire search path as defined by the PATH command, usually included in AUTOEXEC.BAT. A long path string may be cut off when DOS runs out of space to hold it. This is common after you install a program that makes additions to the current PATH statement. Use the SET command to look at the contents of the environment. A truncated path is likely to end arbitrarily in the middle of a word. Add the line `SHELL=COMMAND.COM /E:320` to CONFIG.SYS to increase the environmental space, and then reboot.

Explanation

COMMAND.COM is frequently mistaken as DOS. DOS is actually two hidden programs located on the boot disk. COMMAND.COM just processes commands from the user and sends them to DOS. This relationship between DOS and COMMAND.COM is suggested by the fact that you can substitute another command shell in CONFIG.SYS.

Running a Second COMMAND.COM

Many DOS program can suspend (stop running) themselves, load another copy of COMMAND.COM, and allow standard DOS commands to be used. For example, Microsoft Word has a Library Run Command menu choice to "drop" to DOS. Word is suspended, along with the current documents, and the DOS prompt appears. You can use almost any DOS command, including DIR, COPY, and even FORMAT. Once you have completed your DOS tasks, typing **`EXIT`** returns you to Word.

This use of a second level (or copy) of COMMAND.COM is not the same as just ending the program and returning to the primary level of DOS. In fact, there are several possible problems with this quick access to a second level of COMMAND.COM:

- *Loss of data.* When you use the program's commands to drop to DOS, your data is suspended in memory. If you forget that you are in the second level of DOS, you could lose unsaved data. Some programs modify the prompt to include a message like Type EXIT to return. The best defense is to save any files before dropping to DOS.
- *Limited memory.* When DOS loads the second copy of COMMAND.COM, the suspended program is still in memory. This is likely to leave a small amount of memory available. DOS programs will run with very limited memory. Other programs may not. Run CHKDSK to see the difference in memory used. DOS 5.0 users can use MEM.
- *Attempts to load additional programs.* Although you may be able to run other programs, that may be hazardous to the program currently suspended in memory. Do so only with extreme caution.

SET

The SET command has two uses. One is to place a variable into the DOS environment. Such variables are specific to individual programs and are covered, if necessary, in the program manuals.

The other use of SET is to examine the contents of the environment, mostly to solve problems. As noted earlier, new programs sometimes make changes to the AUTOEXEC.BAT and CONFIG.SYS files. You may not notice a problem until the next time you turn on the computer, because only then will the changes take affect. The most noticeable problem is that an old program no longer works. The changes made by the new program have added data to the environment, and some old data has been pushed out because the environment space was too small.

For example, the following sequence allows you to examine what should be in the path and what really is in the path:

```
C:\>TYPE AUTOEXEC.BAT
@echo off
PATH C:\DOS;c:\batch;c:\norton;c:\pctools;c:\database\foxpro
prompt $p$g

C:\>SET
PATH=C:\DOS;C:\BATCH;C:\NORTON;C:\PCTOOLS;C:\DATABASE\FOXPRO
PROMPT=$p$g

TEMP=C:\DOS
```

The PATH line in AUTOEXEC.BAT sets the path automatically. The PATH= line in CONFIG.SYS had been cut off strangely, possibly suggesting that the environment was full. In this case, it was not.

More information on additional switches for use with COMMAND.COM and the SET command is available in your DOS manual or in other program manuals.

References

Operating Systems (75), History of DOS (88)

NEXT TOPIC: Networks (79)

Compression method unknown

See Compressed Files (80)

Communication parameters

See Modems (56)

Communications (55)

VERSIONS
All ●
Some ○
5.0 ○

Command ○
Program ○
Concept ●
Problem ○

Communications, also referred to as *telecommunications*, relates to connecting one computer to another. The connection may be from PC to PC or from PC to a larger computer.

Problem

Trouble in making the connection. Using one computer to "talk to" another computer requires a number of steps. Each step must be done correctly, or the connection will not work. If you are trying to make the connection and are having trouble, you may need some outside assistance from someone with telecommunications experience.

Explanation

Computer signals sent over the phone lines represent a whole new communication channel. Anyone with a computer, a modem, and communications software can tie into one of the information services now available. Thousands of personal computers across the country are dedicated as information centers, waiting for incoming calls. *Bulletin board systems* (BBS) contain messages and files generated by hundreds of callers each week. Most of these systems are free. A few require a yearly registration fee. As in a small grocery store, the variety may be limited, but the service is personal.

The supermarkets of communications are provided on mainframes and charge by the minute for time spent connected to the main computer. There are dozens of these service bureaus, the largest of which is probably CompuServe, located in Ohio, but available from the nearest phone line. These commercial services provide hundreds of topic areas, massive research libraries, stock quotes, on-line buying services, and much more. Although the range of services is overwhelming, there is likely to be something of interest to everyone.

Making the connection requires an additional piece of equipment and special communications software. A *modem*, discussed more fully in topic 56, translates the computer signal to a phone line signal. A modem on the other end of the connection reverses the process, returning the phone line signal to a computer signal. Modems are rated by the speed, or *baud*, at which they can send signals. Most modems in use now are 2400 baud, although 1200- and 300-baud modems still work, just more slowly. The next (more expensive) speed is 9400 baud.

In addition to connecting the computer to the phone line through the modem, you need software for sending and receiving the signals from the other computer. In most cases, you don't see a character you type on your keyboard until the other computer has received and returned that character. Although this produces a slightly sluggish response, it also tells you that the communications channel is working.

Most communications software keeps a list of phone numbers, dials the numbers, and allows you to send and receive files from the other computer. Advanced features vary but can include having your system act as the host, calling another computer at a preset time, and performing a small program to copy messages from the other computer to yours.

A list of BBS numbers in your area is generally available from a local user group or computer store. Once you make the local connection, you can find a list of national numbers on a local BBS. To find out more about the commercial services available, you can contact (by voice) these companies:

CompuServe	800-848-8990
Delphi	800-544-4005
Genie	800-638-9636
Prodigy	800-822-6922

Within the past few years, another reason to make the computer-to-computer connection has emerged. In normal communications mode, one computer serves as the host to the calling computer. The host runs special software to post messages and transmit files. Typically that's all the host computer does. But software is now available for one computer to completely control another computer.

This method of "remote" communications requires the same brand of software on both computers. The host computer is set up to receive the call. The computer making the call will be able to control the host system completely. With this kind of computer-to-computer communications, users of the phone line can get help from support technicians. A technician can see exactly what a user is having problems with and then make suggestions. This method is also useful for programmers when they need to fix bugs in their software without having to sit in front of the original computer.

When confronted by a screen like that shown in Figure 55-1, some users attempting to use communications software might just forget it. This screen, from ProComm Plus 2.0, is just one of several screens for configuring the program. Fortunately for most users, the more common settings are included here as specific selections. When a user first starts to use ProComm Plus, it also asks some questions that help get the proper settings.

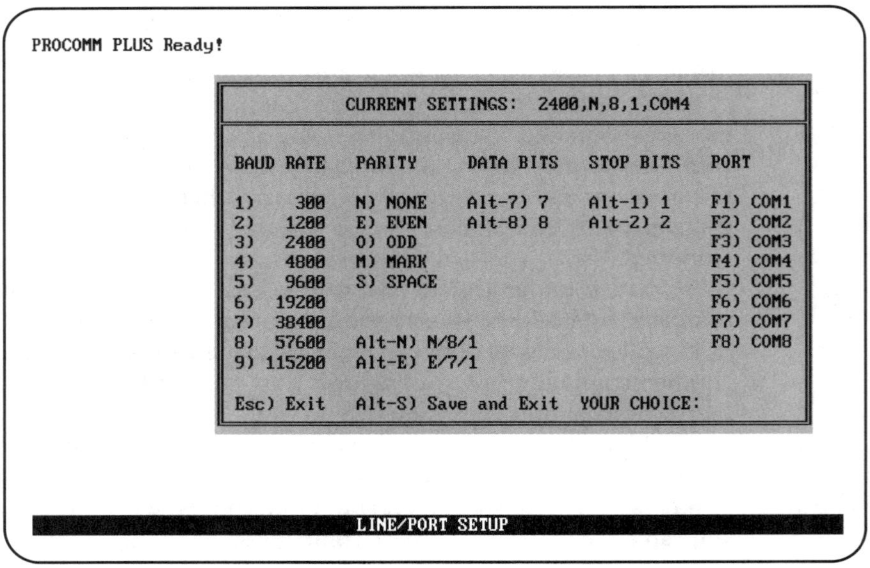

Figure 55-1. The ProComm Plus configuration screen called from the menu with Alt-P.

References

Ports (40), Modems (56), Networks (79)

NEXT TOPIC: Modems (56)

Compatible displays

See Hardware and Software Compatibility (72)

Compatible processors

See Hardware and Software Compatibility (72)

Computer won't work

See Hardware (38)

Compressed Files (80)

VERSIONS	
All	●
Some	○
5.0	○
Command	○
Program	○
Concept	●
Problem	○

Some programs can compress the size of data and program files. These compressed files save storage space on disks and take less time to transmit by modem. Before you can use the files, they must be uncompressed with the same program used to compress them.

Before You Begin

Files (2)
File Names (4)
Command and Program Parameters (34)

Problems

Not enough space on the hard disk. A hard disk is like a closet. You always want to put more into it than you have space for. To solve this problem, you can use a compression program for files you rarely use. Then, when you need the files, you can uncompress them. Although this compression and uncompression process takes time, it still requires less time than locating the floppy disks and copying their files to the hard disk.

File transfer time too expensive. Files are often copied from computer to computer over the phone lines. Because this process is likely to involve the expense of a long distance call or an on-line service, the smaller the file, the greater the savings. Most BBS and commercial services provide the files in compressed form.

Unknown compression method. A compressed file is useless unless you know the compression method. A compression program usually creates a file with an extension unique to that program. A file that does not run has been misnamed by another user. For example, in the process of copying the file FUNSTUFF.ZIP to a floppy disk, someone might accidentally rename it FUNSTUFF.EXE. Typing **FUNSTUFF** to run the file will not work. The only hope is to try as many uncompression programs as possible on the file. You'll have to provide the entire file name as FUNSTUFF.EXE because compression programs assume and expect their own extensions—in this case, ZIP. When you provide the EXE extension, the program uses that entire name as input for the file to be uncompressed.

Explanation

Using special formulas, compression programs can reduce file sizes by as much as 80 percent. A compression program looks at a file to find recurring characters and unused space. Then the program writes a new file to the disk in a format that takes less space. You can use this file just as you use any DOS file. The compressed file requires less space when copied to a floppy disk and less time when transmitted by modem. When you want to use the file again, it must be uncompressed by a program that recognizes the compression method used.

You can recognize compressed files by their file extensions. Common extensions are ARC and ZIP. Some programs perform the compression and then insert part of the uncompression program in the final file. The compressed file contains the original material as well as a program to uncompress the material. This file has the extension EXE because it is an executable program. When run, the program just uncompresses the original file or files to the disk.

Most new programs are stored in a compressed format on the installation disks. Some programs use the commonly available compression programs such as ARC and PKZIP, but others use their own programs. This is one of the reasons that programs must be "installed" to a hard disk. The installation program copies and uncompresses the files from the floppy disk to the hard disk.

Reference

NEXT TOPIC: TYPE — Looking at Files (81)

Confidential data

See Security (95)

CONFIG.SYS (22)

VERSIONS	
All	●
Some	○
5.0	○
Command	○
Program	●
Concept	○
Problem	○

This data file is read as DOS boots the system. The CONFIG.SYS code configures specific DOS functions and sets other system parameters. It is not an essential file but is usually present on hard disk systems.

Before You Begin

Boot/Startup (1)
File Names (4)

Problems

Too many files open. DOS keeps track of open files when any program runs. One statement in CONFIG.SYS tells DOS in advance the maximum number of open files to track. Newer programs may use 15 or more files at a time. If a program presents this type of message, DOS may not have set aside enough "handles" for open files. The `FILES=` line in CONFIG.SYS has a low number. Using any text editor, you can increase the number in the line. After you reboot, the program should run. See the "Exercises" section for the steps to create a CONFIG.SYS file.

Mouse suddenly won't work. DOS must know when certain devices are attached to the computer. The most common device is a mouse. Even though the mouse can be activated by running MOUSE.COM, typically it is activated in CONFIG.SYS with a line like `DEVICE=C:\DOS\MOUSE.SYS`. If the mouse has been working, but now is not, try the following:

1. First check the connection in the back of the computer.
2. Use DIR in the root directory to make sure that the CONFIG.SYS file is still in the root directory.
3. Use TYPE to look at the contents of the file. Make sure that the MOUSE.SYS file still exists in the location referenced, usually `DEVICE=C:\MOUSE.SYS` or `DEVICE=C:\DOS\MOUSE.SYS`.
4. If there is no line with MOUSE.SYS, you can add the line and reboot the system. Then test the mouse again.

Other devices can exhibit this same problem. The process for checking is the same.

Other programs won't work after you install a new program. Some installation programs make changes to both CONFIG.SYS and AUTOEXEC.BAT. If other programs do not work as they did before, check these two files to determine whether changes were made. A backup of the files, with the extension of OLD or BAK, should be in the root directory. The software company that provided your new program should be able to help you solve (by phone) any problems with the altered files.

Explanation

CONFIG.SYS is an ASCII file that DOS reads and acts on before starting AUTOEXEC.BAT. CONFIG.SYS cannot be interrupted, and any changes made in the file do not take effect until the system is rebooted. Making changes in the file is not likely to harm anything but may affect how well the computer operates. Always make a backup copy of CONFIG.SYS before making any changes with a text editor or word processing program that can save the file in ASCII format. Reboot to determine the effectiveness of your changes.

A CONFIG.SYS file might contain the following lines:

```
DEVICE=\DOS\EMM.SYS
DEVICE=\DOS\VDISK.SYS 340 /A
DEVICE=\DOS\MOUSE.SYS
FILES=20
BUFFERS=20
```

The first three lines of this CONFIG.SYS file set up expanded memory, create a RAM disk, and activate the mouse driver. The last two lines set the number of files that DOS can have open at one time, and the number of disk buffers to use for disk access. Most systems will have at least the last two lines, with values ranging from 10 to 40.

Instructions for the CONFIG.SYS file, as well as examples, are provided by the new program or device (or necessary changes will be made automatically). The `FILES` and `BUFFERS` statements may be changed to improve performance. A common value for `FILES` is 20. As mentioned in the "Problems" section, this value does not need to be changed unless an error message appears when a program runs. A larger number in the `BUFFERS` statement improves hard disk speed at the expense of some conventional memory. Hard disk users should have a value of at least 20.

Device drivers are becoming more important in newer systems. With a line like `DEVICE=\EMM.SYS`, DOS modifies itself, using the information in the device files (SYS) as building blocks. Although these devices extend the power of DOS, they can potentially cause problems. Each device block also requires more memory. Additional information about devices is available in your DOS manual or in the manual provided with the device driver software.

Exercises

If CONFIG.SYS is not present in the root directory of the boot disk and you have a hard drive, you may want to create a quick CONFIG.SYS file. Exercise 1 shows you how to look at the file. In Exercise 2, you create a CONFIG.SYS file.

Exercise 1 of 2

This exercise provides the steps to examine your CONFIG.SYS file. You won't change the file or in any way affect how your system works.

TRY	NOTE
`C:\>`**`TYPE CONFIG.SYS`**	Make sure that you are in the root directory of your drive. The TYPE command displays the file. If you get an error message, you don't have a CONFIG.SYS file. Move to the next exercise to create a "quicky."

Exercise 2 of 2

Complete this exercise *only* if you do not have a CONFIG.SYS file in your root directory.

TRY	NOTE
`C:\>`**`COPY CON: CONFIG.SYS`**	This is a quick way to create an ASCII (text) file. You will not see a cursor or a prompt until these steps are through.
`FILES=20` **`BUFFERS=20`**	Although the numbers here can range from 1 to 99, these represent a good compromise for most systems.
`<F6>`	Press the F6 key to end the process.
`1 file(s) copied` `C:\>`	DOS tells you that the file was copied from the CONsole to the disk file.

You must reboot the system (with Ctrl-Alt-Del) to see any changes. One noticeable improvement will be how smoothly a directory listing appears on the screen. Without the `BUFFERS` statement, the default of 3 limits DOS to the number of file names displayed before another disk is read. With `BUFFERS=20`, more file names can be read from the directory before DOS has to reread the disk.

References

TYPE — Looking at Files (81), EDIT — DOS 5.0 Text Editor (98), EDLIN — Line Editor (99), Batch Files — Write Your Own (100)

NEXT TOPIC: DATE (23)

Confusing kilobytes and megabytes

See Bytes and Computer Math (67)

Confusing the / and \ keys

See DIR — Directory (8)

COPY — Files (10)

VERSIONS	
All	●
Some	○
5.0	○
Command	●
Program	○
Concept	○
Problem	○

This command duplicates files, typically from one disk to another. Unless DOS is instructed to change the file name on the second copy, the name remains the same. Unlike a paper copy of a copy of a copy, which gets progressively "fuzzy," each successive copy of a file is exactly the same as the original.

Before You Begin

Files (2)
File Names (4)
DIR — Directory (8)
CD, MD, and RD — Working with Directories (9)

Syntax

`C:\>`**`COPY SAMPLE.TXT A:`** `1 file(s) copied`	Copies SAMPLE.TXT to the disk in A:
`C:\DOCS>`**`COPY *.DOC A:`**	Copies to A: all files with the extension DOC
`A:\>`**`COPY *.* C:`**	Copies all files in the root directory of A: to the current default directory of C:

Problems

Overwriting a newer file with an older file. DOS does not check the target location (destination) for a file of the same name when you copy a file to that location. When the source file is copied to the target location, a file with the same name on the target location is overwritten.

`File cannot be copied onto itself.` If you do not provide the destination for the file, DOS responds with this error message. Without at least a new drive or directory destination, DOS tries to copy the file back into the same subdirectory where the original file (with the same name) is located. DOS does not allow two files with the same name in the same subdirectory. Try again, this time including the destination drive or directory just after the file name.

`File not found`. As with many commands, if the file does not exist or if wild cards are misused, DOS will not be able to perform the COPY action. In this case, nothing happens because DOS cannot find the file(s) to copy. Either use DIR to determine whether the file exists or retype the COPY command line.

Lost file(s). You might think that the command **`COPY *.DOC A`** copies all files with the DOC extension to drive A:. But without the colon after the destination drive (A:), DOS just takes each file in the wild-card list and copies the file to a file named A. The files never reach A:, and they appear to be lost. DELete the file named A. Then retype the command and remember the colon.

Explanation

You must include two pieces of information after the COPY command. The first is the name of the file or files to be copied (the *source*). The second is the location where the files are to be copied (the *destination*). Note the following format:

```
COPY source destination
```

For example, to copy the file named AUTOEXEC.BAT to the disk in drive A:, you use the command

```
C:\>COPY AUTOEXEC.BAT A:
```

The COPY command can use wild cards (* and ?) to copy many files with one command. To copy all the spreadsheet data files in the SHEETS directory on drive C: to drive A:, you use

```
C:\>CD SHEETS
C:\SHEETS>COPY *.WQ1 A:
```

Before beginning this task, you need to know that the files you want to copy are in the SHEETS directory and that the data files for your spreadsheet software have the WQ1 extension.

Because the files are copied as digital images, the destination file is exactly the same as the source file. The computer and the software use error-checking methods to make sure the files match. You can use the /V switch at the end of the COPY command to verify that the destination file matches the source file, but this switch is usually not needed. If DOS has difficulty copying a file, DOS reports the problem with an error message.

Although you can rename the copy of the file during the copy process by providing another name in the destination, this is probably not a good practice. The user can identify matching files by the file size, date, and name. If the file name is changed, that process requires another DOS program, COMP, to compare the files.

As with many DOS commands, COPY can include the entire drive and path name for both the source and destination. If, for instance, you know that you have a sheet named 4Q.WQ1 in the subdirectory \SHEETS\BUDGET on drive C:, and you want to copy that file to a disk in drive A:, you can do so from anywhere in the system, including another drive. The following command does the task:

```
D:\>COPY C:\SHEETS\BUDGET\4Q.WQ1 A:
```

Notice that this command is issued from the root directory of drive D:! The full "formal" name for 4Q.WQ1 is the entire path specified here. It may be easier to use CD to change into that specific subdirectory before you use **COPY 4Q.WQ1 A:** to copy the file to the disk in drive A:.

You should know how to copy files for the following reasons:

1. The most important reason is to prevent the loss of data and time in case the original file is accidentally destroyed. Because you can copy files to another disk so easily and in such a short time, there is little reason not to do so.

2. At times, you may want to make changes to a file but keep the original intact. You can make a copy of the file within the same subdirectory by renaming the second copy of the file. If you have MAINMEMO.DOC and you want to keep that file, you can issue **COPY MAINMEMO.DOC MEMO01.DOC** to make a second copy. You then use MEMO01.DOC for the new document. Later you can use **COPY MAINMEMO.DOC MEMO02.DOC** to make the next version of that file.

3. You may want to make a copy to give to someone else. If you have created an effective spreadsheet for tracking vacation time, you can multiply your efforts by providing a copy to someone else who needs to accomplish the same task.

4. When files are no longer needed on the hard disk, you can save space by "archiving" those files to floppy disks. Once the files are copied to disks, you can delete the original files from the hard disk, knowing that they are accessible on the floppies whenever you need them.

The process of moving files with the COPY command can be tedious. First you have to COPY the files from one place to another, usually from one subdirectory to another. Then you have to DELete the files from the original location.

The MV (MoVe) utility, provided on the accompanying disk, moves files from one directory to another on the same disk. MV replaces the two steps required with COPY and DEL. More information about the MV utility is provided in Part III, "Guide to Using the Disk."

Exercises

Exercise 1 shows all the steps for COPYing a file from drive A: to drive C:, and then back to drive C:. Exercise 2 shows how to speed up file copying with wild cards. Finally, Exercise 3 outlines the process of copying files, along with an example.

Exercise 1 of 3

The key to making copies of files is to know what you want to copy and where you want it to go. You must know the file names (or parts of file names) before you start the COPY command. And you must know where you want those copies to end up. For this exercise, you need to use the disk provided with this book. The task is to copy files from that disk to a subdirectory on your hard disk.

TRY	NOTE
Insert the disk in drive A: `C:\`*???*`>`**`CD\`** `C:\>`**`A:`** `A:\>`**`DIR *.SPL`**	To make sure that you are in the root of C, you use **`CD\`**. Then you move to A: to examine the directory of files on the disk. You are looking for files with the SPL extension.
Look at the screen.	You should see a directory list with files named ONE.SPL, TWO.SPL, and THREE.SPL.

`A:\>`**`COPY ONE.SPL C:`**
`1 file(s) copied`
`A:\>`
	You've just copied the file name ONE.SPL to the current (in this case, root) directory in drive C:.

`A:\>`**`C:`** `C:\>`**`DIR ONE.SPL`**	Move to drive C to look for ONE.SPL.

TRY	NOTE
Look at the screen.	The file should be there. If it isn't, were you in the root directory in the first step?
	Assume that you made some changes to ONE.SPL and you now want to copy it back to the floppy disk in drive A:. Just use this next command line.
`C:\>`**`COPY ONE.SPL A:`** `1 file(s) copied`	Now you have ONE.SPL on the disk in drive A:.

You just copied one file from the floppy disk in drive A: to your hard disk (C:). You worked on that file on drive C: and then copied the file back to A:. What happened to the original copy on the disk in drive A:? DOS did *not* provide a warning that a file by the same name was already on the target location (drive A:). If the file in drive A: had been the newer version, you would have lost it because the older version on drive C: would have overwritten it.

> Always be careful when you know you are dealing with more than one version of a file. Check the file date and time to determine which copy is the newest version of the file.

Each of the SPL files contains one line of text. If you are curious about the contents, refer to the topic TYPE — Looking at Files (81) to learn how to look at those files.

Exercise 2 of 3

One way to save time with a DOS command is to use wild cards (topic 11). In this exercise, you copy all the files with the extension SPL from drive A:, using just one command. Usually you'll want to check the target location before using COPY. In this case, you already know how important the "new" and "old" files are (not very).

TRY	NOTE

`C:\>`**`A:`**
`A:\>`**`COPY *.SPL C:`**
`3 file(s) copied`
`A:\>`
	You moved into drive A: and copied all the files with the extension SPL to drive C:. That's it!

`A:\>`**`C:`** `C:\>`**`DIR *.SPL`**	Move to drive C: to look for the files you just copied.
Look at the screen.	If you are concerned about those three "strange" files on the root directory on C:,

TRY	NOTE
	you can use this next command to remove them. If you want to wait until you learn about the DELete command (topic 30), that's OK too.
A:\> C:\>**DEL *.SPL**	You just deleted all three files with one command. DOS does *not* provide any confirmation that the command took effect. You'll have to use DIR to check.

As in the first exercise, if one or more of those files had already been on drive C:, the COPY command would have overwritten them with the files from drive A:.

Exercise 3 of 3

This exercise outlines the easiest way to copy a file or files. You may want to follow along, using your own files and floppy disk as examples.

1. Change to the drive and subdirectory containing the file(s) you want to copy.
2. Use DIR to make sure that the files you want to copy are there. Use the wild cards if you can. That way, the list produced by DIR will reflect the files copied with the same wild-card combination.
3. To make certain that you are not copying over files in the target location, move there and use the same DIR command. You should not find anything. If you do, you'll want to check the file dates.
4. Move back to the original drive and subdirectory. Just typing the drive letter should do it.
5. Issue the COPY command with the same wild-card combination used in the first DIR command, adding the target destination at the end of the command.

   Here are the steps in action:

```
C:\>CD SHEETS
C:\SHEETS>DIR *.WQ1

Volume in drive D is LEARN DOS
Volume Serial Number is 1681-A996
Directory of D:\QPRO

TEST09   WQ1     2452 12-08-90   2:45p
FLICS    WQ1    13107 04-29-91   9:07a
BMG02    WQ1     2355 04-29-91   9:41a
```

```
FTU      WQ1      5588 05-02-91   8:00p
        4 file(s)

                        3751936 bytes free

C:\SHEETS>A:
A:\>DIR *.WQ1
Volume in drive A has no label
Volume Serial Number is 091-B996
Directory of A:\


File not found

A:\>C:
C:\SHEETS>COPY *.WQ1 A:

4 File(s) copied
```

And, yes, as mentioned in the "Explanation" section, all this could be done without using CD or moving to the drive. The method presented here, though, is the easiest way to keep straight what you are copying and where.

References

Floppy Disks (19), DEL — DELete Files (30), TYPE — Looking at Files (81)

NEXT TOPIC: Wild Cards * and ? (11)

Copying disks with different capacities

See DISKCOPY — Duplicating Disks (63)

Copyright (51)

VERSIONS	
All	●
Some	○
5.0	○
Command	○
Program	○
Concept	●
Problem	○

Commercial software is protected by copyright. You may make copies to protect your investment but you cannot give copies to anyone else.

Problems

Damaged master or key disk. If a program requires a specific disk (called a *master* or *key* disk) to be inserted before the program can run, the disk has a special copy-protection scheme. That scheme prevents the disk from being copied with DISKCOPY and is used to check whether the user has that specific disk before the program will work properly. Because only *that* copy allows the program to work, only one person can use the program at one time. Although these types of protection methods are rare, some programs, especially games and educational software, still use this method. If the key disk becomes damaged, the only recourse is to contact the company and arrange for a replacement disk. You are likely to have to send back the original disk and a fee of $5–$20 for the replacement. Depending on how long this process takes, you may not be able to use the program for several days or even weeks.

Protected program relocated on the hard disk. Because some copy-protected programs can be installed on the hard disk, the key or master disk is not needed to run the program. Typically the master disk becomes inoperable. Such a program copies special hidden files onto the hard disk and records the program's hidden location. When the main program starts, it looks in the hidden spot and, if the program is still there, continues. The problem occurs when other hard disk programs move this hidden file in order to optimize the disk. The file still exists. It is still hidden. But it is not located in the same place. When the parent program looks for this file and cannot find it in its original location, the program stops working. Because the master disk may be disabled, you may not be able to run the program at all. As mentioned, the only solution may be to contact the company for a replacement disk. Note some related problems:

- If you have one or more protected programs installed on the hard disk, you cannot run most disk optimization programs. These programs usually provide a warning about this problem in the documentation.
- If a hard disk crashes and you restore your files to a new hard disk, the hidden files are likely to end up in a different location. The parent program will not work on the newly restored hard disk.
- Because it is possible to "unhide" files, someone may inadvertently find the file and erase it without knowing the purpose of that file. You might be able to use an UNDELETE program to recover the file, but only if the problem is discovered immediately.

Illegal program copies. When you purchase a program, you buy the rights to use that program in any way you choose. Copyright laws protect the value of the program by limiting copies for backup only. Making a copy of a purchased program and handing that program to someone else to use violates the copyright law. If someone asks for a copy of a program you own, you might offer to show them how it works on your system and then provide suggestions on purchasing the software.

Upgrade copies. Now that some program releases are up to version 6.0, you may have several copies of earlier versions, along with their manuals, lying around. Can you sell or give those copies to someone else? Most software companies would respond with a loud "NO!" Your upgrade price is based on successive ownership of upgrades to the original product. If you sell or give away the software, you are terminating your rights to the use of that program. Some companies allow you to give your old copies of the program to educational institutions. Other companies insist that all old program disks and documentation be destroyed within 30 days after you receive the new software. These, and other conditions related to disposal of the old versions, are noted in the software documentation.

Explanation

Software publishing companies, like other businesses, want to make a fair profit as the result of labor and investment. Software makers want people to pay for the products they use. But software is easy to copy. You can make as many copies of most software packages as you like. People can copy a diskette and hand it to someone else to use. Then two people are using the product for the price of one. Because there is no limit to the number of copies you can make from a diskette, virtually any number of people can use one copy of a program. Understandably, people who spend a lot of time writing programs don't like that loss of income.

For years, software publishers created special schemes to prevent casual program copying. The schemes caused problems if a user's only copy of the program was lost or damaged. Over the years, publishers responded to users and removed the software protection methods. Very few programs have protection now.

Some people are not concerned about the legality of "sharing" programs. They see nothing wrong with making copies and giving them out. After conducting a survey several years ago, one software company estimated that for every purchased copy of its software, one illegal copy was also being used. Such a ratio means that millions of illegal copies of a program can exist, representing millions of dollars in lost income for the software publisher.

Software publishers now focus on public education, letting people know that making copies of programs to give to others is theft. Handing a program diskette to someone takes money out of the publisher's pocket. This is a heavy message, but users are beginning to hear it. Responsible users make backup copies for their own safety and don't ask for, or give out, programs they didn't purchase.

Consider the number of programs you use frequently. Do you have the manuals for all of them? Is there any chance that you are violating some copyrights? Promising yourself that you are going to buy a legal copy "some day" is like saying you'll pay your utility bill "some day."

References

Manuals and Documentation (53), Product Registration (54)

NEXT TOPIC: Data File Formats (52)

Correcting command line entries

See DOSKEY (25)

Current drive no longer valid

See A: B: C: — Drive Designation (7)

Cutting expenses

See Sharing Devices (93)

Damaged disk

See Disk Damaged (36)
See also Floppy Disks (19)

Damaged master/key disk

See Copyright (51)

Data (loss of)

See Files (2)
See also Lost Data Files (77)

Data and program files mixed

See File Organization (17)

Data File Formats (52)

VERSIONS	
All	●
Some	○
5.0	○
Command	○
Program	○
Concept	●
Problem	○

Many software programs store data in files on disk. Even though all the programs use standard DOS file names and dates, the method of storing the data can vary radically from program to program. Transferring files between programs is called *importing and exporting* data.

Before You Begin

Files (2)
File Names (4)

Problems

Exchanging data between programs. The success of data exchange between programs depends on several considerations. If the data is being moved between similar programs, there is a good chance that the programs will have menu choices to help the transition. If the data is being moved from one type of program to another, the result depends on the direction of the move and on how the data is organized. More details are provided in the "Explanation" section.

Retaining word processing styles. Exchanging document files between word processing programs may be as simple as making a menu choice to save the file in the receiving program's format. How well the format of the first file is carried over to the second file depends on the first program's capability to make the conversion. Some word processing programs can save a file in an RTF (rich text) format. This is supposed to be a universal format for word processing but it does not always work well. Refer also to the topic ASCII — Character Codes (74).

Maintaining data in two file formats. Although some programs have utilities to translate the data files, transferring the data back and forth regularly may result in a loss of data. Changes in field types and length may be compounded with each exchange. And even if the data exchange is completely accurate, only one person can update the data file at a time. If both users update the data, each using a different format, the data in the files will never be accurate. The only way to keep the file accurate is to keep the data on a floppy disk and pass the disk back and forth between users.

Identifying a file's format. DOS does not include a program to identify the type or contents of a file. Some programs use specific file extensions to identify their own files. For example, Microsoft Word uses DOC as the file extension. But MultiMate uses that extension too. The programs cannot automatically read each other's files, though. If you are not sure whether your program can read the file in question, you won't damage the file if you try. The worst that might happen is that you'll get an error message.

Explanation

Like the languages in different countries, many programs have their own unique way to store data files. Although the natives will argue that their language is best, the real issue is being able to understand (use) the data. If you use only one program and you have no need to use the data with another program, the format of the file makes little difference to you. If, however, you sometimes want data originally created by another program, the file format becomes an issue.

As mentioned, the difficulty of transferring data files depends on the types of programs used and the direction of the move. Some programs can share a data file because they can read and write the same format. Other programs can translate the data into the necessary format, but this is more difficult. For some data movement, the process can occur only once because the data significantly changes in form as it moves from one program format to another.

Some data formats have become fairly standard. The DBF format for dBASE data files is used by a number of database programs. If another database program does not use that format, it is likely to import and export the data in the DBF format.

Another example is the spreadsheet file format originally created by Lotus 1-2-3 with the extensions WKS, WK1, and WK3. Again, many spreadsheet programs can read and write that format. In some cases, though, using that format precludes using some of the features in the second program. To remain compatible, the second program must not add additional features to the file. Once it does that, the file can no longer by used as a WKS file.

For instance, Excel 3.0 can read the Lotus 1-2-3 compatible WKS file format. Excel can enhance the file by adding some of its own features, such as graph links and cell notes. Once it does that, however, Excel cannot save the file back to the original WKS format. The data file, new features included, can be saved in only the Excel format. If you wanted to return the file to someone who uses Lotus 1-2-3, you could make only minor changes in the data and then save the file again as a WKS file.

Data files of word processing programs are the most difficult to transfer. Because there often is so much in a document file—including headers, footers, and special fonts—a standard has not emerged among these programs. This does not seem to be a major problem because document files are rarely shared between users with different word processing programs. When documents are shared, the participants are likely to be in the same department and use the same software.

A number of programs exist that translate document files between formats. Because this is likely to be a one-time move (from, say, WordPerfect to Microsoft Word), the document file can be "cleaned up" and used.

References

Word Processing (43), Spreadsheets (48), Utility Software (50)

NEXT TOPIC: Manuals and Documentation (53)

Data fragments from deleted files

See Security (95)

Data integrity

See Security (95)

Databases (49)

VERSIONS	
All	●
Some	○
5.0	○
Command	○
Program	○
Concept	●
Problem	○

Databases contain data that is organized in a consistent manner and is easily retrievable. A phone book is a database. Database programs allow data to be added, changed, and printed in a wide range of ways.

Problems

Inaccurate records. A database is like a "living thing" because it requires constant attention. Parts of the database become dated almost immediately. A specific schedule for adding, changing, and deleting records is essential in keeping the database as accurate and useful as possible. Once users lose confidence in the accuracy of the database, hours of work may be required to bring the data up-to-date.

Individual records lost. You can sort and view any database of names or other data by any item in the database. If the last name is entered first, it is likely to be the first item on the screen. An accidental change to the first character of the last name puts the whole name in a different location in the sorted database. If the last name is *Smith* and someone accidentally changes it to *zmith*, the record drops to the bottom of the alphabetical list of last names. In a large database, this may put that data thousands of records away. If someone or something is lost, you can search for the record by substituting wild cards in place of the potentially changed data. For example, try looking for *?mith* if the database program allows that kind of search. Or find a unique field item and search for it. The phone number or social security number is a likely candidate.

Poor record design. Even if all the data is in the database, the way that the data is structured can greatly affect the database's usefulness. A field name of NAME, containing both the first and last name, cannot be used to sort on the last name. Finding records with a specific last name requires additional effort. If you are in doubt, divide data into the smallest useful units. A phone number field can have just 7 digits, or it can have 3 digits for the area code, 7 digits for the number, and 4 digits for an extension.

Explanation

Effective use of data requires planning. Unlike word processing or spreadsheets, in which the words and numbers can be entered and endlessly moved around the document, most databases require a consistent format for the data. Because good design is essential for any database, this discussion provides a basic review of the design process.

Imagine collecting on blank sheets of paper the names and addresses of 50 people who are interested in purchasing your new Widget-Walker product. Although most people will probably write their first names first, a few people will write their last names first. What would you guess for *John George* or *George John?* And some people will include home and work phone numbers, but you won't know which is which. If you call during the day, will you reach them? Will you ask for Mr. George or Mr. John? You can avoid such problems by providing a form for everyone to use. And because you know what the data represents on each line, you won't have to guess.

A computer database is unable to guess what the data represents on a blank page. Proper design of this data form is the key to effective use of the database. Although different database programs may use different words for this form, the general database term is a *record*. Each record represents a person or thing. Fifty people interested in buying the Widget-Walker will be in a database with 50 records, one record per person.

Although each record represents, in this example, one person, each line describes something about that individual. That line, in computer database terms, is called a *field*. A field contains specific data about that person. A record can have one or a dozen or hundreds of fields, each designed to contain data on a specific aspect of the person (or object). *People* fields include FIRST NAME, LAST NAME, STREET, CITY, and PHONE NUMBER. Depending on how you want to use the database, the field might also include HAIR COLOR, DATE OF BIRTH, and SEX.

It is the user's responsibility to be sure that the data entered in each field makes sense and is consistent. The database program allows Y in the SEX field, as well as M and F. The data is meaningful only if you can trust its accuracy. The count for SEX = M might be 25. The count for SEX = F might be 24. In a database of 50 people, where did that last person go? (One Y?)

The record and field design is actually the middle of the design process. Real database design begins with questions about what is be tracked by the database. If you want to sell Widget-Walkers to these people, what do you want to know about them? They are your information domain. They represent the small part of the world you want to know more about:

- Who are they, and where do they live?
- Where can you call them during the day and evening?
- Because Widget-Walkers are for kids, how many children are there, and what are their ages?
- In case the adults might also be interested Widget-Walkers, what hobbies do they have?

From these few questions, you might design the following record on paper:

LASTNAME: ____________________ FIRSTNAME: __________________

STREET: ____

CITY: _________________________ STATE: ___ ZIP: ________

DAY PHONE: ______________ EVENING PHONE: ________________

NUMBER OF CHILDREN: _____ CHILDREN'S AGES: ____________

YOUR HOBBIES: ____

This sample record for the Widget-Walker sales prospects contains 11 fields.

Figure 49-1 shows the process of creating the actual record (for the WIDGET database) in PC-File version 6.0. In this case, each field was typed on the screen to correspond with the form the prospects completed. This makes data entry much easier.

Once you have designed the form, each record can be added to the screen (see Figure 49-2). Each screenful of information represents one person who filled out the prospect form.

Gathering and entering the data is like tilling the soil and planting the seeds. What you really want is to gather the harvest. You need to organize the data to help sell Widget-Walkers. You want prospects with lots of children, and you want to talk with those prospects during the day. (You assume that if they give you their daytime numbers, it's OK to call them at work.)

Using the data in your database, you can generate a report that shows the prospects with the most children and where you can reach the prospects during the day and evening. Here are just a few lines of a sample report:

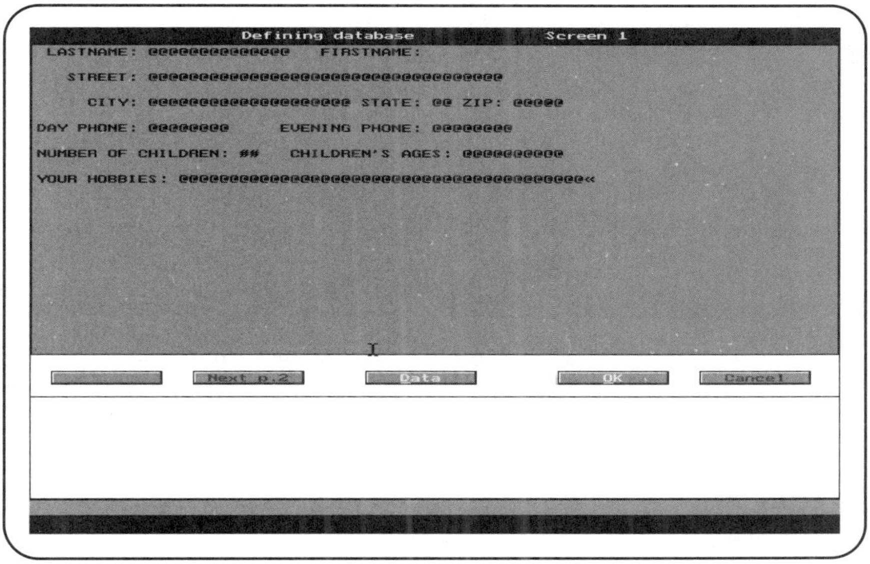

Figure 49-1. A PC-File 6.0 screen containing the record design for the WIDGET database.

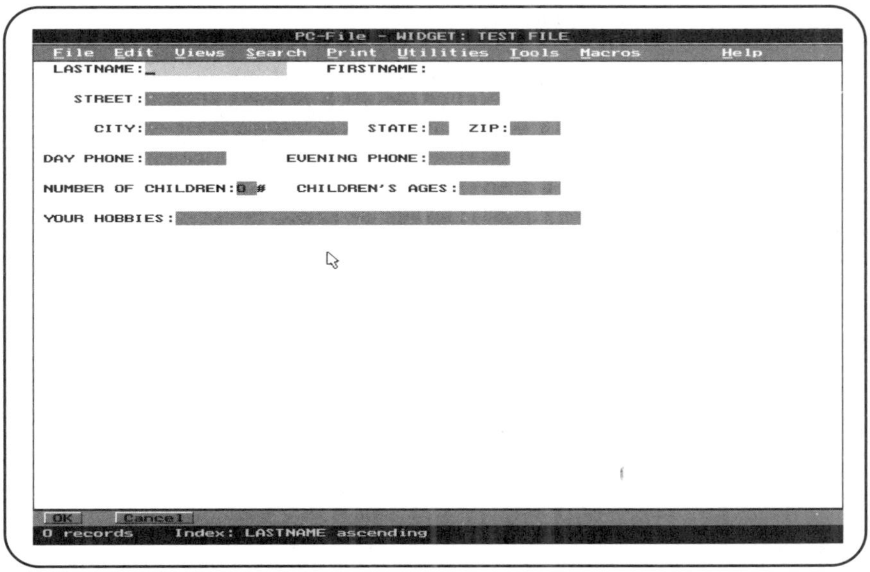

Figure 49-2. The data entry screen for WIDGET.

```
Widget-Walker prospect list                         08/26/91
SORT: Number of children

NUMBER OF    FIRST     LAST       DAY      EVENING
CHILDREN     NAME      NAME       PHONE    PHONE
-----        --------  ---------  -------- --------
  4          Tom       Olivier    555-3423 555-1231
  3          Irene     Wooster    555-1212 555-3412
  3          Beth      Smock      555-4534 555-2312
...
```

You can then use the report to make notes about calling. If a prospect is interested in a home demonstration, you might circle the phone number and arrange to call that evening for an appointment. If the database includes fields with the date and time, you can create another report showing each day's appointments, sorted by time of day. (If that question had been raised earlier, during the design process, these records would include those fields. It's not too late, though. You can change the record.)

Would this project make sense if you had just 15 prospects? For this amount of information, it probably wouldn't. Using the computer to organize data depends on the return of time invested to "till the soil and plant the seeds." If you want to use the database to track each call as well as the subsequent sales and service information, a database with 15 records still might make sense. However, if you just want to call all the people, in no particular order, you might prefer to work from the forms they completed, throwing away the rejections.

Your computerized Widget-Walker database contains one file. The file with the list of prospects has 50 records, and each record has 11 fields. You can sort and print the data however you like. It can help you manage the process of selling those wonderful Widget-Walkers.

Exercise

The most basic database products can handle the information needs covered in this discussion. (Even without database software, you can plan and use a database.) Design a simple database by answering the following questions:

1. *What is the information domain?* All the people in the office.
2. *What do you want to know about them?* First name, last name, extension, birth date, and hire date.
3. *How often do you want to know it?* A revised printed report monthly.
4. *Where will the data come from?* Each person will complete a form with the following blanks:

Last name: ____________

First name: ____________

Phone number and ext.: _______

Birth month and day (*mm/dd*): ___/___

Hire date (*yy/mm/dd*): ___/___/___

5. *How can it be organized to answer your questions?* Alphabetically on last name, alphabetically on first name, sorted by birth month and day, and sorted on hire date.

6. *Who will maintain the data and provide the information?* John will distribute and gather the forms. He'll have new employees fill out the form. He'll update the database and print the main reports monthly.

Although that is just a brief look at database design, it does provide some ideas for getting started.

References

Copyright (51), Data File Formats (52), Security (95)

NEXT TOPIC: Utility Software (50)

DATE (23)

VERSIONS	
All	●
Some	○
5.0	○
Command	●
Program	○
Concept	○
Problem	○

The DATE command sets the *system date*. All files created and changed will show this date. Because some programs use the system date as the current date for processing, keeping the date accurate is important.

Syntax

```
C:\>DATE
Current date is Mon 08-26-1991
Enter new date (mm-dd-yy): 8/27/91 <Enter>

C:\>DATE
Current date is Mon 08-27-1991
Enter new date (mm-dd-yy): <Enter>
```

Problems

Wrong system date. Except on older systems, the date is kept internally. Check the date occasionally with the DATE command. You can make a temporary correction by typing the correct date. Making a permanent change to the system date will depend on your computer. Check the manual for instructions on changing the system date permanently.

Date changes. If you notice that the system date has inexplicably changed after you altered it with DATE, correct the date as instructed in the computer's manual. If, after restarting the computer, the date has changed again, the small internal battery holding the system date may be weak. Replace the battery as instructed in the computer's manual.

Explanation

The DATE command was used much more extensively before computers were able to keep the system date between sessions. Like battery-powered watches, most systems now keep a number of variables, including the date and time. Except for checking the date occasionally, you won't have much use for the DATE command.

Typing **DATE** shows the current date and provides a prompt to enter a new date. You can enter it as *mm/dd/yy* or *mm-dd-yy*. The *yy* may be expressed as *yyyy* to include the century. The day of the week shown on the prompt is calculated by the system. This changed date is maintained only as long as the system remains on. Changing this value may or may *not* change the internal system date on most computers.

Because files are *date stamped* when they are created or changed, the system date should be kept accurate. An accurate date can help when you are determining which files to delete or which version of a file is current. Users of older systems are prompted for the DATE and TIME every time the system is turned on. These systems do not keep a current system date when the power is turned off. Even though you can just press Enter to bypass that prompt, it's a good idea to enter the current date and time for the reasons noted.

Exercise

As mentioned, most systems keep the date internally. But you should check the date occasionally and may need to change it. This exercise steps you through the process.

Exercise 1 of 1

You may be prompted for the date whenever you start your system. Hopefully you look at that date and make a correction if necessary. In this exercise, you can check and change the date from the DOS prompt.

TRY	NOTE
C:\>**DATE** Current date is Tue 01-01-1980 Enter new date (mm-dd-yy):	DOS responds with the current system date. These sample date lines are from an XT system. Systems like it did not keep the date and time between sessions.
8-26-91 <Enter>	Notice that the prompt shows the response format as *mm* for the month, *dd* for the day, and *yy* for the year. You *do not* enter the day of the week. The system calculates that from the date.

If you type a nonexistent date, DOS responds with `Invalid date` and provides another prompt. The date response can use a slash (/) instead of a hyphen (-) and can include the entire year. In just a few years, the century will need to be included at the date prompt.

The internal date table even knows leap years. If you enter **2-29-91**, you get the `Invalid date` response. If you enter **2-29-92**, the system accepts the date because that's a leap year.

References

Hardware (38), Microprocessors (96)

NEXT TOPIC: TIME (24)

Date changes

See DATE (23)

Decreasing PATH search time

See PATH — Program Search (29)

Default Drive (3)

VERSIONS	
All	●
Some	○
5.0	○
Command	●
Program	○
Concept	●
Problem	○

Disk drives contain the media that store the data and program files. The default drive is the drive currently being used for DOS to read and write these files.

Before You Begin

Boot/Startup (1)
Files (2)

Syntax

`C:\>`	The DOS prompt that shows the current default drive.
`C>`	The prompt may be just the drive letter.

Problems

`Not ready reading drive A` and **`Abort, Retry or Fail?`** If DOS attempts to read the disk that is indicated by the drive light but cannot, one of these error messages appears on the screen. Older versions of DOS may respond with `(Abort, Retry or Ignore?)` Insert a disk in the drive and press R (for Retry). If a disk is not available, press F or I. Refer to the topic Floppy Disks (19) for information on correcting this problem.

`Bad command or file name.` Although there are many ways to get this error message, when you are dealing with drive letters, the problem usually occurs when you type a semicolon instead of a colon after the letter or you forget to type the colon. To correct the problem, just type the drive letter again and include the colon.

Explanation

DOS always works from one specific disk drive. The current drive is the *default drive*. Unless DOS is given instructions to use another drive, this is the drive in use. The DOS command prompt shows the current default drive as a letter.

Personal computers contain at least one drive. This floppy drive is referred to as A:. If the system has a hard drive built in, it is drive C:. For drive A:, the DOS prompt on the screen looks like

```
A>
```

or

```
A:\>
```

And the prompt for drive C: looks like

```
C>
```

or

```
C:\>
```

A system can have as many as 26 drives, each labeled as a letter of the alphabet. Table 3-1 shows some typical drive letters and types.

Table 3-1. Some typical drives.

Drive Letter	Drive Type
A	Floppy drive
B	Floppy drive
C	Hard drive
D	Hard drive or RAM drive
E	Hard drive or RAM drive
F	Hard drive or RAM drive
...	...
X	Network drive
Y	Network drive
Z	Network drive

You select the default drive by typing the drive letter followed by a colon. For example, if the prompt shows that drive C: is the current drive, typing **A:** changes the prompt so that A: is now the new default drive:

```
C:\>A:
A:\>
```

If a disk is not in drive A: when it becomes the default drive, an error message appears, as noted in the "Problems" section.

References

A: B: C: — Drive Designation (7), Floppy Drive Failure (32), Hard Drive Failure (33), Networks (79)

NEXT TOPIC: File Names (4)

Defective product

See Product Registration (54)

DEL — DELete (30)

VERSIONS
All ●
Some ○
5.0 ○

Command ●
Program ○
Concept ○
Problem ○

The DEL command deletes files from a DOS directory. The space occupied by that file is then available for use. ERASE and DEL work exactly the same. DOS 5.0 users can recover a deleted file immediately with UNDELETE. Earlier versions of DOS require the use of other programs such as PC Tools or Norton Utilities.

> If you have just deleted a file and you want to recover it now, you must attempt the recovery before using any program that creates files. DO NOT INSTALL OR COPY ANY PROGRAM TO THE HARD DISK BEFORE ATTEMPTING TO RECOVER THE DELETED FILE.

Before You Begin

Files (2)
File Names (4)
DIR — Directory (8)
Wild Cards * and ? (11)

Syntax

`C:\WORDPROC>`**`DEL GOODBYE.TXT`**

The file name GOODBYE.TXT will no longer appear in the \WORDPROC directory.

`C:\WORDPROC>`**`DEL *.DOC`**

All the file names in the \WORDPROC directory with the extension DOC will be deleted.

> Be extremely careful when using wild cards with the DEL command.

`C:\WORDPROC>`**`DEL *.DOC /P`**

DOS 5.0 prompts you before deleting each file.

Problem

Accidentally deleted file(s). Because this is a distinct possibility with the DEL command, many DOS users refuse to delete any files. Or they may delete files one at a time but will not use the * and ? wild cards to save time. But even the largest hard disk eventually fills up. And if a hard disk is not full, the presence of unneeded files slows DOS down and creates cluttered directories for the user. To avoid accidental deletes (or to minimize their damage), be careful in the following ways when you use DEL:

- You can minimize the damage from accidental deletes by keeping your backup files current. All critical files should be located in two places at once. If a large database was backed up the evening before, the loss will be limited to the day's changes.
- If you are unsure which files will be deleted with the wild cards, use the same wild-card combination with the DIR command. Then, if the files listed are those you want to delete, you can use DEL with those same wild cards.
- Practice with the UNDELETE command or a program that undeletes files before you accidentally erase a critical file. This will help prevent panic when you erase a file you need to recover.

Explanation

Like the card catalog in the library, DOS keeps the name and location of files in the directory. Because the library has a limited amount of space, any card "deleted" from the card catalog represents space available on the bookshelf where that book was located. A file can be *undeleted* because the contents of that file actually remain in that space until the space is needed. The book remains on the shelf until pushed off by the new book.

The programs that recover deleted files look in the directory and find files marked as being deleted. (DOS originally marks these files by removing the first letter of the file name.) But not only must the undelete program find those marked files, it must also check on the disk to make sure that the contents of the file still exist. This is why undeleting a file immediately after the deletion is critical. Any program that writes data to the disk is likely to use that space marked by DOS as being "open." Once this happens, the actual file's data is gone and unrecoverable.

If a series of files is accidentally deleted, the same problems and solutions apply. As long as no additional data has been written to the disk, you can recover the files. If data has been written to the disk, some or all of the files may be unrecoverable.

If an immediate solution or help is not available, do *not* turn off the computer while waiting for help. When the system is booted, programs may run that make changes to the disk—changes that may lose the deleted file's data. You may be able to run the system safely for days; you just can't use any program that writes to the disk.

If necessary, you can use programs that read from the disk and then write the changes back to a floppy disk. This minimizes the chances of the undeleted file space being used. For example, if you called up a file, named C:\WORDPROC\LETTER1.DOC, in your word processing program, you could then save the changed file as A:LETTER1.DOC.

Exercise

For this exercise, use the disk provided with this book. A special subdirectory, named EXER30, exists with sample files to be deleted.

Exercise 1 of 1

Make sure that a *copy* of the accompanying disk is in drive A:. You'll be making changes on that disk, so you don't want to use the original.

TRY	NOTE
`C:\>`**`A:`** `A:\>`**`CD EXER30`** `A:\EXER30>`	You move into the EXER30 subdirectory (on the accompanying disk), which contains files to be deleted.
`A:\EXER30>`**`DIR`**	This directory includes 15 files. The names are listed on the screen.

You follow these same steps each time you delete one or more of the files in EXER30. First you'll use DIR, along with your wild-card combination, to check which files you will be deleting. Only then will you use that same wild-card combination to delete the files. For the purpose of learning, you'll then use DIR to look at the entire list of files. Normally you don't need to use DIR to confirm that the deletions were made; when DOS says files are deleted, they are.

TRY	NOTE
`A:\EXER30>`**`DIR LDO001.DOC`**	Even though you want to delete all the files that begin with LDO, you'll do this first one the hard way. This DIR shows one file.
`A:\EXER30>`**`DEL <F3>`**	You could retype the entire line if you like. But pressing the F3 key repeats the rest of the line.

TRY	NOTE
A:\EXER30>**DIR**	Look at the directory. LDO001.DOC is gone. But you want to get rid of all the files that start with LDO. Try the next line.
A:\EXER30>**DIR LDO00?.DOC**	Does this command list all the LDO files? No, it does not include LDO013.DOC because the wild card ? replaces only the sixth character in the file name. Try again.
A:\EXER30>**DIR LDO0??.DOC**	Now you see the remaining three LDO files.
A:\EXER30>**DEL <F3>** A:\EXER30>**DIR**	Now you don't. The three files are gone. You could instead type **DEL LDO0*.DOC** and accomplish the same thing.
A:\EXER30>**DIR *.SPL**	To remove all the files with the extension SPL, use the wild card * for the first part of the file name.
A:\EXER30>**DEL <F3>**	The SPL files are deleted.

But how do you delete files that have no extension? The EXER30 subdirectory has just one file like this, but it will serve as an example.

TRY	NOTE
A:\EXER30>**DIR ***	DOS takes the single * as a wild card and lists all the files, just like **DIR** without the *.
A:\EXER30>**DIR *.**	The period in this example is critical in finding the files you want. This same command is helpful in listing subdirectories within a directory.
A:\EXER30>**DEL *.** A:\EXER30>**DIR**	The one file without an extension is gone. DOS will not erase subdirectories in this way, however.

```
A:\EXER30>DIR *LETR.TXT
 Volume in drive A is LEARNDOS
     Directory of A:\EXER30
LASTLETR TXT         4 08-26-91   12:00a
DWDLETR  TXT         4 08-26-91   12:00a
PJDLETR  TXT         4 08-26-91   12:00a
PJDLETR1 TXT         4 08-26-91   12:00a
4 file(s)                16bytes
                      9216 bytes free
```

TRY	NOTE
	Here you just want to list files with LETR as part of the name. Did this command work? No, the * substitutes for the *remaining* part of the file name, so four files are listed (based on *.TXT).
A:\EXER30>**DIR ???LETR*.TXT**	Now three files are listed. Look carefully at the file named LASTLETR.TXT in the preceding step. That file name has four letters before the LETR in the name. That one just does not fit into the current wild-card pattern.
A:\EXER30>**DEL LASTLETR.TXT**	To get rid of that file, you type the entire file name. Or, as you've probably noticed by now, those four files are the only ones with the extension TXT. You could have just used **DEL *.TXT** and been rid of them all.
A:\EXER30>**DIR *.***	Using *.* with DIR is redundant. But for consistency, use it here. To remove the remaining files from the subdirectory, use this next command.
A:\EXER30>**DIR <F3>** Are you sure (Y/N)?**Y**	Using the wild-card combination *.* is the only time DOS warns you that you're about to clean out the directory.

If you knew you wanted to delete all the files in the directory from the start, you could have just used the **DEL *.*** command. But that would have shortened the exercise, and you would not have had as much fun.

References

ATTRIB — Protecting Files (62)

NEXT TOPIC: UNDELETE (31)

Determining label capacity

See Labels in Printer (69)

Different document file formats

See Word Processing (43)

Different key locations

See Keyboard (39)

Different operating system versions

See Operating Systems (75)

Difficulty tracking your position in the program

See Interfaces (27)

DIR — Directory (8)

VERSIONS	
All	●
Some	○
5.0	○
Command	●
Program	○
Concept	○
Problem	○

The DOS directory contains the file names that you (or, in some cases, the computer) have grouped together. The DIR command lists files in the current directory.

Before You Begin

Files (2)
File Names (4)
A: B: C: — Drive Designation (7)

Syntax

`C:\>DIR`	Lists files in the current directory
`C:\>DIR /P`	Pauses at each full screen
`C:\>DIR /W`	Shows files in five columns across the screen
`C:\>DIR *.EXE`	Shows files with the extension EXE

5

Version 5.0 has the following additional switches:

C:\>**DIR /S**	Shows files in the current directory and its subdirectories
C:\>**DIR /B**	Shows bare format (no heading or summary)
C:\>**DIR /O:N**	Sorts files by name
C:\>**DIR /O:E**	Sorts files by extension
C:\>**DIR /O:D**	Sorts files by date and time (earliest file is listed first)
C:\>**DIR /O:D /P**	Sorts by date and time and pauses each time the screen fills

As the last example illustrates, you can combine various command switches with DIR.

Problems

Mistyped file name. After the DIR command and any switches, you must supply the full file name or wild cards. If you leave any space in the file name, an error message appears.

Misused wild card. You can easily get confused when using wild cards with DIR, or with any DOS command. This is not a serious problem except that you may not see the files you thought you would see. For more information on wild cards, refer to topic 11.

Confusion between the / and \ keys. You can use both the slash (/) and the backslash (\) keys in the DIR command. The backslash separates directories in the path name. And any extra switch at the end of the command requires a preceding slash, as in this example:

```
C:\>DIR \WORDPROC\DOC\*.DOC /P
```

Explanation

Before exploring the DIR command, you need to understand directories in DOS. Knowing how to use the DIR command without understanding directory structure is like being able to look around in one room but not knowing that there are other rooms to move into.

The DOS system of directories is frequently expressed as a tree. Each branch of the tree leads to more branches, those branches lead to additional branches, and so on. The first branch is called the "root" directory. A typical directory "tree" is shown in Figure 8-1.

```
C:\─┬─BATCH
    ├─DATABASE────────┬─VPINFO
    │                 ├─FILE
    │                 ├─FOXPRO
    │                 └─PROSCHED
    ├─DOS─────────────────CONFIG
    ├─GRAPHICS────────┬─3D
    │                 ├─COLLAGE
    │                 ├─FRACGRAF─────────┬─EXAMPLES
    │                 │                  └─HELP
    │                 ├─GENERAL
    │                 ├─GIF
    │                 └─ZOOM
    ├─LANGUAGE────────┬─PBASIC
    │                 └─SOURCE
    ├─NORTON
    ├─PCTOOLS
    ├─TELECOMM────────┬─PCPLUS
    │                 ├─CARBON
    │                 └─ZIP
    ├─UTILS───────────┬─GENERAL
    │                 ├─MOUSE
    │                 └─PRINTER
    └─WORDPROC────────┬─DOCS─────────────┬─MISC
                      │                  └─TRAINING
                      ├─WORD5
                      ├─WRITE
                      ├─HOMEBREW
                      └─LEARNDOS
```

Figure 8-1. A sample directory tree.

It may be more helpful to see each directory as a room. Each room can contain files, or it may just contain doors into other rooms. This arrangement of rooms, the name of the room, and the location are determined mostly by the user. (In some cases, programs create their own subdirectories.) You decide what goes where. The process of organizing your files is covered in more detail the topic File Organization (17).

You are always in a directory in DOS. Any directory under a directory is a *subdirectory*. If you are at the top directory (expressed as the root directory or \), all the other directories are subdirectories. In Figure 8-1, the CONFIG directory is a subdirectory under the DOS directory, which is a subdirectory under the root directory. Each subdirectory has a name, and the names of subdirectories are separated by a backslash (\). For example, the full name for the CONFIG subdirectory is C:\DOS\CONFIG. You have to go through the DOS directory to reach the CONFIG subdirectory. (Note that as a matter of convenience subdirectories are often called just directories.) The process of moving from directory to directory is covered in the next topic, CD, MD, and RD — Working with Directories (9).

The DIR command shows the file names and subdirectories in the current directory. The command can consist of up to three parts: the command, the search files and wildcards, and the switches. The first part is just the command:

```
C:\>DIR

Volume in drive C is LEARN DOS
Directory of C:\

BATCH        <DIR>      08-26-91   9:42p
DATABASE     <DIR>      08-26-91   9:42p
DOS          <DIR>      08-26-91   7:43p
GRAPHICS     <DIR>      08-26-91   9:45p
AUTOEXEC BAT        133 02-27-91   9:45a
COMMAND  COM      48554 06-31-91   5:47a
CONFIG   SYS        269 02-27-91   9:45a
        7 file(s)      48956 bytes
                     5378048 bytes free

C:\>
```

Several pieces of information are provided in the directory list. The lines at the top show the label name, the unique disk serial number, and the name of the directory. This example shows the label name LEARN DOS and a list of the root directory on drive C:. The serial number is a new feature with later versions of DOS.

This list of file names contains four subdirectories (marked as <DIR>) and three files. The three-letter extensions are lined up in a column on the directory list. The files, though, are still referred to as CONFIG.SYS and AUTOEXEC.BAT. Notice that the period is not shown in the directory list, but when you type the file name, you must type the period before the extension. Following the file extension is the size of the file, in characters. To the right of the file name is the creation date and time.

The DIR command also shows the number of files at the end of the list, the total number of characters (bytes) in these files (only in later versions), and the amount of space (empty bytes) on the disk.

The second part of the DIR command can contain a specific file name. This is helpful when you just want to see whether a specific file is within a long directory listing. Note this example:

```
C:\DOCS>DIR LET01.DOC

Volume in drive C LEARN DOS
Directory of C:\DOCS

LET01    DOC        246 08-26-91  10:32p
        1 file(s)        246 bytes
                     5365760 bytes free

C:\DOCS>
```

You can guess at parts of the file name by using wild cards, the asterisk (*) and the question mark (?). In this next example, the asterisk replaces the entire file name. Here you are looking for files with the extension of EXE:

```
C:\DOS>DIR *.EXE

Volume in drive C LEARN DOS
Directory of C:\DOS

DIRSIZE  EXE     24576 08-26-91   9:35a
DEBUG    EXE     20602 08-26-91   5:47a
EDLIN    EXE     12578 08-26-91   5:47a
        3 file(s)      57756 bytes
                     5380096 bytes free

C:\DOS>
```

To list all files beginning with LDO and ending with the extension DOC, you type

```
C:\BOOKS\LEARNDOS>DIR LDO*.DOC

Volume in drive D LEARN DOS
Directory of C:\BOOKS\LEARNDOS

LDO001   DOC      6144 08-26-91   8:42a
LDOINTRO DOC      6144 08-26-91   4:45p
LDORIENT DOC     29696 08-26-91   7:40a
        3 file(s)      41984 bytes
                     3641344 bytes free

C:\BOOKS\LEARNDOS>
```

The question mark substitutes for just one character in the file name. See the topic Wild Cards * and ? (11) for more information about what the wild cards mean and how you can use them in DOS commands.

In this next DIR command, you are looking for all four-letter file names that begin with LDO:

```
C:\BOOKS\LEARNDOS>DIR LDO?.DOC

Volume in drive C LEARN DOS
Directory of C:\BOOKS\LEARNDOS
```

```
LD07      DOC      4566 08-26-91  10:32p
LDOR      DOC        34 08-26-91  10:45p
         1 file(s)       4600 bytes
                      5365760 bytes free


C:\BOOKS\LEARNDOS>
```

The third part of the DIR command can contain a switch to affect how the list is displayed, as in this example:

```
C:\>DIR /P
```

The /P switch produces a pause with the message `Press any key...` on the last line of the screen.

The /W switch creates a five-column "wide" listing without the file size, date, and time information:

```
C:\DOS>DIR /W

Volume in drive C LEARN DOS
Directory of C:\DOS

[.]           [..]          [CONFIG]      EGA.SYS       FORMAT.COM
DISPLAY.SYS   COUNTRY.SYS   B.COM         HIMEM.SYS     BROWSE.COM
CASTLE.BAS    CATAPULT.BAS  KEYB.COM      CLEANUP.EXE   CLEANUP.INF
KEYBOARD.SYS  MODE.COM      CPY.COM       SETVER.EXE    DIAG.TXT
.             .             .             .             .
.             .             .             .             .
PACKING.LST   MORE.COM      README.TXT    DELOLDOS.EXE  COMMAND.COM
TEMP
      116 file(s)    2638228 bytes
                     5355520 bytes free


C:\DOS>
```

(In the preceding example, some of the lines of files were deleted to save space.)

Any DOS command that uses a switch requires the slash key (/). The backslash key (\) is used to separate directories, so a DIR command can include a reference to a directory other than the one you are in.

Now look at the following example:

```
C:\>DIR C:\WORDPROC\WORD5\DOCS\LD000?.*
```

Including the directory path in this command line is like leaning around the corner of the house to look into the back yard. You don't have to walk into the back yard to see what is there. Typically you move into the directory you want to see, and the command is just

```
C:\WORDPROC\WORD5\DOCS>DIR LD000?.*
```

Exercises

The DIR command works in any directory. Exercise 1 demonstrates the use of DIR and the /P and /W switches for all versions of DOS. Exercise 2 covers switches available in DOS 5.0. To learn how to select and show only some files, see the topic Wild Cards * and ? (11).

Exercise 1 of 2

TRY	NOTE
`C:\>`**`DIR`**	This lists all the files in the root (the top) directory of drive C:. The list of files may scroll by too fast to see. In that case, use this next command.
`C:\>`**`DIR /P`**	Now the screen "pauses" the list of files when the screen fills up.
`C:\>`**`DIR /W`**	If you still find it difficult to track the files, use the /W switch to produce a "wide" list. You can even use both switches together: **`DIR /W/P`**.
Insert a disk in drive A:. `C:\>`**`A:`** `A:\>`**`DIR`**	After you move to the disk in drive A:, you now see the files on that disk.

Exercise 2 of 2

5

DOS 5.0 has several new switches available with the DIR command. In this exercise, you look at a more extensive list of files, a list of files sorted by file name, and a list of files sorted by extension.

TRY	NOTE
`C:\>DIR /S`	This list in the root directory is likely to prove quite long because it includes all the files in all the subdirectories on the disk. You can press Ctrl-C to stop the command.
`C:\>DIR /S/P`	Here you add the /P switch to pause the list.
`C:\>DIR /O:N`	This switch lists the *o*rder of of the files by *n*ame. It does not change the directory.
`C:\>DIR /O:E`	This switch lists the files by *e*xtension. Remember to add the /P switch if there are too many files for one screen.

Other switches and combinations of switches are available with the DIR command. As always, your DOS manual lists them all.

References

Wild Cards * and ? (11), File Organization (17)

NEXT TOPIC: CD, MD, and RD — Working with Directories (9)

Directory not empty

See CD, MD, and RD — Working with Directories (9)

Directory not found

See CD, MD, and RD — Working with Directories (9)

Dirty keyboard

See Keyboard (39)

Disk and drive capacities not compatible

See Floppy Disks (19)

Disk Damaged (36)

VERSIONS	
All	●
Some	○
5.0	○
Command	○
Program	○
Concept	○
Problem	●

The surface media on floppy disks and hard disks are fairly delicate. The magnetic signal can become corrupted in dozens of ways. This discussion shows how you can minimize this disaster or recover if disk damage does occur.

Problem

`Unable to read file.` This message, or a variation of it, suggests that the disk no longer has the proper data in a readable format.

Explanation

When a program needs a data file, the program issues the request to DOS. DOS then locates the file and instructs the disk drive to read and transmit the signal from the disk. If that signal does not conform to the standard DOS data stream, DOS attempts to read the data again. This step may occur up to seven times. You can tell because the drive light begins a rhythmic flickering. Only after DOS has attempted to read the data several times does it report the message `Unable to read file`. Only after you read and absorb this error message several times do you accept the fact that you are in trouble.

If the problem occurs when DOS is trying to load a program, the program can't be loaded, and DOS returns an error message. If a program is attempting to read a file, DOS reports the error to that program. Some programs respond with their own error messages and return to a menu. Some will just "crash" and stop working by dropping to DOS or locking up the system.

You can take several steps when you have a problem with a disk:

1. Sometimes persistence pays off. Try to use the file several times. If you finally get the file to read, immediately save the file under a new name. DOS writes the file to a new location on the disk.

2. Some programs, such as databases, do not read the entire file at one time, and the file cannot be resaved under a new name. If the file will not load or does not load completely, return to DOS and attempt to copy the file to another location, either on the hard disk or a floppy. If DOS reports `Disk error reading drive X:` and offers the `Abort, Retry, or Ignore?` prompt, press R (for Retry) several times. If this

does not work, pressing I (for Ignore) will result in a corrupted and highly unstable file. If this is better than nothing at all, use it, but remember that one or more sections of the file will have garbled data. Press A (for Abort) to get out of the error.

3. Try CHKDSK with the /F switch. Don't count on it, but the problem may be cross-linked files, and CHKDSK may solve the problem in its own unique way.

4. At this point in the file recovery, you need one of the commercial utility programs. These programs are even more persistent than DOS when reading a file and, in many cases, will succeed in recovering the file. They automatically move the parts of the file they can recover to another location on the disk and mark the bad areas to prevent later use.

> Disaster recovery programs like PC Tools and Norton Utilities are like fire extinguishers. You really don't want to be caught on the phone trying to order one just after you first smell smoke.

Of course, the best solution to a bad disk file is *prevention*. Both the topics Hard Drive Failure (33) and Floppy Drive Failure (32) provide advice on preventing this kind of problem. If you have observed regular backup procedures (see topic 13), the damaged file may cause you the loss of only a few hours of work because you can restore yesterday's backup file to the hard disk.

If you do have the backup file, make sure you that rename the bad file on the disk. Use something like KEEPFILE.BAD. Then the backup will not be written back to the same location on the disk. Keeping that file active also prevents good data from being written to bad places.

References

Backing Up Data (13), Floppy Drive Failure (32), Hard Drive Failure (33), Hardware (38), BACKUP — Files (41), Product Registration (54)

NEXT COPY: XCOPY — Files (37)

Disk error reading/writing

See Floppy Drive Failure (32)

Disk Full (35)

VERSIONS
All ●
Some ○
5.0 ○

Command ○
Program ○
Concept ○
Problem ●

When a floppy disk fills up, you can get another one out of the box. When a hard disks fills up, the solution is not quite so easy. Regular housekeeping and paying attention to several DOS commands should prevent this problem.

Problems

Program ends with a disk-full message. Any program that automatically creates data is using disk space. Although many programs are able to project the amount of space needed, some cannot. Such programs often do not deal well with the inability to write data to the disk. Once the problem occurs, the only option is to delete some files from the hard disk and start the program over again. In some cases, such as data-intensive programs, a program may not be able to "roll back" the processing, and the files will be corrupted. Check the manual for this potential problem before it occurs.

File cannot be saved. A less data-intensive program, such as a word processing program, might simply declare that it cannot save the file, and return to its main menu. You may be able to save the file to a floppy disk (if an empty formatted disk is available) until you can delete files from the hard disk. Some programs allow you to drop temporarily to DOS. You can then delete files to make room on the disk.

> Always keep several formatted disks available for saving files in case the hard disk fills up when you are saving a file and you cannot complete the save.

Explanation

As discussed more fully in the topic File Organization (17), the way you organize a hard disk is mostly personal preference. But regardless of your organizational skills, *the hard disk will fill up eventually*. You can learn this lesson now or learn it later.

Every time you use the DIR command, you know how much space is left on the disk. Even though the number of bytes remaining is presented without commas, you should occasionally work through that string of digits because it provides a useful gauge. Any number less than one-fourth of the disk's total capacity suggests that housekeeping is necessary. If you are not sure how large the hard disk is, use CHKDSK (topic 20) to find out.

The Disk Meter Deluxe (DMD) utility, provided on the accompanying disk, gives a graphic representation of remaining disk space. DMD is a good program to use for a quick assessment of your remaining disk space. The program can be included in AUTOEXEC.BAT to remind you every time you boot the system how much space remains. More information about DMD is provided in Part III, "Guide to Using the Disk."

Some of the newer programs use a lot of disk space, if allowed, when you install them. Most will ask if you want optional files included in the installation. These may include a sample data file, tutorial programs, extra graphics, or complete typefaces in all 12 sizes. Unless you know that you need these files, decline a program's polite offer. You can install the files later if you need them. In some cases, you'll forget that the files are there, even though they can easily take up an extra three or four megabytes of hard disk space.

Exercise

If you have not checked for the amount of space remaining on your hard disk, do it now. Refer to the topic CHKDSK—CHecK DiSK (20) for instructions. If you find that there is very little space left, read the topic File Organization (17) and get to work.

References

File Organization (17), CHKDSK — CHecK DiSK (20)

NEXT TOPIC: Disk Damaged (36)

DISKCOPY — Duplicating Disks (63)

VERSIONS	
All	●
Some	○
5.0	○
Command	○
Program	●
Concept	○
Problem	○

The DOS DISKCOPY program makes an exact duplicate of the contents of a floppy disk. The disks must be the same size and have the same capacity.

Before You Begin

Floppy Disks (19)

Syntax

`C:\>`**`DISKCOPY A: B:`**	Copies the contents of the disk in drive A: to the disk in drive B:.
`C:\>`**`DISKCOPY A: A:`**	Copies the contents of the disk in drive A: to a second disk swapped into drive A:.

Problems

Exact duplicate of a disk needed. Because the file images are binary, the result of a DISKCOPY (or any other file copy command) is an exact duplicate of the original file. If you need extra assurance, DOS 5.0 provides the /V switch (for *v*erify), which you enter at the end of the command line.

Copying a disk from one capacity to another. If drive A: and drive B: have different capacities, you cannot use DISKCOPY. You must format the target disk and use COPY or XCOPY. For example, if you have a high-density (1.2M) 5 1/4-inch floppy in A: and a high-density 3 1/2-inch floppy in B:, the command to copy all the files is **`COPY A:*.* B:`**. This *does not* make an exact duplicate of the first disk but only copies the files. Naturally if the second disk has less capacity than the first, the second disk may not be able to hold all the files from the first.

Copying a disk when you have floppy drives with different capacities, or just one floppy drive. If drive A: and drive B: have different capacities or if you have just one floppy drive, DISKCOPY works with just one drive. The program provides prompts to `Insert source disk` and `Insert target disk` when needed. A 360K disk can be copied in one pass. Larger disks may require more than one exchange to make a complete copy.

Explanation

The DISKCOPY program duplicates the source disk onto the target disk exactly. The copy includes deleted files and any "garbage" left in the tracks of the source disk. These "deleted" files and miscellaneous bytes are recoverable from the target disk.

Because the source disk's data completely overwrites the data on the target disk, anything on the target disk is totally lost. The one advantage is that the target disk does not need to be formatted before you use it with DISKCOPY. A disadvantage is that the fragmentation of files (gaps caused where other files have been erased) is retained on the target disk.

COPY and XCOPY, when used with the wild cards *.*, would appear to be similar to DISKCOPY. In both cases, all the files are copied from the source to the target disk. But the results can be very different. COPY and XCOPY do not copy hidden files. This includes the hidden system files necessary for a disk to be bootable. Because DISKCOPY copies everything on the disk, those files are also copied. COPY and DISKCOPY procedures do have different advantages.

Use **`DISKCOPY A: B:`** for the following tasks:

- Duplicating a disk with the same capacity
- Copying dozens of files from one disk to another, including all subdirectories

- Copying to an unformatted target disk
- Copying a system (boot) disk

  Use **COPY A:*.* B:** for these tasks:

- Adding files to the current files on the target disk
- Copying just a few files
- Copying with a formatted target disk
- Unfragmenting the files

You use the /1 switch, for copy side 1 only, to maintain compatibility with older systems with single-sided disk drives. DOS 5.0 users can use / V (for *verify*) at the end of the command line. This makes DISKCOPY perform an additional read-and-compare step during the process. If DISKCOPY has trouble reading the source or writing to the target disk, a warning message is displayed when the program is finished. Once completed, DISKCOPY asks `Copy another diskette (Y/N)?` If you answer **Y** (for yes), you are prompted for another target disk.

Exercise

For this exercise, you need two disks, a disk with some files and an unformatted disk (or one containing old files). The disks *must* be exactly the same size and have the same capacity. DISKCOPY can copy a 360K disk to *only* a 360K disk, a 1.2M high-density disk to *only* a 1.2M high-density disk, and so on.

Exercise 1 of 1

If you have not made a copy of the disk included with this book, this is a good time to do so. Before you begin, cover the write-protect notch of the original 5 1/4-inch disk with opaque tape.

TRY	NOTE
`C:\>`**`DISKCOPY A: A:`**	Because most systems now have different sizes for drives A: and B:, you'll have to swap disks several times before DISKCOPY is done.
`Insert source disk in drive A:` `Press any key to continue...`	Insert the original disk in drive A:.

`<Enter>`
`Copying 80 tracks`
`15 sectors per track, 2 sides`
	Depending on the disk capacity, you may have to make the swap several times.

TRY	NOTE
`Insert target disk in drive A:` `Press any key to continue...`	A 360K disk can be copied in one pass. Larger-capacity disks take several exchanges.

If you just made a copy of the accompanying disk in this exercise, put the original in a safe place, other than at the back of the book. Use the duplicate disk for the rest of the exercises in the book.

References

Backing Up Data (13), Floppy Drive Failure (32)

NEXT TOPIC: Redirection < > ¦ (64)

DOS programs that can't be used with SUBST

See SUBST (58)

DOSKEY (25)

VERSIONS	
All	○
Some	○
5.0	●
Command	○
Program	●
Concept	○
Problem	○

This DOS program is new in version 5.0. DOSKEY keeps a history of DOS commands you used previously, allows more extensive editing of the command line, and allows you to create and use macros within DOS.

Before You Begin

File Names (4)

Syntax

`C:\>`**`DOSKEY`**	Installs the DOSKEY program
`C:\>`**`DOSKEY /MACRO`** or `C:\>`**`DOSKEY /M`**	Displays all macros that are in effect
`C:\>`**`DOSKEY /HISTORY`** or `C:\>`**`DOSKEY /H`**	Shows the most recent commands used

Problems

Making a mistake on the command line. If you make a mistake while typing a command, DOSKEY allows you to edit the command line by inserting or overstriking text.

Retyping long command-line entries. DOSKEY keeps the most recent entries in memory. The up- and down-arrow keys enable you to access these lines, which you can then edit and reissue by pressing Enter.

Explanation

You can run the DOSKEY program from the DOS prompt or, more commonly, from the AUTOEXEC.BAT file. Once loaded, DOSKEY enhances DOS in three ways:

- DOSKEY provides greater flexibility for editing the current command and previous commands.

  Your editing of the DOS command line is normally restricted to pressing the Backspace key to erase characters and then retyping them. Once you have typed (entered) a command line, you can press the F3 key to recall that line (only the last command line you entered) and then make changes to the line. You can also use the right-arrow key to recall the command, one character at a time, instead of pressing the F3 key.

  Using DOSKEY, you can fully edit the command line with the right- and left-arrow keys. You can use the Insert and Delete keys to make any changes in the line. The Home key moves you to the beginning of the line, and the End key moves you to the end. A complete list of DOSKEY edit and command keys appears in Table 25-1.

- DOSKEY keeps a history of previous commands to be reused or stored in a macro (a collection of recorded commands or keystrokes).

  You use the up- and down-arrow keys to move to previous lines in the DOSKEY buffer. The line displayed can then be edited and reused. With the Page Up key, you can move to the top of the command history; with the Page Down key, you can move to the bottom.

- With DOSKEY, you can create and use macros stored in memory. These can replace standard DOS commands.

  DOSKEY can create and store commands with specific names. These commands are called macros, and they can be used to replace standard DOS commands. For example, if you always want the DIR command to include the /P switch (for *p*ause), you can create a macro called DIR that includes the command DIR /P. When you type **`DIR`**, DOSKEY finds the DIR macro and uses it instead of the standard DIR command.

Table 25-1. The DOSKEY edit and command keys.

Key(s)	Purpose
Up arrow	Moves up one line in the list of previous commands
Down arrow	Moves down one line in the list
Page Up	Moves to the top of the list
Page Down	Moves to the bottom of the list
F7	Displays all commands in the current list
Alt-F7	Deletes all commands in the current list
nnn, F8	Searches for a command line that contains *nnn*
F9	Prompts for the command-line number to be displayed
Left arrow	Moves left one character
Backspace	Moves left and deletes one character
Right arrow	Moves right one character
Ctrl-left arrow	Moves left one word
Ctrl-right arrow	Moves right one word
Home	Moves cursor to beginning of current line
End	Moves cursor to end of current line
Esc	Clears the line from the current display
F1	Copies character in the current cursor position from last command
F2, *n*	Copies the previous command up to the letter *n*
F3	Copies the rest of the command to the current line
F4, *n*	Deletes the command up to the letter *n*
F5	Copies the current command into the list
F6	Places the end-of-file marker at end of line
Alt-F10	Deletes all macro definitions

In addition to the switches noted earlier in the "Syntax" section, other DOSKEY switches are available. For a complete list, refer to your DOS 5.0 manual.

Exercises

The following exercises focus on the three major uses of DOSKEY. The first exercise demonstrates the line-editing keys. The second exercise examines the list of commands kept by DOSKEY. And the third exercise shows you how to create a small macro.

Exercise 1 of 3

This first exercise demonstrates the editing commands available with DOSKEY. Do not press the Enter key unless it is specifically noted in the TRY column.

TRY	NOTE
`C:\>`**`DOSKEY <Enter>`**	DOSKEY is now loaded. If you have an error message, you may have to change to your DOS subdirectory and try again.
`C:\>`**`LEARN DOS`**	Don't press the Enter key here! You just want a line for practice.
`<left arrow> <left arrow>` **`<left arrow> <left arrow>`**	Press the left-arrow key four times. The cursor should be under the space between `LEARN` and `DOS`.
`<Insert> ING`	When you press the Insert key, notice that the cursor changes. When you type **`ING`**, the letters are inserted in the command. Now the line reads `LEARNING DOS`.
`<Home>`	This moves the cursor to the beginning of the line.
`<Delete>`	Now the line reads `EARNING DOS`.
`<F2> D`	This moves the cursor to the letter D in the command line.
`<Enter>`	DOS responds with the message `Bad command or file name`.

Try a few of the other command keys listed in Table 25-1. You'll find yourself using some keys often, such as the right- and left-arrow keys. However, getting accustomed to pressing the F2 key and then another key to point to a letter may take some time.

Exercise 2 of 3

This exercise focuses on the use of commands previously entered at the prompt and stored by DOSKEY. The total number of bytes available to store commands is 512 bytes (by default). The `/BUFSIZE=` setting can be increased when DOSKEY is started if you want to keep a longer list of previous commands.

You begin by entering some nonsense commands. DOS will fuss at each one. You just want to load the DOSKEY buffer (where previous commands are stored) so that you can look at it.

TRY	NOTE
C:\>**THIS <Enter>** C:\>**IS THE <Enter>** C:\>**LIST OF <Enter>** C:\>**COMMANDS ENTERED <Enter>**	Each time you press Enter here, DOS provides an error message.
C:\>**<up arrow>**	The command line now contains the last line entered.
C:\>COMMANDS ENTERED **<Page Up>**	This moves you to the top of the command history. If you just started DOSKEY with these exercises, that is probably LEARNING DOS.
C:\>LEARNING DOS **<down arrow>**	Press the down-arrow key a few times to look at all the lines you typed. Notice that you see only one at a time.
C:\>**<F7>**	This lists all the lines in the current command history.
C:\>**<F9>** C:\>Line number:**4 <Enter>**	This selects line number 4 to display.
C:\>LIST OF **<Esc>**	You may not see this as line number 4. At any rate, press the Esc key to clear the current prompt.

With these methods, you can easily search for and reuse DOS commands and programs. The length of time spent searching for a previously typed command shouldn't be longer than the time required to retype the command. For some commands, such as DIR, retyping the command is quicker than searching for it with the up-arrow key. In many cases, though, you won't want to retype the entire command line. Suppose, for example, that you want to reuse the command

```
D:\>C:\UTILS\ZIP\PKUNZIP F:\DOWN\NEWFILE.ZIP
```

Once that is finished, you can type

```
D:\>DIR
```

to look at the files. You can then press the up-arrow key twice to redisplay the line. Then you can edit the line to change it to

```
D:\>C:\UTILS\ZIP\PKUNZIP F:\DOWN\NEXTFILE.ZIP
```

Exercise 3 of 3

This brief exercise on macros just touches on the possibilities. Because DOSKEY "sees" the command on the line before DOS does, you can rename any command to suit yourself. You can use batch files to store these macros, and reuse them whenever you boot the system. For this example, which uses the DIR command, assume that you always want the directory sorted by file name.

TRY	NOTE
C:\>**DOSKEY DIR=DIR /O:N <Enter>**	You replace the DIR command with DIR /O:N.
C:\>**DIR**	Now when you type **DIR**, the directory is sorted by name (*o*rder:*n*ame).
C:>**<space bar> DIR**	The space in front of the DIR command tells DOSKEY to ignore the macro by that name and just look at DOS for the command—in this case, DIR.
C:\>**DOSKEY /M** DIR=DIR /O:N	This switch lists the current macros in memory—in this example, just one.

With DOSKEY's macro capability, you can actually redefine all the commands on your system. If you make changes to suit your preferences, you are likely to remember and use them. For more information about setting up regular macros from within a batch file, see the topic Batch Files — Writing Your Own (100), as well as the DOS manual.

References

Command and Program Parameters (34), Batch files — Write Your Own (100)

NEXT TOPIC: PROMPT — Command Line Information (26)

DOSSHELL — DOS 5.0 Menu (44)

VERSIONS
All ○
Some ○
5.0 ●

Command ○
Program ●
Concept ○
Problem ○

The DOSSHELL program is included in both versions 4.0 and 5.0 of DOS. The latest version, which is vastly improved, is the one covered here.

Before You Begin

Files (2)
File Names (4)
DIR — Directory (8)
Wild Cards * and ? (11)
Interfaces (27)

Syntax

C:\DOS>**DOSSHELL**	Starts the DOSSHELL program
C:\DOS>**DOSSHELL /G**	Starts the program in graphics mode
C:\DOS>**DOSSHELL /T**	Starts the program in text mode (opposite of graphics mode)
C:\DOS>**DOSSHELL /B**	Starts the program in black-and-white mode, necessary for some graphic screens
C:\DOS>**DOSSHELL /G/B**	Starts the program in black-and-white and graphics mode (switches can be combined)

Problems

Forgetting basic DOS commands. DOSSHELL provides a full screen of menu choices for moving around the system, starting programs, and manipulating files. If you use DOS commands infrequently, DOSSHELL provides a convenient way to accomplish many essential DOS tasks.

Turning off the computer with programs still active. DOSSHELL allows you to start a program, *suspend* it, and then start another program. You can start as many programs as memory allows. As is true with most programs, abruptly turning off the system or rebooting can cause data loss or corruption. DOSSHELL can multiply that error by having two or more programs suspended but with open files. Rebooting without closing each program properly can leave an even bigger mess. If this happens, run CHKDSK /F immediately to find clusters lost as the result of the reboot.

Programs prevented from running because DOSSHELL requires extra memory. DOSSHELL uses about 40K of memory. Although this is not likely to cause problems with newer systems, the older systems limited to 640K of memory may find that this "overhead" keeps other programs from running.

Using DOSSHELL without a mouse. Because DOSSHELL is a *graphical user interface*, it works much better with a mouse or another pointing device. Although you can use the Tab key and arrow keys to move around the screen, a mouse is highly recommended.

Explanation

DOSSHELL provides solutions to common problems with DOS and adds features not available at the command prompt. Although entire books have been written about DOSSHELL, this discussion focuses on the problems solved, and possibly created, by DOSSHELL.

As explained in the topic Interfaces (27), a graphical menu system presents the user with multiple choices on one screen. DOSSHELL is designed for ease of use, in a stark contrast to the DOS command line prompt. All the options are available in pull-down menus and on-screen dialog boxes. Not only does DOSSHELL show you what is available, but it also provides some functions not available from the DOS command prompt. Here are a few of the extras offered in DOSSHELL:

- *A complete menu system.* Once set up, the menu system can be initiated from within AUTOEXEC.BAT and be structured so that the user sees only those choices. The menu choices can branch to more choices, and a help screen can be provided for each menu choice.
- *A visual directory tree.* Moving from subdirectory to subdirectory and disk to disk is as easy as clicking on the directory name or the letter of the disk. The visual tree can be expanded to show only those directories off the root or all directories on the disk. Once a directory is selected, the files in that directory are shown in another window on the screen.
- *File searching.* Although tricks are available for locating files on the hard disk (see topic 20, CHKDSK — CHecK DiSK), with a simple menu selection in DOSSHELL, you can locate a file based on wild cards in very little time.
- *Program quick start.* Running a program is as easy as clicking on the file name. When the program ends, DOSSHELL returns to the screen.
- *Data file association.* Once a link has been established between a data file and the program file that uses it, you can just select that data file. The program file runs and automatically loads the data file.
- *Task swapping between programs.* When you enable task swapping, you can start a program, suspend it, and then start another program. The programs in the background are inactive, but you can switch between them with a simple key combination.

- *Context-sensitive help.* Whatever command or function is active, pressing F1 or selecting `Help` from the menu system provides information related to that command or function. The help is "sensitive" to the "context" of the request.

Many of the common DOS commands and functions are either available on the DOSSHELL menu or are no longer necessary. For example, the files in the current directory are displayed on the screen. To view all the files, you can scroll the list up and down. You can even select the files to display. All this replaces DIR with wild cards and improves the DIR /P command because you can move up and down the list.

The `File` menu includes `Move`, a command not available in DOS. After selecting the files to move, you still have to type the complete subdirectory into which the files are to be moved. Yet this task requires fewer steps than the DOS COPY and DEL commands.

You can customize DOSSHELL to suit yourself. It allows views with just a menu, with a menu and directory tree, with two trees, and more. You can also set different colors and decide whether you want a text display or graphics display.

Exercises

These six exercises highlight many of the features found only in DOSSHELL (not from the DOS command line). Suggestions are then provided to help you explore your system with DOSSHELL.

The first exercise provides a tour of the DOSSHELL screen and discusses ways to configure the screen. This exercise also contains a brief discussion about using the mouse and the keyboard with DOSSHELL. The next two exercises focus on making menu selections and moving around in the visual tree provided by DOSSHELL.

The fourth exercise covers features available only in DOSSHELL, including `Search`, `Associate`, and `Move`. Exercise 5 explains the DOSSHELL menu system. The last exercise shows how you can use task swapping to switch from program to program quickly within DOSSHELL.

Exercise 1 of 6

The first part of this exercise provides a tour of the DOSSHELL screen. Once you have looked at the sample screens, consider the suggestions for using DOSSHELL to explore your system.

Tour

The DOSSHELL screen shown in Figure 44-1 has been configured for one of eight possible text or graphic settings. The color scheme is the four-color monochrome (black, white, and two grays) of the eight possible color combinations, including `Hot Pink` and `Emerald City`. You can see that the mouse is active, as indicated by the arrow just below the C:\ in the Directory Tree.

Figure 44-1 also shows the main areas of the DOSSHELL screen. The top area provides menu and drive choices. The menu bar contains pull-down menus you activate by either clicking with the mouse or pressing the Alt key. You can use the mouse or keyboard to select the default drive. The files on that drive are then displayed in the Directory Tree immediately below the drive icons.

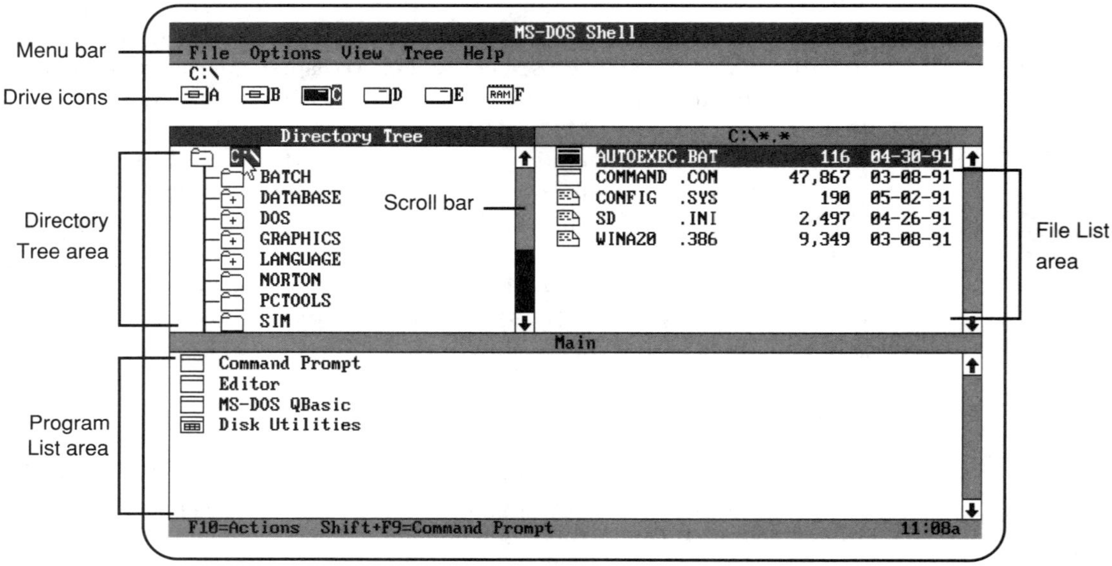

Figure 44-1. The main areas of the DOSSHELL screen.

To the right of the Directory Tree is the *File List* area. In this case, the directory being displayed is the root of C:, as shown in the title bar at the top of this area. As you move the default directory indicator (highlight) on the Directory Tree, the files in the File List change.

The *Program List* area at the bottom of the screen shows the first level of a menu. When DOSSHELL is installed, some basic menu choices are created, as shown in Figure 44-1. You can add your own programs to these menu choices. Exercise 5 explains more about the menu system.

A fourth area, not shown in Figure 44-1, is the *Active Task List*. This area is used for task swapping, discussed later in this topic.

On the right side of each area is a *scroll bar*. This bar contains a slider button when the area is active. Mouse users can click and drag (hold the mouse button down and move the mouse) the slider bar to scroll the contents of the window up and down. Keyboard users just use the Page Up and Page Down keys, and the slider bar moves in relation to the amount of text above or below the current view.

Only one of the four areas can be active at a time. Keyboard users press the Tab key to move from area to area. Mouse users just point and click to activate an area. Once an area is active, you can use the scroll bar and carry out other actions in that area.

With the `View` menu, you can change the number of visible areas on the screen. Of the five choices, this tour just shows three. Figure 44-1 shows the result of selecting the `Program/File Lists` choice. Figure 44-2 shows the result of selecting `Single File List`. If you want to see more of the Directory Tree and File List area, this view provides more space. You can easily change all the available views as needed during a DOSSHELL session.

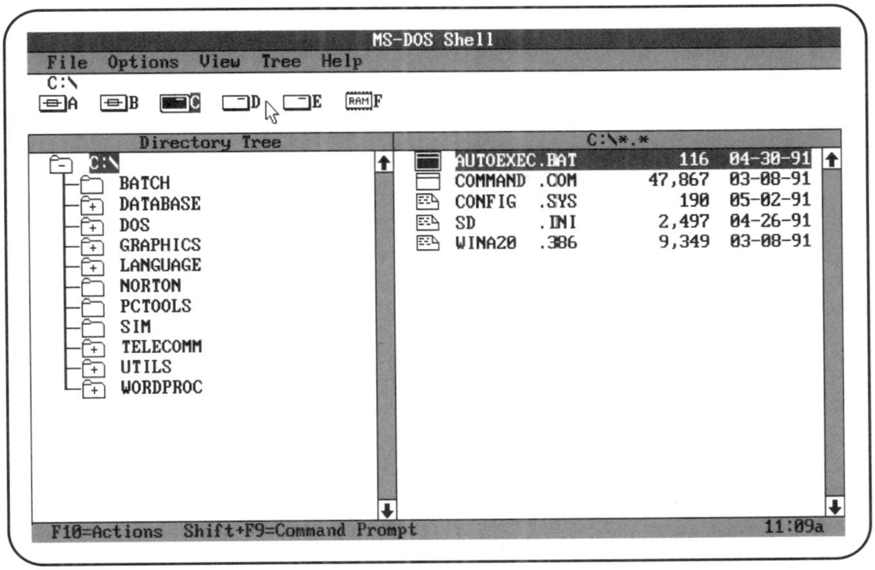

Figure 44-2. The `Single File List` view in DOSSHELL.

If you create an extensive menu system in the Program List area, you can use the `Program List` view to show only those choices (see Figure 44-3). For someone interested in using DOSSHELL only to select and run programs, this view is much less intimidating than the others. Figure 44-3 shows also the Active Task List area, although there are no active tasks at this time.

Each of these areas is covered in more detail in the next exercises. The rest of this exercise discusses the advantages of using a mouse with DOSSHELL.

DOSSHELL is a GUI, or graphical user interface (see topic 27). Making multiple choices on the screen, marking items, and manipulating them are all functions designed for a mouse. Most users can master the moves of a mouse in just a few moments. Nontypists usually respond favorably to the mouse because, for the first time, they can control the computer more quickly than with the keyboard.

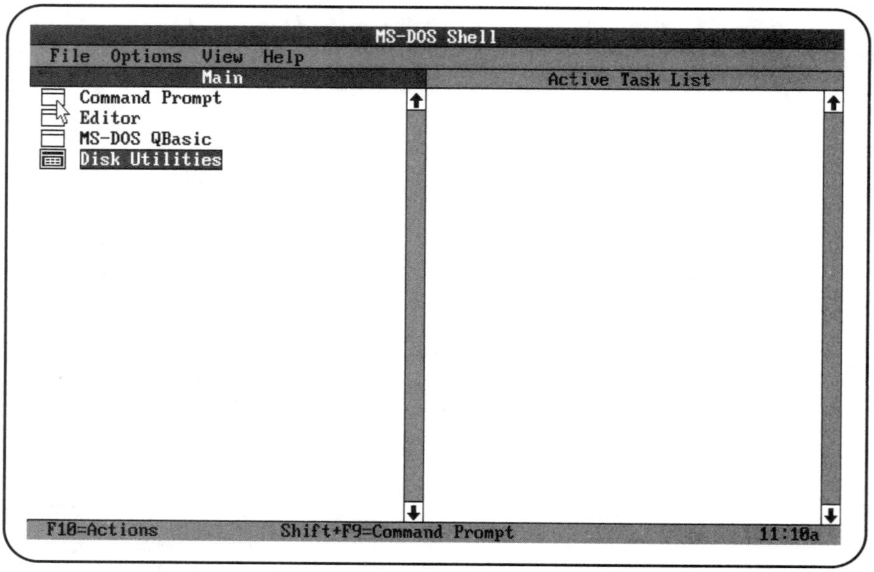

Figure 44-3. The Program List and Active Task List areas.

Suppose that you want to delete a file in DOSSHELL. You use the following steps with the mouse:

1. Point to the file name and click on it.
2. Click on the `File` option in the menu bar.
3. Click on `Delete`.
4. Click on `Yes` to confirm the deletion.

To accomplish the same task, the keyboard user in DOSSHELL must follow these steps:

1. Press the Tab key until the File List area is highlighted.
2. Use the down-arrow key until the file name is highlighted.
3. Press F10 to activate the menu bar.
4. Press F to pull down the `File` menu.
5. Press D for for the `Delete` option.
6. Press Enter to confirm the deletion.

Although the keyboard user can discover some shortcuts, many keystrokes are still required. In short, if you like the DOSSHELL, consider purchasing a mouse. You'll find yourself even more productive, and you'll be ready for more GUI programs.

Explore

If you have not started DOSSHELL yet, type **`DOSSHELL`** at the prompt. If you get the message `Bad command or file name`, change into the DOS subdirectory and try again. Once you have the DOSSHELL screen, practice the following tasks, using either the mouse or the keyboard:

- Move from area to area by pressing the Tab key or clicking within an area.
- Press F10 to activate the menu bar and then press the first letter of the menu choices. Mouse users can click on each menu choice. Examine all the choices in each menu.
- Within the `Options` menu is the `Display` option. Select that option and explore the different screens. Also select `Color` and examine the options listed there.
- When you are done, you can leave DOSSHELL by selecting `File` and `Exit`, or by pressing Alt-F4. If you plan to continue with these exercises, just leave DOSSHELL active on the screen.

Exercise 2 of 6

In this exercise, you look more closely at the menu choices. Some of them duplicate the standard DOS commands, other choices are unique to DOSSHELL, and others are just used to control DOSSHELL itself.

Tour

During this tour, you may want to follow along and look at each menu. Once you press Alt or F10, you can use the right- and left-arrow keys to look at the main menu choices. Because these menus are pulled down from the menu bar, they are referred to as *pull-down menus*. Notice also that one letter of each menu choice is highlighted. If you want to use the keyboard to make menu selections, just press the highlighted letters of the options you want. Some of the choices on a menu may be blank or "grayed" out, indicating that those choices are not available at that time. You can press the Esc key to exit the menus.

The first menu, `File`, does most of the work associated with the command line when you are in the Directory Tree or the File List area (see Figure 44-4). If the Program List is the active window, the `File` pull-down menu offers different choices. (If the `File` menu you are currently looking at on your screen has the word `NEW` at the top, press Esc and then select the Directory Tree or the File List area. Press Alt-F again.) Exercise 5 covers the Program List area of DOSSHELL in more detail. Notice that some of these menu choices have shortcut keys at the right of the pull-down menu in addition to highlighted letters.

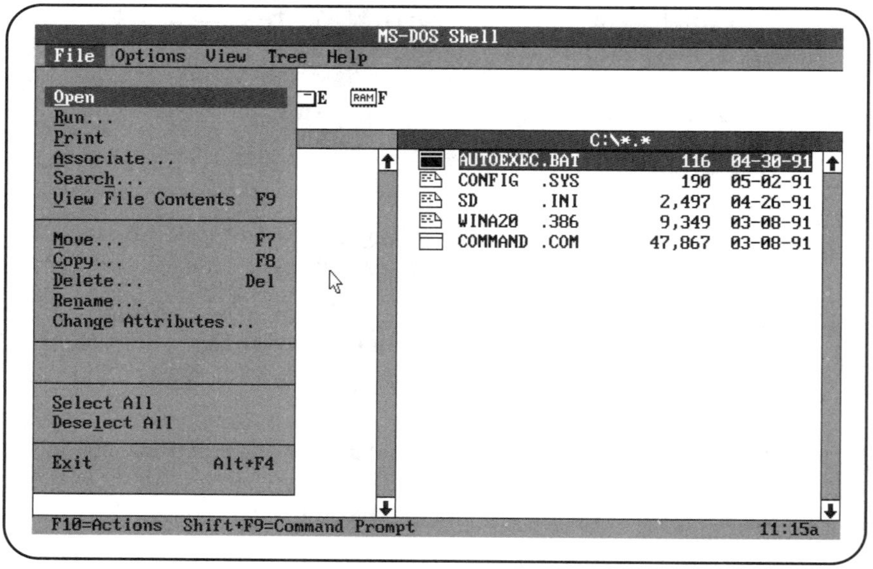

Figure 44-4. The options on the `File` pull-down menu.

Exercise 4 covers the `File` choices that are not standard DOS command line options. These choices include `Associate`, `Search`, and `Move`. You can explore each of these now by pointing to the command and pressing the F1 key for `Help`.

Use the right-arrow key to move to the `Options` pull-down menu, and use F1 again to explore these menu selections. Be sure to look at `File Display Options`. DOSSHELL can show files sorted by name, date, and size in the File List area. The most interesting menu choice here is `Enable Task Swapper`, which is discussed in Exercise 6.

The `View` choice on the menu bar determines the number of areas you can see on the screen at one time. As mentioned in Exercise 1, there are five different ways, or views, to set up the screen. Although you cannot move the areas around or change their size, you can change these views at any time, depending on the task as hand.

The `Tree` menu options affect only the Directory Tree. Menu choices are available to collapse and expand the visual tree. Each of the four choices has a shortcut key as well. After a few minutes in the Directory Tree, you'll find yourself using these shortcut keys instead of the `Tree` menu.

`Help` is the last menu choice. As noted, you can press F1 at any time, and DOSSHELL provides a multiple-layer help system. With this menu, you can select an area of help you want to look at, or just select `Index`. Once you are in the Index of help topics, you use the Page Up and Page Down keys, or the scroll bar, to move the list up and down in the Help window. Press Esc or click on `Close` to return to the DOSSHELL screen.

At the bottom of the screen, notice the Shift-F9 choice. Pressing this key combination is not the same as selecting `File Exit` (or Alt-F4). `File Exit` tells DOSSHELL to stop running and return to the DOS command line. The Shift-F9 option *suspends* DOSSHELL while you perform some DOS commands. When you are done, you simply type **`EXIT`**, and you return to DOSSHELL exactly where you left off. For more information about suspending programs to use DOS, see the topic COMMAND.COM/EXIT (78).

Explore

If you followed along during the tour, you have seen most of the features discussed. Make sure that you know how to do the following tasks:

- Find help on the menu with the F1 key
- Select a menu choice quickly by pressing Alt and the highlighted letter
- Use some of the shortcut keys associated with menu choices
- Understand the difference between temporarily exiting DOSSHELL with Shift-F9 and leaving completely with `File Exit`

Exercise 3 of 6

Although using the subdirectory system is essential to DOS, moving through subdirectories is not necessarily easy. DOSSHELL provides a visual and quick way to move from directory to directory. This exercise focuses on the Directory Tree and the File List area of DOSSHELL.

Tour

When the Directory Tree is activated, you use the up- and down-arrow keys to move the directory highlight. As it moves, the list of files to the right (in the File List area) changes to show the first portion of the highlighted directory. You use the `Options` pull-down menu to determine the order in which these files are displayed.

Each directory entry has a box, or folder, to the left. If the box contains a plus (+), the entry has subdirectories under it. Pressing the plus key (+) expands that directory one level. Pressing the asterisk key (*) expands all branches under that branch. The Ctrl-* key combination expands all the branches on the current drive. Once a branch has been expanded, it shows a minus (–) in that box. Pressing the minus key (–) collapses that branch.

When first accessing a drive, DOSSHELL creates an image of that entire directory structure in memory. The + and –keys allow you to expand or contract the directory. To select a directory, you just move to it. If you are using a mouse, you just point and click.

Figure 44-5 contains a list of directories in drive C:. The subdirectories \DATABASE and \WORDPROC have been expanded to show their subdirectories. The DOCS subdirectory in WORDPROC has additional directories because it contains a plus (+) in the box. To expand the DOCS subdirectory, you move to the word DOCS and press the + key. The current directory, though, is the FOXPRO directory because its name is highlighted in the Directory Tree. The files within that selected directory are listed in the File List area, sorted by file name.

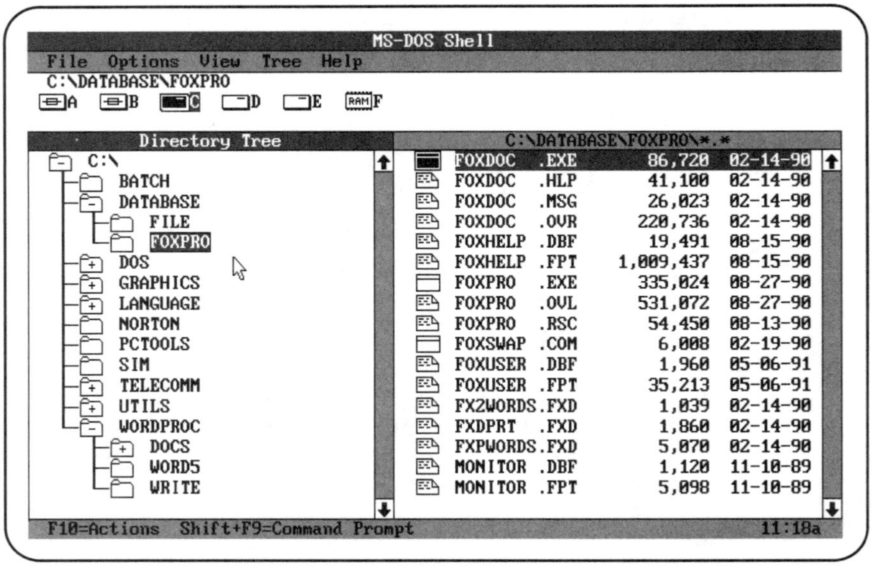

Figure 44-5. The active Directory Tree with the subdirectory FOXPRO selected.

The `File` menu provides options to copy, move, and delete files, as well as perform other actions. Before opening the `File` menu, you must select the file(s) in the File List area. A major advantage of DOSSHELL is that you can select files simply by pointing to them and then work with the files as a group. There are several ways to select files before you work with them.

Assume that you want to copy all the files that begin with the number 2 to a floppy disk in drive A:. They are all grouped together in the File List area because the sort order is by name (see Figure 44-6). You discover, however, that if you point to the second file, the first one is no longer highlighted. The Shift key enables you to highlight a range of file names. Select the first file name with the mouse or keyboard, press and hold down the Shift key, and select the last file name in the group to be copied. If you do this with the keyboard, you will just spread the highlight to the last file name. If you use the mouse, you just point to the last name and click on it. The highlight then expands to cover all the files in between. Now you can use the `File` menu (or F8) to copy the files.

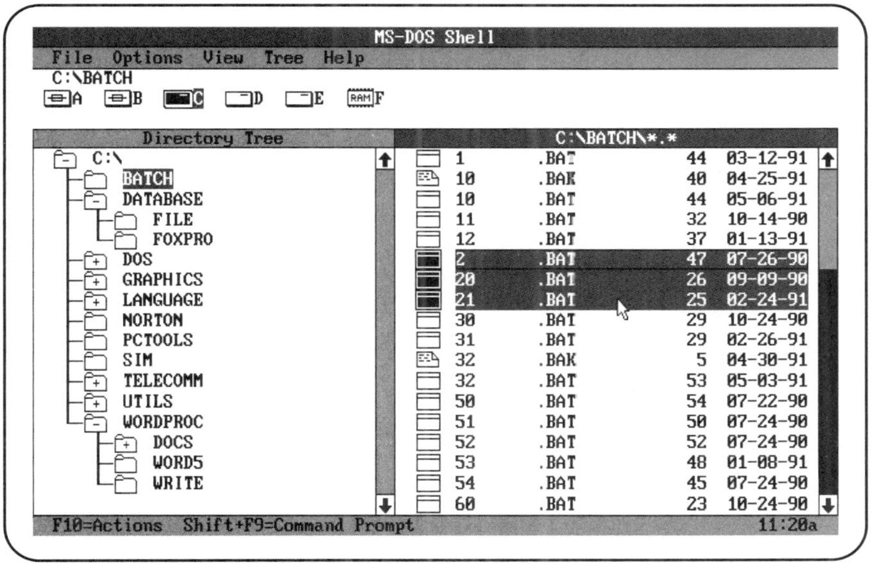

Figure 44-6. A group of files selected for copying.

Now assume that you want to delete a number of files in that same subdirectory. You could point to each file and then press the Delete key. But you prefer to do it all in one pass. Although the Shift key allows a range of files to be highlighted, the files you want to delete are individual files. In that case, if you are using the mouse, you can first press the Ctrl key, which allows multiple files to be highlighted. You just press Ctrl and then highlight one of the files with the mouse. You can select as many individual files as you want (see Figure 44-7).

Keyboard users must use Shift-F8 to turn on the Add files function, as noted at the bottom left of the screen (`ADD`). Once this feature is turned on, you can press the space bar to mark the files. Press Shift-F8 again to turn off the Add files function. You can then proceed with the action in the `File` menu or use the shortcut keys (Del to delete files and F8 to copy them).

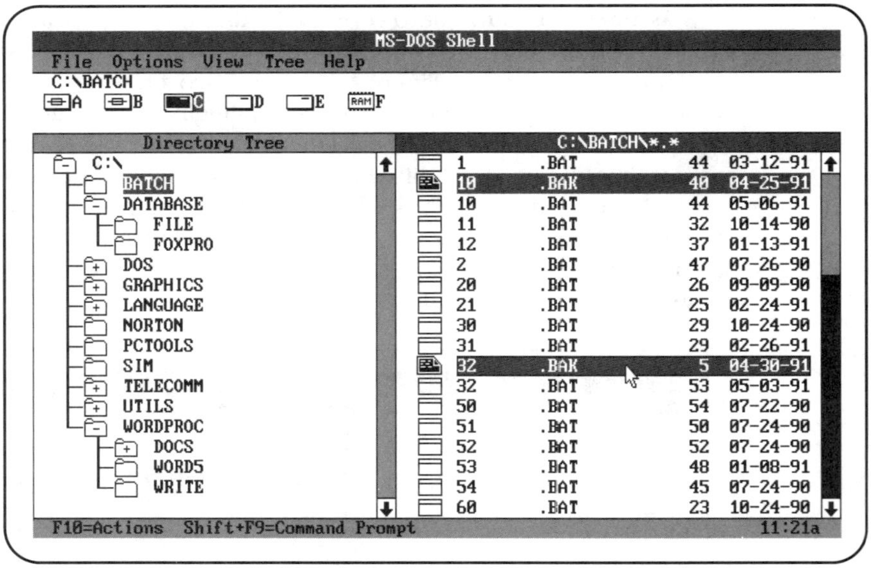

Figure 44-7. Two files selected with the Ctrl key and the mouse.

Explore

The DOSSHELL Directory Tree is a major feature. Practice using it and selecting files. When you are done, you should know how to do these tasks:

- Move up and down the tree
- Expand and collapse individual branches (using the + and – keys)
- Expand and contract entire subdirectory branches (using the * and – keys)
- Select a range of files
- Select several individual files

Exercise 4 of 6

DOSSHELL provides a few extra features not found in the DOS command line. These include the capabilities to associate a program with a data file, search for a file by name or with wild cards, and move files from one location to another.

DEF

Tour

With DOS, you usually must load a program and then, in some specific way, load the data file you want to work with. In DOSSHELL, you can simply point to a data file and, using the `Associate` choice from the `File` menu, tell DOSSHELL that any file with that extension, when selected, requires that a specific program be run. Then, when you double-click on a file name with that extension (in the File List area) or when you highlight such a file name and press Enter, the associated program will run.

For example, if you highlight a file with the extension DBF, select `File`, and then select `Associate`, a dialog box appears (see Figure 44-8). You type the full drive, path name, and program name in the box provided. In this example, you might type **C:\DATABASE\FOXPRO\FOXPRO**. Once you click on `OK` or press Enter, all files with the extension DBF will be "associated" with FOXPRO.

The next time you double-click or press Enter on a file with that extension, FOXPRO will run. Depending on the program, the data file may or may not be automatically loaded. With FOXPRO, the error message `Line too long` will appear on the screen because the data file does not load automatically. In that case, you must load the data file in the normal manner. Some programs such as Microsoft Word, accept a data file name at the command line; the `Associate` option loads Word, and Word loads the data file.

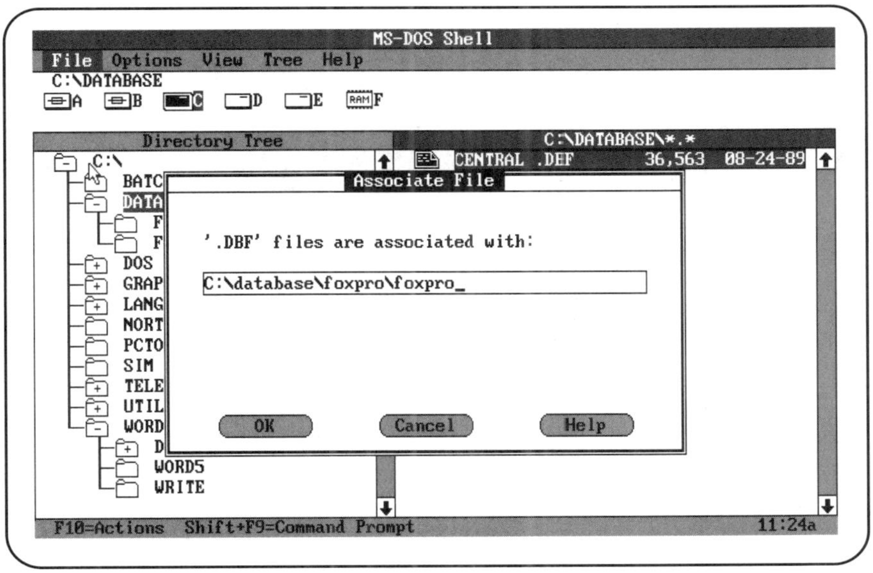

Figure 44-8. The Associate File dialog box after the file CENTRAL.DBF is selected. The full path and file name have been typed.

You can associate more than one extension with a program if it doesn't require a specific extension. For example, you can associate the extensions WP, WP5, and MEM with WordPerfect. You cannot associate more than one program with the same extension, however. You cannot tell DOSSHELL, for instance, to use either EDIT or EDLIN with the file extension TXT.

You may not find that associating a data file with a program file is useful. But it is hard to imagine that you don't occasionally lose track of a file on the hard disk. The `Search` option on the `File` menu is handy and extremely fast. You can search the entire disk or just the current directory. And you can use standard DOS wild cards in the Search File dialog box.

Assume for a moment that you have a request to compare the budget figures from the fourth quarter with those of the current quarter. You have your spreadsheet files organized into several different directories, all named so that you know exactly where to find any file—well, most of the time. You know the name of the Quattro Pro file, but not where it is. You select `File` from the menu bar and then select `Search`. The dialog box that appears prompts you for the file name, and you type **`Q4BUDGET.WQ1`** (see Figure 44-9). Once you press Enter or click on `OK`, the results are almost immediate. The Search screen declares `No files match specifier`. Don't panic yet. You press Esc, select drive D:, and repeat the process. If the file is on that drive, DOSSHELL will find it. You just hope it's there. If not, you'll have to begin digging through your archive disks.

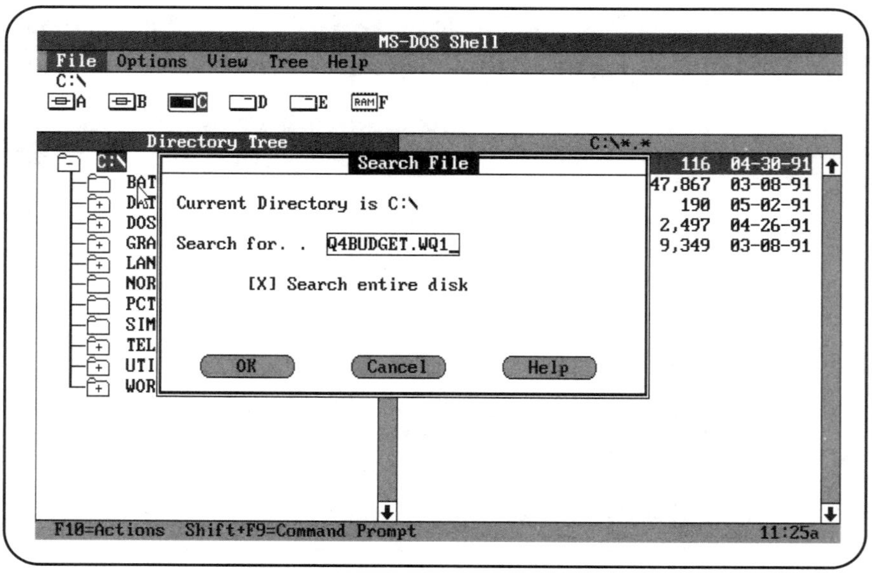

Figure 44-9. The Search File dialog box.

You must have used the DOSSHELL `Move` feature instead of `Copy` when you made the archive copy of Q4BUDGET.WQ1. That's why Q4BUDGET.WQ1 is no longer on the hard disk. `Move` reduces two steps to one. Instead of having to select files in the File List area, use `File Copy` to copy the files, and then press Del, `Move` makes the copy and then deletes the files from the original location.

Now assume that you want to move a file named GORILLA.BAS from the DOS subdirectory on drive C: to the \LANGUAGE\SOURCE subdirectory. You first select the file (GORILLA.BAS) and then select `Move` from the `File` menu. The file name appears in the Move File dialog box, shown in Figure 44-10. You type the To: location and press Enter. GORILLA.BAS is then copied to the target directory and erased from the source directory.

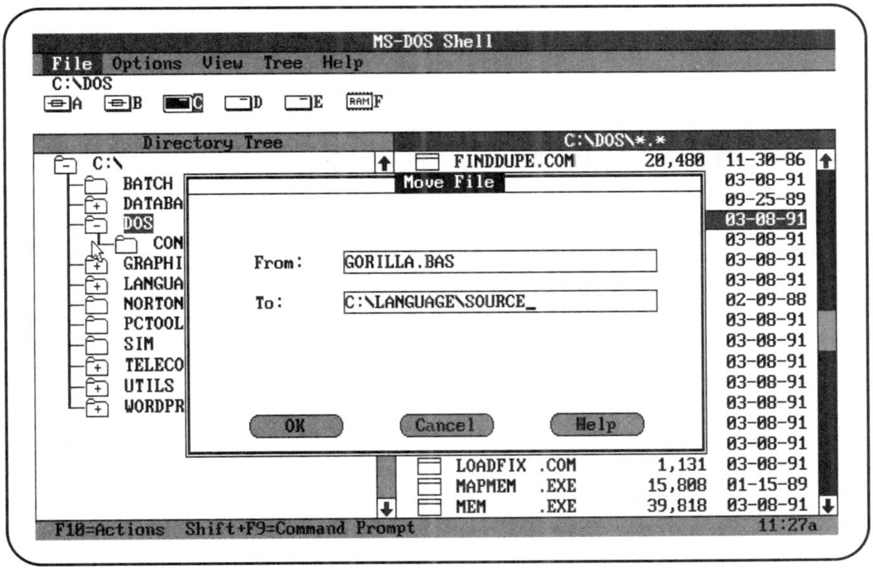

Figure 44-10. The Move File dialog box just after the target directory is typed.

Explore

This exercise covered just some of the DOSSHELL features not available from the DOS command line. As you explore these features on your system, be sure that you can do the following tasks:

- Associate a data file extension with a program file
- Use that data file to start the program file

- Search for a file on the disk
- Move files from one location to another

Exercise 5 of 6

In addition to all the file and directory features, a complete menu system is provided in DOSSHELL. When you select `Program List` from the `View` menu, you see only a series of menu choices. This tour examines those menu selections initially provided in DOSSHELL and shows you how to add both a menu group and a menu selection.

Tour

You may want to follow this tour of the Program List, as the `View` pull-down menu refers to it. Make sure that you have selected the Program List area before you attempt to use the arrow keys with the menu.

The DOSSHELL menu system is similar to the structure of a directory tree. You can have any number of program groups and any number of programs under those groups. As for the root directory, you probably want just a few groups in the first level of the menu system. Depending on how many programs you use, the next level of each group might just contain programs or additional program groups.

The initial menu selections installed by DOS contain three program selections and one additional group selection. The program selections include `Command Prompt` (drops to DOS, just like Shift-F9), `Editor` (runs DOS EDIT), and `MS-DOS QBasic` (runs QBASIC). If you select one of these with a double-click or a press of Enter, that program runs. When you select the `Disk Utilities` program group, the next menu level is displayed. The top choice returns you to the preceding menu. The remaining six menu choices run five DOS programs or commands. (`Quick Format` and `Format` run the same program, but `Quick Format` provides an additional switch.)

The menu system contains many features. These include adding your own help text, requiring a password, specifying memory allocation, and allowing shortcut keys. For this tour, you'll see how a program group and program item are added to the menu.

Your current position within the menu is critical when you want to add programs or groups. Once you select the `File` menu, the dialog boxes step you through the process and create the group or program at the current menu location. Notice that when you press Alt-F, you get a `File` menu with specific selections relating to the Program List area. In this case, you want to create a new entry, so select the `New` option.

A New Program Object dialog box appears, asking if you want to create a program group or program item. To create a group, press the up-arrow key or click on `Program Group`. Press Enter to bring up the Add Group dialog box (see Figure

44-11). The only requirement here is the group title—in this case, *Learning DOS*. Notice that you can also create help text and a password here. Pressing Enter again returns you to the menu, with the new group title added to the list.

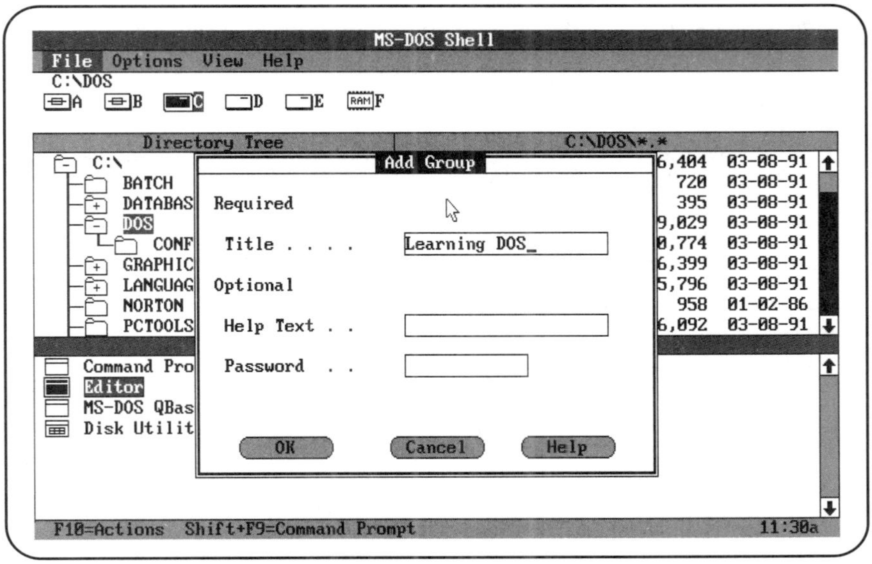

Figure 44-11. The Add Group dialog box used to add a new program group to the Program List area.

To add a program or another group to this new group, make sure that you are within this new group, now named *Learning DOS* (select it and press Enter). The only entry will be the name of the previous group—in this case, *Main*. To add a program item, use Alt-F and `New` again. Because this is a program item, you can press Enter to select `Add Program`. Figure 44-12 shows the Add Program dialog box.

In this case, the `Program Title` is *Microsoft Word*. The command (there can be more than one) is just *WORD*, which is the name of the program to run. (You may need to include the entire path to the program.) The `Startup Directory` tells DOSSHELL the default directory, typically the location of the files you want to use. Once you press Enter, the entry becomes an item under the current group. In this case, the Learning DOS group now has one program choice: Microsoft Word.

Explore

There are dozens of other features in the menu system. If you are interested in using DOSSHELL as a menu system, explore this part of the program. When you are done, you should know how to do the following tasks:

- Move from group to group and run programs
- Add program groups and help text
- Add program items and related passwords
- Change the view to show only the Program List
- Delete a program group or program item

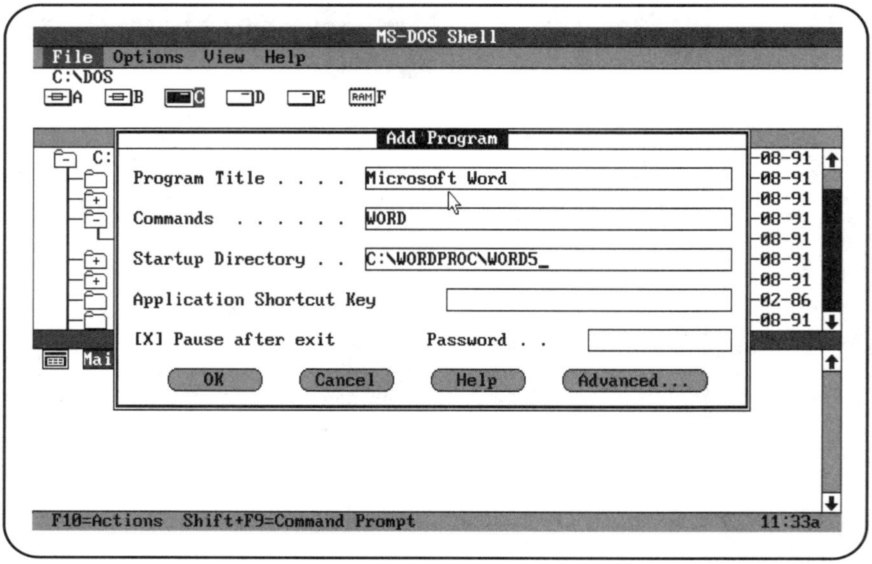

Figure 44-12. The Add Program dialog box, used to add a new program to the *Learning DOS* program group.

Exercise 6 of 6

The final exercise in this discussion covers a feature unique to DOSSHELL. After DOSSHELL starts a number of programs, you can switch between them by pressing a key combination. This is known as *task swapping*. The other programs are inactive, frozen by DOSSHELL. Read through this tour and then explore this feature on your own.

Tour

You must first activate the task-swapping feature of DOSSHELL in the `Options` menu. When you select `Enable Task Swapper`, a diamond appears next to that choice, indicating that Task Swapper is active. An additional area appears if the `View` menu is set for `Program/File Lists` or `Single File List`. The Active Task List area contains a list of the active programs, as shown in Figure 44-13.

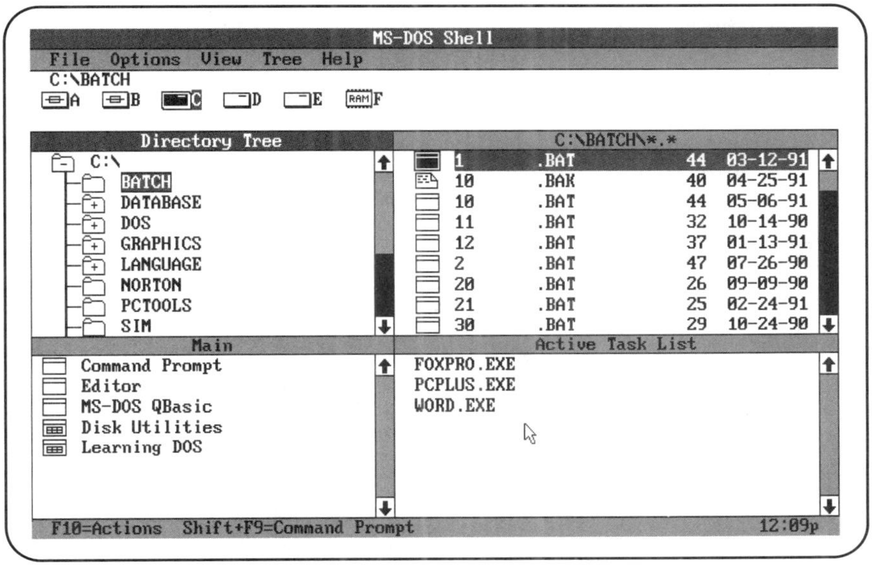

Figure 44-13. The Program/File Lists screen showing Task Swapper enabled with three active programs.

Once Task Swapper is active, you can point to a program or use the `Run` option on the `File` menu. Instead of exiting that program to return to DOSSHELL, you press Ctrl-Esc. You then see the name of program you just started. Run another program. Again, you use Ctrl-Esc to return to DOSSHELL. If you want to return to one of these programs, select the program and press Enter, or just double-click.

You don't need to return to DOSSHELL before bouncing back out to another program. Alt-Tab allows you to jump to the next program in the list. If you want another program farther down in the list, keep your finger on Alt and continue to press Tab until the program you want appears on the screen.

The main advantage of using task swapping is time. The time required to swap from one program to another is much less than the time required to reload each program. In addition, the program returns exactly as you left it when you pressed Ctrl-Esc to return to DOSSHELL or Alt-Tab to switch to another program.

Using Task Swapper is like working on several projects at one time. Each project folder remains on your desk, open to where you last worked on it. The active folder is on top of the stack. If you need another folder quickly, you pull that folder to the top of the stack. Quitting one program and starting another each time you need to change projects is like closing a folder and refiling it before getting out another to work on.

The most immediate example relates to writing this material. The text was prepared in Microsoft Word, but DOSSHELL was available with the Ctrl-Esc key combination. On a 386 system with a 19-millisecond hard drive, the swap took less than two seconds each time. Every step covered in these exercises was tested immediately before and after it was written.

Task swapping does have limitations. Each program must be exited properly for it to be removed from the Active Task List. Just turning the system off is likely to cause havoc with data files. DOSSHELL will not let you exit without properly ending the active programs (see Figure 44-14).

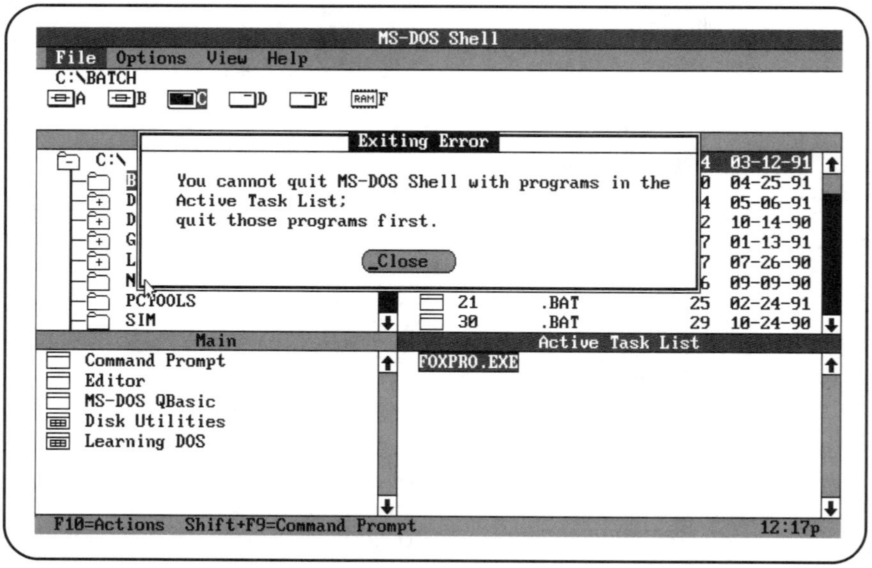

Figure 44-14. The DOSSHELL response when you try to exit with a task still active.

Task swapping is not the same as multitasking. With task swapping, the programs "below" the currently active program are inactive. You cannot start a process in one program and then switch to another while the first program is working. Furthermore, the activity is suspended while you use another program.

Explore

Using task swapping with DOSSHELL will be more a personal preference than anything else. If you spend a lot of time loading and quitting several programs frequently, you may find that this feature saves time. If you tend to use one program for long periods of time and you don't use DOSSHELL for other functions, task swapping may not appeal to you.

Take a five-minute tour to see whether task swapping in DOSSHELL may be helpful to you. Once you are done, see if you have explored the following tasks:

- Enabled task swapping in the Options menu
- Started at least three programs
- Switched between a program and DOSSHELL
- Switched from one program to another
- Exited from DOSSHELL after having exited from the active programs

References

Interfaces (27) and COMMAND.COM/EXIT (78)

NEXT TOPIC: Print — Spooler (45)

DOSSHELL without a mouse

See DOSSHELL — DOS 5.0 Menu (44)

Drive not ready

See FORMAT — Disks (12)

Dry eyes, "pseudomyopia"

See Workspace — User Comfort (85)

EDIT — DOS 5.0 Text Editor (98)

VERSIONS
All ○
Some ○
5.0 ●

Command ○
Program ●
Concept ○
Problem ○

DOS 5.0 includes EDIT, a full-screen text (ASCII) editor. It is useful for creating and editing batch files and other text files. If you want to scroll up and down through a text file, use EDIT.

Before You Begin

File Names (4)
Word Processing (43)
ASCII — Character Codes (74)

Syntax

`C:\>EDIT`	Loads EDIT
`C:\>EDIT AUTOEXEC.BAT`	Loads EDIT with AUTOEXEC.BAT

Problems

Need to examine a long text file. Even though there are ways to examine long files more quickly, EDIT can also serve as an ASCII file viewer. You can load the file and then use the Page Up and Page Down keys to scroll through the file.

Need to edit a batch file. EDIT is an excellent program for making changes to batch files and creating batch files. You do not need any special formatting, just a quick way to enter the file.

Need to write and print a quick note. EDIT contains a print function under the FILE menu. The editor also allows block printing of a section of a file.

EDIT will not load. If you examine the EDIT.COM program, you'll notice that it is quite small. All EDIT.COM really does is find QBASIC.EXE and load the file editor contained in that program. To use EDIT, you must have EDIT.COM and QBASIC.EXE in the same subdirectory or path. In most cases, EDIT and QBASIC are in the DOS subdirectory. If you want to use the EDIT help system, you'll also need to include EDIT.HLP.

Explanation

For the first time, DOS provides a full-screen text-editing program in version 5.0. Before that version, the only editor provided was EDLIN. EDIT can print, search and replace, and copy or delete files and blocks. Furthermore, EDIT has a complete help system available from the menu or with the F1 key.

EDIT is a true text editor rather than a word processor. The distinction lies in several areas. EDIT works with and saves *only* ASCII text. It does not have any spell-checking commands or formatting commands. For example, you cannot create running headers or add italics in EDIT. It does not even wrap words at the end of the line. EDIT's advantages are that it loads quickly, allows full-screen editing, has a comprehensive help system, and works well with a mouse.

The EDIT program provides help in a number of ways. When you first start the program, a Survival Guide window appears if you do not provide a file name to edit. If you press Enter, you are presented with a series of screens explaining how to use EDIT. Figure 98-1 shows the opening screen of the Survival Guide. Use the Tab key or mouse pointer to move to the topics. Click or press Enter to move to the next screen. If you press Esc at this screen, you enter the editor with a blank screen.

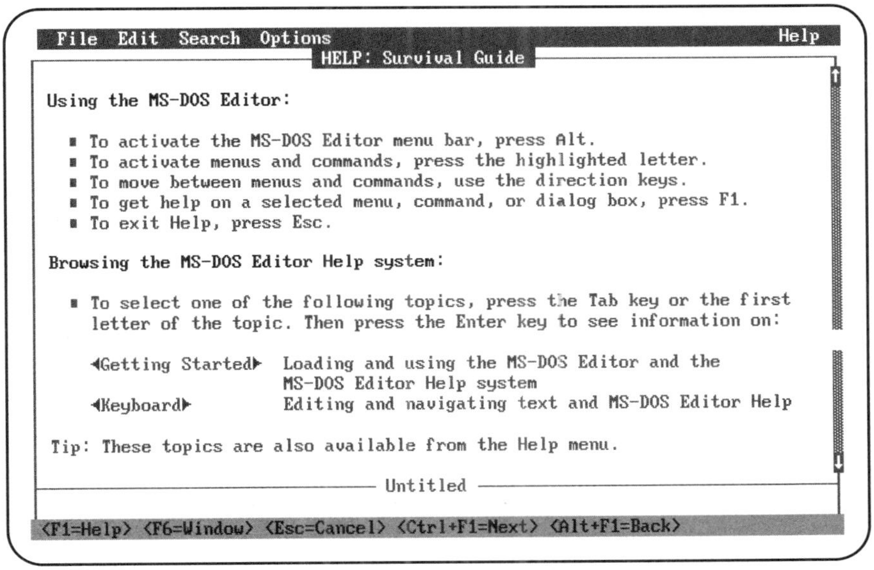

Figure 98-1. The first screen of the Survival Guide.

If you provide a file name on the command line, EDIT immediately loads that file for editing. Figure 98-2 shows the result of typing **`EDIT AUTOEXEC.BAT`**.

The screen includes a menu bar at the top, a help line at the bottom, and slider bars on the right and bottom of the edit window. At the top of the window is the name of the file being edited.

Once you are in edit mode (instead of help), pressing the Alt key activates the menu bar across the top. A quicker way to select a menu choice is to press Alt and the first letter of the choice. Figure 98-3 shows the result of pressing Alt-F for `File`. Once the pull-down menus have been activated, the right- and left-arrow keys shift the selection bar back and forth. The up- and down-arrow keys move the highlight within the pull-down menus.

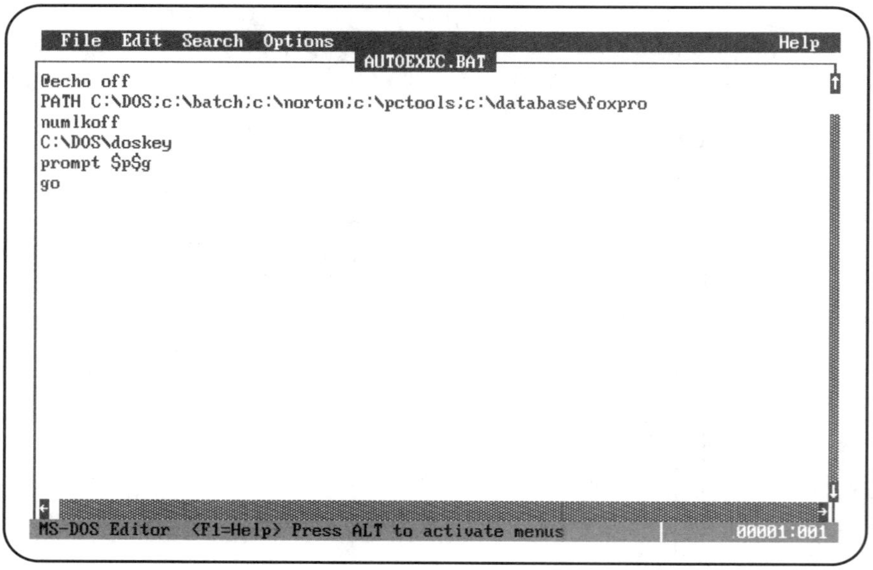

Figure 98-2. The EDIT screen with the batch file AUTOEXEC.BAT loaded and ready to edit.

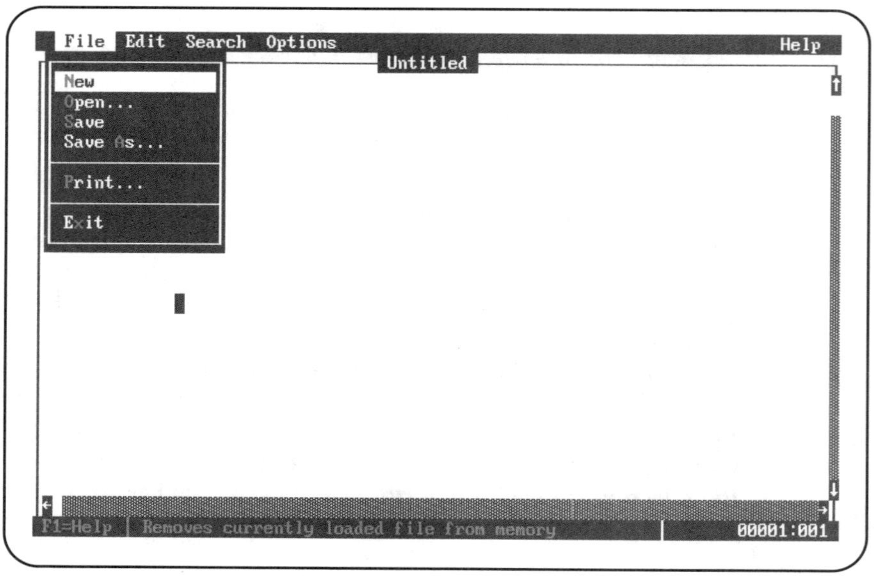

Figure 98-3. The `File` pull-down menu activated with Alt-F.

Working within the text to highlight blocks to be copied, moved, or deleted requires two or three key combinations. Once text has been marked with the highlight, the menu choices under EDIT are active and can be used. The F1 key provides a list of all the key combinations you can use to highlight text. Table 98-1 also shows some basic key combinations that can handle most block-marking tasks. Mouse users can make menu selections, move around in the help system, and mark text with standard point-and-click mouse movements.

Table 98-1. Six easy key combinations for marking text.

Key Combination	Action
Shift-right arrow	Marks character to the right
Shift-left arrow	Marks character to the left
Shift-down arrow	Marks current line
Shift-up arrow	Marks preceding line
Shift-Page Up	Marks screen up
Shift-Page Down	Marks screen down

As noted, the EDIT program has a complete context-sensitive help system available from the menu or with the F1 key. The program starts with the Survival Guide, a tutorial about the EDIT program.

Exercises

These two exercises take you through the process of editing an existing document and creating an original document. If you plan to use batch files or just want to make changes to AUTOEXEC.BAT and CONFIG.SYS, learning to use EDIT is a worthwhile endeavor.

Remember that EDIT is a text editor. It does not have spell checking or provide page formatting. It does not even wrap words at the end of the line. But it does provide a quick way to work on batch files and other ASCII files.

Exercise 1 of 2

This exercise uses a file located in the EXER98 subdirectory of the accompanying disk. You will need to put that disk in drive A: and use EDIT from drive C:. Because you don't do the steps in these exercises at the DOS command line, the steps include `<Enter>` each time you need to press that key.

TRY	NOTE
C:\>**EDIT A:\EXER98\SAMP.TXT <Enter>**	This step loads EDIT and also loads the file SAMP.TXT, located on the accompanying disk in drive A:.
Press the arrow keys.	Use the arrow keys to move around in this small document. How far down can you go?
<End>	This takes you to the end of the line.
<Home>	This takes you to the beginning of the line.
<Ctrl><Home>	This moves you to the beginning of the document.
<Ctrl><End>	This moves you to the end of the document.
<Alt>F	You've opened the `File` pull-down menu.
<right arrow> <right arrow> <right arrow> <right arrow>	As you use the arrow keys, the menus change on the screen. Examine each menu as you move to it. You can call each one directly by pressing Alt and the first letter of the menu.
<Esc> **<Ctrl><Home>**	This returns you to the top of the document, where you can begin editing.
Now is the time	As you type this, notice what happens to the characters on this line.
<Insert> **for all good people**	Because the default mode for EDIT is Insert, pressing the Insert key turns insert off, and you can begin overwriting the material.

You just made a mess of this document, so you need to load the original copy from the disk again, using the `File` menu. EDIT will warn you that you have not saved the current version of the file. In this case, that's OK; you don't want to save this version.

TRY	NOTE
<Alt>F O	This opens the `File` pull-down menu and then opens the Open dialog box.
SAMP.TXT <Enter> `File is not saved.` `Save it now?` **N**	As promised, EDIT warns you. Just say *no* (N). The original version of the file is now on the screen.

At this point, just explore the process of changing this document. Add a word. Use Backspace to make small corrections. To mark portions of the text, try the key combinations in Table 98-1. Note that the editor assumes that you have already marked text in some way before you call up the `Edit` menu. Also try the `Search` menu. When you are done, follow these next steps to exit the EDIT program.

TRY	NOTE
<Alt>F X	Again, EDIT warns you that you have made changes. If you want to save the changes (and usually you will), answer *yes* (Y). If not, answer *no* (N).

Exercise 2 of 2

This exercise provides the steps to create an original document (a new file). As always, the file name must follow the standard DOS file-naming conventions. ASCII files usually have an extension of TXT. That, in fact, is the extension EDIT first looks for when providing a directory of files to load.

TRY	NOTE
`C:\>`**EDIT**	This starts EDIT and presents the opening window.
<Esc> **In times of change, learners inherit the earth, while the learned find themselves beautifully equipped to deal with a world that no longer exists. — Eric Hoffer**	Here you begin with a blank screen. If you typed this as one line, you are now in column 157. Remember that EDIT does not automatically wrap the lines.

TRY	NOTE
<Home>	You are back to the beginning of the line.
Move the cursor to the end of each of the following words and press the Enter key: `while` **<Enter>** `deal` **<Enter>**	Now the lines are on one screen.
<Alt>F A	This opens the `File` menu and the Save As dialog box.
LEARN.TXT <Enter>	This file had not been saved, so you give it a name before EDIT can save it.
<Alt>F X	You exit EDIT.
`C:\>`**TYPE LEARN.TXT**	This step shows you that the file saved is a straight ASCII file.

The `Save As` option on the `File` menu is useful when you have opened a file but don't want to replace the old version with the new one. For example, you could now start EDIT by typing **EDIT LEARN.TXT**. But if you want to keep this version, use the Save As dialog box and type **LEARN02.TXT** to save the version. Then the disk will contain LEARN.TXT and LEARN02.TXT.

Reference

NEXT TOPIC: EDLIN — Line Editor (99)

EDLIN — Line Editor (99)

VERSIONS	
All	●
Some	○
5.0	○
Command	○
Program	●
Concept	○
Problem	○

This venerable line editor provides a quick way to create and edit text files. Because EDLIN is a line editor, you must know the specific commands for making changes in a file, listing it, and saving it.

Before You Begin

ASCII — Character Codes (74)

Syntax

`C:\>`**EDLIN FILENAME.EXT**	Starts EDLIN and loads FILENAME.EXT

Problem

Need to make quick changes to batch files. EDLIN allows quick changes to batch files or ASCII files. Because EDLIN is a line editor, you can use just a few keystrokes to make a change. You then return to DOS.

Explanation

The EDLIN line editor has been with DOS from the beginning. Its original advantage was that it could be loaded quickly and required little memory. In the days of 64K of memory and floppy disks, these were assets. Now that DOS users have hard disks and 640K of memory (or more), these features have little value. Because EDLIN is a line editor, you must know its cryptic commands before you can accomplish anything, even listing a file.

Unless you are a DOS 5.0 user (with EDIT), you should learn how to load and save ASCII files with a word processor instead of learning EDLIN. Practicing with your preferred word processing package may take some trial and error. Keep these points in mind while you explore:

- How does your word processor load ASCII files?
- Does it show hard carriage returns/linefeeds?
- Does it expand tabs to spaces?
- Does it attempt to reformat lines?
- Do you need to use a special command to save the file as ASCII text?
- Because some programs use a specific extension, such as DOC, how do you load a file with a different extension?
- Does your word processor make backup copies of the original version of a file? What extension does the backup copy have?

Reference

NEXT TOPIC: Batch Files — Write Your Own (100)

Editing batch files

See EDIT — DOS 5.0 Text Editor (98)

Erratic system behavior

See Virus (92)

Error in EXE file

See Floppy Drive Failure (32)
See also Hard Drive Failure (33)

Error in writing to device

See Floppy Drive Failure (32)
See also Hard Drive Failure (33)

Examining a long text file

See MORE — Pausing Screen Display (84)
See also EDIT — DOS 5.0 Text Editor (98)

Excessive noise during formats

See FORMAT — Disks (12)
See also Floppy Drive Failure (32)

Exchanging data between programs

See Data File Formats (52)

Exchanging files between different operating systems

See Operating Systems (75)

Extended warranty

See System Maintenance (94)

Extremely long format time

See FORMAT — Disks (12)

FASTOPEN — Speeding Up Disks (70)

VERSIONS	
All	○
Some	●
5.0	○
Command	○
Program	●
Concept	○
Problem	○

The DOS FASTOPEN program decreases the amount of time required to open frequently used files. FASTOPEN works on hard disks only and was first available in DOS 3.3.

Before You Begin

CONFIG.SYS (22)

Syntax

C:\>**FASTOPEN C:** — This loads FASTOPEN from the DOS prompt or as a line in AUTOEXEC.BAT.

C:\>**FASTOPEN C:=100 D:=100** — The default number of files to track is 48 in DOS 5.0. The number can range from 10 to 999. The value is set with an equal sign (=), and up to four drives can be specified.

5

INSTALL=FASTOPEN C: — CONFIG.SYS in DOS 5.0 can contain this line.

Problems

Hard disk access speed. Even though the BUFFERS= line in CONFIG.SYS improves disk access speed, the FASTOPEN program keeps more information about the file location. When you use FASTOPEN, you'll see some improvement with any program, such as a database with dozens of files. You'll see more improvement on a system with a slower hard disk.

Using disk compression or optimization programs with FASTOPEN. These programs "close up" the open spaces in the disk and make sure that all parts of each file are physically located together. Disk optimization programs make changes to file locations without FASTOPEN knowing about the changes. Always reboot after running a disk compression or optimization program if you use FASTOPEN or if the program suggests a reboot when it is finished.

Explanation

The FASTOPEN program enables you to enhance the performance of DOS. Using disk caches and altering the `BUFFERS=` statement in CONFIG.SYS also affect access speed. To discover a good combination of these methods for the best performance on your system, you'll need to experiment. Because FASTOPEN can be installed only once, each change in the settings requires a reboot. The parameters have changed significantly from DOS version 3.3 to version 4.0, and then again in version 5.0. Consult the DOS manual for the proper use of FASTOPEN with your version.

Exercise

A good way to test FASTOPEN is to run any program you have that takes a few moments to load. Note subjectively how long DOS takes to load the program. Then return to the DOS prompt. Type **`FASTOPEN C:`** (or use whatever drive the program is on). Load the program and quit again. Now load the program and see whether it loaded more quickly than the first and second time. If you noticed a difference, you might want to include **`FASTOPEN C:`** in your AUTOEXEC.BAT file.

The second loading of the program after you run FASTOPEN shows FASTOPEN where to look for the file. The load time should be faster because now FASTOPEN knows exacty where to look for the file.

Reference

NEXT TOPIC: New Programs on Old Computers (71)

FAT — File Allocation Table (89)

VERSIONS	
All	●
Some	○
5.0	○
Command	○
Program	○
Concept	●
Problem	○

The hidden File Allocation Table (FAT) stores the location of each part of every file. The FAT is not directly accessible to the user. Because it is such a critical part of DOS, there are actually two copies of the FAT on the disk.

Before You Begin

DIR — Directory (8)

Problem

`File allocation table bad.` This DOS error message occurs when DOS cannot use the file allocation table to locate files. When the FAT is damaged, some or all of the data on the disk becomes inaccessible. Use **`CHKDSK /F`** to attempt to correct this problem. If that is not successful, utility programs from other companies may help in recovering the FAT by referring to the second copy on the disk. Problems with the FAT are serious, and they need to be resolved. It is possible for all the data on a disk to be lost if the FAT is corrupted.

Explanation

The file allocation table (FAT) is a part of DOS that most users never worry about. The FAT contains the actual directory of files on the disk. Both copies of the FAT are always located in the same space on the disk.

The CHKDSK program attempts to recover lost clusters (parts of files) when the /F parameter is included as part of the command. See the topic CHKDSK — CHecK DiSK (20) for more information.

References

CHKDSK — CHecK DiSK (20), UNFORMAT (86)

NEXT TOPIC: MEM (90)

File attributes

See ATTRIB — Protecting Files (62)

File allocation table bad

See Floppy Drive Failure (32)
See also Hard Drive Failure (33)
See also FAT — File Allocation Table (89)

File cannot be copied onto itself

See COPY — Files (10)

File cannot be saved

See Disk Full (35)

File compatibility

See Upgrading Your Software (65)

File exchange between operating systems

See Operating Systems (75)

File name created with a space

See REN — REName Files (76)

File Names (4)

VERSIONS
All ●
Some ○
5.0 ○

Command ○
Program ○
Concept ●
Problem ○

The computer keeps all programs and data in files, located on floppy disks and hard disks. DOS uses file names to keeps track of those files. Each file name can contain up to eight characters and have an extension of up to three characters. A full file name consists of eight characters, a period, and a three-character extension. Blank spaces cannot be included in a DOS file name. Nor can the following characters:

? * < > \ / ¦

Before You Begin

Files (2)
Default Drive (3)

Syntax

`FILENAME.EXT`
`LETTER01`
`DAN.TXT`
	Valid file names

`FILE NAM.EXT`
`LETTER?`
`DAN>.TXT`
	Invalid file names

Problems

Illegal characters. In many cases, the program requesting the name of the file to be saved will check to make sure that the file name does not have any "illegal" characters. If it does, you are prompted to retype the name to correct the error. When you are working at the DOS level, using illegal characters can result in unpredictable errors and the loss of data because such characters means something entirely different to DOS.

Using meaningful names consistently. With DOS file names limited to eight characters, creating original and meaningful names can become a problem as files accumulate. Creating a personal system for naming files can be helpful. Suggestions for file names are included in the "Exercise" section.

Extensions assigned by programs. Some programs automatically add a unique three-letter extension to a file name. They may also allow you to substitute your own three-letter extension. Unfortunately, when you return to the program later, the file name will *not* be displayed because the program shows only files with the expected extension. For example, if a word processing program looks for DOC extensions but you named your file MYFILE.TXT, that file will not be displayed. You'll have to remember it and type the entire file name (MYFILE.TXT) to retrieve the file into your word processing program. The best approach is to let the program add the file extension. Just type the first eight characters.

Adding a file directory to a file name. DOS allows you to add subdirectory names (topic 9) to a file name. The file will be saved on the disk, provided the subdirectory exists. A problem can occur when the file has been placed in another location and you don't know where it is. If the files are usually stored in \DOCS and the file name you enter is \SHEETS\MYFILE.TXT, the file will be saved as MYFILE.TXT but located in another, unexpected subdirectory. Don't add another subdirectory to the name unless you know that you'll remember where the file went.

Explanation

Any program that keeps data entered by the user will request a file name before saving the data. This name becomes the "label" that both the user and DOS use to keep track of the file containing the data.

In some cases, a program automatically adds a file extension, such as DOC or WKS, to the name of the file. If you are not sure whether the program adds an extension, just type the eight-letter name, when asked, and press the Enter key. The program adds the extension when it saves the file. If you look for the file later with the DIR command, you'll have to know the extension or use DOS wild cards (topic 11).

DOS provides certain functions relating to the use of files. These functions are expressed with special characters, which you cannot include in file names. Table 4-1 lists these special characters (invalid in file names).

Table 4-1. Invalid characters in DOS file names.

Character	Invalid Name	Explanation
A space	FILE NM.TXT	DOS stops reading a file name at the first space encountered.
?	NOT?HERE.TXT	DOS uses the question mark (?) as a wild-card character when searching for files.
*	INTRUBL*.TXT	DOS uses the asterisk (*) as multiple question marks (???) when searching for files.
<	FILE<IT.TXT	This is a *redirection* character used to bring data into a program.
>	FILE>IT.TXT	This is another redirection character that sends data out of the program.
/	NAME/IT.TXT	The slash is used as a special "switch" in many programs.
\	WHAT\IS.TXT	The backslash character is used to designate the root directory and subsequent levels of directories.
.	WHAT.IS.TXT	The period can be used only once to signify the beginning of an extension.

Character	Invalid Name	Explanation
¦	WHAT¦IS.TXT	This symbol is the pipe command in DOS.
,	1,000.WKS	The comma is used to divide file names and parameters on the command line.

These special characters are covered in other topics. Wild cards are included in DIR — Directory (8) and in other file-related commands. The redirection characters are discussed in Redirection < > ¦ (64). And the slash (/) and backslash (\) are discussed in various topics, when appropriate.

The file extension (the three characters after the period) is used by DOS and many programs to determine a file's type. Only three extensions signify that a file is actually a program and may be run from the DOS prompt. Files with the extension COM, EXE, and BAT are program files. All other files are data files that programs can use. Common file-name extensions for programs are listed in Table 4-2.

Table 4-2. Some common file-name extensions used by different programs.

Extension	Program
WKS, WK1, and WK3	Lotus 1-2-3
DOC	MultiMate and Microsoft Word
PCX	PC Paintbrush
HLP	Menu programs that use on-line help files
SYS	Special files used by DOS
SCR	Screen-image files
DBF	dBASE data files
TXT and ASC	Generic extensions for ASCII files
BAK and ~BA	Backup files

These file extensions indicate that the data is formatted in specific ways. A file with the extension WKS cannot typically be used by a word processing program. Some newer programs do know how to read other file formats and can read the files of other programs. But if a spreadsheet file were read by a word processing program, the resulting file would be saved with a DOC extension and would not be usable by the spreadsheet program. For more information, refer to the topic ASCII — Character Codes (74).

The FT (FileType) utility program, provided on the accompanying disk, makes an educated guess about a file's type, based on over 80 different patterns. FT does not rely on the file extension but reads the first part of the file instead. More information is provided in Part III, "Guide to Using the Disk."

Exercise

One of the most common complaints about DOS is its limitation of eight characters in a file name. How can the user remember what is contained in all the files that accumulate? The following exercise helps you create file-naming patterns. The exercise does not require the use of a computer.

Exercise 1 of 1

Assume that all the programs you use provide their own file extensions. You therefore have eight characters (letters and numbers) with which to create your file names. Each file that you keep on a floppy disk or in a hard disk directory must have a unique name. If a file is related to other files or is one of a series of files, a part of each file name can stay the same, and another part can change. Deciding on a meaningful file-naming pattern may take some practice.

Who will be using the files? Are you creating a number of files for other people? Or are you creating files just for yourself? In either case, the principle is the same: be consistent when naming files and provide a hard copy (printed) note of the names.

Suppose that you type letters regularly for three people whose initials are PD, KB, and JF. They work in the personnel department and frequently send letters to applicants and employees. Some of these letters are similar. PD, KB, and JF give you a marked-up version of an old letter and want you to create a new letter. They don't care whether you retype the whole letter or find the old version to make the changes. You'd rather find the old version.

You can use the first two letters of the file to represent the author, so every file that PD creates will start with her initials. PD has three basic types of letter. One is a letter in response to a phone call, another is a letter to thank someone for coming to the interview, and the third is a job-offer letter. You can use the next four letters of the file name to categorize the letter. You now have file names that begin with PDCALL, PDTHNX, and PDOFFR. Finally, you can use the last two characters for the version number. Each time that you use an old document file—for example, PDTHNX01.DOC—you can save the newly updated file as PCTHNX02.DOC. (Remember that the word processing software adds the DOC extension.)

Now when PD hands you a marked-up "thanks for coming to the interview" letter, you'll know to look for the last version of PDTHNX. Actually, if the letters do not vary that much, the version numbers may not be necessary. If, though, the versions vary quite a bit and the letter you orginally used to make the changes is three months old, you may have a hard time finding the original file.

Of course, if you included the file name on the letter, you'll know exactly which file to look for. This may be as simple as adding PDTHNX04 after your initials. In other cases, it may be another line, farther down in the document, that includes the notation FN:C:\DOCS\PDTHNX04.DOC. This tells you not only the file name but also the location of the file on your disk. Naturally you'll want to check with the author of the documents to make sure that this additional bit of information is acceptable. When you explain how much time you can save with the addition, how can the author argue?

A second example of file naming pertains to a specific project. Suppose that you create spreadsheets, databases, and documents for the WIDGET project. How can you keep track of them all? Use the same pattern of consistency that you used in naming the letters. Because the project relates to the latest widget, make sure that all the related files begin with WID. Sample file names for the WIDGET project are provided in Table 4-3.

Table 4-3. Suggested file names for the WIDGET project.

File Name	Data Type
WIDBUDGT.WK1	Lotus 1-2-3 spreadsheet
WIDPROP1.DOC	First version of the proposal
WIDPROP2.DOC	Second version of the proposal
WIDPLAN9.DOC	Final version of the planning document
WIDVEND.DBF	List of possible vendors for the project
WIDGRAF1.PCX	A graphic for presentation to the board of directors

In all these cases, the document contains a line with the name of the file, as well as the date and time the document was created. Note this example:

```
FN:WIDBDGT.WK1  08/26/91 12:05 pm.
```

The date and time provide additional information in the event that several versions of a document are circulated.

Using a consistent pattern of file naming and including each file name on the document will save you both time and effort. Additional suggestions are presented in the topic File Organization (17).

References

DIR — Directory (8), CD, MD, and RD — Working with Directories (9), Wild Cards * and ? (11), File Organization (17), DEL — DELete Files (30)

NEXT TOPIC: CLS — Clear Screen (5)

File no longer listed by program

See REN — REName Files (76)

File not found

See COPY — Files (10)
See also Lost Data Files (77)

File Organization (17)

VERSIONS	
All	●
Some	○
5.0	○
Command	○
Program	○
Concept	●
Problem	○

File organization relates to the way files are saved on the hard disk. A specific plan for organizing your hard disk directory and maintaining your files makes finding and using files much easier.

Before You Begin

Files (2)
File Names (4)
DIR — Directory (8)
CD, MD, and RD — Working with Directories (9)

Problems

Too many files in the root directory. The root directory requires only three files, as noted in the "Explanation" section. The remaining entries in the root directory should be subdirectories. You can end up with too many files in the root directory because you copied them there from floppy disks or created them by starting a data file name with a backslash (\). Having a large number of files in the root directory is like stacking all your work papers on top of your desk.

Inconsistent use of subdirectories. Without at least a basic plan for organizing the hard disk, files can easily become lost in a maze of subdirectories. This discussion suggests effective ways to organize a hard disk.

Data and program files mixed. Some programs come with dozens of additional files. If data files are kept in the same subdirectory as the program files, the DIR listing can continue screen after screen of file information. Keeping data files in a separate directory makes finding them easier and backing them up more convenient.

Multiple users. If several users are on a single system, there is an even greater need for organization, regular backups, and a group consensus about how and where to keep files.

Explanation

DEF

Organizing a hard disk directory is largely a matter of personal preference. Whatever method you choose, consistency is the key to effectively using the directory structure that DOS provides. Instead of trying to develop a system that handles every possible program, you can follow a few basic principles for handling the inevitable growth of directories and files on the hard disk.

The advantages of organizing your hard disk become obvious as files accumulate in the hundreds or thousands. Even if your hard disk has been accumulating files for years, you can begin to clean it up the moment you decide how you want to organize it.

Organizing the hard disk system does not stop with a well-designed directory tree. Regardless of the design you choose, regular maintenance is important. At least once a month, a good housekeeping session is necessary. This session may take just a few moments or several hours, depending on how much the system is used. Housekeeping can include some or all of the following tasks:

- *Removing backup and temporary files.* To delete extra files, you can use DOS wild cards with the DEL command. Change into each data subdirectory and type **DEL *.BAK**, or substitute the extension your program uses for the backup files. Doing this manually takes a few minutes, or you may want to use one of the programs that can perform this action across the entire hard disk.

- *Growing (expanding) the directory tree.* If a subdirectory has many files, you can create several new subdirectories and copy groups of related files into those subdirectories. Suppose, for example, that you have named your word processing files consistently, and you notice that several dozen files begin with MEMO and have an extension of DOC. All of them are in the DOCS directory. You could make a subdirectory called MEMO under DOCS and copy all the files, using **MEMO*.DOC**, into that subdirectory. Then just **DEL** those files from the DOCS directory.

- *Pruning the directory tree.* If you no longer use an area of the disk, copy all the files to a floppy and **RD** the directory. Label the floppy and store it. A well-organized system for archiving files helps if you need to find an elusive file later. If you are absolutely sure that you'll never need those files again, just delete them all with **DEL *.***.

- *Backing up and deleting files.* If you notice many old data files, you can use the XCOPY command to copy those files (before a specific date) to a floppy. Label the floppy. List the directory to the printer and keep that list with the disk. Then delete the files you just copied to the floppy. Again, you can do this manually, but a number of utility programs can save time in this process.
- *Listing the directory to the printer.* As you begin to clean up and reorganize, you may want to work from a printed list. Use the **DIR > LPT1:** command. The list of files will then be sent to the printer instead of the screen. DOS 5.0 users can use **DIR/S > LPT1:** to list files in all the subdirectories too. Using the **/S** from the root directory may print dozens of pages, though.

The different approaches to directory organization are based on common rules. Although they are not hard and fast, they do provide a basis for a well-organized hard disk. Here are some rules you can generally follow:

- The root directory should contain the minimum number of files to start the system: COMMAND.COM, AUTOEXEC.BAT, and CONFIG.SYS. All other entries will be subdirectories.
- Program files and data files should be kept in separate directories.
- Directory names should be recognizable, but short and easy to type. They usually do not include an extension, although they may.
- Data files should be grouped by project or data type, or by some other consistent method.
- Depending on the capacity of the hard drive, separate drives may be used for programs and data. (Hard drives can be divided into more than one drive designation, such as C:, D:, and so on.)
- Subdirectories with more than two screens of files (40 or more) become hard to manage because you can easily forget what has scrolled past.
- Using a program (or the DIR /O option in DOS 5.0) to sort the directory listing can be valuable for file and directory maintenance.

Next you take a look at three different ways a hard disk can be organized. These are not the only ways to set up directories on a hard disk. You may want to borrow some elements from each method and create your own directory organization. The key, as always, is to remain consistent to the system you design and implement.

The three methods presented here are called the Deep system, the Shallow system, and the Parallel system. Here is an overview of each of these systems:

- *Deep system.* This method is appropriate if you have more than one program within each group of applications. The root directory has subdirectories with names like SPREADS, DATABASE, and WORDPROC. Within each of these subdirectories are a number of subdirectories containing specific programs. This system can easily have five levels or more.
- *Shallow system.* This method is based on a few applications, typically just one word processing program, one database program, and so on. Each subdirectory in the root directory is named with the program contained in that subdirectory, such as QPRO, WORD, and PCFILE. Below each of these directories is a DATA subdirectory.
- *Parallel system.* If the option is available when you first format your hard disk, you can "partition" a 60-megabyte drive into two drives, a 30-megabyte drive C: and a 30-megabyte drive D:. The parallel system contains two duplicate structures. Drive C: contains the programs, and drive D: contains the data files.

The rest of this discussion provides diagrams and suggestions for setting up each of these systems.

The Deep System

This structure may be more useful for a system with a number of users. The general design is shown in Figure 17-1. The directory levels depend, in part, on data file compatibility.

```
C:\──────┬──DATABASE──────┬──DBASE
         │                ├──PCFILE
         │                ├──VPINFO
         │                └──DATA
         ├──WORDPROC──────┬──WORD──────DOCS──────┬──MINUTES
         │                │                      └──MEMOS
         │                ├──WP────────DOCS
         │                └──NE
         ├──SPREADS───────┬──QPRO
         │                ├──VPPLAN
         │                └──SHEETS
         └──DOS
```

Figure 17-1. The Deep system, with mutiple directory levels.

Although both the DATABASE and SPREADS directories have several programs, each of these directories has only one subdirectory for data. DATABASE has DATA to hold data, and SPREADS has SHEETS to hold data. This arrangement works because all the programs in each group can use the same data file format. Under the WORDPROC directory, WORD and WP each have a DOCS subdirectory for data.

Separate subdirectories are necessary because these two word processing programs have different file formats and cannot share files. If you go even deeper, WORDPROC\WORD\DOCS has two additional directories, one for MINUTES and one for MEMOS.

Here are the full "formal" path names for all the subdirectories shown in Figure 17-1:

C:\DATABASE
C:\DATABASE\DBASE
C:\DATABASE\PCFILE
C:\DATABASE\VPINFO
C:\DATABASE\DATA
C:\WORDPRO
C:\WORDPROC\WORD
C:\WORDPROC\WORD\DOCS\MINUTES
C:\WORDPROC\WORD\DOCS\MEMOS
C:\WORDPROC\WP
C:\WORDPROC\WP\DOCS
C:\WORDPROC\NE
C:\SPREADS
C:\SPREADS\QPRO
C:\SPREADS\VPPLAN
C:\SPREADS\SHEETS
C:\DOS

The Shallow System

The Shallow system has fewer programs but may have more files relating to those programs. Figure 17-2 shows an example of this kind of system.

```
C:\───────┬─QPRO
          ├─WORD
          ├─PCFILE
          ├─BUDGET91
          ├─STAFFING
          └─DOS
```

Figure 17-2. The Shallow system, with all programs and data directories coming off the root directory.

This system contains specific directories based on project or category. Within the BUDGET91 subdirectory are data files with the extensions WQ1, DOC, and DBF. Because each of these extensions is used only by its respective program (Quattro Pro, Microsoft Word, and PC-File), listing the directory of BUDGET91 from within Quattro Pro shows only the WQ1 files.

The Shallow system might be helpful when a number of users share the same system. The programs are in the same location, but each user has a "base" directory. The path for each of these directories begins with a user's name, as shown in Figure 17-3. When Becky wants to use QPRO, she points to the files to use as \BECKY\BUDGET, assuming that her spreadsheet files are located in the BUDGET directory.

```
C:\───────────┬─QPRO
              ├─WORD
              ├─PCFILE
              ├─DOS
              ├─BECKY───────┬─STAFF
              │             ├─BUDGET
              │             └─FREELANC
              ├─JOE─────────┬─STAFF
              │             └─MEMOS
              └─RICHARD
```

Figure 17-3. The Shallow system designed for multiple users.

The Parallel System

The Parallel system requires the partitioning of a hard disk into more than one drive. An advantage to this system is that you need to back up only one drive—the one containing the valuable data. In the sample shown in Figure 17-4, only drive D: needs to be backed up regularly. The programs, of course, are still on their original disks and can be reinstalled easily. The DOS directory does not require a parallel in D:.

```
C:\───────┬─DBASE     D:\────────┬─DBASE
          ├─PCFILE               ├─PCFILE
          ├─WORD                 ├─WORD
          ├─QPRO                 └─QPRO
          └─DOS
```

Figure 17-4. The Parallel system, with program directories on drive C: and data directories on drive D:.

Whether you use the shallow, deep, or parallel system, you'll eventually run out of space and have to clean it up. Considering how quickly a hard disk can accumulate thousands of files, the question is not *if*, but *when*. The longer you wait, the longer the cleanup will take.

The following utilities, provided on the accompanying disk, may help you locate and find files:

- FD (Find Directory). This utility locates a directory and changes (CD) to it, using just the directory name or even a partial name. FD searches all drives on the system, starting with C:.
- MV (MoVe Files). This utility moves files from one directory to another on the same disk. MV replaces the two steps required with COPY and DEL.

More information about these programs is provided in Part III, "Guide to Using the Disk."

Exercises

There is no time like the present to begin the cleanup effort. The first exercise helps you plan the reorganization of your hard disk. The second exercise reviews the steps necessary to reach that goal.

Exercise 1 of 2

This exercise helps you assess what programs you use, how you use them, how your hard disk is currently organized, and how you would like to organize it.

The first step just takes a few moments. On the left side of a plain piece of paper, write the names of the programs you use regularly. Exclude any DOS programs you know and love to use. (They are already well established in the DOS directory.) Don't take too long. Don't worry if you can't remember the exact name of the program. Now, on the right side of the page, write the projects or tasks you work on regularly. Table 17-1 shows what this sheet might look like.

Table 17-1. A sample software and projects/tasks sheet.

Software	Projects/Tasks
Microsoft Word	Letters
Quattro Pro	Invoices
FoxPro	Budget
PC Paintbrush IV Plus	Image design
CorelDraw	Communications
Windows	Books
ProComm Plus	Newsletter mailing list
	Newsletter

For the second step, draw lines from each project or task to the software you use for that project. You may draw one or more lines to or from each item. A sample list, re-sorted for convenience, is shown in Table 17-2.

Table 17-2. The re-sorted list with connecting lines between projects and software.

Software	Projects/Tasks
Microsoft Word	Letters
	Books
Quattro Pro	Invoices
	Budget
FoxPro	Newsletter mailing list
PC Paintbrush IV Plus	Image design
Corel Draw	Newsletter
Windows	
Procomm Plus	Communications

Now, on another sheet of paper, use this diagram to draw a hard disk organization. Figure 17-5 shows one way it can be done.

```
Root──┬──DOS
      ├──WORD────┬──LETTERS
      │          └──BOOKS────┬──SIMCITY
      │                      └──LEARNDOS
      ├──QPRO────┬──BUDGET
      │          └──INVOICES
      ├──FOXPRO────NEWSLIST
      │
      ├──PBRUSH────PICS
      │
      ├──WINDOWS───COREL──────NEWSLTR
      │
      └──PCPLUS
```

Figure 17-5. A hard disk organization for the programs listed in Table 17-2.

Only two steps are left in this organizing effort. The DOS TREE program can provide a quick listing of all the subdirectories on your hard disk. For more information, refer to the topic TREE — Directory Map (87). For now, make sure that your printer is turned on and then type the following from the root directory:

```
C:\>TREE > LPT1:
```

DOS 4.0 and 5.0 users need to add a switch to the command so that the lines print properly:

```
C:\>TREE /A > LPT1:
```

The result will be a complete listing of all the subdirectories on drive C:. If you have more than one drive, repeat the command for each drive.

The final step in this exercise is to make changes to the current list so that it more closely resembles your ideal design. You will probably settle for a compromise between the ideal and the usable, depending on how much work you want to do. If you are willing to do the work, the final design will look a lot like your ideal design. If you don't have much time, you might make just a few changes to the existing design and leave it at that.

Exercise 2 of 2

Rearranging a hard disk is not necessarily an easy task. Taken a step at a time, however, it can be accomplished if you have done adequate planning in Exercise 1. The four steps in this exercise include backing up the entire disk, deleting old files, building the new subdirectory structure, and moving the files from the old to the new structure. Here are the four steps:

1. Use DOS BACKUP, or some other commercial hard-drive backup program, to make a complete copy of your hard disk. Set this copy aside as a special set of disks. Don't include it in your regular backup sequence. This step is important because it captures the exact state of the disk before the reorganization. Do a complete backup of the hard drive on new disks when you finish the process. Keep the old set for at least six months in case you later discover files missing as the result of the reorganization.

2. Using the TREE printout for guidance, move into each subdirectory and delete unnecessary files. You may need to use the programs that created the files so that you can look at each file before deleting it. If possible, use the dates as a guide. If you know that you don't need any letters written last year, you can start by automatically deleting those old files. Also delete any obvious backup files with extensions of BAK and OLD. If you are in doubt, look at the files first.

   If you run into subdirectories containing programs you never use, you can delete all the files in that subdirectory. Again, if you're in doubt, leave the files alone. You will need to decide where those files can go in the new structure, though.

   This process of cleaning up the hard drive may take weeks. Keep at it. Do two subdirectories a day, and eventually you will have the system cleaned up. Use the TREE printout and cross off each subdirectory as you finish.

3. If the new structure is radically different from the old, you may want to create the entire new tree before you begin to move the files. If the tree

is only slightly different, you can do just one branch at a time. Again, your design sheets should help.

4. Using just DOS commands, you'll first need to copy all the files from the old directory to the new. You'll then need to go back and delete the old files. If you use the MV (MoVe) utility provided with this book, you can accomplish these tasks in one step. In some cases, you may have to pull files out of a directory. If all of your document files are in the word processing program's subdirectory, copy the document files to the new subdirectory. Then delete them from the old directory. Afterward, you can copy the remaining program files to the new directory for that program.

With a little—well, a lot of—work, you can get your hard disk organized. The time saved will be well worth the effort.

References

Disk Full (35), BACKUP—Files (41), RESTORE—Files (42), Utility Software (50), TREE — Directory Map (87)

NEXT TOPIC: Software (18)

File transfer time too expensive

See Compressed Files (80)

Files (2)

VERSIONS	
All	●
Some	○
5.0	○
Command	○
Program	○
Concept	●
Problem	○

A file is the basic storage unit on a computer. Each file has a name limited to 11 characters. Files are stored on floppy and hard disks so that you (or the computer) can reuse the data or programs in the files.

Before You Begin

Boot/Startup (1)

Problems

Lost files. Hard disks can have thousands of files. A consistent file-naming method and a well-organized hard disk will help you prevent misplaced files.

Loss of data. The data in a file is stored on magnetic media. Although the computer is reliable, occasionally it will not be able to read a file. Any file that takes a significant amount of time and effort to create should exist in at least two places.

Misnamed files. Even if files are created with a consistent naming pattern, you can misplace them by mistyping their names. For example, you might type O instead of 0, or L instead of 1. Or you might add an additional character at the end of the file name. Many programs alphabetize the list of files for you. LDO01.DOC would be in a completely different alphabetical location than LDOOl.DOC.

Explanation

One of the many functions of DOS is to keep track of data stored on the magnetic media of floppy disks and hard disks. The only evidence that you see of this DOS control is a file, identified by its file name. This file name, discussed in the topic File Names (4), is provided by the original creator of the file. In some cases, a file is a program file and is therefore named by the original programmer. In many cases, the file is created by the user to save data in the format of a letter, spreadsheet, or mailing list.

There are two kinds of DOS files: *program* files and *data* files. Both kinds are stored on the disk in the same way, but they are used differently by the user and the computer.

Program files contain the instructions to run the computer. These instructions are written by a programmer to control the computer system in specific ways. Program files include such applications as word processing, spreadsheets, and databases. The disk operating system (DOS) is a series of programs that controls the computer. The DOS programs actually control the next level of programs, the applications. DOS programs are therefore referred to as "systems programs." One of the main DOS programs is COMMAND.COM.

Program files are easy to recognize because they have an extension of COM, EXE, or BAT. This three-letter extension at the end of the file name—for example, PROGRAM.EXE—tells DOS that the file is a program. It can be loaded and the first instruction in the program begun.

> Running a program at random, without knowing in advance what the program is supposed to do, may be dangerous. Consult the program's manual for information about starting the program.

Data files contain data you have created or data to be used by a program. The data is in a special format that can be used only by a program (or programs) designed to read that format. A specific word processing program, such as Microsoft Word, creates data files containing the documents you enter. In many cases, a spreadsheet program, such as Borland's Quattro Pro, cannot read or use a data file created by

Microsoft Word. Some newer programs are able to read files from other programs. A program's manual can provide additional information about reading different data formats.

In a list of files, the only files that can be used immediately are the program files. You can use any file with COM, EXE, or BAT at the end of the file name just by typing the name of that file. You don't need to type the extension. If the list of files contains

```
WORD    EXE
Q       BAT
SHEET   WKS
LETTER  DOC
```

you can type

WORD

or

Q

and that program file begins to run on the computer. The program takes control of the computer and provides additional directions on what to do next.

If you type

SHEET

or

LETTER

DOS returns the message `Bad command or file name`. These two files are data files, and they can be used only by other programs. Such data file names are created by the user.

The process of creating data files is consistent from program to program. For example, when you type **WORD**, the word processing program begins issuing instructions to the computer. After a moment or two, you begin typing. Even if you just want to print one copy of a document, you may have to spend 45 minutes working on it first. To keep from accidentally losing the file before printing it, you type commands to tell the WORD program to save the file to disk. WORD prompts you for the file name. You type **LETTER** and press Enter. WORD then saves to that file name the data you just typed (LETTER.DOC). WORD adds the DOC extension to help the program determine later that this file is in the special format WORD can use.

Some files on the computer are data files but are not ones the user has created. These files are provided with the programs and are used by them for their own purposes. An example is a file named SPELL-AM.LEX, which is provided with WORD. This data file contains thousands of words that WORD uses to check for proper spelling in a document.

Getting a program started on a DOS computer can be as simple as making a choice on a menu or as basic as typing the program name. In many cases, someone has provided a list of instructions for you to type whenever you want to run a program. These instructions, written on a sticky-note hanging off the edge of the monitor, may look like this:

```
CD\WORDPROC\WORD5
WORD
```

After you type these lines, your program comes up on the screen, and you can then work on a task. Now you know that the second word in this command starts the program called WORD. What the additional command (CD) does and where the WORD file is located will become clear as you learn about directories and file organization in the next few topics.

The FT (File Type) utility program, provided on the accompanying disk, makes an educated guess about a file's type, based on over 80 different patterns. FT does not rely on the file extension but reads the first part of the file instead. More information about FT is provided in Part III, "Guide to Using the Disk."

References

File Names (4), DIR — Directory (8), File Organization (17), Application Software (46)

NEXT TOPIC: Default Drive (3)

Files lost

See Files (2)

FIND — Searching Files (82)

VERSIONS
All ○
Some ●
5.0 ○

Command ○
Program ●
Concept ○
Problem ○

The DOS FIND program searches one file at a time for a string of text and displays the entire line containing the search string.

Before You Begin

ASCII — Character Codes (74)

Syntax

`C:\>FIND "NICE" LOOKFILE.TXT`	Displays any line containing the word *NICE*
`C:\>FIND /I "NICE" LOOKFILE.TXT`	Looks for the word *NICE*, *nice*, or any combination, such as *nIcE* (ignores case)

Problem

Need to locate a specific word or phrase within a file. The DOS FIND program is limited to searching one ASCII file at a time. Other public domain or commercial programs can search multiple files at one time for more clearly specified phrases.

Explanation

The DOS FIND program is fairly limited because it can work on only ASCII files, and it does a literal search. A search for *the* will find *theme*, *theory*, and *scythe*, as well as dozens of lines with *the*.

You can use several switches with FIND, immediately following the command and before the search string. Here are a few:

/V Shows all lines *not* containing the specified string

/C Counts the number of lines containing the string

/N Shows the line numbers with the lines

/I Ignores the case of characters

One of the best uses for the FIND program is covered in the topic Lost Data Files (77). You use the CHKDSK program and FIND to locate specific files on the disk.

Exercise

Refer to the topic Lost Data Files (77) for an exercise on the use of FIND.

References

ASCII — Character Codes (74)

NEXT TOPIC: MODE — Configuring System Devices (83)

Finding a file

See Lost Data Files (77)

Finding and erasing hidden files

See ATTRIB — Protecting Files (62)

First track unusable

See FORMAT — Disks (12)

Floppy Disks (19)

VERSIONS	
All	●
Some	○
5.0	○
Command	○
Program	○
Concept	●
Problem	○

Floppy disks allow data files to be permanently stored away from the computer. The disks also contain programs, typically copied onto the hard drive inside the computer. Because the medium is plastic and the data is stored magnetically, the data may be lost from improper use of the disks.

Before You Begin

Files (2)
Default Drive (3)
FORMAT — Disks (12)

Problems

Damaged disk. Disks inside the plastic covers are made of plastic and are coated with a magnetic film. The plastic can be melted, creased, cut, or damaged from liquids accidentally spilled on it. The magnetic image can be erased by magnets, motors, and ringing phones. There is no solution once damage has occurred. Treating your disks carefully is the best way to prevent this problem.

Incompatible disks and drives. Floppy disks come in two incompatible sizes. The 5 1/4-inch format is older than the 3 1/2-inch format. Many software packages contain both sizes. Check the package before purchase. If data is to be provided or received in both sizes, the easiest solution is to have disk drives of both sizes installed in the computer. Connecting two computers with drives of different sizes is possible, through the serial ports, but requires special cables and software.

Disk and drive capacities not compatible. Not only can disks have different physical sizes, but they can also have different capacities. A high-density (HD) drive can read double-density (DD) disks as well as high-density disks. A double-density drive can read and write to a double-density disk only. A high-density (HD) floppy cannot be read in a double-density drive.

Keeping archived disks. Even with a large hard drive, files should be copied eventually to floppies and deleted from the hard drive. You should keep those disks for a specified period of time, usually for two years. Any financial records should be kept permanently, of course. Maintain these disks just as you would any archival records, keeping in mind that disks are sensitive to heat and magnetic fields. A number of programs are available to keep a list of all disks, as well as all the files on each disk. The programs can then locate files by name, extension, or date.

Explanation

The computer reads and writes data to floppy disks by magnetizing parts of the disk. The data is written in binary code that is useful to only the computer. Before data can be written and read from the disk, you must format the disk. For specific instructions on formatting disks, refer to the topic FORMAT — Disks (12).

The disk's *storage capacity* affects the amount of data a disk can hold and may limit its usefulness. Figure 19-1 compares the amounts of data that can be stored on different sizes of disks. Because each byte equals one character and one page of typed text contains 2,000 characters, a 360,000-byte disk can hold approximately 180 typed pages. Although this may seem like a lot of storage, almost any disk will fill it up quickly if you use it often.

Floppy disks come in 5 1/4-inch and 3 1/2-inch sizes. The larger size is truly a "floppy" disk because the cover is just thin plastic. The smaller size is contained in a rigid plastic case that protects the disk inside. Figure 19-2 shows the distinguishing characteristics of each disk.

5 1/4-Inch Disks

This disk size includes two capacities. The 360,000-byte 5 1/4-inch disk, more commonly referred to as a 360K disk, is currently the smaller-capacity disk. Although the original floppy disk held only 180K, that format is hard to locate now. The 360K disk is found in older XT computers. There is nothing wrong with this capacity disk, but it represents the least efficient floppy disk you can use for data storage. However, it is the format that almost anyone with a 360K drive can use.

Newer computer systems may contain a 1,200,000-byte 5 1/4-inch drive, which handles disks of that size. This disk is called a 1.2-megabyte (or 1.2M) high-density disk. (One megabyte equals 1 million bytes. Refer to topic 67, Bytes and Computer Math, for more about computer measurements.) Computers that contain this drive size include the AT, 386, and 486 systems. These disks hold 3 1/3 times more data than the 360K disks.

The 5 1/4-inch disks in both capacities look exactly the same, with the possible exception of the manufacturer's label stating that the disk is a high-density (HD) disk. The less expensive, generic high-density disks may not have this label. If a disk has no distinguishing characteristics, trial and error may be required to determine the capacity of the disk. The better approach is to apply your own label immediately (in the upper left corner of the disk) and write *HD* somewhere on the label. Remember that a high-density disk will not work in a double-density drive. If the 360K drive cannot format the disk, the disk is HD. If a high-density drive formats the disk without errors, the disk is HD. If FORMAT declares many `Bad sectors` or reports `Format failure`, the HD drive is trying to format a double-density disk as a high-density disk. That won't work. Reformat the disk as a 360K disk with **`FORMAT A:/4`**.

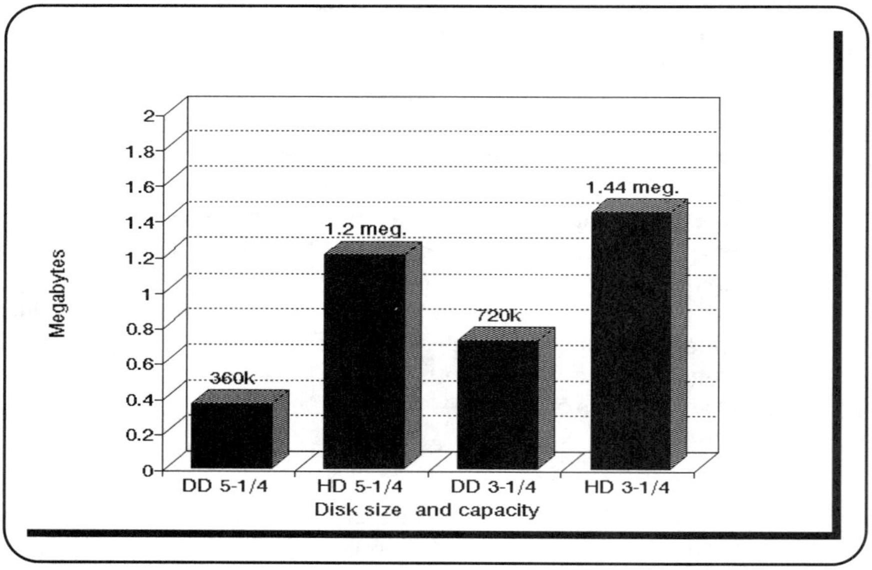

Figure 19-1. A comparison of disk storage capacities.

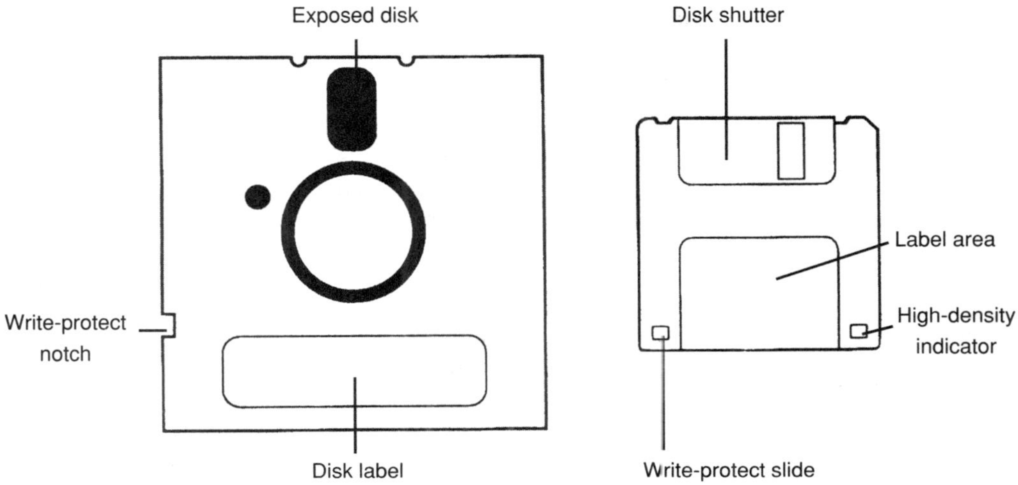

Figure 19-2. The 5 1/4-inch and 3 1/2-inch disks.

3 1/2-Inch Disks

This disk size also includes two capacities. The double-density disk holds 720,000 bytes (720K). This size was originally popular in the first laptop computers and is the standard in the IBM PS/2 Models 25 and 30. The high-density 3 1/2-inch disk holds 1,440,000 bytes (1.44M). One of these disks stores 4 times the amount of the standard 5 1/4-inch 360K disk.

Fortunately you can identify disks with these two capacities in at least one way, and usually two. As shown in Figure 19-2, the upper right corner of all 3 1/2-inch disks has a write-protect slider. If the disk has a second hole in the upper left corner, it is a high-density disk. Many manufacturers also print the letters HD on the lower left corner and possibly on the metal slide.

Floppy Disk Care

The 5 1/4-inch floppy disks require more care than the 3 1/2-inch disks. Because the larger disks consist of a thin sheet of plastic sandwiched between two thin pieces of plastic, the disk can easily be damaged. Here are some common causes of disk damage:

- You cause a crease in the disk by inserting it in the drive too quickly (and missing). This can ruin the disk.
- You place something on the disk or smash it in a book. This can prevent the inside disk from spinning.

- The actual disk surface is exposed when the disk is not in its paper *sleeve*. Any fingerprint on this inner surface can prevent the entire disk from being used.

The 3 1/2-disk design has corrected many of the vulnerabilities of the 5 1/4-inch disk. The 3 1/2-inch disk is enclosed in a hard shell. Inserting the disk quickly cannot crease the disk or hurt it in any way. The shell can withstand quite a bit of pressure before the inner disk is affected. And the disk surface is always covered by the metal shutter.

These disks, like 5 1/4-inch disks, can still be damaged by heat, liquids, and magnets. The mylar plastic inside the case is very thin in both disks. Any temperature much over 100 degrees for any length of time can warp the thin plastic disk inside. If the disk is warped, it cannot spin in the jacket or be read by the computer. The quickest way to fry a disk is to leave it in a hot car in direct sunlight.

Any device with moving parts can be damaged by liquids. Even a small amount that seeps into the inside will ruin the disk. There are reports of users damaging 5 1/4-inch disks this way and still recovering the data on the disk. They have apparently clipped the edge off the cover, slipped the disk out, rinsed it off, and let it dry completely. Then they sacrifice another disk by opening that cover, replacing that good disk with the cleaned disk, and then immediately making a copy of the disk! All the disk parts are discarded, but the data now resides on a good disk. Fact or fiction? If the data is valuable enough, it may be worth a try.

Magnets and magnetic fields cause irreparable damage to both types of disks. The data is stored on the disk magnetically. A small magnet placed within an inch of the disk for several seconds will erase a spot on the disk. Even a small blank spot can keep the disk from being read. Any device with a motor or electromagnetic coil also creates a magnetic field. Leave a disk next to a telephone with bells when the phone rings, and the data may be gone. Here are some other sources of magnetic fields:

- Paper clip holders
- Paper clips
- Answering machines
- Magnetic paper holders
- Screwdrivers
- Electric clocks

As with all computer-related disasters, careful attention to keeping duplicate copies of files can make the loss of data on a disk a minor inconvenience. But if it's the only copy of a 400-name mailing list. . . .

Exercise

This exercise helps you examine a floppy disk as you never have before. You'll get a new perspective, and the floppy disk will never be the same.

Exercise 1 of 1

Locate an old disk of the type you normally use. Make sure that nothing of value is on the disk because it will be destroyed as the result of your educational efforts.

Look closely at the disk. Which parts can you safely touch and which parts need to be protected? Locate the write-protect notch. If the disk is a 5 1/4-inch floppy, see how much the disk will bend before it develops a permanent crease. If it is a 3 1/2-inch disk, slide the metal cover back to look at the exposed disk surface.

Use scissors to cut or pry open the sleeve. Remove the inner disk. Notice the cushion for the disk. Imagine how nicely this would soak up anything spilled on the disk. Flex and then crease the inner disk. Imagine how hard it would be for the disk to turn in the sleeve if it were creased like that.

Do not try to put the disk back together again. Just toss the remains in the trash. Do not try this exercise on your hard disk.

References

Floppy Disk Failure (32)

NEXT TOPIC: CHKDSK — CHecK DiSK (20)

Floppy Drive Failure (32)

VERSIONS	
All	●
Some	○
5.0	○
Command	○
Program	○
Concept	○
Problem	●

Floppy disk drives use removable disks with a wide variety of sizes and storage capacities. Because they are electronic and mechanical, they can fail any number of ways.

Before You Begin

Boot/Startup (1)
Files (2)
Floppy Disks (19)

Problem

Floppy drive failure. Disk drives are mechanical, so they can (and do) break down. A floppy drive may not be able to read or write to a floppy disk. DOS can report various errors, some caused by mechanical failure.

Explanation

Drives may fail to read a disk for several reasons. Some relate to the drive and disk density, and others relate to mechanical failure. If DOS attempts to read the disk, indicated by the drive light, and cannot, DOS returns one of many error messages. The following steps can help you determine the problem and the solution. In most cases, after each step is attempted, you should respond to the DOS error message. If the problem still exists, DOS will return the message again.

1. Check the disk drive door or button. Make sure that it is turned down or pressed in completely.
2. Make sure that the disk is inserted properly. Like a piece of bread in the toaster, a 5 1/4-inch disk can be inserted eight different ways. Unlike the toaster, only one way works. Remove the disk and make certain that it is right side up in the drive and that the exposed portion (a long oval) goes in the drive first. You can insert a 3 1/2-inch disk only one way.
3. Check the drive capacity. If it's a 360K drive (present on older XT-class computers), it will not be able to read a high-density disk.
4. Try a different floppy disk. This step determines whether the problem is with the disk drive or that particular floppy disk. If the second disk can be used, the first disk is probably damaged. See the topic Utility Software (50) for more information on recovering a damaged floppy disk or file.
5. If a third disk fails, the problem is likely to be the drive. If the drive still makes noises but cannot read the disk or has caused intermittent problems, the disk heads may be dirty. You can use a head cleaning kit to attempt to solve the problem.
6. If, after the heads have been cleaned, the drive still does not read any of the disks with the proper capacity, the disk drive needs service. Because floppy drives are not readily repaired, the entire unit is likely to need replacement.

Both floppy drives and hard drives operate by spinning a disk with magnetic material between brackets (heads) that can read the signal on the disk. A more technical explanation could include access speed and head-seek tolerance. The important information relates to the care of disk drives. Proper care of floppy disks is covered in the topic Floppy Disks (19).

Because floppy drives just read the disks you insert, failure of the disk is not quite as critical. Data is not lost when the disk fails. You just can't get to the data on the floppy disk or copy data to and from your hard disk. Only two points should be mentioned about the care of floppy disk drives:

- The heads that read the data become covered with small particles from the floppy disk. Some users advocate using a disk-drive cleaning kit regularly. Other users suggest that cleaning the heads is necessary only when the drive has problems reading and writing to the disk.

- Because air is pulled through the computer to keep the electronics cooled, a lot of air comes through the open drive. So much dust can accumulate that the disk drive will not work. Removing the cover of the computer and simply looking inside can determine if this is the problem. Gently blowing the dust out may be the solution.

References

Hardware (38), Utility Software (50), Product Registration (54)

NEXT TOPIC: Hard Drive Failure (33)

Forgetting basic DOS commands

See DOSSHELL — DOS 5.0 Menu (44)

Forgetting the colon

See A: B: C: — Drive Designation (7)

Forgetting to use the Shift key

See A: B: C: — Drive Designation (7)

FORMAT — Disks (12)

VERSIONS	
All	●
Some	○
5.0	○
Command	○
Program	●
Concept	○
Problem	○

New disks must be prepared for use before DOS can use them. The FORMAT program has a number of switches to accommodate a variety of drive and disk sizes. MS-DOS 5.0 is able to unformat a disk formatted with version 5.0. With other versions of DOS, all the existing data is lost with FORMAT.

Before You Begin

Default Drive (3)
A: B: C: — Drive Designation (7)

Syntax

`C:\>`**`FORMAT A:`**	Formats a disk in drive A:
`C:\>`**`FORMAT B:`**	Formats a disk in drive B:
`C:\>`**`FORMAT B: /T:80/N:9`**	Formats a 720K disk in a high-density 3 1/2-inch drive
`C:\>`**`FORMAT A: /4`**	Formats a 360K disk in a high-density 5 1/4-inch drive
`C:\>`**`FORMAT A: /S`**	Formats the disk and installs DOS (*s*ystem)

Problems

Excessive noise during formats, extremely long format time, and more than two bad tracks. These three conditions may suggest that you are trying to format a double-density disk as a high-density disk in a high-density disk drive. Because double-density and high-density 5 1/4-inch disks look identical, you might be trying to format a 360K disk in a high-density (1.2M) drive. Look for the letters HD on the label. If there is no label, assume that it is a 360K disk and use **`FORMAT A: /4`** (or B:). If a `Media type mismatch` message appears, you may have other problems with the drive. The hard, plastic 3 1/2-inch disks are easier to identify. They have two square holes in the upper corners of the disk. And they usually have the letters HD on the lower part of the disk. To format a 720K disk in a high-density (1.44M) drive, use **`FORMAT A: /T:80 /N:9`**.

First track unusable. A high-density disk cannot be formatted or used in a double-density drive. Use a standard double-density (360K) floppy disk.

`Drive not ready.` The disk drive sends DOS a signal that the drive door is not closed. DOS then responds with this error message and waits for corrective action. One or more of these actions should solve the problem:

1. Make sure that a disk is in the drive.
2. Check and close the drive door or latch.
3. Pull the disk out and reinsert it.
4. Examine the disk to make certain that the disk is spinning freely in the jacket.

`Bad command or file name.` If you type **`FORMAT A:`** and DOS responds with this message, the program is not in the current subdirectory. The quickest way to solve this problem is to CD (change directory) into the DOS subdirectory with the FORMAT program. The longer-term solution is to modify the PATH statement. See the topic PATH — Program Search (29).

DEF

Explanation

Floppy disks (topic 19) are totally blank when shipped from the manufacturer. (Some new disks are now preformatted as a convenience.) The FORMAT program marks this magnetic space with tracks and sectors. As it makes these markings, it reads and writes to each part of the disk. When FORMAT does this, it is testing to make sure that all parts of the disk are usable. If any unusable spots are found, FORMAT automatically marks them and will not try to use them later to write or read data.

Once a disk has been formatted, it does not need to be formatted again. The only reason to reformat a disk is to erase the directory information quickly, leaving the disk relatively blank. With the newer versions of DOS and with some third-party software, the data can be recovered. If the data is truly sensitive, use special programs that totally erase the disk.

The DOS FORMAT program has some optional switches. A *switch* gives special instructions to a command (see topic 34, Command and Program Parameters). The most common switches pertain to formatting double-density disks in high-density drives. Other useful switches include /V to place a volume label on the disk when you format it, and /S to copy the DOS operating system to that drive. Additional switches are listed later in this discussion.

If you routinely format the disks appropriate for your drive's capacity—for instance, a high-density (HD) disk in a high-density drive—the only form of this command that you'll need is **`FORMAT A:`** or **`FORMAT B:`**.

If you use mixed sizes of disks, you'll need to include some switches to tell FORMAT that you want a double-density format. For example, if you have a high-density 5 1/4-inch floppy drive, formatting a high-density disk in that drive provides 1.2M of space on that drive. You can use **`FORMAT A: /4`** to tell the FORMAT program to format the disk in the drive as a double-density 360K disk.

Or you may have a high-density 3 1/2-inch drive that normally formats disks to 1.44M. If someone else has a laptop or a system that can handle only 720K disks, you'll need to use **`FORMAT B: /T:80 /N:9`** to format the disk to that lower density. Then the disk can be used in both drives (with different capacities).

5

DOS 4.0 and 5.0 provide some additional switches:

/Q Performs a quick format

/U Performs an unconditional format

/B Allocates space for the operating system on the formatted disk

/N: Formats specified number of sectors per track

/T: Formats specified number of tracks per disk side

As always, your DOS manual contains a complete explanation of all the options and switches available with FORMAT. Once you determine the command line options you need to use, you might want to write the exact command in the margin on the first page of this topic.

Exercises

These two exercises show the process of formatting a disk. In the first exercise, the disk is new and must have a complete format. The second exercise shows DOS 5.0 users how to use the /Q switch for a quick format of a previously formatted disk.

Exercise 1 of 2

For this exercise, you need a new floppy disk or a previously formatted disk that does not have important files on it. You need to know whether it is a double-density disk or a high-density disk. If you are not sure, read the topic Floppy Disks (19).

Finally, you need to know your drive's capacity. If you have an XT (8088) system, you probably have a double-density drive. If your computer is an AT or a 386 system, you are likely to have a high-density drive. Use a high-density disk in the high-density drive.

TRY	NOTE

Insert the disk in drive A:.
`C:\>`**`FORMAT A:`**
`Insert new diskette for drive A:`
`Press ENTER when ready`
	Because the disk is already in the drive, just press Enter.

`<Enter>`
`Checking existing disk format.`
`Saving UNFORMAT information.`
`Verifying 1.2M`
`Format complete`
	The disk drive begins working. Depending on your version of DOS, you may see a progress report as the disk is formatted. (This is DOS 5.0.)

`Volume label (11 characters,` `ENTER for none)?` **`PARTY TIME`**	The newer versions of DOS request a volume label. Older versions request one if you include the /L switch on the command line.
Look at the screen.	FORMAT provides additional information relating to the disk capacity and outcome of the format operation. FORMAT then asks this next question.
`Format another (Y/N)?` **`N`**	In this case, you say *no* (N). If you have a box of new disks, you might want to format all of them now.
Attach a blank label to the disk.	To signify that the disk is formatted, you can attach a blank label. This step is optional.

Figure 12.1 shows the entire process of formatting a high-density disk. Remember that if you are using a lower-density disk in a high-density drive, you'll have to add one or more switches (see the "Syntax" section for the most common switches).

```
C:\>format a:
Insert new diskette for drive A:
and press ENTER when ready...

Checking existing disk format.
Saving UNFORMAT information.
Verifying 1.2M
Format complete.

Volume label (11 characters, ENTER for none)? PARTY TIME

   1213952 bytes total disk space
   1213952 bytes available on disk

       512 bytes in each allocation unit.
      2371 allocation units available on disk.

Volume Serial Number is 2D5D-12EC

Format another (Y/N)?n

C:\>
```

Figure 12-1. The entire process of formatting a high-density disk.

Exercise 2 of 2

5 Here DOS 5.0 users can use the /Q switch for a quick format. In this case, FORMAT does not read and write to all tracks on the disk, but just cleans out the directory. In that same process, FORMAT saves the information to a hidden file on the disk. This allows the UNFORMAT program to restore the directory. Because the actual data is not removed, the disk returns to its original form. See the topic UNFORMAT (86) for more information.

TRY	NOTE

Leave the preceding disk in drive A:.
`C:\>`**`FORMAT A: /Q`**
`Insert new diskette for drive A:`
`Press ENTER when ready`
`<Enter>`
	The disk drive begins working. Depending on your version of DOS you may see a progress report as the disk is quick-formatted.

```
Volume label (11 characters,
ENTER for none)? PARTY TIME
```

With a quick format, DOS still requests a volume label.

The rest of the steps are the same as those for a normal format. Figure 12-2 shows the result of the /Q switch.

```
C:\>format a:/q
Insert new diskette for drive A:
and press ENTER when ready...

Checking existing disk format.
Saving UNFORMAT information.
QuickFormatting 1.2M
Format complete.

Volume label (11 characters, ENTER for none)? PARTY TIME

   1213952 bytes total disk space
   1213952 bytes available on disk

       512 bytes in each allocation unit.
      2371 allocation units available on disk.

Volume Serial Number is 3D0D-12EF

QuickFormat another (Y/N)?n


C:\>
```

Figure 12-2. The result of using FORMAT /Q in DOS 5.0.

References

Floppy Disks (19), UNFORMAT (86)

NEXT TOPIC: Backing Up Data (13)

Frequent headaches and muscle tension

See Workspace — User Comfort (85)

Gather your patience

See Solving Problems (14)

General failure

See Hard Drive Failure (33)

Generic and specific paths

See PATH — Program Search (29)

GRAPHICS — Printing Screens (66)

VERSIONS
All ○
Some ●
5.0 ○

Command ○
Program ●
Concept ○
Problem ○

The DOS GRAPHICS program allows graphic images to be printed as they appear on the screen. Once the GRAPHICS program has been loaded, pressing Shift-Print Screen prints the image. DOS versions vary greatly in how well this program works.

Before You Begin

Printers (15)
Monitor (61)

Syntax

```
C:\>GRAPHICS
<Shift><Print Screen>
```

Pressing Shift-Print Screen produces on your printer a graphic image with black letters on a white background.

```
C:\>GRAPHICS /R
<Shift><Print Screen>
```

Now you get a reversed graphic image (one that matches the screen) on the printer.

5

```
C:\>GRAPHICS LASERJET
```

DOS 5.0 users can specify the printer type.

Problems

Garbage prints after you press Shift-Print Screen. If the screen is in graphics mode, you need to run GRAPHICS to get the proper image. Load the GRAPHICS program. Or, if you're using DOS 5.0, you may not have specified the proper printer. Remember that EGA and VGA screens will not work with older versions of DOS. Try to load GRAPHICS again. If the program is already loaded, you may have other printer problems.

Printer ejects pages continuously. If you try to use the Shift-Print Screen keys to print the image on the screen without GRAPHICS loaded, the printer may eject pages continuously. You may be able to turn the printer off. Wait a second and turn it back on. Try this a few times to clear the printer buffer. You'll have to turn the printer off when the printer stops printing. Line the page up with the top of the printhead and turn the printer back on.

Explanation

The Shift-Print Screen key combination instructs DOS to send to the printer the characters that are on the screen. As long as the screen is in text mode, there is no problem. When the screen is in graphics mode, the signal becomes more complicated. This is the time that GRAPHICS can help. Instead of trying to duplicate the characters on the screen as printer output, the GRAPHICS program reads each dot on the screen and sends the signals to the printer so that those dots are duplicated. Because the images (including any letters) are usually white on black, GRAPHICS reverses the image so that it appears black on white.

The older versions of DOS performed this screen dump in CGA mode only. At the time, this graphics screen was the only type available. Newer systems with EGA or VGA screens will not work with the GRAPHICS program. DOS 5.0 is able to use EGA and VGA screen images to send to the printer.

Until DOS 5.0, GRAPHICS would work only if an IBM or Epson graphics printer was attached to the computer. The program had the special codes required just for those printers. DOS 5.0 supports a number of printers listed in a special file named GRAPHICS.PRO. You can view this ASCII file to see all the printers supported. Because DOS versions differ greatly, the DOS manual will be your best source for more information about GRAPHICS.

If you are interested in printing high-quality graphics, consider using one of the many graphics programs now available. You will be able to view, change, and print better images than you can get by dumping images to the printer with the GRAPHICS program.

Exercise

The GRAPHICS program has so many variables that you'll have to explore the possibilities on your own. To see the basic result, just type **GRAPHICS**. Load a program that displays a graphic image of some sort and then press Shift-Print Screen to see what the image looks like on the printer.

5

A DOS 5.0 user can examine the GRAPHICS.PRO file to see whether a specific printer is listed. Typing **GRAPHICS printername** can produce fairly good images on the printer.

References

Printers (15)

NEXT TOPIC: Bytes and Computer Math (67)

GUI — Graphical user interface

See Interfaces (27)

Hard disk access speed

See FASTOPEN — Speeding Up Disks (70)

Hard disk size or remaining space unknown

See CHKDSK — CHecK DiSK (20)

Hard Drive Failure (33)

VERSIONS	
All	●
Some	○
5.0	○
Command	○
Program	○
Concept	○
Problem	●

Disk drives contain the magnetic media for storing data files and program files. A hard disk is built into the drive to provide high-storage capacity and fast access. The hard disk is located inside the computer and cannot be removed on most systems. When the drive fails, all the data is lost on that disk. The terms *hard disk* and *hard drive* are generally interchangeable. Hard drives are also called fixed disks and Winchester drives.

Before You Begin

Boot/Startup (1)
Files (2)

Problem

Hard drive (disk) failure. Hard drives are more critical than floppy drives. A hard drive contains 30 to 300 times more data than a single floppy. If the drive fails, all the data on that drive is lost. (Some services can recover portions of the data but at a considerable expense.) Maintaining a regular schedule of backing up files on the hard disk is extremely important.

Explanation

Because the hard drive contains the magnetic media for storing hundreds or thousands of files, failure of the drive means loss of all that data. Recognizing the impending failure of a hard drive and backing up all the files can prevent the loss of important files. For more information on backing up files, refer to the topic Backing Up Data (13). Once the hard drive has failed, there is nothing you can do to recover the data. Symptoms leading to failure, in reverse significance, include the following:

1. If the DOS messages `Seek error drive C:` or `Disk read error` occurs more than once a week, begin backing up files daily.

2. If the normal whine of the drive becomes lower in pitch and then returns to normal, the bearings or motor may be wearing out. If this occurs several times a day, get out the backup disks and get busy.

3. If the amount of time required for the disk to load files or save data increases noticeably, load several other programs. If they also take longer to load, a serious problem with the hard disk may be developing.

4. When you cold-boot the computer, if the system returns a `Hard disk failure` message or the number 1701 in the upper left corner, turn the system off. Wait 10 seconds and then turn it back on. If the system does boot, the next task is to back up the entire disk. If the message returns again, try at least two more times. If the computer still does not boot by the fifth attempt, the hard disk has failed. Locate your most recent set of backup disks and hope that they are recent.

5. If your hard disk drive does fail and you have no backup disks, there are some companies that can *attempt* to recover the data from the hard disk. This process is likely to cost hundreds of dollars and take two or more

weeks. Contact a local computer store to locate this kind of service. If you cannot afford this recovery, you'll have to use your original program disks to begin to reconstruct your system on a new hard drive. The data files you've created are gone.

Floppy drives and hard drives operate by spinning a disk with magnetic material between brackets (heads) that can read the signal on the disk. A more technical explanation could include *access speed* and *head seek tolerance*. The important information relates to the care of disk drives. Proper care of floppy disks is covered in Floppy Disks (19).

Hard disk drives are self-contained. Also called *fixed disks*, they are located inside the computer, and most types cannot be removed. They contain large amounts of data that can be accessed quickly because the hard disk containing the magnetic material spins very fast. To read the data, the heads move back and forth across the disk, but they do not actually touch the disk surface. The heads ride on a small wave of air created by the high speed of the spinning disk.

Understanding *how* the hard drive works is important to ensuring *that* it works properly. Whenever the computer is on, the hard disk is spinning and the heads are "flying" over the surface, reading and writing data. A movement of the computer or a sudden blow to it may cause the head to *crash* into the spinning disk. The drive is likely to fail completely or at least lose data where the surface has been scratched by the head. As noted before, any data on a hard disk is lost when the drive fails.

> Take steps to prevent a hard disk crash and loss of data!

To prevent your hard disk from crashing, keep the following suggestions in mind:

- Don't ever move the computer, even an inch, while it is running. Turn it off when you must move it.
- Keep the main part of the computer on a sturdy table or desk. If you can wiggle the table at all, that movement can easily cause a head crash.
- Make sure that all cables to the computer are completely tucked out of the way. Some of the cables may be firmly attached in back. If someone tugs on one of the cables or trips over a cable, the accident could jerk the computer violently and prove fatal for the hard drive.
- Don't stack heavy books or other objects where they could fall on the computer.
- Always perform a complete backup of the data on the hard disk before you move the computer.

- Because a hard disk constantly spins when the computer is on, the hard disk does wear out. Although the average time before a failure occurs is increasing with newer computers (hard disks now last longer), a user of an older hard disk should be careful to back up the data frequently if the system has been in use for more than one year.

- Always "park" the heads before moving the computer more than a few feet. Even when the computer is turned off, some hard drives may suffer damage if the heads have not been moved to a safe location on the disk platter. Most drive manufacturers provide a program called PARK.COM, PARK.EXE, or SHIPDISK.COM, which moves the heads to the landing zone on the disk to prevent damage if the computer is bumped. When you run PARK, you get a message to turn off the computer immediately. The heads will be left in the proper location so that the computer can be moved.

- When you move the computer, if you drop it even an inch, you should suspect hard disk damage. Run a hard disk diagnostic program to check the surface of the disk, or watch for any unusual error messages concerning disk access. Popular programs include Spinrite, Norton Utilities, Mace Utilities, and PC Tools.

- If a computer comes in from the cold, let the system warm up to room temperature for 24 hours. Contraction from the cold is enough to change the tight tolerances within the drive. Let the system return to room-temperature operating conditions before doing anything with it.

Standing a computer with a hard disk on its side has caused some concern. With the computer on the table top, the disk spins horizontally, like a vinyl record. With the computer on its side, the disk spins vertically, and the heads are pulled sideways by gravity.

Experience shows that thousands of computers positioned on their sides can work properly. Hard drive manufacturers indicate that the drives can tolerate any position unless the computer is resting on its back. Because the cables are located in the back, that position is very inconvenient for the cables as well as the hard disk.

Some problems have been reported with systems used on their sides for several years and then placed in upright positions. The theory is that the drive mechanism had "settled" in the first position but got out of alignment when the drive was repositioned. The drive cannot read data in the new position but can return to reading data in the old position. Reformatting the drive in the new position may correct this problem.

References

Backing Up Data (13), Floppy Disks (19), Disk Damaged (36), BACKUP — Files (41), Utility Software (50), Product Registration (54), System Maintenance (94)

NEXT TOPIC: Command and Program Parameters (34)

Hardware (38)

VERSIONS	
All	●
Some	○
5.0	○
Command	○
Program	○
Concept	●
Problem	○

Hardware is the physical part of the computer system, made of metal, plastic, and glass. Hardware is one of the three areas in which problems can develop. The other two are software and the user.

Problem

Computer won't work. When something goes wrong with a computer system, it may be difficult to determine whether the problem is related to the hardware, the software, or the user. You may need to enlist the help of a repair technician. Depending on how much the technician knows, he or she may attribute the problem to the user, which the technician knows the least about. Determine that the technician has performed at least some basic diagnostic tests. Ask exactly what could cause the problem and the best way to fix it. Get a second opinion if you have the time, especially if the proposed solution is expensive.

Explanation

The physical part of the computer system, the hardware, needs the same amount of care you would provide to a stereo system. The following are guidelines for the care of any computer system:

- Keep all liquids away from the keyboard, monitor, and main system box. Do not set coffee cups and soft drink cans anywhere near the system. Liquid spilled in a system will destroy it and may create a fire hazard.
- Keep the system well ventilated, especially in the back. Most systems have a fan to cool the interior. If the vent is blocked, the system may overheat. Don't stack books on the monitor or system box. Keep the computer out of direct sunlight.
- If the room temperature is uncomfortable for the user, the system should not be used. If the room is too cold, the hard disk may not read and write properly. If the room is too hot, the system may overheat and cause erratic problems.

- Remove the cover at least once a year and blow out the dust. If the environment is extremely dusty, you may need to do this more often. Dust can affect the cooling of the chips and may prevent the floppy drive from performing properly.
- Secure all cables to eliminate the possibility that someone may accidentally pull one out. Many cables include clips or screws for a secure connection.
- A system with a hard drive should never be bumped or moved while the system is running. Read the topic Hard Drive Failure (33) for more information.
- A dust cover placed nightly over both the keyboard and the monitor can help reduce dust accumulation.

References

Software (18), Ports (40), Manuals and Documentation (53), Product Registration (54), Modems (56), Monitor (61), System Maintenance (94), Security (95)

NEXT TOPIC: Keyboard (39)

Hardware and Software Compatibility (72)

VERSIONS	
All	●
Some	○
5.0	○
Command	○
Program	○
Concept	●
Problem	○

MS-DOS systems are made by dozens of manufacturers. Although there used to be concerns about how well a computer actually runs MS-DOS software, the concern now is whether the programs that users want to run will work at all on their systems. With so much diversity among systems, compatibility between hardware and software has become a complicated issue.

Before You Begin

Hardware (38)

Problems

Incompatible processors. A more powerful processor can run software intended for older systems. But some programs require newer processors. You need to know what kind of computer you have before buying software. Check the box or ask the sales representative what the *minimum system configuration* is for that software (the least powerful computer that will run the program). Then ask for an optimal system. Software that states an AT level system as a minimum may work well only on a 386SX or faster system. See the topic Microprocessors (96) for more information.

Incompatible displays. In addition to the power "under the hood," the next biggest problem is the display. There used to be two types of displays, one for clean text and one for poor text and graphics. Now a number of displays are available. You might have an EGA display yet want to use a program that requires a VGA display. But as VGA displays become more specialized, programs will require Super VGA and beyond. A program might run, although poorly, on a system with less power, but if a VGA screen is required, the program won't run at all on an EGA or CGA monitor. Refer also to the topic Monitor (61).

Explanation

The old test of hardware and software compatibility on PC or XT systems was to see whether you could run Microsoft Flight Simulator or Lotus 1-2-3. Any problems of compatibility among DOS systems were pretty much resolved in the mid-1980s.

At the heart of the compatibility issue was the main microprocessor chip originally based on the 8088 family of chips designed by Intel. Other companies were able to design chips that did exactly the same thing without violating the Intel copyright. The first versions were close but not always exact functional copies of the originals. This is what caused compatibility problems, eventually resolved by better design and testing.

References

New Programs on Old Computers (71)

NEXT TOPIC: Memory (73)

Higher-capacity disks

See Floppy Disks (19)

History of DOS (88)

VERSIONS
All ●
Some ○
5.0 ○

Command ○
Program ○
Concept ●
Problem ○

This topic provides a small history lesson about DOS. Just as you can drive a car without knowing who Henry Ford was, you can use DOS without knowing who Bill Gates is. But it is kind of interesting to know.

Explanation

DOS—or more formally, MS-DOS—was first originated in July, 1980. IBM, working on a secret project to develop a personal computer, contacted Bill Gates at Microsoft. At that time, Microsoft was known for its version of BASIC. IBM first approached Gates about writing a version of BASIC for a new 16-bit system. When the IBMers mentioned that they were also looking for an operating system, Gates and company jumped at the chance to develop what would become PC DOS.

Bill Gates found someone who had already written most of an operating system for the new 8088 microprocessors. He struck a deal with the programmer and then marketed the finished version to IBM. Microsoft supplied both DOS 1.0 and BASIC to IBM for its new IBM PC.

Initially DOS was called PC DOS. As a shrewd businessman, Gates obtained the rights to market DOS to other computer manufacturers. These versions were typically named to correspond with the manufacturers' system names. In time, all of these versions were recognized as MS-DOS.

Version 1.0 was originally released with the new IBM PC in 1981. In 1982, version 1.1 added the capacity for double-sided floppy disk drives. In 1983, version 2.0 was released to support the newly released IBM XT. Because that system included a hard disk, the operating system had to support subdirectories.

Version 3.0, released in 1984, supported networked systems. Each increment in versions 3.0 to 3.1, 3.2, and 3.3 added to the networking capabilities. Additional utilities were also provided, including FASTOPEN, XCOPY, and finally in version 3.3, support for 1.4M 3 1/2-inch floppy disk drives.

By 1988, hard drive storage capacity had exceeded DOS's capability to keep track of the data. Version 4.0 was introduced to allow *partitions* (sections of the hard disk) to be larger than 32 megabytes. This version also introduced the DOS Shell, a program that puts many of the DOS commands on a menu. And DOS 4.0 began to recognize the additional memory available on 80286 systems (and later).

5

MS-DOS 5.0, released in mid-1991, adds many new features, including a very functional Shell and advanced memory management. Several new utility programs include UNDELETE, UNFORMAT, and MIRROR. These programs, originally written by Central Point Software, help prevent data loss. Additional features include EDIT, QBASIC, and help for all DOS commands and programs. The capability to recall and edit previous commands is provided by DOSKEY.

Although MS-DOS appears to be the "standard" operating system, others are available for systems based on the 80x86 Intel microprocessor. Some are completely compatible with DOS, including Digital Research's DR-DOS 5.0. Others, like OS/2 and UNIX, require programs written specifically for those operating systems.

References

Learning More (28), Operating Systems (75)

NEXT TOPIC: FAT — Fat Allocation Table (89)

Identifying a file's format

See Data File Formats (52)

Illegal characters in a file name

See File Names (4)

Illegal program copies

See Copyright (51)
See also Product Registration (54)
See also No One to Help (59)

Inaccessible features in software

See New Programs on Old Computers (71)

Inaccurate records

See Databases (49)

Inaccurate results

See Spreadsheets (48)

Incompatible displays

See Hardware and Software Compatibility (72)

Incompatible processors

See Hardware and Software Compatibility (72)

Inconsistent program commands

See Interfaces (27)

Inconsistent use of subdirectories

See File Organization (17)

Incorrect DOS version

See History of DOS (88)

Individual records lost

See Databases (49)

Insert diskette for drive x:

See Floppy Drive Failure (32)

Installing Programs (60)

VERSIONS	
All	●
Some	○
5.0	○
Command	○
Program	○
Concept	●
Problem	○

Many programs must be installed on a hard disk before they will run. Installation includes copying the files to the proper subdirectory and telling the program what the default settings should be.

Before You Begin

Files (2)
DIR — Directory (8)
CD, MD, and RD — Working with Directories (9)

Syntax

Installation programs with purchased software do not have a consistent name. Some companies are standardizing the program name SETUP or INSTALL. The syntax presented here shows how these programs might work.

```
C:\>A:SETUP C:\NEWDIR
```

This runs SETUP on A: and tells it to put the new program in C:\NEWDIR.

```
C:\>A:
A:\>INSTALL
```

Some programs can run only from the floppy in A: and may require moving to that drive first.

Problems

Not enough room on the hard drive. Even though a program comes on two 360K disks, the installed version may require more than just 360K + 360K on the hard disk. Many programs are compressed on the original disks and are expanded when installed. Check the program documentation for an estimate of the final size. It is not unusual for programs to double or triple in size when uncompressed.

Some installation programs check the amount of free space on the hard disk before the installation. If there is not enough space, they provide a warning and quit. Other installation programs do not check. You may be almost finished, and the installation program suddenly locks up. The disk is out of space, and the installation program does not know what to do about it. You'll have to reboot and reinstall the software after erasing files from other areas of the disk.

Previous versions overwritten. Some programs locate previous versions and overwrite those old files. This is likely to happen if you use the default path suggested by the installation program. Some installation programs will at least ask whether you want to overwrite those files. If you have enough space on the hard disk, do *not* overwrite the files. The default settings you may have worked so hard to perfect can be lost when the installation program copies the new files over the old files.

Program won't run from the original disks. Unless a program specifically says that it will run from the original floppy disks, it may need to be installed, even on another floppy disk. Running a program from the original disks is not a good idea because the original files might be changed as you run the program. Then you would not have an original backup copy of the program.

Unknown changes made to AUTOEXEC.BAT and CONFIG.SYS. Some installation programs "look at" and make changes to these critical system files. Most programs ask permission, but some do not. Keeping a copy of CONFIG.SYS and AUTOEXEC.BAT in the DOS subdirectory is a good idea for this reason as well as others.

Other programs will not run. If other programs will not run after you have installed a new program, check the AUTOEXEC.BAT and CONFIG.SYS files. They may be missing or have additional lines that affect the other programs.

Explanation

Unless otherwise instructed, you should always use a write-protect tab or move the metal slider on the original disks before installing a new program. This prevents the disk from being accidentally changed. Some installation disks cannot be written on because they do not have an open notch or hole in the disk.

Purchased programs come with installation programs for at least three reasons: (1) the programs can be provided on fewer disks, (2) you can choose how much of the program to install (how much space to use) on the hard disk, and (3) you know what the initial defaults will be even before you run the program the first time.

Newer programs with dozens of advanced features have their price. They require more powerful computers and more disk space. The sizes of the programs can translate into over a dozen disks. But if the programs are compressed on the original disks, the number of disks can often be reduced by half. One of the installation program's purposes is to expand those files into usable programs and data on the hard disk.

Because the programs that you purchase can require so much space when expanded, you may not want to copy all the files that come with these programs. A checklist of files is usually provided at the beginning of the program, with a running total of the bytes required to include those files. The "extras" may include sample files and tutorials. In some cases, they include a complete set of fonts. The installation program and manual should give suggestions on which files you actually need on the disk. As a novice, you may want to run the tutorial and use the sample files to explore the program. If you are upgrading from a previous version, you'll probably want to save disk space and decline to install those files on the hard disk.

Most programs have *defaults* settings, which are used unless you change them. These settings include, for example, the type of printer and printer port to use. Although the settings may not prevent the program from running initially, other settings, such as screen type and work drive, can keep the program from working properly, even the first time you try to run it. By making the appropriate choices during installation, you should be able to run the program the first time you use it. Some programs don't include menu choices to make changes to the default settings. In those cases, you may need to rerun the installation program to reset the defaults.

References

Program Versions (47), Copyright (51)

NEXT TOPIC: Monitor (61)

Insufficient disk space

See Disk Full (35)

Insufficient memory

See Memory (73)

Intentional reboot or power down

See CHKDSK — CHecK DiSK (20)

Interfaces (27)

VERSIONS	
All	●
Some	○
5.0	○
Command	○
Program	○
Concept	●
Problem	○

Technically an *interface* (also called a *port*) is the connection between electronic devices. The term *interface* is used also to refer to the way the software "communicates" with the user. This topic covers the command line, menu, and pull-down interfaces, as well as the newer GUI (graphical *u*ser *i*nterface).

Problems

Inconsistent program commands. Many programs have a unique series of steps for performing specific tasks. The problem is that you can learn one program's method of saving a file—for example, pressing Alt-F and then S. But another program might use a completely different set of keystrokes, such as Ctrl-S. Interface conventions create a consistent way for users to perform the same basic tasks. Companies are now creating some consistent conventions, such as pressing F1 for on-screen help. Even more consistency is available in the Windows environment.

Difficulty in tracking your position in the program. To accomplish any task with software requires a series of steps. These steps represent a number of choices you make toward completing the task. An effective system shows you each step as you complete it and allows you to return to the preceding step. If the interface does not show your progress, only time and experience will help you remember which steps you have completed and which steps you still need to take.

Speed versus ease of use. Much debate has taken place over the speed of a program's interface versus its ease of use. Often the choice is simply one of personal preference. Commands used frequently can be easily remembered and typed for quick results. Actions performed infrequently are likely to be quicker if the choices appear on menus on the screen. Even though using a menu may take several steps, it is generally more efficient than remembering infrequently used commands.

Explanation

The program-to-user interface is accomplished in several ways. When a user needs to signal a choice or enter some data, the system must provide some indication that a response is needed. In most cases, this indication is a prompt on the screen, or a sound, such as a beep. The user responds by pressing keys or moving a mouse. Another alternative is a voice command, although it's not commonly used yet.

There are several methods by which the user can be prompted on the screen: a command line, a menu system, a pull-down system, and a GUI (graphical user interface). With the first method, the user must respond with the keyboard. With the other three methods, the user can usually respond with the keyboard or the mouse. The oldest and most difficult method is the *command line*. The command line program provides no additional information on the screen, so the user must know what to type.

A *menu system* typically uses the keyboard for input, with the possible choices listed on the screen. The user can just press a character or number that corresponds to a choice on the menu. In some cases, the mouse pointer also works.

A *pull-down system* is a menu system whose main choices are presented across the top of the screen. Only when a choice is made do additional choices become evident in a box which "pulls down" from that choice.

A *graphical user interface*, abbreviated GUI and pronounced GOOey, is the most recent and, some say, the most sophisticated way to communicate with a computer system. The images are likely to be pictures, called *icons*, which can be manipulated easily with a mouse or another pointing device.

Command Line

The standard DOS interface is a command line. The user must know exactly what to do or type in order to control the system. The burden is on the user to remember all the possible ways to control the system. A command line is arguably the quickest interface to use. In most cases, the command and any switches are on one line and initiate the required action.

Knowing how to use a command line interface can be compared to driving a car. You have to remember which control to use and how much to use it so that you can move the car, head the car in the right direction, and stop the car. Once you learn these fundamentals, they become second nature. Because you don't need to think about how to issue commands at the command prompt, you can concentrate on the task at hand: getting from point A to point B.

Menu Choices

With a menu-based interface, the choices are presented on the screen. Most application programs are designed with menu choices. A program provides a screenful of choices, and after you make your selections, performs an action. Some menu systems show the choices and the work area on the same screen. Figure 27-1 shows a sample menu screen from PC-File 5.0, a database program.

Some menu systems are *shallow*. They do not require many choices to achieve the result you want. A shallow menu system may be just a simple program or may present many choices on one menu screen. A *deep* menu system lists only a few choices at each step but may require that you make five or more choices before reaching a final result. Such a system provides less confusion initially but requires more keystrokes to get the work done. Once you become familiar with the sequence of keystrokes to accomplish certain tasks, you can use a deep menu system efficiently.

Making choices from a shallow menu system or a deep menu system can be compared to making choices from a fast-food menu or a menu at a nice restaurant. A fast-food menu provides many choices right at the beginning. Once you have selected from the list, you have no further options. At a nice restaurant, you may have fewer initial selections, but once you have decided on the entree, you can specify how it will be cooked, the vegetables, and the dressing for your salad. Each of these choices represents another menu of choices: broiled, baked, or blackened; corn, potatoes, asparagus, or green beans; and Thousand Island, French, or Blue Cheese. Then, if you select the potatoes, you can have them fried, mashed, or. . . .

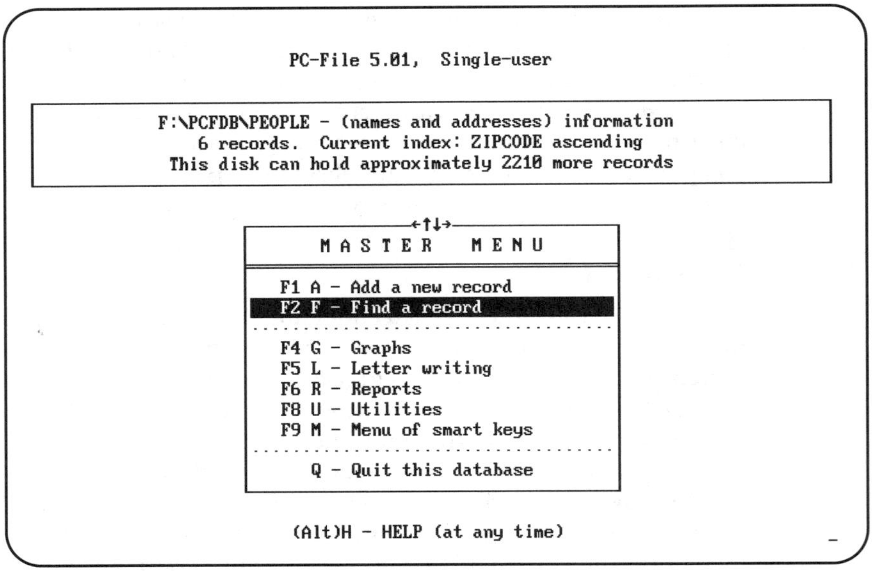

Figure 27-1. A menu screen from PC-File 5.0.

Pull-Down Menus

Pull-down menus have become popular because they allow a large part of the screen to be used as a work surface while providing quick access to menu choices. This type of menu system is illustrated in Figure 27-2, which shows a screen from the FoxPro database program. You can still see most of the screen even after the main menu choice has been made.

Pull-down menu systems provide a window-like response. They also lend themselves to use of a mouse. You place the mouse pointer on the menu bar at the top and then click. The pull-down menu appears. Point to a menu choice and click again. The action (of that choice) is taken with just two small moves and two clicks.

Most GUIs include pull-down choices. The difference between a pull-down system and a GUI is that the pull-down menu is not based on icons but relies instead on pressing keys or clicking on words.

Graphical User Interface (GUI)

A graphical user interface (GUI) is also a menu system. You make selections based on choices presented on the screen. The notable examples are the Macintosh interface and Windows for DOS. There are several differences between a generic, character-based menu system and a graphical one. Figure 27-3 shows a GUI from Windows 3.0.

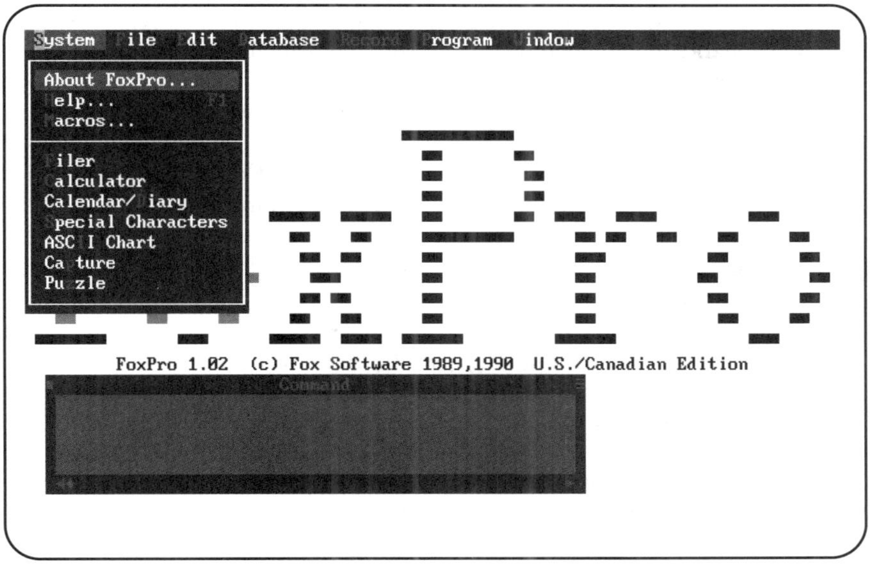

Figure 27-2. A menu screen from the FoxPro database program.

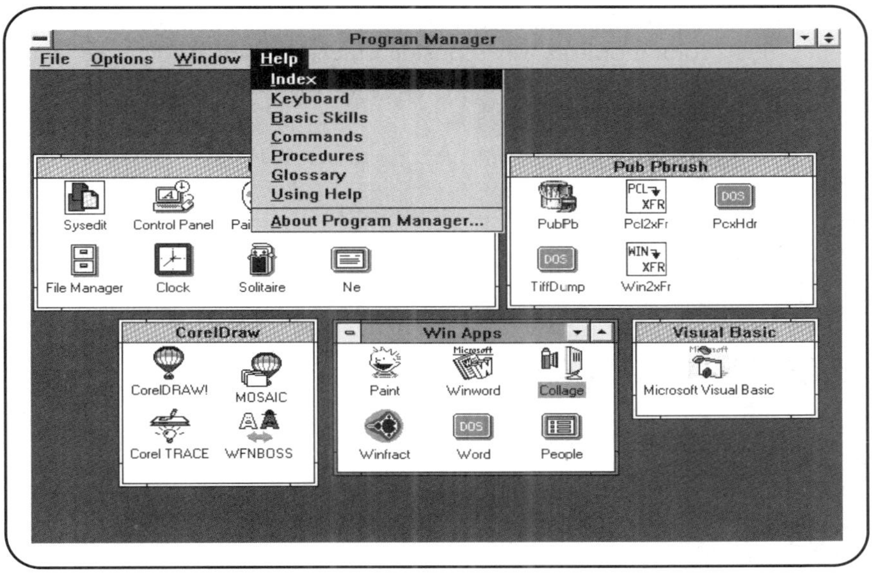

Figure 27-3. An example of a GUI interface from Windows 3.0.

Because the GUI can present pictures as well as words, the user may understand more easily the meanings behind the choices. The image of a trash can represents the action of throwing away files. A disk drive is represented by the image of a floppy disk. The passage of time (which means a delay in processing) is indicated by an hour glass.

With the GUI, you can make your selections with a pointing device. In most cases, this is a mouse or a trackball. Depending on the hardware, the pointing device can also be a light pen or a touch-sensitive screen, both of which require physical contact with the screen. This method of interaction does not rely on typing speed for quick results.

But the GUI goes beyond images (icons) and pointing. When all the programs that run under the GUI use the same icons and menu choices, the user knows immediately how to perform basic tasks in any of those programs. Add to this the capability of exchanging data between programs, and the GUI begins to look even better.

There are disadvantages to the GUI as well. The monitor must be able to display many small images easily. The system must have enough power to move all those images and control the programs associated with those images. A mouse or another pointing device is essential in getting the most out of the interface. If you don't have the appropriate hardware, software, and peripherals, a GUI may not be the best interface for your system.

Whether users like it or not, the GUI appears to be the wave of the future. Just as color monitors were considered extravagant 10 years ago, a non-GUI system will probably seem primitive in less than five years.

References

DOSSHELL — DOS 5.0 Menu (44)

NEXT TOPIC: Learning More (28)

Invalid COMMAND.COM

See COMMAND.COM/EXIT (78)

Invalid directory

See PATH — Program Search (29)

Invalid drive in path name

See PATH — Program Search (29)

Invalid drive specification

See A: B: C: — Drive Designation (7)

Invalid parameter — x:

See SUBST (58)

Invalid parameter(s)

See Command and Program Parameters (34)

Invalid path

See CD, MD, and RD — Working with Directories (9)

Invalid switch

See Command and Program Parameters (34)

Irregular backups

See Backing Up Data (13)

Keeping track of the current version

See Program Versions (47)

Key pressed but nothing happens

See `Strike a key when ready...` (16)

Keyboard (39)

VERSIONS	
All	●
Some	○
5.0	○
Command	○
Program	○
Concept	●
Problem	○

The keyboard is the standard device for giving instructions to the computer. The alphabetic keys are the same as on a typewriter. A computer keyboard, however, has additional keys that perform many functions.

Problems

Key locations vary. Even though the letter keys and number keys are arranged as they are on a typewriter, some key locations are not standardized. Each computer manufacturer places keys in different locations, depending on the perceived usefulness of the key and the location. Some keyboards have removable keys and software that tells the computer which keys stand for which letters. Once you have spent a few days on a keyboard, you can usually adjust to its key locations. If you use many different computer systems, you may have to study each keyboard for a few moments to locate the different keys.

Dirty keyboard. Even a careful user's keyboard will begin to collect dust and grime. These can make the keys sticky and may affect the key contacts. You can blow out dust by inverting the keyboard and using pressurized air or lung power. The grime presents a difficult problem. Try a semimoist cloth with a mild cleaner on the tops of the keys. Cotton swabs with cleaner can be used for the the sides of the keys. Do not allow the cleaner to drip into the keyboard. If the keys are very dirty, you can remove them and soak them in cleaner. You may want to put the keyboard face down on the copy machine first so that you'll know where the keys go. Check carefully to make sure that the keys can be removed and replaced without damage before you remove them.

Keyboard feels strange. How a keyboard feels is important to some typists. Some prefer a "clicky" feel, and others like a soft touch. Because keyboards on DOS-compatible systems are interchangeable, you can usually find a keyboard you like, which you can then use with any system. The old XT systems have a different keyboard. Most of the manufacturers provide a switch for XT or AT on the bottom of the keyboard. AT works with all the newer computers.

Low typing speed. One of the frustrations of using a computer has to do with typing proficiency. Nontypists are at a disadvantage when learning how to use the computer. Because so much of the learning is trial and error, a slow typist simply does not have the chance to try as many things out. A number of computer programs are available to help you learn the keyboard and improve your typing speed. The best advice to high-school students who are worried about learning to use the computer is to *learn to type*.

Explanation

A keyboard represents a series of switches to the computer. Some of the switches always produce the same result. For example, when you press the A key, the computer code for the lowercase letter *a* is transmitted to the software. (DOS is responsible for this transaction.) Some keys, when used with other keys, can produce different results. If you press the Shift key and the A key together, the transmitted letter is a capital A.

The computer can handle thousands of switches. The newer keyboards have 101 or more keys. There are special keys for paging up, paging down, going "home," and getting to the end. One key is labeled Insert, and another is labeled Esc (for escape). Other keys are simply labeled F1 through F10 or F12. The purpose of these *function keys* is not as obvious as that of the A key. To make matters even more confusing, each program can define what a special key does when pressed. In some word processing programs, the Home key moves the cursor to the top of the screen. In others, the Home key sends the cursor to the left of the current line.

In addition to all the different keys, there are key sequences, key toggles, and key combinations. You use key sequences all the time. A *key sequence* is a series of two or more keystrokes in which each key is pressed and released, in turn, one at a time. Typing the words in this book required many key sequences.

A *key toggle* switches back and forth from one condition, or mode, to another. The first time you press the key, the toggle is "on." Examples of toggle keys are the Caps Lock, Num Lock, and Scroll Lock keys. Newer keyboards include lights for these keys. When each key is toggled, the light is on. Press the key again, and the light goes out.

A *key combination* is two (or more) keys that must be pressed together. How you press the keys is important in achieving the effect you want. You must press and hold down the first key while you then press the second key. For instance, to get a capital A, you must first press and hold down the Shift key and then press the A key. Another example, Ctrl-Alt-Del, requires that you press and hold down the Ctrl and Alt keys while you then press Del. Combinations are always required with the Ctrl (Control) and Alt (Alternate) keys. Like the Shift key, these keys do nothing by themselves. But when used with other keys, they can supply many keyboard actions. In fact, if you use the Ctrl key with each of the other keys on the keyboard, you've just doubled the possible combinations. Do the same thing with the Alt key, and the possibilities have increased again.

You can use the special keys (such as Shift, Ctrl, and Alt) with the function keys as well. The computer keyboard has 10 or 12 function keys, labelled F1 through F10 or F12. Using each of these with the Shift, Ctrl, and Alt keys increases the number of possibilities to 40 or 48 special functions.

The most important point about key combinations is that you press the special key (or keys) first, leave your finger on it, and then press the second (or third) key. The odds are against you if you try to press both keys at exactly the same time. The difference in key contact may seem insignificant to you, but to the computer, which measures time in *nano seconds* (billionths of a second), there is a big difference.

DOS programs use a number of special keys and key combinations. Table 39-1 shows some examples.

Table 39-1. Some DOS keys, key combinations, and their results.

Key(s)	Result
Ctrl-Alt-Del	Reboots the computer
Esc	Frequently reverses the last action and may also terminate or interrupt a program
Ctrl-C	May terminate a program
Ctrl-Break	May terminate a program
Shift-Print Screen	Copies contents of the screen to the printer
Ctrl-Print Screen	Echoes each DOS command and result to the printer
F3	Repeats the last DOS command line
F6	Inserts an end-of-file character (Ctrl-Z)
Ctrl-Z	Inserts an end-of-file character
F1	Frequently provides HELP in programs

References

Hardware (38), System Maintenance (94)

NEXT TOPIC: Ports (40)

Keyboard feel

See Keyboard (39)

Label stuck in printer

See Labels in Printer (69)

Labels in Printer (69)

VERSIONS
All ●
Some ○
5.0 ○

Command ○
Program ○
Concept ○
Problem ●

Self-adhesive mailing labels require special programs to print and extra care to use in the printer. Mailing labels for laser printers require a program that can print on the special label sheets designed for laser printers.

Before You Begin

Printers (15)
Paper in Printer (68)

Problems

Label stuck in printer. This is the most common problem associated with self-adhesive, continuous-form labels. The paper path in continuous-feed printers is made to move paper only one way. Attempting to save a few blank labels by backing the labels out of the printer is likely to roll a label off inside the printer. Because this point is so important, here is it again:

> Do *not* attempt to roll continuous-form labels backward out of the printer. Tear them off behind the paper-feed tray and roll the remaining few forward out of the paper path.

Determining label capacity. Although labels come in different sizes, most programs can use standard sizes. A fairly standard label is 15/16 of an inch tall and 3 1/2 inches long. If your printer is printing 6 lines per inch and 10 characters per inch (horizontally), this label will print 5 lines of 35 characters each. This is the capacity of that label. But if the printer is set for 8 lines per inch and 16 characters per inch, the label has a different capacity. The label capacity is determined by the printer, printer settings, and software being used. Check the software documentation for the label sizes supported by that software. You may have to discover a label's capacity through trial and error.

Explanation

Self-adhesive labels are usually provided in one continuous column for personal computers. When printing labels of this design, you must readjust the tractor feed and watch the labels carefully. Some programs can now print 2 or 3 labels across the page. These sheets of labels are easier to use and print more quickly. Check your program's documentation to see whether you can use label sheets.

Labels for laser printers always require software that can print specifically to a laser sheet format. Typically these label sheets contain 3 labels across and 10 down. Both the top and the bottom of the sheet have a half label to compensate for the nonprinting area on a laser printer.

Caution is necessary when using laser labels. A one-cent label stuck in a laser printer may end up costing $100 to be removed. Here are some suggestions:

- Although label sheets in similar sizes are available for copiers, check the specifications on the package. Some can be used in laser printers, and some cannot. Use copier labels on a laser printer only after careful testing.

- Never try to reuse a partial sheet of labels for several reasons. The sheet has been dried once from the heat of the laser. The remaining labels may be more likely to stick somewhere inside. The missing labels also create an uneven surface for the rollers, which may cause a label to come loose inside.

- Some laser printers have difficulty picking up a heavier sheet of labels from the paper-feed tray. You may need to hand-feed the label sheets.

Whether the labels are on laser sheets or in one continuous column, extra labels are always left over. Even if you don't worry too much about blank paper, blank labels actually have a number of uses:

- Mailing labels are very handy as disk labels. Most mailing labels on disks peel off readily but don't come off in use. Some disks have a manufacturing residue that prevents these labels from sticking well. If the label begins to peel up, pull it completely off. Don't try to insert a disk (in the floppy drive) with an edge of the label sticking up.

- Blank labels are useful for recycling file folders. Just stick a blank label over the old tab.

- If you do not have a blank copy of a form, small sections of labels can be used to "blank" the form. A copy machine will then create a new blank form.

- Place several labels on the back of the computer to mark which slots contain which ports. Make additional notes about when the computer was installed, how much memory it has, and the last time it was cleaned.

- Fold a blank label around each end of a cable. Note at each end what the other end is attached to.

- Roll the label into a loop and use several to put posters or maps on the wall. Be careful when taking them down, though. The adhesive may bring the paint with it.
- Blank labels are useful at home. Use them to mark leftover containers in the refrigerator.
- And (are you ready for this?) use blank labels to remove lint from clothing.

When you have to peel labels, the trick is to do it very slowly. Most labels can be removed from anything if enough time is taken in the process. If a label begins to tear, start from another corner and peel even more slowly. Do not brag to others about your newfound skill. Becoming a full-time label peeler is not a good career move.

References

System Maintenance (94)

NEXT TOPIC: FASTOPEN — Speeding Up Disks (70)

Learning More (28)

VERSIONS	
All	●
Some	○
5.0	○
Command	○
Program	○
Concept	●
Problem	○

Learning about computers can be a confusing process. Fortunately a number of resources are available to help you identify and solve problems. This discussion covers several kinds of resources and provides tips for getting the most out of all of them.

Problem

Limited resources. Often users are faced with learning how to use computers, along with the programs they run, without the appropriate resources. Formal (or informal) training may not be offered, and a well-defined support system may not be established for handling simple questions. At times, not even the most basic resource—the computer manual or the software documentation—is available. (At least you have this book for reference.) Such users have great difficulty in solving computer problems. In fact, many users get so frustrated that they give up long before they discover how useful the computer is for accessing, storing, and manipulating massive amounts of data. A number of good resources are available; you just need to know which ones can be of help to you.

Explanation

To learn how to use the computer and to solve problems that may arise, you'll need resources. Where can you learn more? Who can help? Some possible resources, both structured and unstructured, include classes, corporate training, user groups, support services, tutors, software, video tapes, and books.

Classes

Many high schools and most colleges provide evening classes that teach the use of computers. If you need a structured setting and you have a few hours each week for several weeks, these classes can improve your skills. Here are several things to do before signing up for a computer class:

- Decide what you want to get out of the course. If you want to learn how to use Lotus 1-2-3, consider taking to class some examples of spreadsheets you use at work, and learn how to create them with the instructor's help. If you just want to know what Lotus 1-2-3 does, you may not need to take a full course. A seminar that presents an overview of the product might be more appropriate.

- Talk with others who have taken the class. Find out if their goals were met and how well structured the class was. Ask what they thought of the instructor and the equipment. Were there many lab nights with no instruction?

- Talk with the instructor. Find out in what ways the instructor has used the software and for how long. Ask for a specific description of the instructor's last project with the software.

- Call the department head about the lab equipment. Ask about the type of computer and the version of software used in the course. You'll want to compare them with the computer and software you have access to at work (or home). If the school's is older, you may be frustrated by the limitations imposed in class. If your equipment is older or if you are using an older version of the software, you may need to decide whether to improve your system or upgrade your software. You may also learn a few features in class not available at work.

- Find out when you can drop the course and still get a refund. If you attend the first class and don't feel that the course will help you, at least you'll know that you can drop it and get a partial or full refund.

After the course has begun in earnest, remember that the more you put into the course, the more you'll learn. You are taking the class to learn how to use the computer, not just to get a grade. If the instructor does not know the answers to your questions, ask someone who does. If the equipment fails, make sure that you get compensation time later. Attend class even if it is scheduled as an "open lab" and you can do the work on a computer elsewhere. The instructor may provide some "nuggets" of information you won't want to miss. Insist that the instructor use the full class period as scheduled. Part of the benefit of taking the class is to have access to resources. Allowing the instructor to dismiss class an hour early wastes your tuition money.

Corporate Training

Corporate training usually provides short, noncredit courses in the business environment. These courses may last from a few hours to several days. They may include time spent on a computer or may just present a lecture. Such a course may be designed for a specific company or application, or may be a general course available to anyone who is interested. Corporate training can be structured in two ways. The first method is especially helpful to learning, and the second method, though useful, is less effective.

With the first method, the course is designed specifically for your company or department and uses examples from your daily work. The students either work with the software or see what other people in the company have done with it. Lecture time and computer time have a ratio of about 1 to 2. An hour spent explaining the concepts and providing examples leads to 2 hours of computer time. Each student uses a computer similar to the system at the office. Students are allowed to attend for a variety of reasons, including a need to use the software, general interest, and previous experience on the computer. Sessions are no longer than 4 hours, are held once a week, and last 4 to 6 weeks. Students are encouraged to review the material at work after covering it in class. Short review sessions are conducted 6 weeks and 3 months after the initial course. Classes contain 8 to 16 students.

The second, less effective method is to provide a full lecture with an overhead display. The course is open to anyone interested in paying. The students may or may not have worked with the software, and they have no access to computers in the course. Classes may contain over 100 students, who simply sit and follow a course outline. The course lasts 2 or 3 days, and there are no review sessions. Although this training method is less effective, such a course can provide an introduction to the software, familiarize you with useful resources, and give suggestions for getting additional help.

User Groups

Any semiregular gathering of computer users can be designated as a *user group*. Its purpose is for the members to help each other learn more about computers and software. Some groups are organized for specific computers, and other groups focus on software packages. Six people may casually meet every week in a restaurant, or the group may be large enough to have paid officers. Whatever the level of organization, user groups can be a valuable resource for all levels of experience.

Computer stores in your area usually know about local user groups and can provide information or a copy of a group's newsletter. Attend a meeting and don't be afraid to ask questions. The members remember their first struggles with the computer, and they'll be happy to help you avoid some of that frustration.

If the group is large enough, it is likely to have special interest groups (SIGs). These groups focus on specific software or applications. Various SIGs may meet after the main meeting to discuss such subjects as accounting software and the basics of communications.

Large companies may have user groups. They can meet at lunchtime and provide all the services of noncompany user groups. The company may even allow someone to work part-time in organizing the group, as well as provide a meeting place and demonstration equipment.

Support Services

When you have a computer problem, who can you call for help? Depending on the size of the company and the number of computers, the *computer support services* may consist of several technicians or one person casually answering questions while replacing hard drives and installing new software. Larger companies have entire departments dedicated to supporting all computer users within the company. Regardless of the size of the company and the support staff, the problems are still yours to solve, but with help if possible.

Some problems, such as those relating to hardware, must be solved by someone else. Other problems you can solve yourself, although you may still decide to call support services. (In that case, a technician may bluntly suggest that you handle some minor problems yourself.) If you do need help in solving a computer or software problem, be sure that you understand the solution so that you can fix the problem if it occurs again. Ask the technician for a full explanation; if necessary, take notes and review them later.

Tutors

Casual tutoring occurs all the time in the computing office environment. An advantage of tutoring is that you and the tutor focus on the immediate task at hand. Another advantage, of course, is that you enjoy a "one on one" relationship with the tutor. A disadvantage is that you may become too dependent on the tutor to solve problems yourself.

The tutor's responsibility is to help you learn how to solve a problem, not to sit at the keyboard and fix the problem for you. Remain at the keyboard while the tutor explains the solution. Take many notes so that you remember both the problem and the solution.

Software

Computer-assisted instruction (CAI) software exists for most major software programs. Some of these instruction programs require that you own the program you are trying to learn. Other CAI programs run on their own. Quality and flexibility vary from package to package.

One effective way to use CAI is to purchase the CAI program to evaluate the appropriateness of the application software you are considering. Spending $40 on the CAI program and two hours may save $400 if you learn that the software is not right for your application. Or the time you spend may help you understand the category of software better so that you can take another look at similar programs.

CAI provides consistent training for users within a work group. A good training method uses CAI to introduce the software, followed by sessions that teach members how to use the software for specific tasks. Make sure that everyone has used the software before the training session.

A problem with CAI (as with the next two methods of training) is that the user must be motivated to use it in order to get anything from this kind of instruction. Unlike CAI, classes are scheduled sessions, and the student who attends regularly is bound to learn something. With computer-assisted instruction, the learner has to take the time to sit in front of the computer and learn. The learning process depends on the schedule set by the user. CAI, then, is ***user-structured learning***.

To get the most out of user-structured learning, consider the following suggestions:

- Establish a buddy system. Users pair up to discuss their schedules and goals for learning the software. This may include many of the methods noted.

- Create a small reward for completing a user-structured course within a period of time. Even though learning something new can be motivation in itself, a good lunch is nice too.

- If you are working with a group, set a specific schedule for using the software. If the program takes approximately six hours to use, an hour per week may help everyone set a schedule and stick with it.

- For a designated period every week, declare a "learning break" of one to two hours. Everyone uses CAI, watches a video, studies a computer book, works on a team, or spends time learning something new about computers. Treat this time as if it were a staff meeting—except that everyone remains in his or her office. No calls or interruptions of any kind are allowed.

- Provide some token of completion. A certificate may cover a hole in the wall, but a T-shirt covers more (and is more useful). One popular T-shirt proclaimed "I learned how to computer peck with RCA and Ivy Tech."

Video Training

Video training is gaining popularity because users can relax in front of the TV while "learning" how to use the computer. This form of training can be quite helpful in providing an overview of software or in showing what the software can accomplish. A video tape can use actors or computer experts to illustrate the steps in using the software. This added element of "live action" makes learning more interesting. Video training that requires you to sit with the computer, VCR, TV, and manual may not make the best use of the medium.

Because video and computer users are conditioned to expect entertainment just after popping in a video tape, most tapes still come across as pretty dull. There is very little music and few moving images—just people who talk to the camera. And there's absolutely no plot! Here are some tips on using video training tapes:

- Use the video tape to get an overview of what the software does. Don't worry about writing down each step. Just knowing that the task can be completed with the software is enough.
- Watch the tape in short segments. Unless the material is extremely interesting, most adults can't concentrate for more that 15 or 20 minutes. Some videos are structured to include breaking points every 20 or 30 minutes.
- Watch the tape with other people. Stop the tape when someone has a question to see whether other viewers can answer it.
- Circulate the tape before a training class. The tape can present important concepts before the class meets, because the time in class is usually spent on procedures (for example, which keys to press).
- Make your own tapes. The hardware to connect a PC to a video tape deck costs well under $1,000. The video tape will show exactly what appears on the screen. (Aiming the camera at the screen works but also creates a very annoying flicker.) The results will be rough but tailored specifically to your work group's needs.

Books

Even with all the high technology, books are still the most convenient way to learn about computers. As discussed in the topic Manuals and Documentation (53), the printed material provided with software is not always presented effectively. Users with great faith in computer manuals look first in those books for answers. More experienced users typically own at least one book on each of the major software packages they use regularly.

Now that you have purchased this book to solve your DOS problems, here are a few tips on purchasing and using additional computer books:

- Determine the experience level of the targeted reader of the book. The levels are usually beginner, intermediate, and advanced. Unlike shoe sizes, these experience levels have no standard measurements, just rough guidelines.
- Open the book randomly to a page. Read a few paragraphs to see if they make any sense at all. Take time to repeat this process. If the book is loaded with words you don't understand, it may be written for a more knowledgable reader than you.
- Scan the table of contents. Are the chapter and topic headings descriptive enough? Can you find what you need?
- Look in the index. How large is it? Do the indexed words have multiple cross-references?
- Flip through several pages. Does the material have an "open look" without being too sparse? Is there a lot of dense text? Can you easily find the sections you need? Do the drawings illustrate important points or just take up space?
- Examine several books on the same topic. Some books are thicker because the publishers use heavy paper. Look at the final page counts for a better comparison.
- Select a topic you already know about. See how quickly you can find the answer to a question about that topic. Try several questions. If you can verify the answers you already know, you can probably find answers to questions you don't know.
- Don't be afraid to write in your books. Insert notes that will help you the next time you are confronted by the same problem. Use "sticky notes" to mark pages you refer to frequently.
- If your books tend to "walk away," write your name on the spine or the inside cover. Although this may remind you of school, students use the same technique for the same reason.

Book prices, like everthing else, continue to increase. But the return on the investment comes quickly with computer books. Assume that your time is worth $10 an hour. You spend $29.95 on a book about a program you use all the time. Even though you cannot possibly measure the amount of time you save because of the book, suppose that you can save three hours in one month by referring to the book. That savings has paid for the book in a month. (This does not take into account the reduced tension because you've solved a stubborn problem.)

References

Solving Problems (14)

NEXT TOPIC: PATH — Program Search (29)

Light images

See Printers (15)

Limited resources

See Learning More (28)

Loading EDIT

See EDIT — DOS 5.0 Text Editor (98)

Loading labels

See Printers (15)
See also Labels in Printer (69)

Loading paper

See Paper in Printer (68)

Locating a specific word or phrase within a file

See FIND — Searching Files (82)

Looking at the contents of batch files

See TYPE — Looking at Files (81)

Looking at the screen

See Solving Problems (14)

Loss of data

See Files (2)
See also Lost Data Files (77)

Lost Data Files (77)

VERSIONS
All ●
Some ○
5.0 ○

Command ○
Program ○
Concept ●
Problem ○

A hard disk can have dozens of subdirectories and thousands of files. Keeping these files organized is the first line of defense against losing track of your data. Using the DOS FIND program with CHKDSK can help you locate a file.

Before You Begin

Files (2)
File Names (4)
DIR — Directory (8)
CHKDSK — CHecK DiSK (20)

Syntax

`C:\>CHKDSK /V ¦ FIND "TARG"`	Searches every directory on the disk and finds all file names with the letters TARG

Problems

Using the ¦ character. Notice in the syntax line that the vertical bar is behind the /V and in front of FIND. This special character, discussed in the topic Redirection < > ¦ (64), allows FIND to accept the data from CHKDSK /V output. Note that the ¦ character is a shifted key and is located in a different place on various keyboards.

Case-sensitive input. Many programs recognize the difference between upper- and lowercase letters. Although DOS makes no distinction between *dir* and *DIR*, those letters may make a difference as used by the program. In the example with FIND, the program searches for exactly what you type. Because the directory list is always uppercase, if you type the search letters in lowercase, you'll never find a match.

Explanation

Even with a well-organized hard disk, files sometimes get lost. You can use a trick with the CHKDSK and FIND commands to help you find all occurrences of the file name you are looking for. Although the method is slow, it will get the job done. Notice that the search string must be in quotation marks and does not use wild cards. The smaller the search string, the more "hits" you'll have.

This trick with CHKDSK and FIND just hints at the possibilities available by combining DOS programs with commands. In this case, the infrequently used /V switch on CHKDSK lists the files as CHKDSK performs its check on each file. The vertical bar (¦) is a pipe command, which says, "Instead of sending the output to the screen, send it to the FIND program." The FIND program then uses the data from CHKDSK and performs its search for the specified string. When a match is found, FIND lists the entire line to the screen. Because the line includes the complete path of the file name, you've found your file or files.

If your search string is too small, you'll get a long list of files. For example, if the search string is *EX*, you'll come up with hundreds of files because many program extensions are EXE. Notice also that you *cannot* search for dates. The /V switch on CHKDSK lists only the file name and path name.

The disk accompanying this book contains a utility that can locate files more quickly than the CHKDSK and FIND method. This utility, also called FIND, uses standard DOS wild cards to search a disk drive for specified files. The DOS FIND program looks only within a specific file or CHKDSK output for a text string. The FIND utility searches all drives for the file name. You may have to rename your DOS version of FIND before using the FIND utility. More information is provided in Part III, "Guide to Using the Disk."

Exercise

Here you practice using CHKDSK and FIND to locate a file by name. Because this method is slow, you may want to read about the FIND utility in Part III. Knowing how to use CHKDSK with FIND is useful, however, because the method works on any system. You don't need to have the FIND utility available to find a file.

Exercise 1 of 1

This exercise uses a file extension commonly found on all hard disks. If you try and don't find anything, try another extension.

TRY	NOTE
`C:\>CHKDSK /V ¦ FIND ".DOC"`	This may be a huge list of files. If the list scrolls off the screen, do the next command. Remember to use capital letters between the quotation marks.
`C:\>CHKDSK /V ¦ FIND ".DOC" ¦ MORE`	Notice the use of the period in the search string. Because you are looking for files with the extension DOC, you don't want files with DOC as part of the file name.
`C:\>CHKDSK /V ¦ FIND "ABC"`	Substitute three letters that you know are likely to be found in a file name on your hard disk.
`C:\>CHKDSK /V ¦ FIND "ABC" > LPT1:`	If you want the results to go to the printer, use the redirection character > to LPT1:.

Using the /V switch and the pipe (¦) with FIND makes this exercise work. Depending on the speed of your hard disk and the number of files, the action can take several seconds. Consider also using the FIND utility covered in Part III.

References

FIND — Searching Files (82)

NEXT TOPIC: COMMAND.COM/EXIT (78)

Lost file(s)

See Files (2)
See also COPY — Files (10)
See also Lost Data Files (77)

J K L

Lost network connection

See Networks (79)

Lost subdirectories

See CD, MD, and RD — Working with Directories (9)

Maintaining data in two file formats

See Data File Formats (52)

Maintenance agreements

See System Maintenance (94)

Making a mistake on the command line

See DOSKEY (25)

Making quick changes to batch files

See EDLIN — Line Editor (99)

Making the connection

See Communications (55)

Manual replacement

See Manuals and Documentation (53)

Manual storage

See Manuals and Documentation (53)

Manuals and Documentation (53)

VERSIONS
All ●
Some ○
5.0 ○

Command ○
Program ○
Concept ●
Problem ○

Although it would be nice to assume that you could effectively use all software without any kind of instruction manual, software isn't always that nice. And most computer hardware requires at least a manual for installation and maintenance.

Problems

Storing manuals. Software manuals are valuable. Although the software may be easy to copy (even if copying is illegal), duplicating the manual takes more effort. The manuals should be within reach but not necessarily within view. If manuals have a habit of "taking a walk," you may want to resort to printing your name or department name on the manual with a marker.

Missing manuals. If the software manual is not readily apparent, the first question is, Do you have a legal copy of the software? The absence of a manual is an indication that the software on your system may not be legitimate.

Replacing manuals. Some software companies are willing to replace software manuals if the software has been registered. This is especially true in the case of a disaster, such as a fire or water damage. A statement from your insurance company may be required.

MNO

Explanation

Software and hardware manuals trigger frequent complaints from users:

- The users are expected to know more than they do.
- The terms are not well defined.
- The manual is either too technical or not technical enough.
- The information is not presented in a logical order.
- Answers to problems are difficult to find.

Although some of these complaints are valid, users often expect too much from manuals. The manuals may explain all the menu choices in the software and provide hints on more advanced features, but there just aren't enough pages in a manual to explain everything in complete detail. This book (*Learning DOS*), along with other computer books, can supplement the manual. The most critical DOS commands and concepts are featured and discussed here in some detail. But if *everything* in the DOS manual had been included in this book, and discussed on the same level of detail, *Learning DOS* could easily have been 1,500 pages!

Some complaints about software manuals are understandable. The people who write the manuals are frequently the same people who design the programs. They already know the program intimately, so they tend to ignore basic concepts and use technical words that first-time users may not know. This approach to writing manuals has changed in the last few years, however. The larger companies now have people dedicated to writing manuals. They are not hired because they know all about computers but because they can explain complicated software in plain English. In fact, these writers may take pride in not knowing the technical details of the program. As they learn the program, they write about their discoveries.

The software companies have their complaints about users too. The people on the telephone support lines spend a great deal of time answering questions that users don't bother to answer themselves by looking in the manual. Picking up the phone even before you look for the answer in the manual is, well, not very smart. If the manual is not helpful, invest in a book written about the software—like this one. Sometimes using the manual along with another book provides enough examples for you to answer most questions. You won't have to make that call after all.

The terms *documentation* and *manual* are sometimes used interchangeably. The manuals are the actual books provided with the software or hardware. Documentation refers to all the information gathered about the product. In addition to the information in the user's manual, the documentation includes the Help section of the program, as well as the technical specifications you won't see. The only time to worry about documentation is when someone is writing a program for you. You'll want the complete system documentation as part of the programmer's efforts. The programmer may or may not include writing the user manuals as part of the work.

Exercise

Conduct an inventory of your software manuals. Are they easily available? Do you use them frequently? How long do you struggle with a problem before opening the manual? Do you have other books about the software programs you use (besides *Learning DOS* for MS-DOS)?

References

Copyright (51), Product Registration (54)

NEXT TOPIC: Product Registration (54)

Manuals missing

See Manuals and Documentation (53)

Manufacturer's warranty

See System Maintenance (94)

Meaningful file name

See File Names (4)

MEM (90)

VERSIONS
All ○
Some ○
5.0 ●

Command ○
Program ●
Concept ○
Problem ○

This DOS 5.0 program displays memory status, including extended memory, expanded memory, and all memory used. Additional switches can show the size and location of each of your programs.

Before You Begin

CHKDSK — CHecK DiSK (20)
Memory (73)

Syntax

`C:\>MEM`	Shows used and free memory in the system.
`C:\>MEM /P`	Shows the status of programs in memory. You can use /PROGRAM instead of /P.
`C:\>MEM /D`	Shows programs, internal drivers, and other information. You can use /DEBUG in place of /D.
`C:\>MEM /C`	Shows program memory usage. /CLASSIFY may be substituted for /C.

Problems

Not enough memory. Each program you load takes up memory. When too many TSR programs (see next problem) are loaded at once, there may not be enough memory for the main program you want to run. Use **MEM /P** to determine which programs can be eliminated from the stack. Modifications to the AUTOEXEC.BAT and CONFIG.SYS files may be necessary to reduce this list.

Memory conflicts between terminate-and-stay-resident (TSR) programs. Some programs are called TSR because they remain in memory (after their first use) and perform specific functions. **MEM /C** can help determine what programs are in memory and the order in which they were loaded. For example, DOSKEY and PRINT are TSR programs. These programs are stacked in memory, waiting for trigger events, such as the pressing of specific keys or the appearance of certain characters in a printed file. When the event occurs, the program becomes active and performs its task. Problems can arise when two or more programs are waiting for the same event to occur. The key combination used or the order in which the programs were loaded can affect these problems. The only solution is to load each program manually and test for the problem. Then load the next program. When you find the problem occurring, you at least know one of the two "problem" programs. Some programs enable you to change the trigger event, which may help resolve the conflict.

Explanation

The DOS 5.0 MEM program provides a quick way to see how much memory is being used by various memory-resident programs and how much is left for standard programs. With the advanced memory capability of DOS 5.0, the MEM command is necessary to fine-tune the system.

Using the MEM command without switches is usually sufficient in determining the amount of conventional memory available and the largest executable program size. Note the first and third lines in the following example:

```
C:\>MEM

    655360 bytes total conventional memory
    655360 bytes available to MS-DOS
    601280 largest executable program size

   3145728 bytes total contiguous extended memory
         0 bytes available contiguous extended memory
    770048 bytes available XMS memory

           MS-DOS resident in High Memory Area
```

Notice the amount of conventional memory made available by DOS 5.0. This version of DOS can now load itself into high memory, leaving more memory for conventional programs. The amount shown here could have been even higher, but a number of device drivers and other programs have also been loaded.

The /C switch shows the programs and the amount of memory they use:

```
C:\>MEM /C
Conventional Memory :

  Name                Size in Decimal        Size in Hex
-------------       ---------------------   -------------
  MSDOS               13824       ( 13.5K)       3600
  SETVER                400       (  0.4K)        190
  MOUSE               12624       ( 12.3K)       3150
  HIMEM                1184       (  1.2K)        4A0
  SMARTDRV            13312       ( 13.0K)       3400
  ANSI                 4192       (  4.1K)       1060
  RAMDRIVE             1184       (  1.2K)        4A0
  COMMAND              2624       (  2.6K)        A40
  DOSKEY               4128       (  4.0K)       1020
  FREE                   64       (  0.1K)         40
  FREE                  112       (  0.1K)         70
  FREE               601424       (587.3K)      92D50

Total  FREE :        601600       (587.5K)

Total bytes available to programs :   601600   (587.5K)
Largest executable program size :     601280   (587.2K)

   3145728 bytes total contiguous extended memory
         0 bytes available contiguous extended memory
    770048 bytes available XMS memory
           MS-DOS resident in High Memory Area
```

Exercise

When you use the MEM program, you are peeking into the state of memory. If you have specific problems with TSR programs (terminate-and-stay-resident programs) or you want to fine-tune your memory usage, the MEM program is quite helpful.

Exercise 1 of 1

You can use the > character to redirect the output of all of these commands to either an ASCII file or the printer. Just add **> LPT1:** for the printer or add **> MEM.TXT** (or some other file name) to create the ASCII file.

TRY	NOTE
C:\>**MEM**	This provides the basic memory information.
C:\>**CHKDSK**	Compare the output of MEM with the memory information provided in CHKDSK.
C:\>**MEM /C**	Of all the switches, /C produces the shortest output with MEM. You may want to add **> LPT1:** to examine the results more closely.
C:\>**MEM /P ¦ MORE**	This produces a longer listing with more detail. Using the pipe (¦) with MORE is the only way you can see everything on one screen.
C:\>**MEM /D ¦ MORE**	For the technically inclined, this provides memory locations as well.

Another interesting exercise with MEM is to load a program that allows you to "drop" to DOS. Then, at this second level, run MEM to see how much memory the program is using and gauge how much memory remains. If enough memory is left, you may be able to run a second program under this second level of DOS. As always, save any data in the first-level program before dropping to DOS and performing your "experiments."

References

ASCII (74), COMMAND.COM/EXIT (78)

NEXT TOPIC: MIRROR (91)

Memory (73)

VERSIONS	
All	●
Some	○
5.0	○
Command	○
Program	○
Concept	●
Problem	○

A system loads programs and data into computer memory. Older systems were limited to 640K of memory. Newer systems can use up to 16M or more.

Before You Begin

Bytes and Computer Math (67)

Problems

`Not enough memory.` This DOS error message occurs if the system does not have enough memory to run a program. Here are some possible causes:

- The system may have only 512K of memory when it needs 640K. Check the program manual for memory requirements.
- Other programs have been loaded into memory, and there is not enough remaining memory to run the current program. Determine how many programs have been loaded and which ones you can do without. You may need to examine the AUTOEXEC.BAT file for programs that load automatically, and remove the lines that load one or more of these programs. Reboot and try to run the program again.
- You may have dropped to DOS from another program. Try typing **`EXIT`** at the DOS prompt. This should return you to the other program. Exit that program normally and try to run the current program again.

`Parity error.` This DOS message indicates a physical problem with the memory chips. You'll have to reboot the system. If the error persists, the bad chips in the system must be located and replaced. This problem can occur also if the system is accidentally shocked by a static discharge.

What's a RAM drive? A RAM drive uses part of memory to act like a standard DOS drive. A special program must be run to set up this drive. Once created, a RAM drive reads and writes files very quickly. But when the computer is turned off or rebooted, all the files in the RAM drive are gone. A RAM drive, then, is a place to store and use temporary files.

Explanation

Memory is like a scratch pad for the computer system. Programs and data are loaded to be used for processing. When additional memory is available, more and larger programs can be loaded. After the programs are loaded, memory is used to hold data being worked on by the programs.

Unlike the contents stored on floppy disks or hard disks, the contents of memory exist only when the computer is on. The electronic program and data images are held in place by electricity. Data storage on disks is based on magnetic images, like music on a cassette tape. Once the power is turned off, only the data you've saved to disk will be available when you turn the computer on again. This is why you should not turn the computer off while you are creating a word processing document without saving it first. The document is in memory but not on disk until you save it.

Having a bigger gas tank won't make a car go faster. Likewise, having more memory won't make a computer work faster. The bigger gas tank will allow the car to travel farther before it has to refuel, though. More memory will allow more programs to be loaded at one time and larger documents or spreadsheets to be loaded.

Memory capacity and disk storage capacity are frequently confused. They are both measured in bytes, yet they are different to the computer. But here is the confusing part: memory can be used as disk space, and disk space can be used as memory. Table 73-1 shows the differences and similarities in memory and disk storage.

Table 73-1. Memory and disk storage compared.

Memory	Disk Storage
Contained in microchips	Contained on magnetic media
Contents lost when power is turned off	Contents permanent until deliberately deleted
Programs loaded into memory before they can be run	Program files stored on disk but must be loaded into memory before they can be run
Accessed by DOS only	Accessed by DOS and the user
Permanent part of the computer	Data can be transported on disks

You can use memory as if it were a disk, known as a *RAM disk*. You load a device driver into CONFIG.SYS to create a disk that DOS can use just like any other drive. Typically it becomes the next disk drive in the line. For example, if you have a C: hard drive, the RAM disk becomes the D: drive. You can copy files to drive D: just as you copy files to any disk.

The advantage of a RAM disk is its extreme speed in file reading and writing. No physical access to the magnetic media is needed. The disadvantages include the loss of data on the drive when power is turned off and the use of memory space. If you remember to save the contents of the disk to a real disk before you turn off the computer, you will not lose anything. If you have enough memory to create a RAM disk and also run your programs, the extra speed of the RAM disk may prove helpful with disk-intensive programs.

Disk space can also be used as memory. In almost all cases, this process is controlled by the individual programs. Some programs, finding that enough memory is not available to perform specific operations, *swap* parts of memory to the disk to free up memory space. When that part of the program is done, the old part is loaded back into memory. The only time that the user may be aware of this activity is when a program produces an error message indicating that there isn't enough room on the hard disk for parts of the program to be swapped.

RAM and *ROM* are terms commonly used in referring to memory. The discussion so far has been completely about RAM (*r*andom-*a*ccess *m*emory). This memory can be written to and read from the computer. ROM (*r*ead-*o*nly *m*emory) represents internal memory, with data and programs permanently located in the chip. Because these cannot be changed, the data is simply read from the chip and then used.

There are several types of RAM memory. Conventional memory is located in the first 640K in the computer. Even though all MS-DOS computers may actually have one megabyte of memory, only the first 640K is available for programs. The top third is reserved for video memory and ROM.

Extended memory consists of one yardstick on top of another—up to 16 stretched end to end. This kind of memory is available on AT (80286), 386 (80386), and larger systems. Some programs use extended memory when they find it. It can be used also for RAM disks.

Expanded memory is a software "trick" developed to provide more memory than normally is available in a system. This memory requires a special device driver in CONFIG.SYS and is automatically recognized by some programs. Additional information on memory and setting up RAM drives is available in the DOS manual and in computer books.

References

Bytes and Computer Math (67)

NEXT TOPIC: ASCII — Character Codes (74)

Memory allocation error

See Memory (73)

Memory conflicts

See Networks (79)

Memory use

See PRINT — Spooler (45)

Memory used

See DOSSHELL — DOS 5.0 Menu (44)

Menus

See Interfaces (27)

Microprocessors (96)

VERSIONS	
All	●
Some	○
5.0	○
Command	○
Program	○
Concept	●
Problem	○

The microprocessor is the heart of a computer. This topic briefly describes how microprocessors work and covers the evolution of the 80x86 family of chips.

Before You Begin

Hardware (38)
Bytes and Computer Math (67)

Explanation

Computers are based on *microprocessors*. These chips are combined to create a system of processors. Some chips are dedicated to accepting input from the keyboard. Others control the monitor, and still others control the disk drives. In the middle of these chips is the *c*entral *p*rocessing *u*nit (CPU)—the base for all the other chips in the computer.

MS-DOS computers use a family of chips originally designed by Intel. The first chip was numbered 8088. The original IBM PC had this chip for the CPU. These systems first contained 64K of memory even though the 8088 could use 1M of memory (64K x 16). Because some memory was needed for monitors, the 8088-based systems (and the later 8086-based systems) used a maximum of 640K. It is now rare to find a system based on the 8088 without 640K of memory. These systems are not capable of running most of the new software released today.

The family numbers expanded by a digit when the 80286 was introduced in the IBM AT. This system was capable of addressing (using) up to 16M of memory. The AT systems are typically shipped with 1M of memory. Design problems prevent the 80286 from using the full 16M of memory effectively, but these systems are still fairly useful for basic computing tasks.

The 80386 was the next chip in succession. Although IBM stamped the PC XT and AT names on the computers at that time, the current crop of systems based on the 80386 is simply referred to as "386" systems. These systems are fully capable of using the 16M of memory first promised in the 286 systems. A slightly more limited version of the 80386 is used in some systems and designated 386SX. The main differences between the 80386 and the 80386SX are speed and cost. The SX costs somewhat less and is slightly slower in performance.

The latest readily available chip is the 80486. Because systems based on this chip are even faster, they are much more expensive. Plans are undoubtedly being made for the 80586 (and higher) processing chip. Each new chip will bring more speed and power to personal computers.

An optional chip in all systems is a *math coprocessor*. When this chip is present in a computer, the chip takes over parts of the main processor's math tasks. This "off loading" of the processing can provide significant increases in speed. The drawback is that the software must specifically detect and use the math coprocessor in order to benefit from the improved speed. Programs that use the math coprocessor include computer-assisted drawing programs and graphics programs. If a program requires a math coprocessor to run, the software makes the statement on the package.

Table 96-1 provides a summary of the chips and the systems that use them.

Table 96-1. The 80x86 family of chips, the systems that use them, and the math coprocessor chip.

Chip	System	Math Chip
8088	PC and XT	8087
8086	Some clones	
80286	AT	80287
80386SX	'386SX	80387SX
80386	'386	80387
80486	'486	Built-in
80586	???	???

References

History of DOS (88)

NEXT TOPIC: Partitions — FDISK (97)

MIRROR (91)

VERSIONS	
All	○
Some	○
5.0	●
Command	○
Program	●
Concept	○
Problem	○

This MS-DOS 5.0 program saves the current disk directory to a separate file, enabling you to recover the files on the disk with the UNFORMAT program. The /T switch adds the deletion-tracking function to the MIRROR program, which can then be used by UNDELETE and UNFORMAT.

Before You Begin

DEL — DELete (30)
UNDELETE (31)
UNFORMAT (86)

Syntax

`C:\>MIRROR C: D:`	For drives C: and D:, saves the FAT in the root directory of each drive
`C:\>MIRROR /PARTN`	Saves to a floppy disk the partition information about the hard disk
`C:\>MIRROR C: /TC`	Saves the FAT and installs the deletion-tracking program for drive C:

Problem

Recovering accidentally deleted programs or formatted disks. You can ensure the quick recovery of accidental deletions if you use MIRROR regularly. Because the MIRROR program restores a disk to the conditions that existed when it was last used, MIRROR is usually part of the AUTOEXEC.BAT file. If you use an old version of MIRROR.FIL located in the root directory of the disk to be recovered, you may lose a lot of data.

Explanation

MIRROR is one of three programs originally developed by Central Point Software and included in DOS 5.0. Although both UNDELETE and UNFORMAT can work without MIRROR.FIL, they are more reliable if they have this data file to use.

MIRROR actually has two functions. The first is to create a data file that has a copy of the file allocation table (FAT) and the root directory of the disk. This file, named MIRROR.FIL, along with its backup file MIRROR.BAK, is kept in the root directory of the disk. When you run MIRROR with

```
C:\>MIRROR C: D:
```

both hard disks C: and D: will have those files in the root directory. Those files, by the way, are read-only and cannot be erased unless you change the read-only attribute with the ATTRIB command.

The second function of MIRROR is invoked with the /T switch, which tells MIRROR to track all file deletions. Depending on the size of the disk, the default number of entries can range from 25 to 303. These entries represent the last files deleted and their locations. Although DOS can undelete files, the MIRROR tracking program keeps a list of file names and locations. It also keeps the first character of the file name. Without MIRROR, you must supply the first letter of each file to be undeleted.

You can increase the number of entries when you use the /T switch. To provide additional deletion protection for drive C:, use the following MIRROR command line:

```
C:\>MIRROR C: /TC-500 /TD-500
```

This extra protection costs some disk space. The greater the number of files to be tracked, the larger the size of MIRROR.FIL. Because the default for a 32M drive is 202 entries, the additional numbers used here may not be necessary.

Keeping the deletion tracker active also increases the amount of time necessary to delete a file. While DOS is removing the first character of the file name to signify that the file is deleted, MIRROR is writing that information (and more) to the MIRROR.FIL file. This does produce a noticeable delay in the DOS response from the time you type **DEL FILENAME.EXT** to the time you return to the DOS prompt. You'll have to decide if the slightly delayed response time is worth the insurance of quick file recovery.

You can remove the deletion-tracking program from memory with the /U switch. As with all memory-resident programs, this can cause problems if additional programs were loaded after the MIRROR program.

Exercise

Because MIRROR is used for both UNDELETE and UNFORMAT, the MIRROR program must be active in order to keep track of the deleted files. This exercise provides the steps to insert a line in your AUTOEXEC.BAT file so that MIRROR runs whenever you boot the system.

Exercise 1 of 1

Adding a line to the AUTOEXEC.BAT file uses COPY's capability to add the contents of one file to another. In this exercise, you just add a new first line to your AUTOEXEC.BAT file. If you know how to use EDIT or EDLIN, you can accomplish the same thing more easily.

TRY	NOTE
C:\>**MIRROR C:**	This lets you see what the MIRROR program does. But because you want to run this every time you boot, you'll put it in your AUTOEXEC.BAT file.
C:\>**COPY CON: TEMP** **MIRROR C:** **<F6>** One file(s) copied C:\>	Here you create a small temporary file with one line: **MIRROR C:** If you have more than one hard drive, include those drives on that line.
C:\>**COPY TEMP + AUTOEXEC.BAT AUTOEXEC.NEW**	This adds the one-line **TEMP** file to your current AUTOEXEC.BAT file as the first line.
C:\>**TYPE AUTOEXEC.NEW**	In this listing, you should see MIRROR C: as the first line.
C:\>**REN AUTOEXEC.BAT AUTOEXEC.OLD** C:\>**REN AUTOEXEC.NEW AUTOEXEC.BAT**	Now the new version of that batch file will run every time you boot your system.

You may want to reboot your system now to make sure that the AUTOEXEC.BAT program works as you expected. If it does not, you can type **DEL AUTOEXEC.BAT** and **REN AUTOEXEC.OLD AUTOEXEC.BAT**.

References

Lost Data Files (77), EDIT — DOS 5.0 Text Editor (98)

NEXT TOPIC: Virus (92)

Misnamed files

See Files (2)

Missing AUTOEXEC.BAT

See also AUTOEXEC.BAT (21)

Missing or unclear prompt

See PROMPT — Command Line Information (26)

Missing parameter

See Command and Program Parameters (34)

Missing the first cluster

See UNDELETE (31)

Mistyped command

See `Bad command or file name` (6)

Mistyped file name

See DIR — Directory (8)

Misunderstood asterisk

See Wild Cards * and ? (11)

Misused wild card

See DIR — Directory (8)
See also Wild Cards * and ? (11)

MODE — Configuring System Devices (83)

VERSIONS	
All	●
Some	○
5.0	○
Command	○
Program	●
Concept	○
Problem	○

MODE is a multipurpose DOS program. It can configure the serial ports, redirect parallel output to a serial port, change the display configuration, and do even more.

Before You Begin

Ports (40)
AUTOEXEC.BAT (21)

Syntax

`C:\>`**`MODE COM1:96,N,8,1,P`** `COM1: 96,N,8,1,P`	Sets the serial port for a printer
`C:\>`**`MODE LPT1:=COM1:`** `LPT1: redirected to COM1:`	Redirects to COM1 the output usually sent to the printer port LPT1:

Problem

Setting up the serial printer. Because some software does not recognize the use of the COM1: port for printing, DOS can redirect to COM1 the printing directed to LPT1:. This requires two steps: (1) initializing the serial port COM1: with MODE and (2) redirecting the output from LPT1: to COM1:. The sample command lines in the "Syntax" section show the steps in this process. Once you initiate this action, anything sent to LPT1: will print on the serial printer attached to COM1:. The process may take some trial and error before it works.

Explanation

The DOS MODE program performs a number of functions, including the more exotic functions of setting code pages and adjusting the display width and location on the screen. The more practical uses for MODE include redirecting the printer output from a parallel port to a serial port and, for DOS 4.0 and 5.0 users, controlling the *typematic rate* (screen character repeat).

> In this discussion, LPT1: can actually be LPT1:, LPT2:, or LPT3:, depending on which ports you have in your system. COM1: can also be COM2:.

As noted in the "Problem" section, some printers require a serial connection rather than a parallel connection. Instead of sending the printing through LPT1:, the printer can receive the signal through COM1: only. There are advantages and disadvantages to both port types. The important thing to know is that if a printer uses the serial port, the DOS MODE program must be used. MODE must *initialize* that port before the system can use the port for printing.

The printer manual should provide information about using MODE to initialize the port. The manual should show the exact line to type. You can try the line first from the command prompt to see if it works. Once you know that MODE works, typically you insert in the AUTOEXEC.BAT file a line that looks like the one you just typed at the command prompt. Again, depending on the printer and which port you are using, the line might look like this:

```
C:\>MODE COM1:96,N,8,1,P
```

This line in AUTOEXEC.BAT automatically initializes the port to be used by your software to send printing to the serial printer. Your software must have a setting for the printer port so that you can select COM1: for the serial port. Once you've done that, it makes no difference that the printing signal is going out the serial port instead of the parallel port.

If your software does not have any setting for the printer port, MODE can redirect the LPT1: output to COM1:. This is accomplished with the command

```
C:\>MODE LPT1:=COM1:
```

After you issue this command, MODE redirects to COM1: any printing sent to LPT1:. Again, you can test this at the command prompt. Once you know that it works, you can insert the line in AUTOEXEC.BAT, just below the preceding MODE command.

Your DOS manual has information on the MODE command not covered here, including more about CODE pages and display mode.

5 DOS 4.0 and 5.0 users may want to explore several enhancements to MODE, including MODE's capability to report the status of all the system devices and the typematic rate.

If you type **MODE**, you get a listing of the current status of the system devices. Because this list more than fills the screen, you can use the ¦ (pipe) character through MORE to pause the screen:

```
C:\>MODE ¦ MORE
```

If you want to print a list of all the system devices, you can redirect the output to the printer. If, however, you are having trouble getting your serial printer to work and you want to use MODE to view the settings, you will not be able to redirect the output to the printer. To redirect the output, use

```
C:\>MODE > LPT1:
```

The typematic rate defaults to 20 characters per second with a delay of half a second. MODE may be able to change these defaults on *some* systems. Some keyboards apparently do not recognize this part of the MODE command. The range for the characters-per-second repeat is from 2 to 30 characters. The value entered on the command line is 1 to 32. If you set the rate, you must also set the delay.

The delay is the time in which a key must be pressed before it begins repeating the character. The possible delays are 0.25, 0.50, 0.75, and 1 second. These are represented as 1, 2, 3, and 4. If you want to set the delay, you also have to provide the rate.

To slow down the repeat rate and the length of the delay before triggering the repeat, use

C:\>**MODE 2 4** (2 characters a second, 1 second delay)

To speed up the number of characters and shorten the wait time, try

C:\>**MODE 32 1** (32 characters a second, 0.25 delay)

Remember that the default is the same as entering

C:\>**MODE 20 2** (20 characters a second, 0.50 delay)

References

Printers (15)

NEXT TOPIC: MORE — Pausing Screen Display (84)

Modem signal drops

See Modems (56)

Modems (56)

VERSIONS	
All	●
Some	○
5.0	○
Command	○
Program	○
Concept	●
Problem	○

A modem is a piece of hardware that translates the computer signal into a phone-line signal. The purpose of a modem is to connect and exchange data with another computer.

Before You Begin

Ports (40)
Communications (55)

Problems

Unmatched communication parameters. To communicate successfully, the computers at both ends must have matching parameters (baud rate, parity, number of data bits, and number of stop bits). Your software manual explains how to change these settings. But first you must know the settings required by the host computer. Fortunately personal computers have fairly common settings. The baud rate is the maximum transmission speed your modem can handle—in most cases, 2400. So the settings, in order, are 2400 baud, parity = none, 8 data bits, and 1 stop bit. You'll also need to know which serial port your modem is using. If you are not sure, use trial and error to determine the port (COM1:, COM2:, COM3:, or COM4:).

Noisy phone line. The occasional static heard during a phone conversation may be annoying but tolerable. This same static completely destroys the computer signals sent during a communication session with another computer. A noisy line may cause a random series of characters to appear on the screen. If the signal is consistently bad, the connection between the systems may be broken. In some cases, reestablishing the connection provides a "cleaner" line. If the problem is persistent, the phone company can check the lines to your house or office. Ask about a charge for this visit. Some phone companies charge for a service call even if nothing wrong is found with the lines.

Modem signal drops. As noted, line static may affect the connection. A more common problem is *call waiting*, a feature provided by the phone company to allow a user to answer an incoming call while talking on the phone. The tone used to signal the incoming call is the same tone that disconnects a modem. You may have to cancel the call-waiting feature before a communication session. Contact the phone company for the sequence of numbers to cancel call waiting.

Explanation

Modems have become fairly standard in the past few years. Hayes Microcomputer Products was one of the first companies to provide modems and, as a result, created the established commands for modems. These commands, referred to as the AT command set or Hayes command set, determine how your communications software controls the modem. Some modem companies add additional commands to use the extra features in their products.

Modems can be either *external* or *internal*. An external modem is a small box attached to a serial port with a 9- or 25-pin cable. External modems require separate power through a transformer. They also have indicator lights and are slightly more expensive than internal modems. Because an external modem is outside the computer case, the modem is more portable and easier to install.

An internal modem is a self-contained board plugged into the motherboard of the computer. This modem uses internal power and, because it has a direct phone-line socket, does not require connection to a serial port. Internal modems do not provide a visual signal about the progress of the connection, as external modems do. Installation of an internal modem requires removing the computer cover and inserting the board in an open slot.

Both types of modems include speakers to allow you to monitor the progress of calls. Usually the speakers are set to turn off after the high-pitched tone of the modem connection. The external modem must be connected to an existing serial port, usually COM1: or COM2:. You'll need to know the number of serial ports in your system before deciding where to plug the modem. If you use a mouse in the serial port and you have only one port, you can plug and unplug these devices if needed. Internal modems have the advantage of providing settings for COM3: or COM4:. In this way, an internal modem provides its own serial port.

References

Ports (40), Communications (55)

NEXT TOPIC: SHARE (57)

Monitor (61)

VERSIONS	
All	●
Some	○
5.0	○
Command	○
Program	○
Concept	●
Problem	○

The monitor, also known as the screen or CRT, displays the characters and images from the system. The quality of the monitor can affect your visual comfort level.

Before You Begin

Hardware (38)

Problems

Wrong monitor type. To work properly, some programs require a specific type of monitor (see the "Explanation" section). Be sure to compare your monitor with the monitor requirements listed on the software box. Most programs on the market today will declare whether the monitor attached to your system will work. If the monitor cannot be used, the program quits.

Blurry screen. If the characters on the screen appear blurry, you can adjust the contrast and brightness to compensate. Blurry characters usually mean that the brightness is set too high. Blurry images are hard on the eyes.

Reflections on the screen. Bright lights shining on the screen create "hot" spots. These make the images on the screen difficult to see and may cause eye strain. See the "Exercise" section to determine how to locate and alleviate hot spots.

Poor color combinations. Some color combinations on color monitors may not be easy to view. Although software companies try to provide helpful screen colors, most programs allow the default colors to be changed. If you are having trouble seeing the characters on your screen, you may be sensitive to certain color combinations. Take time to try different combinations and keep trying until you find one you like. And don't worry if the screen doesn't match the office decor.

Explanation

The computer monitor provides the most immediate output from the computer. Each time you press a key, the system echoes that key on the monitor to confirm that the key you pressed is the key the CPU received. In most cases, the output is text-based. Most word processing and database programs use text-based screens. Graphics programs and educational software require graphics screens. Graphical user interfaces (GUIs), such as Windows, require a graphics monitor.

Table 61-1 shows the different monitor types. Because more programs are using graphics, the minimum screen now is an EGA screen. But there is such a small difference in cost between EGA and VGA monitors that a VGA monitor is highly recommended.

Table 61-1. Different monitor types.

Abbreviation	Type
Monochrome	Text programs only, no color
Hercules	Some graphics programs, no color
CGA	Poor graphics, very limited colors
MCGA	Graphics, color (but not compatible with all software)
EGA	Good graphics, 16 colors
VGA	Good graphics, up to 256 colors
Super VGA	Excellent graphics, up to 256 colors

The images on the screen are made up of tiny dots. When the dots are smaller, the image is sharper. This ratio of dots to screen size is known as *resolution*. A graphics display is rated by the number of dots across by the number of dots down and possibly *times* the number of colors for each dot (across × down × colors). An

EGA screen can display 640 dots across by 480 dots down. These dots can have one of 16 colors. A VGA screen has at least two different resolutions: 640 x 480 or 320 x 200. The lower resolution (fewer dots on the screen) has the advantage of providing up to 256 colors. Even with that lower number of dots, the addition of 240 colors makes an image on VGA monitors very photographic.

Exercise

Before turning on your system, look at the screen for bright spots or reflections. Although these are not as evident when the monitor is turned on, they can affect your ability to see and may cause eye strain. Try moving the light source away from the front of the screen. Or shade part of the light that falls on the screen. See the topic Workspace — User Comfort (85) for more ideas on creating a comfortable work setting.

References

Workspace — User Comfort (85), System Maintenance (93)

NEXT TOPIC: ATTRIB — Protecting Files (62)

MORE — Pausing Screen Display (84)

VERSIONS	
All	●
Some	○
5.0	○
Command	○
Program	●
Concept	○
Problem	○

This DOS program pauses the screen display when it becomes full. Pressing any key advances the display to the next screenful of text.

Before You Begin

Redirection < > ¦ (64)
ASCII — Character Codes (74)

Syntax

`C:\>TREE ¦ MORE`	Accepts TREE's output and displays it on the screen, pausing at each screenful
`C:\>MORE < LONGFILE.TXT`	Reads LONGFILE.TXT and displays its contents on the screen, pausing at each screenful

Problems

Program output scrolls off the screen. The screen output of some DOS programs, such as TREE and TYPE, often scrolls by more quickly than you can read it. To pause the display at each screenful, use the first example in the "Syntax" section.

Viewing long ASCII files. The MORE program can accept an ASCII file directed into MORE with the < character, as noted in the second example in the "Syntax" section. A functional equivalent is **TYPE LONGFILE.TXT ¦ MORE**.

Explanation

The DOS MORE program accepts the output from another DOS program or command and displays that output one screen at a time. At the bottom of the display, MORE prompts with — More —. Pressing any key advances the display.

MORE can also accept an ASCII file as input if you use the redirection character < (the less-than symbol). If, after you type **TYPE LONGFILE.TXT**, the file quickly scrolls off the screen, you can use the MORE program to pause that file. Use

```
C:\>MORE < LONGFILE.TXT
```

to see the contents of the file one screen at a time. You cannot use the Page Up key to review previous material. To stop the display, press Ctrl-C or Ctrl-Break.

The DOS MORE program is more useful with other programs. See the topics CHKDSK—CHecK DiSK (20), Lost Data Files (77), and TYPE—Looking at Files (81) for examples of how to use MORE.

References

CHKDSK — CHecK DiSK (20), Lost Data Files (77), TYPE — Looking at Files (81)

NEXT TOPIC: Workspace — User Comfort (85)

More about This Book (101)

This topic provides details about how and why this book was written. For those who are curious about how a computer book is written, the author steps out from behind his words and explains himself.

MNO

Explanation

A computer book editor prefers that the author leave the *I* out of the book. After all, the book is about computers, not the author. I agree with this approach. But now I want to provide a few more details about how and why this book was written. I can't do that without explaining myself.

Ever since personal computers have been around, I have been involved with computers in some way. I bought the first IBM PC in 1981 when it had a whopping 64K of memory. I struggled then with DOS (and still do now). But I enjoy a challenge, and DOS provides one. I hope that this book will reduce that frustration for you.

After a few years of learning about computers and DOS, I became an independent computer consultant. During this seven years, I taught many classes on spreadsheets, word processing, and databases, as well as DOS. The DOS classes were always the hardest to teach. More than once I had students looking at the screen through tears of frustration. If anything keeps people from using their computers more effectively, it is an unfriendly operating system like, well, DOS.

I have written *Learning DOS* to help MS-DOS computer users (including you) use their computers with as little trouble as possible. The format of this book, as you have seen, is unlike anything I've found in computer book publishing. I remembered the types of questions my students used to ask. These became the basis for selecting the topics and addressing the problems within those topics.

This book about DOS is by no means complete. Many times, I had to stop writing and delete material. I kept telling myself, "Just tell them enough to get the job done." For example, you don't need to know that a floppy disk has tracks, sectors, and clusters to be able to use the disk. You need to know only how to format it and use the files on it.

I hope that you can find in this book the answers to the problems you have with DOS. I'm interested in hearing from you. If you encounter a problem that you think should have been in the book, write to me in care of Macmillan Computer Publishing, 11711 N. College Ave., Carmel IN 46032. I can't answer your questions individually. But if I have a chance to include the material in the next edition, I'll certainly give you credit.

And, as I've mentioned elsewhere, if you use the Learning Guide program and would like to send a copy of your Learning Guide disk, I'll use it to compile a profile of readers. Send a disk of any size and a self-addressed stamped envelope. I'll return the results after I've received the first hundred disks.

Every word is written for you, the reader. Again, I hope that you can use this book to get your DOS problems out of the way. Then you can move on to using the computer as a powerful personal tool for information management.

More than two bad tracks

See FORMAT — Disks (12)

Mouse suddenly won't work

See CONFIG.SYS (22)

Moving the computer

See Ports (40)

Multiple ports

See Ports (40)

Multiple users

See File Organization (17)

Needing exact duplicates of a disk

See DISKCOPY — Duplicating Disks (63)

Network connection error

See SHARE (57)

Network crashes

See Networks (79)

Networks (79)

VERSIONS
All ●
Some ○
5.0 ○

Command ○
Program ○
Concept ●
Problem ○

A network allows individual computers to be connected so that they can share files and printers. Typically one computer serves as the *host* (main system), and the other computers are connected to the host.

Problems

Lost network connection. Once your computer makes the initial connection to the host system, that connection is maintained by both the host and your system's network software. A number of factors can cause this connection to be broken. Depending on your software, reestablishing the connection may be relatively easy or fairly difficult. You need to know what to do if you receive an error message about a dropped connection. The most extreme way to reconnect will be to reboot your system. As with any system reboot, you may lose data in the process. Ask your network administrator for guidelines on what to do when the connection is dropped.

Network crash. When the network host stops processing the network traffic, this is known as a *network crash*. It may mean that the host computer is turned off or the network software has simply stopped working. Again, depending on your software and how much you rely on the network, you may lose data. Network crashes are frustrating because they are unpredictable.

Memory conflicts. The software needed to maintain the connection with the network requires memory. Some network programs take as little as 40K, and others need 160K or more. The network system administrator sets up the local system. But remember that the network software is interacting, and in some cases, replaces DOS. This may lead to an `Out of memory` message as well as other problems. If you are on a network, you have another potential source of system errors.

Explanation

Personal computers used to be personal. Users ran programs and accomplished work. They decided what to do, and when. Everything was under local control. Mainframe and minicomputer systems depended on a host computer to do all the work. A user had a terminal, but without the host, the terminal was useless. Terminals could not do any processing on their own. The system was controlled by the person who controlled the host.

Mainframes were good for sharing data, sharing expensive pieces of equipment, and maintaining consistency of data processing. Personal computers stood alone in their use of data and equipment. Consistency in data processing was up to the individual user. Then came networks.

Networks combine both the good and the bad of personal computing and mainframe computing. The processing is handled locally on the personal computer. In fact, the personal computer can still function even if the network is down. The network provides access to common data and can use common devices, such as high-speed printers and modems. Networks also feature electronic mail, known as *e-mail*. Each user on the network can send messages to other individuals or groups.

But the network can be used to restrict users as well. Personal computers can be set up more like terminals. Take away the hard disk, a local printer, and even a local floppy, and the computer must rely totally on the network to load and run programs, create and use data files, and print files. The computers just become terminals, incapable of doing anything without the network connection.

Anyone connected to a network should understand five points about network access:

1. *Access to data and programs can be totally controlled by the network administrator.* When you log on, you or your system provides an ID and password. These must already be established by the network administrator. That individual also determines the areas of the network you can use and which areas are inaccessible to you. At the DOS level, you will not "see" some areas of the directory tree.

2. *Everything you do on the network can be monitored by the system.* Because the network functions as a data channel, this channel also records traffic. It is possible, although not yet common, to log all activity to and through the network.

3. *At the DOS level, the network simply looks like additional drives and printer ports.* Your system may be completely menu-driven. If you do not normally drop to DOS, the only difference you may see is that some data is stored on drives like Y: and Z:. If you have a local printer, your network printer may be LPT2: or LPT3:. For users who have access to DOS, the network drive should respond to normal DOS commands. There may be additional commands you can use. Refer to your network manuals for more information about these commands.

4. *Network mail should never be considered private.* All e-mail sent on the network is stored until the receiver picks up the mail. Although the software is designed so that usually only the sender and receiver can view and delete the mail, the network administrator *may* be able to read those e-mail files. This is not to suggest that someone is reading your e-mail, but it is possible. Furthermore, once the receiver has read the mail and deleted it, it may not be removed from the system. Those e-mail files may just be copied to a backup area and saved. Recent court cases have brought both these facts to user awareness.

5. *Data and program files may be temporarily unavailable.* Depending on the software being used, when you attempt to access a specific file on the network, you may get the message that the file is "locked" (unavailable). The specific software package has not been designed to let more than one person use the data file at one time. As with a library book, once the file is "checked out," only one person can use it. Other programs allow multiple users to access the same data file. These programs are more sophisticated because they keep track of how the data is being used and they attempt to resolve the conflicts on a lower level. You can still get a "locked" message, but it is more likely to occur when two users are trying the change the same record.

Networks have many different layouts. Some must run a cable to each individual machine. Others require that systems be linked like cars in a train. The actual wiring method is not as important as the power of the engine and how many cars are attached. From the user's perspective, the more users attached to the network, the more power is required from the host. This contention for server resources is what causes processing delays. Requirements vary greatly, but slow response time on the network significantly impairs the work flow and is frustrating to users as well.

References

Communications (55)

NEXT TOPIC: Compressed Files (80)

New bugs

See Upgrading Your Software (65)

New disk

See FORMAT — Disks (12)
See also Floppy Disks (19)

New Programs on Old Computers (71)

VERSIONS
All ●
Some ○
5.0 ○

Command ○
Program ○
Concept ●
Problem ○

Software programs are constantly being improved. Features are expanded or added with each new version. Some features may require a faster computer to use. Whole new categories of programs have also been created because the more powerful computers can run them.

Before You Begin

Application Software (46)
Program Versions (47)
Upgrading Your Software (65)

Problems

Program runs slowly. If you have just installed a new version of an old program, you may notice that the menus do not work as quickly and the screen takes longer to change. The new version may require a new computer too. If the program is new, make sure that the software is "rated" for your type of system. If you have an XT system and the program states that it needs an AT or a 386 system, you'll need to return the program and request a refund. If your system is listed, check the manual for tips on optimizing the software with your current system.

Inaccessible features. Newer programs contain features that require newer equipment. For example, if you have a monochrome (text) screen and the program requires graphics, you won't be able to use the program at all. If the program supports a mouse and you don't have one, you may not be able to use the program as effectively. Don't think that you automatically have to get the new equipment, though. Consider how important the features requiring new hardware are to your productivity before investing in that new software and hardware.

Explanation

Although millions of XT-type computers may be in use, the newer programs require at least an AT system. Some programs now require a 386 or larger system. (See also topic 96 on microprocessors.) Each successive system has more power "under the hood." The programs require this power to handle the extra features that are built-in.

These additional requirements leave users of older computers without a path for upgrading their software. Although human nature compels us to get the newest and latest of anything, look carefully at what you need to get the job done. The topic

Upgrading Your Software (65) considers new software and software upgrades. Upgrading hardware is even a more expensive matter. If you decide that you can use the features in a newer program, how do you decide what to change in your computer system?

The first consideration is, of course, How much can you spend? Because there are so many possibilities, consider an example.

Suppose that you have an XT computer with 256K of memory, two 360K disk drives, and a monochrome (text only) screen. Your software is three years old, but it works well to prepare the newsletter and 400-member mailing list for your group. You are interested in making the newsletter look better with two columns and some graphics. Because your membership roster is growing, you would also like to track dues and committee assignments. Your current system cannot display graphics or store the data on just one floppy. Should you upgrade your system or start over?

You would need to add a 20M hard drive ($300), 384K of memory ($250), a VGA monitor and display card ($500), as well as buy new software. The total cost for the upgrade would be over $1,000, including labor. All these additional parts are still based on a slow processor (the XT computer). The warranty will cover only the parts, not the computer itself. However, an AT-type computer includes 1M of memory (640K + 384K), a VGA monitor, and probably a 40M hard drive. The AT system is 10 to 20 times faster, is covered under warranty, and is not likely to cost much more.

Although comparing costs is important, your primary consideration is, How do you need to use the computer? If your tasks need powerful software that requires more powerful hardware, making changes makes sense. Just be clear on your needs before you make the investment in time and money.

References

Application Software (46), Program Versions (47), Upgrading Your Software (65)

NEXT TOPIC: Hardware and Software Compatibility (72)

No backups

See Backing Up Data (13)
See also BACKUP — Files (41)

No directory status in prompt

See PROMPT — Command Line Information (26)

No One to Help (59)

VERSIONS
All ●
Some ○
5.0 ○

Command ○
Program ○
Concept ●
Problem ○

When you get stuck on a problem, where can you turn for help? A number of resources are available. The best approach is to know where to turn before you are really in trouble.

Problems

One-person office. If you are *it* when it comes to using *the* computer in your office, you need to cultivate some "help" resources:

- Get active in a local user's group. Attend the evening meetings and find out who uses the same software. If you join, you'll receive the newsletter and may have access to the "help line" that many groups now run.
- Make sure that you have registered all your software.
- Create a support sheet with the name of each software package you use, your registration number, the version number, and the phone support number (and hours) of each software company.
- Make sure that the budget has room for additional books on the software packages you use.

Unusual program. One of the dilemmas of using a nonmainstream program is that local help may not be available. You may have to rely on the support staff of the software company. Keep this limitation in mind when deciding to purchase unusual software.

Unregistered software. When you call a company support line and are asked for a serial number, the company won't know who you are unless you have registered your software. The support staff may refuse to help you. You might get an answer by declaring that you have the registration card in hand (because you do), and you'll mail it immediately after hanging up the phone. Then do it.

Illegal copy. If you do not have the manuals to the software and are not registered with the company, you can't expect help from the company. You'll have to find local help. You might want to consider purchasing the software.

Explanation

You may want to read the topics Solving Problems(14) and Learning More (28) for more ideas on getting help and dealing with computer problems.

References

Solving Problems (14), Learning More (28)

NEXT TOPIC: Installing Programs (60)

No support

See Product Registration (54)

Noisy phone line

See Modems (56)

Nonsystem disk or disk error

See Boot/Startup (1)

Not a directory

See CD, MD, and RD — Working with Directories (9)

Not an ASCII file

See PRINT — Spooler (45)

Not an available program

See `Bad command or file name` (6)

Not enough memory

See Memory (73)
See also MEM (90)

Not enough space on the hard drive

See Installing Programs (60)
See also Compressed Files (80)

Not ready reading drive

See Default Drive (3)
See also A: B: C: — Drive Designation (7)

Nothing appears on the screen

See Boot/Startup (1)

Nothing happens when you turn on the switch

See Boot/Startup (1)

Old version of RESTORE

See BACKUP — Files (41)

Older software versions

See Upgrading Your Software

One-person office

See No One to Help (59)

Operating Systems (75)

VERSIONS
All ●
Some ○
5.0 ○

Command ○
Program ○
Concept ●
Problem ○

This book covers DOS, which stands for *d*isk *o*perating *s*ystem. Other operating systems include OS/2, UNIX, and the Macintosh operating system.

Before You Begin

Software (18)
Hardware (38)
Application Software (46)

Problems

Exchanging files between different operating systems. Because operating systems control everything about the computer, including disk formats, the exchange of data between different operating systems presents two problems:

- *Physical media.* Some systems have special boards that can read a foreign disk format. MS-DOS systems can use the Option Board from Central Point Software to read Macintosh disks. If both systems are connected to a network, the files can only be copied to the host and then copied back from the host. You could have the files uploaded to a BBS (by modem) and downloaded by the second system. Systems can be connected directly through serial cables and communications software used to exchange the files.
- *Data format.* With some exceptions, different operating systems create different files formats, just as most DOS programs create unique file formats. A data file must be converted to a format the receiving system can use. In many cases, this format is ASCII. Some software companies are trying to provide universal formats to allow direct transfer of the files to different systems.

What version of DOS do you have? The DOS VER command shows the version number and source for your version of DOS.

Using different operating system versions. Like programs, operating systems change from version to version. Some of the features discussed in one manual may disappear completely in the next. Keep all older versions of the software and their manuals until you are sure that all compatibility problems have been resolved.

Explanation

An operating system controls the hardware and software in every computer system. In some cases, the operating system is built into the computer. This prevents the operating system from being upgraded easily. In most cases, the operating system is loaded first and then allowed to take control of the computer. As the system designers learn how to take better advantage of the hardware, they can improve the operating system software.

The operating system is the most critical part of the computer. A very average hardware design can be maximized by a good operating system. But even the best system design can be wasted if the operating system does not use all the features available in the hardware.

DOS has gone through several releases of PC DOS (created for IBM) and MS-DOS (released by Microsoft). The first two version numbers, 1.0 and 1.1, were released by IBM only after being written by Microsoft. The next release, 1.25, was Microsoft's. From that point, the releases of PC DOS and MS-DOS coincided. Although there are some differences in these designs, notably fewer programs in the PC DOS versions, the features were quite similar through versions 2.0, 3.0, 3.1, 3.2, 3.3, 4.0, and now 5.0. To find the exact version you are using, type **VER** at the command prompt.

References

Communications (55), History of DOS (88)

NEXT TOPIC: REN — REName Files (76)

Other programs will not run

See Installing Programs (60)

Other programs won't work after installing a new program

See CONFIG.SYS (22)

Out of environment space

See PATH — Program Search (29)
See also COMMAND.COM/EXIT (78)

Overwriting a newer file with an older file

See COPY — Files (10)

Panic RESTORE

See RESTORE — Files (42)

Paper in Printer (68)

VERSIONS	
All	●
Some	○
5.0	○
Command	○
Program	○
Concept	○
Problem	●

Loading paper in printers requires patience, stamina, and a lot of practice. This topic provides information on paper types, paper loading, and paper-loading problems.

Before You Begin

Printers (15)

Problems

Trying to load paper. Some olders printers were so difficult to load with paper that an office specialist was needed every time new paper had to be loaded. Newer printers have autoload features. Laser printers load single sheets of paper and don't require lining up the printer sprocket holes. Nonetheless, you can still have some problems:

- With large boxes of continuous (perforated) paper, the interval between paper reloading may be weeks or months. Each time you load the paper, you relearn the process. The first time you load the paper successfully, remove the paper immediately and do it again. Reload the paper several times. Once you figure out how to load the paper, get someone else in the office to learn the process too. Learning how to load or change paper easily may help reduce the number of memos sent out on greenbar paper.

- When loading continuous paper, plan the paper path. Anticipate a 50-page report piling up as the printer continues to feed paper from the stack. Otherwise, the incoming paper may stop feeding from the weight of the outgoing paper. Because the small pins on the sprocket pull the paper through the printer, a torn sprocket hole may result in all 50 pages printing on one line.
- Most *tractor-feed* (holes on both sides) sprockets are movable to allow for different widths of paper. Each sprocket has a small lever to lock the sprocket in place once the paper has been loaded. Although the width of the paper is generally consistent, leaving the left sprocket unlatched allows it to move slightly along the bar. This movement may prevent the paper from pulling apart or creasing if the paper width does change slightly.

Paper jam. Murphy's law suggests that an unattended printer is the same as a jammed printer. The longer or more urgent the report, the higher the likelihood that the printer will jam within the first two pages. Returning 20 minutes after the report should be finished only enhances the prospect that the printer has stopped on the first page. If constant monitoring of the printing is not practical, at least watch the first few pages to make sure that the paper is feeding properly and that the output pile is well established.

Explanation

Computer paper is instantly recognizable because it has green stripes across the page and holes down each side. More technically called greenbar, form-feed, or continuous paper, it is commonly used for printing massive reports. The green bars help the reader scan the page, and the continuous paper forms stay together. The holes can be used to keep the paper in a binder.

Now that personal computers can generate hard copy, green lines and holes down the side have become less appealing. Laser printers have eliminated any appearance of computer-generated paper. These printers deal with the paper one sheet at a time. The method for getting the paper into the printer is called "sheet feed." The originals from a laser printer look just as if they came from a copy machine.

Form-feed printers (for continuous paper) and sheet-feed printers (for single sheets) have little in common for loading paper. Each method has its own tips, covered next in this discussion.

The most important part of loading paper is to *practice*. With the large boxes of 2,500 sheets of paper, it may be weeks or months before you have to reload the paper. The next time you do load the paper, you may have trouble remembering how to do it. Just take the paper back out and load it again. Two or three loadings will help you remember later. Here are some tips:

- Unless your printer has autoload, always load the paper with the printer turned off. The paper roller will turn more smoothly.
- Tear the first sheet off cleanly and then double it over. It may be easier to feed the double thickness of paper through the printer.
- Some printers have a pressure lever. With the lever on, you can pull the paper through. Afterward, make sure that the pressure lever is off. The *tractor-feed* sprockets pull the paper through when the printer is feeding the paper. Having the pressure lever on with tractor-feed paper is a frequent cause of paper jams.
- Check to make sure that the printer ribbon does not get pushed off the printhead (the part that moves back and forth) as you push the paper edge through the printer. The printed image will be a little light without a ribbon in front of the printhead!
- Sometimes leaving the tractor-feed lever (just behind each sprocket) off on the right side will help the paper feed through. The position lever locks the tractor-feed sprocket in place. When the right lever is left off, the sprocket can move slightly if the width of the paper or the location of the holes shifts.
- You can remove 8 or 12 strips (containing the holes) along the edges of the paper at one time if you bend the edges back and forth several times before tearing them off.
- Paper thickness is measured in pounds. An 18-pound paper is a fairly standard weight. Twenty-pound paper is a bit heavier and may be easier to work with. Fifteen-pound paper is very flimsy but cheaper. It may be useful for archival reports if the material will not be used much and if cost and space are considerations.
- Continuous paper (for form-feed printers) comes in various sizes and types, including Rolodex and index cards. Some stationery companies can print your business letterhead on continuous paper.

Laser printers and copy machines use the same kind of paper (single sheets). The image is based on plastic (called *toner*) melted onto the paper. The quality of the paper affects the final image. Note some other tips:

- Paper for copy machines and laser printers has a top and a bottom. Check the package for an arrow indicating which side is the “first” side for printing.

- Paper left out for weeks or months absorbs moisture. The paper may stick together or not feed properly through the printer. If the paper keeps jamming, try a new package of paper.
- The heat inside the laser printer dries out the paper. Reused paper may tend to jam. Trying to print on the backside of previously printed paper may leave extra toner in unexpected places.
- Letterhead paper with a rough surface texture may not hold an image well. Parts of the image may not adhere to the "valleys" in the paper.
- Some printed letterhead uses a plastic ink, usually to produce a raised look to the image. This plastic image is likely to come off on the hot rollers and be repeated down the page along with the printed image.

Exercise

Starting with an empty printer, conduct an office competition to find out who is the quickest to load the paper, align the paper at the top of the page, and turn the printer on. You'll have to think up your own prize.

References

Printers (15), Labels in Printer (68), Networks (79), Sharing Devices (93)

NEXT TOPIC: Labels in Printer (69)

Paper jam

See Paper in Printer (68)

Parity error

See Memory (73)

Partition selected (x) is not bootable

See Partitions — FDISK (97)

PQR

Partitions — FDISK (97)

VERSIONS	
All	●
Some	○
5.0	○
Command	○
Program	●
Concept	○
Problem	○

A partition, among other things, allows DOS to treat a hard disk as separate drives. Before DOS 4.0, the largest partition was 32M. Partitions can be used also to keep different operating systems on the same hard drive.

Before You Begin

FORMAT — Disks (12)
Hard Drive Failure (33)

Syntax

A:\>**FDISK**	Prepares one or more parts of a hard disk to be formatted

Problems

`Partition selected (x) is not bootable.` If you use FDISK to switch partitions and you attempt to boot from a partition without boot tracks, you get this message. Run FDISK again and reselect the primary partition.

Using system setup. Most systems come with a disk or have built-in programs to make changes to the system controls. Many systems provide instructions for accessing these programs on the screen as the system boots. The programs include formatting the hard disk as well as resetting the system date and time. Be sure that you understand the results of any changes you make with these programs. You could lose data or prevent the system from running at all.

Explanation

DOS uses *partitions* to organize parts of the hard disk into logical drives. You see these drives as C:, D:, E:, and so on. Before version 4.0, a partition could be no larger than 32M, so a 40M hard disk could have drives C: and D:. Because the user can determine the size of the partition, these drives could be divided any number of ways. Usually they were divided evenly as two 20M drives, or one 32M drive and one 8M drive. Versions 4.0 and 5.0 allow partitions of any size. Although partitions are intended to allow more than one operating system to exist on the same hard drive, their use was limited in versions before 4.0 because a partition could be only 32M.

Setting up a hard drive is not an everyday task for most people. But because anyone with access to DOS can potentially destroy an entire disk full of data, you should understand how a hard disk is prepared for use. Deleting FDISK from your hard disk helps prevent disaster because you can't accidentally run a program if you don't have it on your hard disk.

> WARNING: DO NOT TRY TO DUPLICATE THE STEPS OUTLINED HERE. This information is provided only for you to understand what happens when disks are formatted. See your DOS manual and your computer manual for specific instructions.

The FORMAT program prepares a floppy disk for immediate use. On a totally unformatted disk, FORMAT marks the tracks and sectors and creates the directory space. FORMAT recognizes that the disk to be formatted is a floppy and handles all the necessary steps at once. Hard disks require a few more steps.

A new hard disk from the factory requires three preparatory steps before it can be used. The hard disk must first be low-level formatted. This step includes determining the proper interleave. The hard disk controllers in XT systems had the program built into ROM. A few instructions in DEBUG started the process. AT systems (and later) provided this step as part of the software used to set up the system.

Once the hard disk has been low-level formatted, the DOS FDISK program sets up the partitions on the hard disk. A partition is just a small section of data that is written to the hard disk and that DOS reads when booting the system. If this partition data is lost or changed, the hard disk becomes unrecognizable to DOS, and the data is totally lost! Because FDISK can change the partition information, exploratory use is not recommended.

After one or more partitions have been set up by DOS, each partition is formatted with the FORMAT program. The primary partition is formatted with the /S switch to make that disk bootable. Once the first drive has been formatted, the disk is usable. If more than one logical disk is created with FDISK, each of those disks must be formatted.

> Initiating a low-level format or changing the partition with FDISK will result in loss of data!

Most *clone* systems (non-IBM but functionally similar systems) have diagnostic and setup programs built into ROM. While the system is booting, the screen provides instructions to access these programs; usually you press the Delete key or a combination of keys. Although a number of useful programs may be accessible in clone systems, there are also a number of ways you can lose the data on your hard disk. Be extremely careful if you use this setup program.

References

Operating Systems (75)

NEXT TOPIC: EDIT — DOS 5.0 Text Editor (98)

PATH — Program Search (29)

VERSIONS	
All	●
Some	○
5.0	○
Command	●
Program	○
Concept	○
Problem	○

The DOS PATH command provides a list of directories that DOS searches so that program files can run. If, after searching the current directory and looking at all the directories in the PATH setting, DOS cannot find the program to run, the system returns the message `Bad command or file name`.

Before You Begin

File Names (4)
DIR — Directory (8)
CD, MD, and RD — Working with Directories (9)
File Organization (17)

Syntax

`C:\>`**`PATH=C:\DOS;C:\WORD`**	DOS will be able to find and run programs in the \DOS and \WORD subdirectories.
`C:\>`**`PATH`** `C:\>`**`PATH=C:\DOS;C:\WORD`**	You type **PATH** without additional parameters to check the current path.

Problems

`Bad command or file name.` The PATH command accepts any string of characters. Only when DOS begins searching for a program along the path will the system report this problem. Type **PATH** to make sure that all the directories are valid. This error message is especially likely to appear after a major reorganization of the hard disk. Because this message has many possible causes, it is covered more completely in topic 6.

`Invalid drive in path name`. This error message is issued only if DOS reaches the portion of the PATH with a drive designation or directory that does not exist. Type **PATH** to make sure that all the drives and directories exist. This problem may occur just after you reorganize your hard disk and delete or rename directories.

Decreasing PATH search time. Some systems set the path in the AUTOEXEC.BAT file and never change it. This results in a long path string, which works in most cases. Other systems change the path in the process of using a menu system. Changing the path for each application is more efficient when some programs that use the PATH setting are run. A path change causes problems if you reorganize the hard disk but don't carefully check the menu or batch system that changes paths as it operates. If AUTOEXEC.BAT contains a long PATH statement, your system is based on the *generic path*. If the PATH statement is limited or missing, the menu system probably makes changes to the PATH as it operates.

`Out of environment space`. This error message has several possible causes. The most common is a PATH statement that is too long and therefore fills up the amount of space DOS has set aside for the environment. See the topic COMMAND.COM/EXIT (78) to solve this problem with the /E:*nnnn* parameter.

Explanation

The DOS PATH command provides flexibility when you run programs on a hard disk system. To run a program, you must usually be in the directory containing the program. But if the PATH statement includes the directory with that program, you can type the program name regardless of the current subdirectory.

The capability of DOS to look down the set path creates some of the confusion between DOS commands and DOS programs. Commands like DIR, DEL, and COPY are internal DOS commands. They work anytime. Other DOS "commands" are actually programs that are provided with the operating system. These programs, such as FORMAT and XCOPY, are usually located in a subdirectory, usually called DOS. With `PATH=C:\DOS`, typing **`FORMAT A:`** works like a command because DOS uses the PATH string to find the program FORMAT.COM under the \DOS directory.

A long PATH makes DOS look through each subdirectory before the system reports that you have typed a `Bad command or file name`. The line

```
PATH C:\DOS;C:\BATCH;C:\WORDPROC;C:\PCTOOLS;C:\DATABASE\FOXPRO
```

causes DOS to look in the C:\DOS subdirectory, then the C:\BATCH, then the C:\WORDPROC, and so on. If each subdirectory has 50 files, DOS may have to look through 250 files on the hard disk before finding the program name you typed. This is not to say that you should avoid long PATH statements, just that you should put the most important subdirectories at the front of the string. Also consider the importance of the subdirectory. If you always change the directory (CD) before using PC Tools, you don't need to include that subdirectory in the path.

Many installation programs now add their subdirectories to the PATH line in the AUTOEXEC.BAT file. This can increase the time required to search the path and can create such a long string that DOS runs out of environment space. You may see evidence of this if the PATH string is cut off in an odd place. DOS has simply run out of room to store that information. See COMMAND.COM/EXIT (78) for the use of the /E:*nnnn* parameter to increase the storage space for a long PATH statement.

If a program lets you decide whether AUTOEXEC.BAT can be changed, allow changes to be made as long as the program makes a second copy of the AUTOEXEC.BAT file. If problems develop after a new program has been installed, you can examine the new AUTOEXEC.BAT in solving the problems.

Exercise

This exercise explores the use of the PATH command. Usually, once you have found the optimum PATH statement, it needs to be changed only when you add new programs to the hard disk. If you use a menu system exclusively, you may not need to worry at all about the PATH setting. The menu program automatically puts you in the proper subdirectory for the program to run.

Exercise 1 of 1

In this exercise, you explore how the PATH setting affects your system. Remember that the PATH command can be used both at the command prompt and in a batch file, usually your AUTOEXEC.BAT. If you do want to make permanent changes to your PATH, you'll need to alter a line of your AUTOEXEC.BAT file.

TRY	NOTE
`C:\>`**`PATH`**	The response to this command will be either a series of subdirectories or the response `No Path`.
	If you have a listing for the path, examine each of the portions separated by the semicolons. Each portion points to a hard disk area containing programs you can use when you are elsewhere in the directory tree.
`C:\>`**`PATH;`**	Using the semicolon immediately after PATH erases the current PATH setting.
`C:\>`**`TREE`**	Try to run the DOS TREE program from the root directory. Unless you have all your DOS files in the root, the program shouldn't run. (If you have all those files in the root, read topic 17 on file organization soon.)

TRY	NOTE

`C:\>PATH C:\DOS`
`C:\>PATH`
`C:\>PATH=C:\DOS`
	You have created a path now that looks into the subdirectory named DOS. (If your subdirectory name is different, use it instead.)

`C:\>TREE`	Now when you run the DOS TREE program, DOS looks down the path and finds the program in that subdirectory.
`C:\>AUTOEXEC`	If you originally had a PATH setting, running the AUTOEXEC.BAT file restores it.

References

TREE — Directory Map (87)

NEXT TOPIC: DEL — DELete Files (30)

Path suddenly not working

See COMMAND.COM/EXIT (78)

Poor record design

See Databases (49)

Ports (40)

VERSIONS	
All	●
Some	○
5.0	○
Command	○
Program	○
Concept	●
Problem	○

A *port* is the hardware connection the computer uses to get input and provide output. Standard ports include the keyboard for input and the monitor for output. Users must usually deal with the printer and serial ports on the back of the computer.

Before You Begin

Printer (15)
Hardware (38)

Problems

Many cable connections. The back of the computer system contains a number of sockets. When connecting a printer, modem, or mouse, you must determine which cable goes into which socket. Although physical differences may prevent you from inserting a plug in the wrong socket, sorting out the sockets may take time. To help you make the connections later, have the sockets labeled when the computer is installed.

Multiple ports. Although a system has only one keyboard and usually one monitor attached, the system may have up to three printers and two or more serial devices. DOS calls each by a unique name, depending on the hardware inside the computer. From the outside, you cannot tell which of two serial ports is COM1 and which is COM2.

Moving the computer. Before moving the computer, use tape to label each cable and socket with a number or letter. If the system has a hard disk, review the topic Hard Drive Failure (33) to prevent such a failure from occurring as the result of the move.

Explanation

If you examine the back of your computer, you are likely to see at least three connections: the power cord, the monitor cable, and the keyboard connector. Each of these cables can be attached in the socket designed just for that cable. There may also be printers, a mouse, and a modem attached. All the cables (except the power cord) represent the flow of data in and out of the computer.

> Because a signal may be traveling in the cables, always turn off the computer before plugging or unplugging cables. And always touch something metal first to prevent a static electric discharge from you through the computer.

The two types of ports of interest are *parallel* and *serial*. The parallel port is commonly used for a printer, and each serial port can be used for a modem or a mouse. Some printers also use serial ports.

A printer cable is easy to match with the proper parallel socket. Either the cable goes in or it doesn't. Notice that the shape of the connection may require turning the cable around before it will fit. You may have difficulty if the system has more than one printer port. If the ports are not labeled, it may take some trial and error to connect the printer to the right port. Make the connection, turn on the system, and then try to print. If a `Printer not ready` message appears, turn the system off and try the other port. Hint: A printer port in the same slot with the monitor cable is probably LPT1:. Once you make the connection, label the ports appropriately.

Serial ports are not quite as easy to connect because they come in two sizes: 25-pin and 9-pin. For most connections, the difference in the number of pins is not significant. There is, though, a difference between the cable that fits the 25-pin port and the cable for the 9-pin port. When confronted with a 25-pin cable and a 9-pin connection, you will need a 9- to 25-pin adapter. If the situation is reversed, you'll need a 25- to 9-pin version. Once you make the connection through the adapter, you should not have any difficulty.

The problem just noted with parallel ports is true also with serial ports. Unless the sockets are marked, you cannot tell which port is which. Again, trial and error may be necessary to find the right port. Most mouse software can search the ports to find the port with the mouse connection.

Serial printers not only require the proper connection but also must be redirected with the MODE program. See the topic MODE — Configuring System Devices (83) for more information about connecting a serial printer to a serial port.

As mentioned, DOS has a unique name for each port. Table 40-1 shows the ports and the DOS names. The specific devices are based on interrupts (switches) set when the ports are installed in the computer. Most programs enable you to set the port for input/output, using the DOS name. The default (standard) setting for a program using a printer is LPT1: or PRN:, and the default setting for a serial port is COM1:.

Table 40-1. DOS ports and names.

Port	DOS Name
Screen/keyboard (console)	CON:
First serial	COM1: or AUX:
Second serial	COM2:
First parallel	LPT1: or PRN:
Second parallel	LPT2:
Third parallel	LPT3:
Dummy device	NUL:

The parallel and serial ports use the designations listed in Table 40-1 because they describe the transmission of data through the port. Parallel ports send the data eight bits at a time, broadside through the port. Serial ports send the data only one bit at a time, single file. This difference in data transmission means that parallel ports send the data more quickly. Serial ports are slower and have a variety of settings, including baud rate, number of data bits, and parity. See the topics Communications (55) and Modems (56) for more information on using the serial port with a modem.

References

Printers (15), Communications (55), Modems (56)

NEXT TOPIC: BACKUP — Files (41)

Postponed recovery

See UNDELETE (31)

Power failure

See CHKDSK — CHecK DiSK (20)

Practice RESTORE

See RESTORE — Files (42)

Press Ctrl-Alt-Del

See Solving Problems (14)

Press Ctrl-C or Ctrl-Break

See Solving Problems (14)

Press the F1 key (or another help key)

See Solving Problems (14)

Preventing accidental file deletions

See ATTRIB — Protecting Files (62)

Previous versions

See Installing Programs (60)

PRINT — Spooler (45)

VERSIONS	
All	●
Some	○
5.0	○
Command	○
Program	●
Concept	○
Problem	○

The DOS PRINT program allows multiple ASCII files to be printed while you use other DOS commands. Any formatting of the text must already be contained in the file.

Before You Begin

Files (2)
File Names (4)
Printers (15)

Syntax

`C:\>PRINT /D:LPT1 TEXTFILE.TXT`	Prints TEXTFILE.TXT to LPT1:
`C:\>PRINT /D:LPT1 *.TXT`	Prints all files with the extension TXT to the printer
`C:\>PRINT`	Gives the status of the print queue

Problems

Not an ASCII file. If the results on the printer don't look right (you get printer garbage), use the PRINT /T switch immediately to terminate PRINT (stop the printing). PRINT can print only standard ASCII files with line breaks. Use the TYPE command (topic 81) to look at the file on the screen. If the file is readable, you can use PRINT. Document files from most word processors will *not* work with PRINT. They must be printed from within their own programs.

PRINT not printing. When a file is first placed in the print queue and the printer is off-line, an error message is not returned. Only if the PRINT command is issued again does DOS respond with `Errors on list device indicate that it may be off-line. Please check it.` PRINT will hold that file in the queue until you do one of the following:

- Turn on the printer so that the file can be printed.
- Cancel the file with **`PRINT FILENAME.EXT /C`**.
- Cancel all files with **`PRINT /T`**.
- Reboot the system.

Attempting to print a file from another program while PRINT is running. You can use other DOS programs while PRINT is sending files to the printer. Do *not* try to print anything from another program while PRINT is still sending files to the printer, however.

Stopping PRINT tasks. After you've placed a list of files in the print queue, PRINT continues until all the files have been sent to the printer. If you need to stop PRINT because the printer is jammed or the wrong file is printing, use **`PRINT /T`** to stop all printing. Use **`PRINT FILENAME.EXT /C`** to cancel the printing of a specific file in the queue.

Explanation

The PRINT program is limited to printing only text (ASCII) files. The first time PRINT is run, it must be told which printer to use. If the /D switch is not used on the command line, PRINT prompts you for the printer. Once PRINT has been loaded, you can add files to the queue without specifying the printer. (PRINT complains if you try to add the device again.) Note this example:

```
C:\DOS>PRINT text.prt
Name of list device [PRN:] <Enter>   (Use default PRN: = LTP1:.)
C:\DOS>PRINT
C:\DOS\TEXT.PRT is currently being printed.
```

A good use for the PRINT program is to send a number of text files or a long text file to the printer and then continue with other tasks. For example, if a directory has 15 batch files you want printed, you can type

```
C:\BATCH>PRINT *.BAT
```

to list them all on the printer. Each file will start on a new page under PRINT's command.

PRINT has a number of additional switches relating to buffer size and printer control. Table 45-1 shows some of these switches. Refer to the DOS manual for details on fine-tuning the PRINT program.

Table 45-1. Some switches you can use with PRINT.

Switch	Description
/D:*device*	Indicates the print device, usually /D:LPT1:
/B:*size*	Specifies internal buffer size in bytes
/Q:*qsize*	Specifies the number of files in the print queue (default is 10)
/T	Removes all files from the print queue
filename /C	Cancels the printing for that file only

You can print ASCII files to the printer in several ways if you don't want to use the PRINT program. The quickest way is to use the redirect character > with the TYPE command. This method does not allow the system to continue with other DOS tasks while it works. To print the file TEST.TXT to the printer, use

```
C:\>TYPE TEST.TXT > LPT:
```

The file prints, but the page does not advance to the top of the next page. You'll have to use the form-feed button on the printer to advance the page. Use Ctrl-Break to stop printing the file.

To use the previous PRINT *.BAT example without placing each batch file on its own page, you can issue the COPY command to "copy" the files to the printer:

```
C:\>COPY *.BAT LPT1:
```

As with TYPE and the redirect character (>), this method does not allow you to use DOS until the printing is finished. Again, use Ctrl-Break to stop printing the files.

PQR

Exercise

Although the DOS PRINT program has a rather narrow purpose, if you frequently print many ASCII files, this exercise may be helpful.

Exercise 1 of 1

In this exercise, you use several files in the EXER45 subdirectory on the disk that comes with this book. These files are ASCII files and are long enough to allow you to place them in the PRINT queue and then cancel them. The exercise works entirely from that disk, placed in drive A: (or B:).

TRY	NOTE
C:\>**A:** A:\>**CD EXER45** A:\EXER45>	This puts you in the subdirectory with the sample text files.
A:\EXERN45>**DIR**	Each of these files contains one page of text.
A:\EXER45>**PRINT** Name of list device [PRN:]	When you first start the PRINT program, it needs to know which printer is to receive the output.
<Enter>	Pressing the Enter key accepts the default of PRN. PRN is also the same as LPT1:.
A:\EXER45>**PRINT** PRINT queue is empty	Once PRINT has been loaded, typing PRINT as a command just lists the status of the queue.
A:\EXER45>**PRINT SAM01.TXT**	PRINT begins printing the file. There is no response from DOS after you initiate this command. Type the next lines as quickly as you can.
A:\EXER45>**PRINT SAM02.TXT** A:\EXER45>**PRINT SAM03.TXT** A:\EXER45>**DIR** A:\EXER45>**PRINT**	You've loaded the second and third files into the PRINT queue. Using DIR here simply shows that you can perform other DOS actions while PRINT is working. Then you see the status of the queue.
A:\EXER45>**PRINT /T**	The /T (terminate) switch cancels the current print job and removes the remaining file names from the queue.

Remember that PRINT stays in memory until the system is rebooted. PRINT will not interfere with other programs that print, but it does not help either. If you have a print job running and you start another program, PRINT may or may not continue with the print job. If you also try to use the program to print to the printer, the results are unpredictable. The best approach is to remain at the DOS prompt while PRINT is still sending files to the printer.

References

Redirection < > ¦ (64), GRAPHICS — Printing Screens (66), ASCII — Character Codes (74), TYPE — Looking at Files (81)

NEXT TOPIC: Application Software (46)

PRINT not printing

See PRINT — Spooler (45)

Printer continues to eject pages

See GRAPHICS — Printing Screens (66)

Printer garbage

See GRAPHICS — Printing Screens (66)

Printer off-line

See Printers (15)

Printer problems

See Printers (15)

Printers (15)

VERSIONS	
All	●
Some	○
5.0	○
Command	○
Program	○
Concept	○
Problem	●

Printers provide a hard copy of the data entered in the computer. Although speed and quality vary from printer to printer, problems are common to all printers.

Problems

Printers probably cause more trouble than any other part of the computer system. Their mechanical parts break down and require regular maintenance. You must load paper, ribbons, or toner and may need to press buttons to control the line status, paper feed, and print quality. Five of the most common problems are covered here.

Printer off-line. When sending something to the printer, a program is actually sending the data to DOS. DOS controls the flow of data to the printer through a parallel or serial port. (See topic 40 on ports.) Before sending the data to the printer, DOS checks whether the printer is available. If DOS sends a message to the printer and does not get a response, the printer is off-line (not available). This condition may have a number of causes:

- The printer may not be turned on. Turn the printer on and try to print again.
- The on-line light is out, which means that the printer is not "paying attention" to the computer. Press the on-line button. A light should turn on. Try to print again.
- The printer may be out of paper. Load the paper and press the on-line button.
- The paper may be jammed in the printer. When this occurs, many printers go off-line. Clear the jam, reload the paper, and press the on-line button.
- The paper may be improperly loaded. Most printers have an "out of paper" switch under the paper path. If the paper is not loaded properly, that switch is open, and the printer remains off-line. Check the switch and make sure that the paper is loaded properly.
- The cable in the back of the computer or printer may be loose. If the printer cable is not attached properly, it may pull out slightly. Push the cable in on both the printer and the computer. Check the on-line button.
- Laser printers go off-line if the toner supply is exhausted. Check the toner light and replace the cartridge if this light is on.

- Some ribbons are "single pass." They can be used only once. Check the status of the ribbon.

Light images. Although laser printers signal when the toner cartridge is out, ribbon printers just continue to circulate the ribbon regardless of the amount of ink remaining. If you have to look twice at an image to read it, the ribbon is too dry. Replace it. If the image begins to lighten on a page and then quits completely, the ribbon is probably jammed, and the printer just ate a hole in the ribbon. Replace it. Watch the next ribbon to make sure that it is being pulled through.

Loading labels. Using printer labels is not easy. The labels come in a variety of sizes and columns. Even if the label software supports the label size, you must adjust the printer to hold the labels. Because each label is a "page," pressing the form-feed button just wastes labels. You may need to move the label to the top of the printhead manually. *Do not ever roll the labels backward in the printer.* The labels are likely to peel off inside the printer and jam everything else coming in. Then you'll need to take the printer apart to remove the label mess. See also the topic Labels in Printer (69).

Wrong print type. Almost all printers can generate several types of printed images. Some have draft, NLQ (*n*ear *l*etter *q*uality), and condensed print. Others have dozens of fonts (typefaces) and sizes you can choose. Most programs are able to send the codes to the printer to select the proper type. But some programs forget to reset the printer back to the standard print when they finish. This results in the next print job coming out in the wrong typeface. You'll want to return the printer to the normal typeface. Laser printers usually have a "reset" button to return the printer to the normal, power-on settings. Other printers may need to be turned off to reset the typeface. Move the paper to the top of the printhead and then turn the printer back on.

Strange characters printed. The printing of strange characters, frequently referred to as "printer garbage," can have several causes. Some are related to hardware, and one is related to software:

- The printer cable may be only partially attached. If the connector has been pulled off at an angle, the system may think that the printer is attached and may send the data signal. But because not all the lines in the cable are connected, the data is garbled, and the resulting characters make no sense. Check all cable connections.

- Improperly shielded printer cables can cause occasional characters or lines of garbage. Printer cables are shielded to prevent stray signals. Unshielded cables are readily identified because they are flat instead of round. Although these cables can be used for short distances (no more that three feet), for longer distances the signal is likely to be corrupted. Replace the ribbon cable with round, shielded cable.

- Even shielded cable cannot reliably carry the printer signal more than 10 or 15 feet. Using an extension cord to connect the printer is likely to cause this trouble too. Move the printer closer to the computer and attach the printer with one cable. Special equipment is available if the printer must be located farther away from the computer.
- Software sends data in specific formats based on the type of printer used. If the printer has been changed but the printer settings in the software have not been changed, a complete mess will be printed in very little time. Check the printer settings in the software. Also note that if your system uses more than one printer, you must pay attention to the port being used by the software. (Ports are covered in the "Explanation" section as well as in topic 40.)

Explanation

Printers provide a wide range of quality that varies with the method used to apply the images to paper. The two most important considerations for a DOS user are the connection port used by the printer and the limitations of the method used for placing images on paper.

Each computer system consists of a box with drives, power supply, and processing unit. Although the calculations are done in this box, the value of the work is expressed when the results are produced as output for you, the consumer. The monitor (screen) provides immediate output. Sending the data to the printer provides permanent output. The channels for these outputs are referred to as *ports*. Printers can use both parallel and serial ports to receive the signal sent from the processing unit. DOS controls all data sent to the printer through these ports.

Understanding the names that DOS uses for these ports is important. The parallel printer ports are referred to as PRN:, LPT1:, LPT2:, and LPT3:. Although it is possible to have a computer without a printer port, it is rare. Most systems have at least one port addressed as LPT1: or PRN:. (It can be referred to by either name.) If the hardware has been installed in the computer, LPT2: and LPT3: may also be available. Having several ports in the same system allows both a laser printer and a dot-matrix printer to be attached. You can use either of these printers simply by telling DOS which port to send the data to. You must know which printer is attached to which port so that you can easily switch back and forth between printers.

DOS can also use the serial ports, COM1: and COM2:, as printer ports, provided the printer specifically uses that signal type. More information about how serial ports can be used is covered in the topic Ports (40). The special settings for a serial printer are mentioned in the DOS MODE program (topic 83).

New printer technology constantly provides a better image, produced more quickly at a lower cost. The two most common printer types are dot-matrix and laser. Recent versions of software can, when properly installed, use these types of printers to their best advantage.

Less expensive printers strike the paper with a series of wires or pins. As the printhead sweeps across the paper, the image is built from a series of dots. These dots, placed in a matrix for each character, create the output on dot-matrix printers. The least expensive type of dot-matrix printer creates the image with 9 pins. A much better image is built with 24 pins. Although dot-matrix printers are noisy and relatively slow, they can be used effectively for large reports and draft printouts. They also cost less to use.

Laser printers create images on paper similar to those produced by copy machines. The difference is that the image is sent from the computer instead of being copied from another sheet of paper. Lasers can provide dozens of fonts and sizes within the same document if the software is capable of sending the proper codes. Lasers print more quickly but are limited to standard-sized or legal-sized sheets. These printers can cost up to 25 cents a page to use. (Making multiple copies on a laser printer is an expensive way to save time at the copy machine.)

Both these types of printers, as well as other types, have a wide range of features. Unfortunately, each feature requires a set of codes unique to that printer. It is not uncommon for you to choose from a list of over 100 printers when installing software. Once a program knows which printer it will send the signal to, the program creates the best possible image for the printer.

Some standards exist. Epson, IBM ProPrinter, and Hewlett Packard LaserJet are printer brand names that provide standards. If a printer claims to emulate (copy) the codes for these printers, the software can be instructed to use those standard codes.

Exercise

Printer supplies are frequently a problem. This exercise provides a checklist to help you keep your printer supplied and maintained.

Exercise 1 of 1

Complete this checklist to prevent potential problems with the printer. These can include running out of toner or ribbon and using the wrong size of paper or labels.

1. What is the model and brand of the printer? ____________________
2. When and where was it purchased? ____________________
3. When does the warranty run out? ____________________
4. Where is the manual? ____________________
5. Who provides service? ____________________
6. Is the cable securely attached at both ends? ____________________
7. What supplies do you need for the printer?

Supply	*Type/Size*	*Current Stock*
Continuous paper	______________	______________
Single sheet	______________	______________
Labels	______________	______________
Ribbon/toner	______________	______________

References

Hardware (38), Ports (40), Manuals and Documentation (53), Product Registration (54), Sharing Devices (93)

NEXT TOPIC: `Strike a key when ready...` (16)

Printing strange characters

See Printers (15)

Product Registration (54)

VERSIONS	
All	●
Some	○
5.0	○
Command	○
Program	○
Concept	●
Problem	○

Most software and hardware manufacturers provide a registration card for you to complete when the product is installed. There are a number of good reasons to complete and mail the cards you receive.

Problems

No support. Some companies insist that you be registered before the support staff provides answers to your questions. If you have not registered, you may be able to claim that you just installed the software and the card has not arrived. That trick will work only once! Send the card.

Defective product. Most software and hardware products are covered by warranty. If you have not submitted the registration card, you will have to provide clear proof of purchase in order to get warranty repair or replacement.

Explanation

As you sort through the material that comes with your software or hardware, you'll find a registration card. This card is the second most important part of the package—after the diskettes (in the proper size) or cables, of course. There are several reasons why you should complete and return the registration card.

By returning the card, you establish ownership. You paid for the product; returning the card is your proof. Most companies provide a 30-day, 90-day, or 1-year warranty. If something happens to the product within the warranty period, the company will replace it free of charge, provided you have registered your copy of the program.

Registration also enables the software companies to inform you of new versions of the program. Many companies provide new and improved software versions to current owners at a significantly reduced price. An updated version is usually more powerful, has more features, and may fix any bugs (problems) in the older version.

When you receive an update notice, you don't have to upgrade to the next version. If the version you're using does everything you want and you've not discovered any bugs, you may want to stay with that version. You will still get a notice about the next update, and you'll have the option of adding the newer features.

In some cases, software companies automatically send new program versions. This may happen if many users discover a problem and call the company for help. If a large number of users experience a software problem or if a problem might result in the loss of data, the company may send a notice or new program diskettes.

Other software companies may put your name on a mailing list if you send in your card. Although some people love poring over new computer catalogs, others would rather avoid the extra mail. If you fall within the second category, make a note on the registration card. State that you do not want your name to be sold or rented for other mailings. Any company that values customer relations will make sure to keep your name out of the general mailing-list database.

If you want to make doubly sure that your name is not passed around, make a slight change in your address. Make the change small—one that won't keep you from getting the mail but will be easy to identify if you get a label with that change. For example, you could rename yourself slightly, from Robert to Roberto. If you get junk mail addressed to "Roberto," take the software company to task and request that the company remove your name from the mailing list. If you make a habit of changing your name slightly, start a list with the name variations and the companies to which you gave each name. This technique works and will be worth the effort if you really don't like junk mail.

When software companies develop and market a program, they target their efforts to a particular type of consumer. The registration cards provide an idea of who is buying the company's product. Your responses to questions on the card help the company focus design efforts on revisions or new products. As a result, you can get products that better meet your interests and needs.

Exercise

Now is the time for all good people to dig through those software boxes and make sure that all the product registration cards have been sent in. While you are at it, you may want to create a database or just fill out a sheet of paper with the following information for each software package:

Program name: ______________________________

Date of purchase: ____/____/____

Place of purchase: ______________________________

Sales rep. name: ______________________________

Cost: ______________________________

Version number: ______________________________

Serial number: ______________________________

Support phone number: ______________________

Registration card sent (date): ____/____/____

References

Copyright (51), Manuals and Documentation (53)

NEXT TOPIC: Communications (55)

Program does not support subdirectories

See SUBST (58)

Program ends with *Disk full* message

See Disk Full (35)

Program output scrolls off the screen

See MORE — Pausing Screen Display (84)

Program runs slowly

See New Programs on Old Computers (71)

Program too big to fit in memory

See MEM (90)

Program Versions (47)

VERSIONS
All ●
Some ○
5.0 ○

Command ○
Program ○
Concept ●
Problem ○

Most software packages include a version number, such as 1.02 or 4.0. What do these numbers mean? What features change from version to version? How often do the versions change?

Problems

Keeping track of the current version. Registering your software will put you on the company's mailing list. Most companies are eager to have you purchase a newer version and will send you information about upgrading.

When should you get the newer version? If you feel that the newer version provides features you can use, you may want to upgrade the software. Consider upgrading if the newer version has a whole new number, especially if you use the software often. Smaller increments—for example, from version 1.01 to 1.02—may not be significant enough to worry about. See also the topic Upgrading Your Software (65) for guidance about upgrading.

Explanation

When a new software product was offered to the public years ago, it was usually numbered version 1.0. Then users began to accept the advice "Don't buy any software with a version number 1.0." Now new software is likely to be introduced as 1.01 or 1.1. Because no standards exist for the version numbering of software, the following information is presented as a guideline.

A whole number increase, such as from version 2.0 to 3.0, usually means that the software has major changes. In some cases, the newer version hardly looks like the preceding version. File formats used by the program are likely to change with a new version number. New kinds of bugs (errors) are possible at this level as well. The company may push hard for current users to upgrade but will probably charge a lot because the software package includes new manuals and disks.

Increments of one-tenth, such as from version 3.2 to 3.3, suggest minor changes that may or may not be of interest to users. You should take a close look at the added features before deciding to upgrade. If you have discovered bugs in the current version, those bugs are likely to have been fixed at this level of upgrade. The company may announce the change and offer the newer version for a modest fee. A completely new set of disks may be provided, but the software additions may be explained in a manual supplement.

Maintenance upgrades are relegated to increments of hundredths—for example, from version 1.01 to 1.02. Upgrading to this version is unnecessary unless you have discovered a bug. When contacted, the company is likely to offer this latest version for only slightly more than the cost of shipping the upgrade disks. In some cases, these disks just contain the files needed to replace the "buggy" program, but no additional documentation except for directions on installing the "fixed" programs.

To provide even more confusion, some companies regularly improve their software packages without incrementing the version number. The best way to tell whether your software is the latest "release" is to check the dates on the main program files. These companies may offer the new disks for a modest material and shipping fee. You won't need to worry about this type of upgrade unless you've discovered bugs.

Software companies sometimes use the terms *version* and *release* interchangeably. To be specific, the release is the date the product ships, and the version is the number attached to that release date. In some cases, the software is "rereleased" but retains the same version number. Confused yet? And then there is the term used for prerelease versions, called the "build."

There is absolutely no consistency in the amount of time between version changes. Some companies release software and then announce a newer version within weeks of the first release. The newer version may just fix bugs found in the first release. Some companies have gone three or four years between versions. Many of these companies have waited too long, and their customers have switched to more recent programs to find the latest features.

Most major programs seem to make significant changes every 12 to 18 months. Depending on the size of the company and the perceived interest in the market, the product may be rewritten for use in other operating systems. The effort to create programs that are compatible with Windows is one example. This redirection of effort may delay or halt the progress on the original product.

As with any equipment purchase, you should record some basic information about the purchase. With software, this includes the version number. The topic Product Registration (54) provides a form for keeping track of your software purchases.

References

Copyright (51), Product Registration (54)

NEXT TOPIC: Spreadsheets (48)

Programs won't run off the original disk

See Installing Programs (60)

PROMPT — Command Line Information (26)

VERSIONS
All ○
Some ●
5.0 ○

Command ●
Program ○
Concept ○
Problem ○

The DOS PROMPT command provides command line information, including the current drive and directory. You can customize the prompt by adding the line `DEVICE=ANSI.SYS` to your CONFIG.SYS file.

Before You Begin

DIR — Directory (8)
CD, MD, and RD — Working with Directories (9)

Syntax

`C>`**`PROMPT $p$g`**	The $p is for path, and the $g is for >.
`C:\DOS>`**`PROMPT $d $p$g`** `Mon 08-26-1991 C:\DOS>`	The $d is for current date.

Problems

No directory status in prompt. Although the plain DOS prompt provides the current (default) drive, the current directory may not be indicated. The most commonly used PROMPT command is **`PROMPT $p$g`**. The $ signifies a special character or information. In this case, the $p provides the drive and path, and the $g provides the > character.

Missing or unclear prompt. You can use the special prompt commands to change or eliminate the DOS command-line prompt. When confronted by a strange prompt, use **`PROMPT $p$g`** to reset the prompt. Remember that the DOS prompt is just repeated every time you press Enter.

Explanation

The DOS PROMPT command provides information for the user on the command line. Changing the prompt does not affect DOS in any way. Typing **`PROMPT`** without additional parameters returns the prompt to the default, which is just the drive letter and the greater-than sign (`C>`). Any characters typed after PROMPT become part of the prompt, except for some characters preceded by the dollar sign. These special characters are included in Table 26-1.

Table 26-1. Special characters used in the PROMPT command.

Character	Use
$q	= (equal sign)
$$	$ (dollar sign)
$t	Current (system) time
$d	Current (system) date
$p	Current drive and path
$v	MS-DOS version number
$n	Current drive
$g	> (greater-than sign)
$l	< (less-than sign)
$b	¦ (pipe character)
$h	Backspace (erases preceding character)
$e	Escape code (ASCII code 27)
$_	Carriage return and linefeed

The special PROMPT characters offer an unlimited number of possibilities. Table 26-2 provides a few examples.

Table 26-2. Uses of the PROMPT characters.

Command	Result
`PROMPT $p$g`	`C:\>`
`PROMPT $t $p$g`	`23:00:01.01 C:\>`
`PROMPT $t$h$h$h$h$h$h $p$g`	`23:00 C:\>`
`PROMPT Yes boss? $p$g`	`Yes boss? C:\>`

`PROMPT $d$_$t$_$l$p$g`	`Mon 08-26-1991`
	`23:00:01.01`
	`<C:\>`

You can enhance the PROMPT by using the ANSI.SYS device driver provided with DOS. If your CONFIG.SYS file contains the line `DEVICE=ANSI.SYS` or `DEVICE=\DOS\ANSI.SYS`, special ANSI commands can be included in the PROMPT. These provide even more possibilities for the system prompt. Figure 26-1 shows a whimsical DOS PROMPT contained in a batch file that uses some special ANSI sequences. Figure 26-2 shows the resulting prompt.

```
REM P.BAT
@ECHO OFF
CLS
PROMPT $e[2C┌────╖$_$e[2C│      ║$_$e[2C└▄▄▄▄╜$_╓─────────╖$_╙──────────╜$_$p$g
```

Figure 26-1. A batch file containing a DOS PROMPT that uses ANSI sequences.

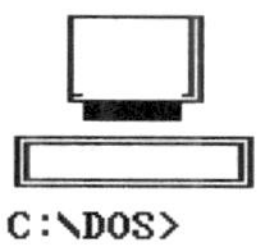

Figure 26-2. The resulting prompt.

This example, along with several others, is included on the accompanying disk. For more information on creating the special ASCII characters, see the topics ASCII — Character Codes (74) and Batch Files — Write Your Own (100). Remember that whatever you do, don't have fun while creating these kinds of prompts. Computers are for work, not play.

Exercise

This exercise shows several possibilities with the DOS PROMPT command. Using pg with PROMPT is the most common.

Exercise 1 of 1

The current setting for PROMPT remains in effect only until the system is rebooted. Whatever you create in this exercise will be gone the next time you reboot. The line with PROMPT is usually included in the AUTOEXEC.BAT file so that the settings are consistent for each session.

TRY	NOTE
C:\>**PROMPT** C>	Use the PROMPT command alone to return to the default. Look at the system prompts closely in these steps to see what does change each time.
C>**CD DOS** C>**CD** C>	Notice that the current subdirectory path is no longer part of the prompt.
C>**PROMPT pg** C:\>	Look back quickly at Table 26-1, and you'll see that the $p stands for the current path and the $g stands for >.
C:\>**PROMPT d_t_pg** Mon 08-26-1991 20:41:32.01 C:\>	The $d is for date, and the $t is for time. The $_ (underscore) is for a carriage return. That's how you get three lines for this prompt.

Tables 26-1 and 26-2 show the wide range of PROMPT possibilities. Remember that typing **PROMPT** always return you to the default C>. If you want to do away with the prompt completely, type **PROMPT hh**.

References

ASCII — Character Codes (74), Batch Files — Write Your Own (100)

NEXT TOPIC: Interfaces (27)

Proper default directory before running

See Batch Files — Write Your Own (100)

Protected program relocated on the hard disk

See Copyright (51)

Pull-down menus

See Interfaces (27)

Pushing the computer off onto the floor

See Solving Problems (14)

Quick changes to batch files

See EDLIN — Line Editor (99)

Read fault error

See Floppy Drive Failure (32)
See also Hard Drive Failure (33)

Reading the manual

See Solving Problems (14)

Recovering accidentally deleted programs or formatted disks

See MIRROR (91)

Redirection < > ¦ (64)

VERSIONS	
All	●
Some	○
5.0	○
Command	○
Program	○
Concept	●
Problem	○

Many DOS commands can *redirect* their output (send it somewhere other than the screen) with the > (greater-than) character. Some programs can use the < (less-than) character to accept input from a source other than the keyboard. The vertical bar (¦) is called the pipe character and can work in both directions.

Before You Begin

Command and Program Parameters (34)

Syntax

`C:\>`**`DIR > TEMP.TXT`**	Creates an ASCII file named TEMP.TXT from the directory listing
`C:\>`**`DIR > LPT1:`**	Sends the directory to the printer instead of the screen
`C:\>`**`CHKDSK /V ¦ FIND "BAK"`**	Searches every location on the disk and locates all the file names containing the letters BAK

Problem

Need to capture program output to a file or printer. Almost any command that displays information on the screen can have that information sent to another device with the > character.

Explanation

Redirecting the results of a DOS command is like saying, "Well, usually you go over here, but this time I want you to go over there." The "over here" is the monitor. The "over there" can be the printer, another file, or another program. The most useful redirection is to the printer or to an ASCII text file. The redirection characters include the following:

>	Directs output to a device or file
>>	Adds to a previously created file
<	Inputs data from a file
¦	A pipe for the MORE, FIND, and SORT programs

Of the commands covered so far in the topics, the DIR command can be used most effectively with redirection. Use

```
C:\>DIR > LPT1:
```

to send the directory list to the printer instead of the screen. If you want to list the directory to a file, use

```
C:\>DIR > DIRLIST.TXT
```

to create a text file called DIRLIST.TXT. You can then load that file into a word processor to examine.

Another use of redirection, covered in more detail in the topic Lost Data Files (77) is to send the output of CHKDSK /V into the FIND program so that FIND can search for a file name or portion of a file name. To find all files with the letters BAK, you type

```
C:\>CHKDSK /V ¦ FIND "BAK"
```

This command line includes the ¦ (pipe) character. The pipe tells DOS to take the output from one command or program (CHKDSK) and use the output as input in a second program (FIND). Because the pipe is redirecting the output, you will not see anything on the screen unless it passes through the FIND program. If that list is too long, you can add both a second pipe character and the MORE program:

```
C:\>CHKDSK /V ¦ FIND "BAK" ¦ MORE
```

These redirection combinations can be quite elaborate. When the redirection characters are used in this book, they are included in examples and explained. The other uses for the < and >> characters are covered in your DOS manual.

Exercise

Many of the commands covered in this book contain the redirection characters. In this exercise, you see how to send a directory listing to the printer and to a text file.

Exercise 1 of 1

Make sure that the printer is turned on before attempting to send output to it. You'll have to press the form-feed button to eject the page.

TRY	NOTE
C:\>**DIR > LPT1:**	The directory listing appears on the printer instead of the screen.
C:\>**DIR > DIRTEST**	The directory listing is sent to the file DIRTEST. (You can name the file anything you want.)

TRY	NOTE
C:\>**MORE < DIRTEST**	The MORE program takes the contents of DIRTEST as input.
C:\>**TYPE DIRTEST ¦ MORE**	This is functionally the same command. In both these cases, if the directory listing is short, the command result won't be very interesting. Pick a long directory to see what really happens.

References

CHKDSK — CHecK DiSK (20), TYPE — Looking at Files (81), MORE — Pausing Screen Display (84)

NEXT TOPIC: Upgrading Your Software (65)

Reducing file transfer times

See Compressed Files (80)

Reflections on the screen

See Monitor (61)

REN — REName Files (76)

VERSIONS
All ●
Some ○
5.0 ○

Command ●
Program ○
Concept ○
Problem ○

The DOS REN command changes file names. The date, time, and file attributes remain the same.

Before You Begin

File Names (4)

Syntax

C:\>**REN OLDN.EXT NEWN.EXT**	OLDN.EXT is now NEWN.EXT. The contents of the file are exactly the same.
C:\>**RENAME OLDNAME.EXT**	Notice that the new name no longer has an extension.

Problems

File no longer listed by a program. If you change the extension of a file name, the original program may not recognize the file. For example, if you use **`REN LT0076.DOC LD0076`** and then press the F1 key in Microsoft Word to load the file, LDO076 does not appear in the list. Word lists only those files with the default extension of DOC. You must type the file name as LDO076 or rename the file to include the DOC extension.

File name created with a space. Some programs allow you to create a file name that contains a space. Even though you can see this file in the directory, you cannot copy or delete it because DOS stops recognizing a file name at the first space. You can use the wild card ? to rename the file. If the file name is BROWN 01.DOC, you can rename it with **`RENAME BROWN?01.DOC BROWN01.DOC`**. (Yes, you can also use the ? in the COPY command and in other DOS commands, but why not rename the file with a legal name first?)

Renaming with wild cards. The REN command supports the ? and * wild cards. For example, you can use **`REN LD00??.DOC LD0??`**.TXT to change the extension of all files that begin with LDO0. But be very careful whenever you use wild cards.

> You can lose track of many files if you use wild cards improperly with the REN command.

Explanation

The REN command can be used as either REN or RENAME. You type **`REN`** or **`RENAME`**, then the old file name, and then the new file name. The new name must conform to standard DOS file-naming conventions.

If you try to rename a file to a name that already exists, DOS refuses by providing the message `Duplicate file name or file not found`. You can add a drive and directory to the original file name, but the newly named file remains in the original directory:

```
C:\>REN C:\DOCS\OLDNAME.EXT NEWNAME.EXT
```

Trying to use any drive/path with the second name produces the DOS message `Invalid parameter`. For example, the following line won't work:

```
C:\>REN C:\DOCS\OLDNAME.EXT C:NEW\NEWNAME.EXT
```

Remember that using RENAME is not the same as making a COPY of the file with a new name in the same directory. Don't rename a file and then work on that new file name, thinking that the old file is still on the disk.

Exercise

File naming and renaming are user-oriented features. DOS just requires a unique file name for every file in the directory. If the name contains meaningless characters, it won't matter to DOS. File names that contain eight characters plus the three-letter extension are simply a convenience for the user.

Exercise 1 of 1

This exercise uses files in the subdirectory EXER76 on the accompanying disk. Change to drive A: and that directory before beginning the steps.

TRY	NOTE
`A:\EXER76>`**`DIR`**	Take a look at the nine files in this directory. After each of the steps, use DIR to examine the results of the RENAME.
`A:\EXER76>`**`REN OLD.TXT NEW.TXT`** `Duplicate file name or file not found`	Oops! DOS provides two possible reasons why it cannot rename the file. In this case, NEW.TXT already exists.
`A:\EXER76>`**`REN OLD.TXT NEW01.TXT`**	This works.
`A:\EXER76>`**`REN OLD OLD.EXT`**	You just added an extension to the old file name.
`A:\EXER76>`**`REN OLD0?.TXT NEW0?.TXT`**	The file OLD4.TXT did not get renamed. Notice the position of the 4 in the name.
`A:\EXER76>`**`REN *OLD.TXT *NEW.TXT`**	This command does not work because it misuses the *. DOS ignores anything after the asterisk in the name or extension.
`A:\EXER76>`**`REN ??OLD.TXT ??NEW.TXT`**	This works.
`A:\EXER76>`**`REN *.TXT *.DOC`**	Be careful out there. This just changed many file extensions in one command.

TRY	NOTE
A:\EXER76>**RENAME OLD*.DOC NEW*.DOC**	This renames all files beginning with OLD to NEW.
A:\EXER76>**RENAME OLD NEW**	This renames the last file with the word OLD to NEW.

Making all these changes to file names at once is unusual. At least you followed a pattern and changed all the parts of the file names with OLD to NEW. If you make changes to file names without good reasons, you may have trouble remembering the new file names the next time you want to use those files.

References

COPY — Files (10)

NEXT TOPIC: Lost Data Files (77)

Renaming with wild cards

See REN — REName Files (76)

Repeating command-line entries

See DOSKEY (25)

Required parameter missing

See Command and Program Parameters (34)

RESTORE — Files (42)

VERSIONS	
All	●
Some	○
5.0	○
Command	○
Program	●
Concept	○
Problem	○

The DOS RESTORE program copies files created with BACKUP. Practice using RESTORE before you actually need it.

> If you are attempting to restore only some parts of a hard disk, perform a second BACKUP on the current disk before restoring the first set of backed-up files.

Before You Begin

BACKUP — Files (41)

Syntax

`C:\>`**`RESTORE A: C:\*.* /S`**	Recovers all the files, including those in subdirectories created with BACKUP, to a *new* hard disk
`C:\>`**`RESTORE A: C:\ACCNT\*.AR`**	Recovers all the files with the extension AR in the ACCNT subdirectory
`C:\>`**`RESTORE A: C:\*.* /S/N`**	Restores files that no longer exist on the *current* hard drive

Problem

RESTORE panic. If you are reading this now in a state of panic because you have lost important data files, do the following:

1. Take a few breaths and try to relax. If you have the backup disks and a DOS disk with RESTORE in your hand, you have what you need to get started.
2. If the entire disk crashed and you are starting over with a new hard disk, make sure that it has been properly formatted and has the boot system installed. RESTORE does not put the boot (hidden) files back on the disk. See the topic ATTRIB — Protecting Files (62) for more about hidden files.
3. Make sure that RESTORE.EXE has been copied to the DOS directory on the new hard disk. Type the following command and insert the first disk in the drive:

   ```
   C:\>\DOS\RESTORE A: C:\*.* /S
   ```

4. The best approach is to practice using RESTORE before you need it. Study the switches to determine which ones you are likely to use. Complete the exercise at the end of this discussion to be certain that you understand the RESTORE program.

Explanation

The RESTORE program copies all or selected files created with BACKUP (topic 41). Many switches allow selective restoration of files (see Table 42-1).

Table 42-1. The RESTORE switches. (Older versions of DOS may not use all of these switches.)

Switch	Description
/S	Restores files in all subdirectories
/P	Prompts before restoring read-only files or files changed since the last backup (if appropriate attributes are set)
/B	Restores only the files last changed on or before the specified date
/A	Restores only the files changed on or after the specified date
/E	Restores only the files changed at or earlier than the specified time
/L	Restores only the files changed at or later than the specified time
/M	Restores only the files changed since the last backup
/N	Restores only the files that no longer exist on the destination disk
/D	Displays files on the backup disk that match specifications

All these switches provide various ways to restore files to the hard disk. Take plenty of time to determine exactly what you need restored before using the switches. If you are not careful, you might accidentally copy old files over new files on the hard disk. Create a second backup of the current disk or subdirectories before attempting to restore the old files.

The corruption of files from a power loss is a common problem that BACKUP and RESTORE can help you overcome. The following example shows the steps in recovering from this serious problem.

Suppose that you are preparing to generate the monthly mailing-list labels. The database contains 4,034 names. You last backed up the list with BACKUP on Monday. It is now Friday, and you need to print the labels. By 8:30 a.m. the labels are loaded in the printer, and the program begins to print the labels in ZIP code order. Usually the process takes an hour and a half, but this time disaster strikes 10 minutes after you start. The power goes out for two seconds. The printer stops, the system reboots, and you return to the DOS prompt. When you restart the mailing list program, you get an error message. The files have been corrupted and are no longer usable.

The first thing you realize is that all the changes made during the week are lost since the files were backed up on Monday. Although that represents only about three hours of work, you still have the add/change forms used during the week. (You keep each weekly batch for a month.) The first step is to gather the three disks from the last set of backup disks. Then you get three new disks and locate the add/change forms processed since last Monday. You are now ready to go to work.

The data files are in C:\LIST. You label each disk with the word TEMP and the current date. You number the disks 1, 2, and 3. Then you type

```
C:\>BACKUP C:\LIST\*.* A: /F/L:\TEMP.LOG
```

All the files, including the corrupted files, will be backed up on the new disks after they are formatted. A file named TEMP.LOG is created in the root directory of the hard disk. This set of disks provides protection against an accident with RESTORE.

Next you are ready to restore the corrupted files. If you had dozens of disks, you might want to do a selective restore based on dates and times. In this case, you just want to restore all the files to their Monday status. You use

```
C:\>RESTORE A: C: /S
```

Because these backup disks contain only the mailing list files and they were in the LIST subdirectory, RESTORE automatically puts all those files back into that subdirectory. If the backup disks had more files or were from an incremental backup, this restoration would take a bit more planning.

Once the RESTORE is complete, you take a look at the files in the LIST subdirectory:

```
C:\>CD \LIST
C:\LIST>DIR
```

All the files have the date from last Monday. The next step is to use the add/change forms to update the data in these files. Three hours later, you have the files back to the condition they were in at 8:30 this morning. You run the add/change report to show the changes to the mailing list. Satisfied that the data is now accurate, you consider the possibility of the power going out again—within the hour and a half it takes to print the labels. This time, you perform the BACKUP before you begin printing the mailing labels. The few minutes required to back up the files is well worth the time to ensure that you won't lose another morning's work because of a power failure.

Exercise

Before you do this exercise, be sure that you have completed the exercise in the topic BACKUP — Files (41). If you have changed files in the TEST area since completing the BACKUP exercise, you might overwrite that file with old data. Do the BACKUP exercise again before proceeding with this exercise.

Exercise 1 of 1

Here you use RESTORE with several switches. Start by inserting in drive A: the first disk of the backup set.

TRY	NOTE
`C:\>`**`RESTORE A: C:`**	RESTORE provides the message `WARNING: No files to restore!` If you have more than one disk, RESTORE searches all the disks before making this pronouncement.
`C:\>`**`RESTORE A: C:/S`**	In almost all cases, RESTORE requires the /S switch to include subdirectories. Because the files were in a subdirectory, they have to go back to that same subdirectory.
Erase two files in the TEST subdirectory.	Don't do this step if the files are critical and you do not have additional copies.
`C:\>`**`RESTORE A: C:/S/N`**	Only the missing files are restored with the /N switch.
`C:\>`**`RESTORE A: C:/S/D`**	The /D switch lists all the files on the backup disk. To send this list to the printer, add **`> LTP1:`** at the end.

Just these few minutes with RESTORE can help you if the time comes when you must recover critical files back to your hard disk.

References

BACKUP — Files (41)

NEXT TOPIC: Word Processing (43)

Retaining word processing styles

See Data File Formats (52)

Retyping long command lines

See DOSKEY (25)

Running other programs with PRINT

See PRINT — Spooler (45)

Running out of space on the hard disk

See Compressed Files (80)

Screen clears too soon

See CLS — Clear Screen (5)

Sector not found

See Hard Drive Failure (33)

Security (95)

VERSIONS
All ●
Some ○
5.0 ○

Command ○
Program ○
Concept ○
Problem ●

The data contained in the computer is valuable and easily corrupted. Various methods are available for reducing the chance that your data will be corrupted or destroyed intentionally or accidentally. These security measures include password protection and physical containment.

Before You Begin

Boot/Startup (1)

Problems

Confidential data. Because computer files are so easily copied, confidential files can be quickly duplicated. You can maintain data security by both restricting physical access to the computer and encrypting the sensitive files.

Data fragments from deleted files. Even after a file has been deleted or reformatted, parts of the file remain on the disk. Data recovery programs can recover those erased files. Special utility programs can wipe the file or disk completely clean to remove those file remnants.

Data integrity. Small changes in critical data files may have a profound effect on decision making that relies on the data. An unprotected system is vulnerable to this type of deliberate corruption.

Explanation

Mainframe computers and minicomputers have a central location, usually behind locked doors. Data security is based on passwords and access levels to the data. Few people have physical access to the data. Personal computers are quite different, however.

By their nature, personal computers are very accessible. The files can be easily copied from the hard disk to floppies. Anyone with access to the system can run programs and make changes to the data. In most cases, users don't consider this accessibility a problem. The problem occurs only after someone copies confidential files or corrupts important data.

Data can be secured at both the system level and the physical level. System-level security includes passwords and file encrypting. Physical-level security includes locking cables and restricting the location of the system.

At the system level, you can use password protection for system access or even file access. When the system is first booted, the user must enter a password. Some menu programs allow password protection on each menu choice. In most cases, these protection methods can be circumvented by booting from a floppy disk.

The lowest level of protection is at the individual file level. Each file can be *encrypted* by special utility programs. The user provides a password, and the program scrambles the data according to that password. If the user forgets the password, the data is lost forever.

Sensitive data can also be "scrounged" from deleted files. Any deleted area of the disk, especially floppy disks, should be "wiped" by special utility programs to remove the data left behind by the DEL command. A disk copy of a floppy disk also copies those deleted tracks. Even formatting a disk does not remove the data. A special "wipe disk" program is needed to clean off the disk completely.

Restricting physical access to the system can include using special locks or just choosing a safe location for the computer. Several companies provide locks that cover the power switch or disk drive. Although this prevents casual access, the system must also be secured to prevent the whole computer from being stolen. The best method is to have the computer locked in an office or large cabinet. This prevents casual access and deters premeditated access.

Data security is important not only to prevent copying or destroying files but also to prevent the corruption of data. A knowledgeable user can make subtle changes to an unprotected system. Unless the original data is reviewed in detail again, the changes may never be noticed, yet they may affect the outcome of decisions for months or years before the corruption is discovered. Small changes to payroll files are an example of data corruption.

Exercise

Do a security assessment. Consider the following questions to determine if you need to restrict access to your system or files:

- Would loss or corruption of the data affect your company financially?
- Was much time spent in compiling the data to create a unique database?
- Is the data based on sources available only to specific people?
- Was the data provided to you in confidence?
- Would public knowledge of the data result in embarrassment or possibly a legal action?
- How critical is the accuracy of the data?
- How vulnerable are you to lost or stolen data?

References

Backing Up Data (13), System Maintenance (94)

NEXT TOPIC: Microprocessors (96)

Seek error

See Hard Drive Failure (33)

Sending output elsewhere

See Redirection < > ¦ (64)

Serial printer setup

See MODE — Configuring System Devices (83)

SHARE (57)

VERSIONS	
All	○
Some	●
5.0	○
Command	○
Program	●
Concept	○
Problem	○

The DOS SHARE program is necessary on systems connected to networks. SHARE provides file sharing and file locking.

Syntax

`C:\>SHARE`	Installs SHARE with default values
`C:\>SHARE /F:4096 /L:40`	Doubles the file space and number of locked files

Problems

`Share already installed.` If you attempt to reinstall SHARE, DOS provides this message. No harm is done. The only way to remove SHARE is to reboot the system.

Network connection error. Many networks require that SHARE be resident in DOS for the program to function properly. Because SHARE is usually started in the AUTOEXEC.BAT file as a step in connecting to a network, something may have happened to the AUTOEXEC.BAT file or the PATH setting.

Explanation

If your system is connected to a network, the network system administrator will already have installed the SHARE program. Running SHARE is one of the steps in making the connection to the network. Contact your network support staff if you have problems with network connections.

The /F: switch sets aside the amount of space, in bytes, for file-sharing information. The default in DOS 5.0 is 2,048 bytes. The /L: switch sets the number of files that can be locked at one time. The default is 20.

References

Networks (79)

NEXT TOPIC: SUBST (58)

SHARE already installed

See SHARE (57)

Sharing Devices (93)

VERSIONS	
All	●
Some	○
5.0	○
Command	○
Program	○
Concept	●
Problem	○

Expensive peripheral devices, such as laser printers or high-speed modems, can be shared between two or more computer systems. Although networks are designed for sharing devices, other lower-cost methods are available also.

Before You Begin

Printers (15)

Problem

Cutting expenses. Because printers and modems are not used constantly, they can be shared between two or more systems. Special switching devices manage the data stream traffic to prevent print jobs from being mixed. Still, someone has to manage the paper tray and distribute the printed material.

Explanation

The keyboard and monitor are integral parts of the computer system. You can't use the computer without them. Other parts of the computer are known as *peripherals*, or extras. Printers and modems are peripherals. You can use the computer even if a printer or modem is not attached. These peripheral devices can be shared between two or more systems.

The main reason to share a device is to get the most use from an expensive piece of equipment. A $5,000 color laser printer is a candidate for sharing; a $400 dot-matrix printer is not. Before you consider sharing a device, several conditions should be met for all users connected:

- Does each user have a low volume of work involving the device to be shared?
- Is one user willing to manage the device?
- Are all the users within quick walking distance, probably no more than 50 feet? (Line of sight is even better.)
- If the device is a printer, does everyone need to use only one type of paper?
- If the device is a modem, can all outgoing calls be charged to the same account?
- Is the device readily accessible to all connected users?

Printers and modems can be connected with *switch boxes*. These boxes have two or more connection ports to attach to the systems. One port connects to the device. The most basic switch box must be set manually to accept the input from each system. This arrangement works only if the systems are sitting side by side and the box is accessible to both users.

More sophisticated switch boxes watch for incoming signals and provide traffic control. These boxes usually include print buffers. This extra memory in the switch box allows the connected systems to send the printing to the box even if the printer is working on another job. When that job is finished, the box then sends the second job held in memory.

The most expensive but useful switch boxes can be software-controlled and handle eight or more users at one time. The box really is a computer dedicated to accepting the output of the connected computers and routing it to one or more printer. Sharing printers and modems with such a system always requires an expert to manage the printers, cable connections, and inevitable jams.

Before seriously considering connecting several people to one printer, you should look carefully at the extra time required when users must walk to the printer to retrieve work. Consider the lost time when a 200-page print job holds up a 2-page memo. And if users want to print on letterhead paper, who will insert the paper? What if someone else begins printing before the letterhead job gets to the printer?

Like printers, modems can be shared. Since 2400-baud modems cost under $150, only the more expensive 9600-baud versions (costing over $600) or direct-connect modems are good candidates for sharing.

References

Modems (56), Paper in Printer (68), Networks (79)

NEXT TOPIC: System Maintenance (94)

Sharing spreadsheets

See Spreadsheets (48)

Sitting on the tree branch you are trying to remove

See CD, MD, and RD — Working with Directories (9)

Software (18)

VERSIONS	
All	●
Some	○
5.0	○
Command	○
Program	○
Concept	●
Problem	○

A computer system consists of both software and hardware. The software controls the hardware. Also called programs, software is written by programmers to tell the hardware exactly what steps to take to perform certain tasks. These tasks include putting the characters on the screen (system level) and adding a column of numbers a user has entered (application level).

Problems

Task definition. Do you know what the software is supposed to accomplish? Do you know if it will help you accomplish what you want to do? (Usually the answer is "No.")

Complexity. Are the steps that are necessary to accomplish the goal too complicated for you to understand? Will you spend more time learning to use the software than doing the task manually? Will the effort to use the software detract from the effort put into the final project?

Support. Who can help you with the software? How is the program best used? What can you reasonably expect to achieve, based on the amount of support provided for the software? Refer to the topics Product Registration (54) for more information about software support.

Versions. Does your current version provide all the features you need? Will the new version add more complexity? Does it require a more powerful computer to run well? Are you "upgrading" to the new version just because you think you might miss something?

Explanation

Every time you prepare food from a cookbook, you are using a "program." Someone wrote the steps for you to follow. The result is consistent (more or less) with the original design. Gather the ingredients, measure them carefully, process them (mix and bake), and you get something that did not exist before.

Because the computer is both accurate and consistent, the result is always the same *provided* the same "ingredients" are added in the same proportions each time. Computer programs are written to provide this consistency. When you type the letter A, you expect to see the letter A appear on the screen. Someone wrote the software to make that A appear on the screen very quickly (it looks immediate) after you press the key.

The computer not only can combine the data to produce results but also can provide additional information based on "rules" the programmer wrote into the program. Because the computer can compare two numbers and determine which has the greater value, the software can branch to different actions based on that comparison. If the current month's expenses (a total of numbers) are higher than the budgeted amount (another number), the program can make the current month's amount red. This happens only if the programmer thought that a deficit in the budget should show up as red on the screen, and wrote the steps to make that happen.

The inconsistencies frequently blamed on the computer are usually missing or incorrect steps in the program. If the programmer forgot to write the steps to check the difference every time the expenses are totalled, some over-budget numbers may show as red, and some may not. If the programmer thought to check each time for a difference but did not include steps to handle a condition in which both numbers are equal, the program may "crash" (stop running entirely). Both these problems are considered *bugs*.

A well-designed and tested program has all the bugs fixed before it is offered for sale. Most programs go through a series of versions as features are added. In some cases, minor bugs are discovered and removed in the subsequent versions. (Of course, new bugs may creep in with the new features.) Users often find and report bugs to the companies distributing the software. If too many users find too many bugs, the program (and company) may fail in the marketplace.

A program that is well designed and tested does what it claims it will do. Consumers are told that they will be able to accomplish specific tasks with the software. And, for the most part, those goals can be achieved. But what about the consumer who has little or no experience with software? As far as that consumer is concerned, the product may *not* do what it claims. The company, however, can have someone sit down and demonstrate exactly how the program works. That person has worked with the product for weeks or months and is therefore more experienced than the average consumer. Often those who promote and sell the software assume that the consumer is as knowledgeable as the person who demonstrates the product.

Understanding the software's objective is often a problem for the user. Is the purpose of word processing to provide printed documents? Yes, in the most basic sense, it is, just as the purpose of a hammer is to drive nails into wood. But in a general sense, a hammer is used to build things. Word processing software, then, helps you communicate through the printed word. It is this broader view that a user often struggles with when using the computer. Mastering the first few menu choices to produce a report seems to be the goal when, in fact, the *real* objective should be to provide a well-constructed message.

The use of the computer, both hardware and software, is just a link in the chain of events leading to a goal. A programmer writes a program to run on the computer, which then performs the steps you need to accomplish your task. If the program has been designed to minimize the learning and maximize the contribution to the goal, the programmer has contributed to your success.

References

Hardware (38), Application Software (46), Spreadsheets (48), Databases (49), Utility Software (50), Manuals and Documentation (53), Product Registration (54), Installing Programs (60)

NEXT TOPIC: Floppy Disks (19)

Software programs that do not support subdirectories

See SUBST (58)

Solving Problems (14)

VERSIONS	
All	●
Some	○
5.0	○
Command	○
Program	○
Concept	●
Problem	○

This topic provides some suggestions for solving a variety of problems related to DOS, software programs, and the computer.

Explanation

When the soup begins to boil over the edge of the saucepan, the cook knows to turn down the heat. This comes from experience and watching others prepare soup. Think, though, of all the other possible "solutions" to this problem:

- Remove the pot from the burner.
- Dip liquid out of the pot.

- Add cold liquids.
- Turn the burner completely off.
- Curse at the soup boiling over.
- Leave the kitchen.

As with cooking, most of your computing experiences are not likely to include watching someone else for very long. If you do watch someone use software, you are likely to focus on the task (getting soup on the table), not what to do when a problem arises. When a problem does occur, the knowledgeable user (or cook) usually proclaims, "Oh, I've seen that before. I'll fix it," and whips through the solution. The task is, after all, making soup.

Because computers are complicated and can present many kinds of errors and problems, too many users develop one standard solution to a problem: turn the computer off. This solves the immediate problem. They don't have to look at the screen anymore. They can start the task over and hope that the problem does not occur again. But the real opportunity is lost—that of learning to solve the problem so that it won't be a problem the next time.

In this case, a "computer problem" is defined as "anything that prevents you from completing your task and for which you do not know the solution." By this definition, almost all of DOS represents a problem! But learning how to deal with DOS problems can prevent them from recurring. Ah ha! That's where *Learning DOS* can help.

The orientation to this book suggested many ways to use *Learning DOS*. Yet even before you reach for the book, you can take some steps in attempting to solve problems with DOS:

1. Gather your patience.
2. Look at the screen.
3. Press the F1 key (or another help key).
4. Read the manual.
5. Press the Enter key.
6. Press other keys.
7. Ask others if they've encountered the problem.
8. Press Ctrl-C or Ctrl-Break.
9. Press Ctrl-Alt-Del.
10. Turn the computer off.
11. Push the computer onto the floor.

Just kidding about step 11! Keeping your sense of humor doesn't hurt a bit, though. Each of these steps deserves some explanation. Although some problems occur again and again, others may happen only once. Some problems are minor, but others are serious and can cause a great deal of damage, especially to your data files. To find solutions, try the following steps in the order presented:

1. *Gather your patience.* Waiting until the last minute to do a required task does not help you keep your patience or your humor. The purpose here is to solve the problem as quickly as possible and move on. Sit back and decide exactly what the problem is. Ask yourself these questions:

   Does the computer respond to your keystrokes?

   Do you know what to do next?

   Do you know where to start?

   Have you seen this problem before?

   If so, what was the solution?

2. *Look at the screen.* If the problem is related to a specific program, the answer is likely to be on the screen. Many programs provide information on the bottom of the screen about what to do next. Study the screen carefully for a clue. If the problem is "Where do you start?" you may have to skip to step 4.

3. *Press the F1 key (or another help key).* Many programs provide additional on-screen help when you press the F1 function key. Usually the help you receive relates to the part of the program you were using when you requested help. This is called *context-sensitive* help. With some programs, you may need to press Shift-F1, Alt-F1, Ctrl-F1, or another key combination for help. The program manual can provide guidance on which key(s) to use for help.

4. *Read the manual.* Find the manual. It is right over there in the bookcase, isn't it? If it isn't, you may want to read the topic Manuals and Documentation (53). The problem may be common and therefore listed in a special section about problems. Check the procedure you were working on in the manual. Did you do anything different? If you do find the solution in the manual, *mark the page!* There's a good chance you'll need it again.

5. *Press the Enter key.* At this point in solving the problem, you may be just trying to get the system to respond in some way. Pressing the Enter key tests whether the software is still active. The response may be an error message, or the program may proceed.

6. *Press any key.* Now you are becoming desperate. Methodically pressing function keys and then alphabetical keys may get some response from your computer. Do this fairly slowly. Otherwise, you may not notice which key produced the response.

7. *Ask others if they've encountered the problem.* Sit back and think about other people who know how to use the program. If you have thought ahead a little bit, you may even have a list of those people. Talk to them. This step is a difficult one because it takes some time and you must admit that you don't know everything about the computer.

   Write down the steps you took to get into this problem (if you can remember them). Make a note of what you have done to solve the problem. If you call someone, remain in front of your system so that you can tell the person what you see on the screen, and you can carry out any instructions immediately. (See topic 54 for more information about calling the software company's support number.)

   If someone comes to you to help, remain seated in front of the computer. Unless the problem is highly technical and you are not likely to have to solve it again, remain at the keyboard and let the person guide you through the solution. Computer "techies" like to solve problems. That's how one of them becomes the local guru. But a guru may be inclined to solve the problem instead of showing you how to do it. If you stay at the keyboard, you'll get to do the typing. (Taking your local guru out to lunch is also a good hedge against a time when you'll need lots of help.)

8. *Press Ctrl-C or Ctrl-Break.* If you cannot find anyone to help, you'll have to resort to more serious tactics. From this step on, you are likely to lose the work you have completed since the last time you saved the file. You are now trying to *stop* the program from running. Unfortunately, with word processing or spreadsheets, you'll lose your most recent work. With databases and more complicated programs, you risk losing vast amounts of data.

9. *Press Ctrl-Alt-Del.* This step is almost guaranteed to solve an immediate problem with locked-up software. Unfortunately it guarantees also that you will lose your data because it restarts the computer from the beginning. For more information on rebooting, see the topic Boot/Startup (1).

10. *Turn the computer off.* The good news is that the problem is gone. The bad news is that all recent data is gone too. Files may be lost, and you still don't know what caused the problem.

11. *Push the computer onto the floor.* Just kidding! Hardware warranties don't have a clause that covers damage caused by an irate user.

The most radical idea wasn't even in the preceding list. It is too scary to contemplate when you are confronting a problem. Save this idea for the post-problem celebration. If you have the time and patience, *re-create the problem!*

> Gasps come from the crowd! Strong men faint. Stronger women catch them and then curse. The crowd grows ugly. They scream, "What kind of idea is this? We just got out of the problem. We can now cruise merrily on our way. Why should we look back on the most recent cause of our distress?"

Re-creating the problem serves several purposes. It helps prevent the problem from happening again because you can now see exactly what caused the problem. You get to solve the problem again, and that helps you remember the solution. Repeating the steps that led to the problem can help you watch for it the next time too.

If there is no solution, re-creating the problem helps you to explain to someone else exactly how the problem developed in the first place. If the problem is reproducible, it may be a bug that needs to be reported to the software company. If the problem is not a bug, at least you know what *not* to do next time.

> Placated, the crowd returns to their computers. They immediately look for their software manuals, ask each other who uses what software, and make a lunch date with the local computer guru. (Is that the phone ringing now?)

References

Learning More (28), Copyright (51), Manuals and Documentation (53), Product Registration (54)

NEXT TOPIC: Printers (15)

Speed versus ease of use

See Interfaces (27)

Spreadsheets (48)

VERSIONS	
All	●
Some	○
5.0	○
Command	○
Program	○
Concept	●
Problem	○

Spreadsheets, as tools for organizing numbers, have been around long before computers. Electronic spreadsheets on personal computers have been available only since the early 1980s.

Problems

What does a spreadsheet do? Unlike word processing in which the result (a document) is similar to that of typing, a spreadsheet requires an understanding of how to manipulate numbers to get answers. You need to know how to design the sheet, write the formulas, test the results, and enter the data. Even if you know how to make menu choices and type numbers, you may not be able to use spreadsheet software effectively. Learn how to design and use a basic spreadsheet before you attempt to use a computerized version.

Inaccurate results. Even a well-designed spreadsheet can be totally misleading if the formulas are not thoroughly tested before the final numbers are plugged in. Use round numbers (with easily calculated results) to test the formulas before committing the company's fortune, or yours, to the bottom line.

Sharing spreadsheets. Designing and testing a template (a reusable spreadsheet) can save you a lot of time. Once designed, it can be used repeatedly with each daily, weekly, or monthly reporting cycle. Providing the spreadsheet for others to use takes another level of skill entirely. You'll need to consider the following questions:

- Are the data entry locations obvious?
- Can formulas be overwritten?
- Does the sheet contain internal documentation about its function?
- Who will answer the inevitable questions about the template?
- Who will take the heat if something goes wrong with the results on "your" spreadsheet?

Explanation

Spreadsheet software is to numbers what word processing is to words. Word processing arranges words to convey thoughts. Spreadsheets arrange numbers to communicate results (the bottom line). The power and flexibility of the computer simplify the process of entering and calculating the numbers. When changes are made to a spreadsheet on paper, all the numbers affected by that change must be recalculated. In the computer version, the results ripple throughout the sheet within seconds of the change.

If you work with a paper spreadsheet more than a few hours a month, you can gain much from using a computer version. Once you have mastered the basics, the ease with which you can change numbers and compare results makes possible a more thoughtful consideration of those results. The time you save can be invested in questions:

- What if we increase the price per pound to 27 cents?
- How many more units must we sell next month to make the quota?
- How will an across-the-board 7 percent raise affect the bottom line?

The first popular electronic spreadsheet was VisiCalc for the Apple II personal computer. Accountants bought Apples just to use VisiCalc. Then Lotus 1-2-3 became the darling of the MS-DOS world and still dominates the market. Originally almost any spreadsheet "clone" had to look like Lotus 1-2-3 to sell. Recent lawsuits have suggested that a program's "look and feel" can be copyrighted, so the new spreadsheet packages look different. Both Excel from Microsoft and Quattro Pro from Borland are popular packages. Even though spreadsheet programs look different, the basic concepts used are the same. Once you learn one spreadsheet program, you'll have much less trouble learning the next.

Figure 48-1 contains a screen from Quattro Pro, a popular program from Borland. The sheet in this example is used to track time spent working for a company. The bottom of the column (just off the screen) automatically calculates the total hours and minutes and displays the total invoice based on the hourly rate.

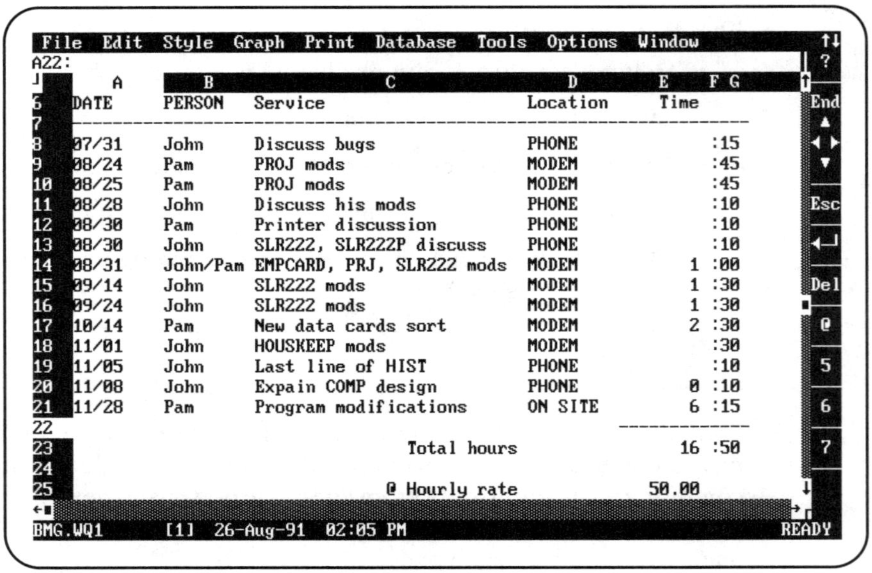

	A	B	C	D	E
6	DATE	PERSON	Service	Location	Time
8	07/31	John	Discuss bugs	PHONE	:15
9	08/24	Pam	PROJ mods	MODEM	:45
10	08/25	Pam	PROJ mods	MODEM	:45
11	08/28	John	Discuss his mods	PHONE	:10
12	08/30	Pam	Printer discussion	PHONE	:10
13	08/30	John	SLR222, SLR222P discuss	PHONE	:10
14	08/31	John/Pam	EMPCARD, PRJ, SLR222 mods	MODEM	1 :00
15	09/14	John	SLR222 mods	MODEM	1 :30
16	09/24	John	SLR222 mods	MODEM	1 :30
17	10/14	Pam	New data cards sort	MODEM	2 :30
18	11/01	John	HOUSKEEP mods	MODEM	:30
19	11/05	John	Last line of HIST	PHONE	:10
20	11/08	John	Expain COMP design	PHONE	0 :10
21	11/28	Pam	Program modifications	ON SITE	6 :15
23			Total hours		16 :50
25			@ Hourly rate		50.00

Figure 48-1. A sample spreadsheet created with Quattro Pro.

Exercise

If you work with numbers in any way and have not seen what spreadsheet software can do, find one or two people who can show you how they use their favorite spreadsheet programs.

References

Databases (49), Product Registration (54)

NEXT TOPIC: Databases (49)

Stopping PRINT tasks

See PRINT — Spooler (45)

Strike a key when ready... (16)

VERSIONS	
All	●
Some	○
5.0	○
Command	○
Program	○
Concept	●
Problem	○

This is one of several messages provided by DOS and other programs. Usually nothing happens until you press a key. This message may be the result of a PAUSE in a DOS batch file.

Syntax

Variations of this message include the following:

```
Press any key when ready...
Press Enter to continue
```

Problems

Which keys can you press? When you see this message, you can press almost any key on the keyboard, including the space bar and the Enter key.

Which keys can you *not* press? Many programs respond to the Esc key by stopping completely. The Ctrl-C and Ctrl-Break key combinations may also stop a program from running. If you stop a program with these keys, you may lose data.

You press a key, but nothing happens. In some cases, pressing a key will not get immediate results. Wait for at least a few moments to determine whether the program is working. Press a key again and observe the results. Try another key.

If the program still does not respond, you may need to take other measures. See the topic Solving Problems (14) for additional ideas.

Explanation

Providing the message `Strike a key when ready...` is simply a generic way of stopping the program until you perform a specific action. In some cases, you may need to insert a disk or check to be sure that paper is in the printer. Some programs wait a predetermined period of time (usually from 30 seconds to 5 minutes) and then resume processing.

References

Command and Program Parameters (34)

NEXT TOPIC: File Organization (17)

SUBST (58)

VERSIONS	
All	○
Some	●
5.0	○
Command	○
Program	●
Concept	○
Problem	○

The DOS SUBST program allows you to substitute a drive letter for a subdirectory.

Before You Begin

Default Drive (3)
DIR — Directory (8)
CD, MD, and RD — Working with Directories (9)
CONFIG.SYS (22)

Syntax

`C:\>`**`SUBST`**	This displays SUBSTituted drives.
`C:\>`**`SUBST G: C:\SIMCITY`**	G: now equals C:\SIMCITY.
`C:\>`**`SUBST G: /D`**	G: connection is deleted.

Problems

Software programs that do not support subdirectories. Older programs may not recognize subdirectories. Using SUBST allows a subdirectory on the hard drive to be treated as a drive, usually drive B:. For example, if you used **`SUBST B: C:\PAYMENT`**, every time your program thought it was using B:, it would actually be using C:\PAYMENT. (You should seriously consider upgrading your software.)

DOS programs that can't be used with SUBST. Because SUBST establishes a software connection only, a number of DOS programs should not be used on a SUBSTituted drive: BACKUP, CHKDSK, DISKCOPY, FDISK, FORMAT, LABEL, RECOVER, RESTORE, SYS, and the DOS 5.0 program, MIRROR.

`Invalid parameter -x:`. If the CONFIG.SYS line `LASTDRIVE` contains a letter earlier in the alphabet than the letter you typed (*x*) as part of a command or if the letter is not in CONFIG.SYS at all, DOS provides this message. You can insert `LASTDRIVE=Z` in CONFIG.SYS to solve this problem.

Explanation

The DOS SUBST program establishes a *virtual* (simulated) drive instead of a physical drive. With the exception of some DOS programs noted in the "Problems" section, most programs use just the drive letter, so DOS directs the file operations to the subdirectory specified as the virtual drive.

In addition to compensating for older programs, the SUBST program enables you to move efficiently between subdirectories because you can type the drive designation **`F:`** more quickly than you can type **`CD\GRAPHICS\PCPAINT`**. Using SUBST is a matter of personal preference. Remembering which drives represent which subdirectories may take more time than typing the full CD command line. Incidentally, a subdirectory is still available through its own name even when the SUBST command has assigned it a drive designation.

You may want to consult your DOS manual for information about the ASSIGN command. With ASSIGN, you can substitute drive A: for drive B: (or drive B: for drive A:). This command is handy when you are installing a program from drive B: and the program insists on using drive A: to find the disk.

Exercise

If you have an older program that does not use subdirectories or you just like the idea of substituting a drive letter for a long subdirectory name, this exercise will be helpful.

Exercise 1 of 1

For this exercise, it is assumed that you don't already have drive E:. If you do, these commands won't work. You'll have to substitute another drive letter. Just keep trying letters until you find one that works. If you get to H: and the commands still do not work, you may have to insert the line `LASTDRIVE=H` (or even Z) in CONFIG.SYS and then reboot the system.

TRY	NOTE
`C:\>`**`SUBST`**	Running SUBST without any parameters checks whether any substituted drives are already set.
`C:\>`**`SUBST E: C:\DOS`**	If you do not have a directory named \DOS, substitute another directory.
`C:\>`**`E:`** `E:\>`**`DIR`**	The directory looks strangely like the C:\DOS directory. It is.
`E:\>`**`SUBST`** `E: => C:\DOS`	SUBST reports the current substituted drive(s).

`E:\>`**`SUBST E: /D`**
`Invalid parameter`
`E:\>`
	The /D switch deletes that drive substitution. In this case, you just get an `Invalid parameter` message, possibly because you are trying to delete the drive you are currently in.

`E:\>`**`C:`** `C:\>`**`SUBST E: /D`**	This deletes the reference to drive E:.

If you like, you can set all your major subdirectories to drive letters. The problem with using multiple drive letters is that you may have trouble remembering the drive letters you substituted for all the directories.

References

Upgrading Your Software (65)

NEXT TOPIC: No One to Help (59)

Support

See Software (18)

System date

See DATE (23)

System halted

See Boot/Startup (1)

System Maintenance (94)

VERSIONS	
All	●
Some	○
5.0	○
Command	○
Program	○
Concept	●
Problem	○

Like a car, a computer system can benefit from regular maintenance. Although the computer does not require oil to run or the corresponding oil changes, some steps are necessary to help keep the system in good working order.

Before You Begin

Hardware (38)
Ports (40)

Problems

Manufacturer's warranty (what's covered?). Most computer systems come with a one-year warranty on parts and labor. The terms vary greatly and should be clearly explained before the purchase. In most cases, you have to bring the system to the store for repairs. There may or may not be any guarantee about how quickly the system will be returned. The repair center may or may not provide a loaner system while your system is being repaired.

Extended warranty (is it worth it?). At the time of the sale or before the warranty has expired, the company or computer store may offer to extend the warranty for an additional cost. Examine the conditions on an extended warranty before deciding whether the insurance is worth the cost. You may want to consider paying more and getting a maintenance agreement.

Maintenance agreement (what do you get?). Paying for a maintenance agreement usually provides more complete service for systems. It usually includes on-site service and a loaner system if your system must be taken in for repairs. This agreement should also include a yearly maintenance checkup. Most agreements include all parts and labor. You might be able to negotiate a lower per-system cost if you pay for any parts needed for the repair. Because the maintenance agreement covers just the labor for the repair, the vendor then assumes a lower risk for repairs to your system.

Explanation

A computer system is a piece of equipment, like an appliance. Despite the "magic" created, the physical part still needs regular maintenance. For the soft side of maintenance, see the topics Backing Up Data (13) and File Organization (17).

The maintenance tools that you need include several sizes of flat-blade and Phillips screw drivers, and a soft brush or can of compressed air. A program to check the condition of the hard drive is also helpful, such as Norton Utilities, PC Tools, or Spinrite II. But even without these tools, you can still perform some of the tasks outlined here.

With the exception of testing the hard disk, you should complete all of this work with the computer system unplugged.

Weekly maintenance. Check the cable connections by pushing each cable into the back of the system. If clips or screws are included with the cable or port, use them to ensure a tight connection. Make sure that the ventilation fan is not blocked. Wipe the monitor screen with a damp cloth or a special screen-cleaning packet.

Monthly maintenance. Turn the keyboard upside down and blow the dust out. You can clean any grimy spots with a slightly moist cloth and a mild cleaner. Run the hard disk testing program if you have it. Use **CHKDSK /F** to look for lost clusters.

Yearly maintenance. Remove the cover of the system and blow the dust out. Check the back fan grill for dust. Push lightly on the cards and connections. Grasp and gently wiggle the disk drives. If one is loose, tighten the screws as necessary. While the cover is off, use a mild cleaner on the cover to remove dirt.

You can handle the weekly and monthly maintenance yourself, but you may want to have a computer store do the yearly checkup for you. Make sure that you back up the entire hard disk before you take the system in.

Exercise

Look at your system. Does it need attention? Just do it.

References

Printers (15), Floppy Drive Failure (32), Hard Drive Failure (33), Manuals and Documentation (53), Product Registration (54), Paper in Printer (68), Labels in Printer (69), Security (95)

NEXT TOPIC: Security (95)

System prompt

See PROMPT — Command Line Information (26)

System setup

See Partitions — FDISK (97)

System time

See TIME (24)

Task definition

See Software (18)

Terminate batch job (Y/N)?

See Batch Files — Write Your Own (100)

TIME (24)

VERSIONS	
All	●
Some	○
5.0	○
Command	●
Program	○
Concept	○
Problem	○

The DOS TIME command sets the system time in 24-hour format. All files created and changed will show this time. Some programs use the system time for processing.

Syntax

```
C:\>TIME
Current time is  8:28:14.30p
Enter new time: 20:50 <Enter>
C:\>TIME
Current time is  8:50:03.30p
Enter new time: <Enter>
```


Problem

Wrong system time. Except on older systems, the time is kept internally. If the system does not keep time between sessions and a time is not supplied when the system is first turned on, the clock starts at 00:00 (midnight). You can make a temporary correction by typing the correct time. Making a permanent change to the system time depends on your computer. Check the manual for instructions on changing the system time permanently.

Explanation

The TIME command was used more extensively before computers were able to keep the system time between sessions. Like battery-powered watches, most systems now keep a number of variables, including the date and time.

The time can be entered as just *hh:mm* for hours and minutes, or it may include *hh:mm:ss.00* for seconds and hundredths of a second. DOS 4.0 and 5.0 can include a or p for AM or PM. These designations are shown at the prompt and are calculated by the system. A changed time is maintained only as long as the system remains on. Changing the time value may or may *not* change the internal system time on most computers.

Because files are *time-stamped* when they are created or changed, the system time helps determine exactly when the file was last worked on. This time can help you decide which files to delete and which file is the current version. The current time can be printed by many programs at the exact time a report is prepared. If several slightly different versions of a report are gathered in a stack, the inclusion of the time makes it clear which is the latest printout. Consult your software manual for instructions on inserting the current date and time on a printout.

A user of an older system may be prompted for the DATE and TIME every time the system is turned on. Older systems do not keep a current system date or time when the power is turned off. Although it is possible just to press Enter to bypass this prompt, it is a good idea to enter the current date and time for the reasons noted.

Exercise

As mentioned, most systems keep the time internally. If you need to check or change the time, this exercise steps you through the process.

Exercise 1 of 1

You may be prompted for the time whenever you start your system. You can then check the time and make a correction if necessary. Or you can check and change the time from the DOS prompt.

TRY	NOTE
`C:\>`**`TIME`**	DOS responds with the current time.
`Current time is` **`8:26:51.40p`**	Note the p at the end of the time.
`Enter new time:`	

TRY	NOTE
20:50 <Enter>	To correct the time to 8:50, you have to use the 24-hour clock. You don't need to attempt to include the seconds or hundreds of seconds. The time takes effect when you press the Enter key.

If you type an invalid time, DOS responds with `Invalid time` and provides another prompt. The response must include at least the hours and minutes. This can take the form of *hh:mm* or *hh.mm*. A partial response is interpreted as the one's place. For example, typing **3.3** sets the time for 03:03.00.

References

DATE (23), Hardware (38)

NEXT TOPIC: DOSKEY (25)

Time required to learn how to write batch files

See Batch Files — Write Your Own (100)

Too many files in the root directory

See File Organization (17)

Too many files open

See CONFIG.SYS (22)

TREE — Directory Map (87)

VERSIONS	
All	●
Some	○
5.0	○
Command	○
Program	●
Concept	○
Problem	○

The DOS TREE program provides a visual display, or map, of all the subdirectories and files on the disk.

Before You Begin

DIR — Directory (8)
CD, MD, and RD — Working with Directories (9)
ASCII — Character Codes (74)

Syntax

`C:\>TREE`	Shows all subdirectories on the C: disk
`C:\>CD BOOKS` `C:\BOOKS>TREE /F`	Shows directories and files in the subdirectory \BOOKS
`C:\>TREE ¦ MORE`	Pauses at each screen of text
`C:\>TREE /A > LPT1:`	In DOS 5.0, sends the text to the printer and uses standard ASCII characters

Problem

What directories are on the hard disk? Because directories and files are added as you need them, an overall picture of the hard disk may be difficult to keep. The TREE command, especially when redirected to the printer, provides a good idea of how organized you hard disk is. Use **TREE > LPT1:** to get this printout.

Explanation

The DOS TREE program examines the disk from the current default directory and reports on all subdirectories. The longer listing that you get with the /F switch shows all subdirectories and their files. Use that switch only if you have much time and paper. Since a good-sized hard disk can have over 2,000 files, TREE could use 33 pages of paper for that list!

Version 3.3 (and earlier) presents an uninspiring rendition of a tree. The listing is all text with plenty of blank spaces. The newer versions of DOS provide a symbolic tree with branches representing the subdirectories. These look nice on the screen because the display uses the ASCII extended characters. Many printers cannot print these characters properly, so newer versions of TREE include the /A switch to display the lines with hyphens and vertical bars (standard ASCII characters).

By moving into a lower directory and using TREE, you can see the subdirectories and files below the current default. For example, if you maintain a subdirectory called LISTS that is further divided into BOARD, BUILDING, and INVNTORY, you get a display like that shown in Figure 87-1 if you have DOS 4.0 or 5.0.

Notice that the current subdirectory name (LISTS) is not displayed. To show all the files in that directory, use the /F switch, as shown in Figure 87-2.

Regardless of your version of DOS, using just **TREE** produces a long list that scrolls by too quickly to do you much good. Use

```
C:\>TREE ¦ MORE
```

so that the output of TREE is paused at every screenful. If you would like a more leisurely look at the files (other than redirecting output to the printer with **TREE > LPT1:**), you can redirect to a file. To create a file with all this information, type

```
C:\>TREE > TREE.TXT
```

This creates an ASCII file named TREE.TXT. It will be located in the root directory and can be called into almost any word processing software.

```
C:\LISTS>TREE

Directory PATH listing for Volume LEARN DOS
Volume Serial Number is 1681-A996
D:
├───BOARD
├───BUILDING
└───INVNTORY
```

Figure 87-1. The LISTS subdirectory displayed with TREE.

```
C:\LISTS>TREE /F

Directory PATH listing for Volume LEARN DOS
Volume Serial Number is 1681-A996
D:
├───BOARD
│       MEMBERS.DBF
│       MEETDATE.DBF
│       EXPENSES.WKS
├───BUILDING
│       MAINTAIN.DBF
│       PURCH.DBF
└───INVNTORY
        EQUIP.DBF
        SUPPLY.DBF
```

Figure 87-2. The same directory displayed with TREE and the /F switch.

Exercise

This exercise shows you how to use TREE to display information on the screen. But more important, it shows how to create a file with a list of all your subdirectories. You can then use this list in your word processing program.

Exercise 1 of 1

All the commands in the first part of this exercise work with all versions of DOS. The last step works with only versions 4.0 and 5.0.

TRY	NOTE
`C:\>TREE`	This produces a lot of information, but it scrolls by too quickly on the screen.
`C:\>TREE ¦ MORE`	Using the vertical bar *pipes* the output from TREE into MORE. Now you get a screenful of information at a time.
`C:\>TREE > TREE.TXT`	You won't see anything on the screen while TREE runs, but it is putting the output in an ASCII file called TREE.TXT.
Look at the file with your favorite word processor.	Remember that the file is located in the root directory. You'll have to type **\TREE.TXT** for the file name.
`C:\>CD\WORDPROC` `C:\WORDPROC>TREE`	Notice that TREE reports only on the subdirectories below the current directory.
`C:\>TREE /A`	DOS 4.0 and 5.0 users can convert the lines on the screen to ASCII characters with the /A switch. These characters will print more readily on most printers.

Use TREE to create a "map" of your system. By importing the map into your word processor, you can clean it up, print it, and use it as a reference for all your subdirectories.

References

File Organization (17), Redirection < > ¦ (64)

NEXT TOPIC: History of DOS (88)

Trouble in connecting two computers

See Communications (55)

TSR memory conflicts

See MEM (90)

Turning off the computer

See Solving Problems (14)

Turning off the computer with programs running

See Boot/Startup (1)
See also CHKDSK — CHecK DiSK (20)
See also DOSSHELL — DOS 5.0 Menu (44)

TYPE — Looking at Files (81)

VERSIONS	
All	●
Some	○
5.0	○
Command	●
Program	○
Concept	○
Problem	○

The DOS TYPE command displays the contents of a single file on the screen. Unless the file is in ASCII format, the results will be meaningless.

Before You Begin

Wild Cards * and ? (11)
ASCII — Character Codes (74)

Syntax

`C:\>TYPE FILENAME.TXT`	Displays the contents of FILENAME.TXT on the screen
`C:\>TYPE FILENAME.TXT > LPT1:`	Sends the contents of FILENAME.TXT to the printer attached to LPT1:

Problems

Quickly examining the contents of a file. You can use the TYPE command with any file. If the file is in ASCII format, the file will be readable. Program (executable) files will be unreadable and will cause unpredictable patterns. If the source file is in a word processing format, some of the file may be readable.

Looking at the contents of batch files. If you are not sure what a batch file will do, you can use the TYPE command to look at the file. Batch files are always in ASCII format.

Explanation

The TYPE command instructs DOS to display the contents of a file on the screen. TYPE does not change the file in any way. Wild cards cannot be used with the TYPE command.

You can achieve the results of the TYPE command by using MORE or COPY instead. The commands presented here are functionally similar, each with its own advantage. The standard TYPE command

```
C:\>TYPE LONGFILE.TXT
```

just displays on the screen the contents of the file. You can press Ctrl-S to pause the display. Pressing any other key continues the display. Ctrl-C stops the file display.

The redirection character > sends the results of the TYPE command to the printer attached to LPT1:

```
C:\>TYPE LONGFILE.TXT > LPT1:
```

In this case, you may need to eject the last page from the printer.

The MORE program is covered more completely in the topic MORE — Pausing Screen Display (84). Basically MORE works like TYPE but pauses after each 24 lines have been displayed:

```
C:\>MORE < LONGFILE.TXT
```

Like TYPE, the MORE command does not accept wild cards.

The advantage of the TYPE command is that it is a DOS internal command. MORE is an external DOS program. It may take a few moments to load the program and then the file before MORE begins to work. TYPE is better for short files, but MORE is worth the wait for longer files. Neither command allows you to move back up to look at previous text.

The LOOK utility program, included on the accompanying disk, enables you to examine a file more easily than with TYPE or MORE. With LOOK, you use the arrow keys and the page keys to move up and down in the file. If the lines are longer than the screen is wide, you can scroll sideways to look at the file. More information on LOOK is provided in Part III, "Guide to Using the Disk."

A variation of the COPY command "copies" the file to the device name CON: (console). You can press Ctrl-S to pause the display. Pressing any other key continues the display. Ctrl-C stops the display of the file. This use of the COPY command *does* allow wild cards. The command

```
C:\>COPY *.TXT CON:
```

displays on the screen all the files with the extension TXT. The Ctrl-S and Ctrl-C key combinations will also work in this instance.

Exercise

If you plan to work with batch files or you need to examine the contents of data files quickly, TYPE is the command to use. Consider also exploring the LOOK utility program explained in Part III.

Exercise 1 of 1

This exercise uses files on the disk included with this book. Make sure that the disk is in drive A: and that you have changed to the subdirectory EXER81 before starting these steps.

TRY	NOTE
A:\EXER81>**TYPE SHORT.TXT**	This is a short ASCII file.
A:\EXER81>**TYPE LONG.TXT**	This long file scrolls off the screen.
A:\EXER81>**TYPE LONG.TXT ¦ MORE**	This command pauses the output of the LONG.TXT file when the screen is full.
A:\EXER81>**MORE < LONG.TXT**	This does the same thing but more quickly and with fewer keystrokes.
A:\EXER81>**TYPE SHORT.TXT > LPT1:**	The contents of the file SHORT.TXT are sent to the printer.

The TYPE command enables you to look at the contents of files. In most cases, other methods are better for this task, including the use of MORE and utility programs like LOOK.

References

ASCII — Character Codes (74), MORE — Pausing Screen Display (84)

NEXT TOPIC: FIND — Searching Files (82)

Typing speed

See Keyboard (39)

Unable to read file

See Disk Damaged (36)

UNDELETE (31)

VERSIONS
All ○
Some ○
5.0 ●

Command ○
Program ●
Concept ○
Problem ○

Available in version 5.0 only, the DOS UNDELETE program allows single or multiple files to be undeleted. If you use UNDELETE right after an accidental deletion, you have a better chance of recovering the file.

Before You Begin

DIR — Directory (8)
DEL — DELete Files (30)

Syntax

`C:\>UNDELETE`	Prompts for recovery of each deleted file in the current directory
`C:\>UNDELETE /LIST`	Lists all deleted and recoverable files
`C:\>UNDELETE /ALL`	Undeletes files with the use of prompts

Problems

Postponed recovery. If the process of recovering a deleted file is delayed, parts of the file may be missing. UNDELETE will not be able to recover that file. Other commercial programs, such as PC Tools and Norton Utilities, may be able to recover parts of the missing file.

Missing first cluster. Even if parts of a file can be recovered by a special program, the first section typically contains the "header" data. Without the header, the original program cannot use the file. A specially written program may be required to use even some of the data from a file with a missing header.

Explanation

As explained more completely in the topic DEL — DELete (30), data in files is not lost until new data is written over the old data. UNDELETE allows immediate recovery of the files containing the old data.

UNDELETE provides several ways to recover deleted files. The /LIST switch shows the files that can be recovered from the current directory:

```
C:\BOOKS\LEARNDOS>UNDELETE /LIST

Directory: C:\BOOKS\LEARNDOS
File Specifications: *.*

    Deletion-tracking file not found.

    MS-DOS directory contains   6 deleted files.
    Of those,    3 files may be recovered.

Using the MS-DOS directory.

        ?DO024    BAK     4096  3-26-91  8:39a  ...A
        ?ALPHA    PRG      749  3-09-91  2:05p  ...A
     ** ?ETTOP    BAK      322  3-09-91  1:52p  ...A
     ** ?ALPHA    BAK      767  3-09-91  2:02p  ...A
     ** ?TOPICS   BAK      794  3-09-91  1:59p  ...A
        ?ETTOP    PRG      329  3-09-91  1:52p  ...A

   "**" indicates the first cluster of the file
        is unavailable and cannot be recovered
        with the UNDELETE command.
```

If all the files shown with the /LIST switch are to be recovered, the /ALL switch, when added to UNDELETE, provides immediate undeletion of all the recoverable files. The # replaces the first character of the file name. You won't see the substituted # for each file name until you run DIR after the UNDELETE. Note this example:

```
C:\BOOKS\LEARNDOS>UNDELETE /ALL

Directory: C:\BOOKS\LEARNDOS
File Specifications: *.*

    Deletion-tracking file not found.

    MS-DOS directory contains   4 deleted files.
    Of those,    2 files may be recovered.

Using the MS-DOS directory.

        ?OPICS    BAK     6459  3-21-91  7:58p  ...A
```

STUV

```
File successfully undeleted.

      ?DO027   BAK     2048  3-26-91  9:12a  ...A

File successfully undeleted.

   ** ?ETTOP   BAK      322  3-09-91  1:52p  ...A
Starting cluster is unavailable. This file cannot be recovered
with the UNDELETE command.  Press any key to continue.

   ** ?ALPHA   BAK      767  3-09-91  2:02p  ...A
Starting cluster is unavailable. This file cannot be recovered
with the UNDELETE command.  Press any key to continue.
```

In this example, ?OPICS.BAK, ?DO027.BAK, and ?ETTOP.BAK are renamed as #OPICS.BAK, #DO027.BAK, and #ETTOP.BAK. You could use the REName command (topic 76) to change the file names of these recovered files.

You can use wild cards with the UNDELETE program. Typing **UNDELETE** is the same as typing **UNDELETE *.***.

In the next example, the first file that has been deleted is located but cannot be recovered. The second file can be recovered, and the first letter of L is provided. If **^C** (Ctrl-C) were not used to terminate UNDELETE in this sequence, UNDELETE would prompt with (Y/N)? for every deleted file in the directory. Here is the output of UNDELETE:

```
D:\BOOKS\LEARNDOS>UNDELETE
Directory: D:\BOOKS\LEARNDOS
File Specifications: *.*

    Deletion-tracking file not found.

    MS-DOS directory contains   13 deleted files.
    Of those,    7 files may be recovered.

Using the MS-DOS directory.

   ** ?DO023   BAK     4096  3-26-91  8:25p  ...A
Starting cluster is unavailable. This file cannot be recovered
with the UNDELETE command.  Press any key to continue.

<space bar>

  ?DO027   BAK    2048  3-26-91  9:12a  ...A  Undelete (Y/N)? Y
      Please type the first character for ?DO027  .BAK: L

File successfully undeleted.
```

```
?DOTEST  BAK     18048  3-28-91  7:07a  ...A  Undelete (Y/N)?
^C
```

Exercise

If you have DOS 5.0, you should practice UNDELETE before you discover that you really need it. For this exercise, you need to use the disk provided with this book. The files are located in subdirectory EXER30.

Exercise 1 of 1

If you have just completed the exercise in the topic DEL — DELete Files (30), you are ready to practice UNDELETE. If not, one special step here will ensure that you have some deleted files to undelete.

NOTE	NOTE
Make sure that the accompanying disk is in drive A:.	
C:\>**A:** A:\>**CD EXER30** A:\EXER30>**DIR**	If there are files in this directory (besides . and ..), use the following step to delete them all.
A:\EXER30>**DEL *.*** Are you sure (Y/N)? **Y** A:\EXER30>	Now all the files are gone. Well, actually, they are not gone. They are just no longer listed.
A:\EXER30>**UNDELETE /LIST**	This shows a list of all the deleted files in the subdirectory.

What you see with this listing will depend on how long ago you erased the files. If you just erased the files, you'll see all the file names except for the first character of each one. If you've made changes by adding or copying other files to the disk, all of the files cannot be recovered. Some of these next steps may not work if some of those files have been overwritten.

TRY	NOTE
A:\EXER30>**UNDELETE DWD.DOC**	You can specify a file just by typing the original file name. UNDELETE prompts for the first letter if the file can be recovered.
A:\EXER30>**UNDELETE *.SPL**	You can use wild cards to locate deleted files—in this case, the two files with SPL as the extension.

TRY	NOTE
`A:\EXER30>`**`UNDELETE /ALL`**	This switch recovers all the files, replacing the first letter of each file name with the # character.
`A:\EXER30>`**`DIR`**	Notice that some of the files now have the # for the first character.

You have recovered all the files in this subdirectory. But what happens when one or more files are not recoverable? You explore that question after you erase all the files again.

TRY	NOTE
`A:\EXER30>`**`DEL *.*`** `Are you sure (Y/N)?` **`Y`** `A:\EXER30>`	They're all gone again.
`A:\EXER30>`**`UNDELETE /LIST`**	See what can be undeleted.
`A:\EXER30>`**`COPY \*.*`**	This copies all the files in the root directory into this directory. What happens to the deleted files?
`?A:\EXER30>`**`UNDELETE /LIST`**	Are some of the deleted file names missing? Depending on the number of files copied from the root directory, one, two, or all of the deleted files may no longer be listed.

The key to undeleting files is to do it immediately after they are deleted. The longer you wait, the less chance you will have of recovering the files.

References

Utility Software (50), REN — REName Files (76), UNFORMAT (86), MIRROR (91)

NEXT TOPIC: Floppy Drive Failure (32)

Unexpected batch file results

See Batch Files — Write Your Own (100)

UNFORMAT (86)

VERSIONS
All ○
Some ○
5.0 ●

Command ○
Program ●
Concept ○
Problem ○

If a disk that contains data is formatted with DOS 5.0, the disk can be unformatted immediately with the UNFORMAT program. All the data will be recovered.

Before You Begin

FORMAT — Disks (12)
Floppy Disks (19)

Syntax

`C:\>UNFORMAT A:`	Begins the recovery process on the disk in drive A:
`C:\>UNFORMAT A: /J`	"Just checking" switch helps determine whether the disk can be unformatted

Problem

Disk formatted accidentally. If a disk containing data files is accidentally formatted, the UNFORMAT program can recover the files if you use UNFORMAT immediately after the mistake is made. The disk must have been formatted again with DOS 5.0 FORMAT.

Explanation

The location of each part of each file is kept in the FAT (File Allocation Table) on the disk. The latest version of DOS, 5.0, looks at a floppy disk before beginning the format process. If DOS finds data on the disk, the FAT is saved to a hidden file on the disk. DOS next erases the current FAT and quits. When DOS then reads this disk, the empty FAT signals an empty disk, and files are written anywhere on the disk.

The UNFORMAT program knows to look for that hidden copy of the FAT. UNFORMAT copies that special file back into the normal FAT location. Because the actual data was not erased, DOS can now find those files again, and the data is restored.

There's a catch: unformatting a disk works only if you run UNFORMAT immediately after accidentally formatting the disk. If you begin to write files to the disk, they will begin filling up the FAT and writing over the old data on the disk. If you then unformat the disk, the old FAT replaces the new FAT. The old version reports files in locations now occupied by the new files. So the old file names in the FAT do not match the new data in those locations. In short, you'll have quite a mess.

The amount of data you recover from an accidentally formatted and reused disk is unpredictable.

The UNFORMAT program has a number of switches that enable you to determine what will happen with UNFORMAT, but they won't make any changes to the disk. UNFORMAT produces more warning messages and explanations on the screen than any other DOS program. Use the "Exercise" section to explore the UNFORMAT program.

Table 86-1 describes the switches you can use with UNFORMAT. Notice that they are grouped in three different UNFORMAT commands. As always, refer to your DOS manual for more information about UNFORMAT.

Table 86-1. The UNFORMAT switches with three UNFORMAT commands.

Command #1: **`UNFORMAT N: /J`**

Switch	Description
N:	Specifies the drive to unformat
/J	Just checks the hidden FAT files against the current FAT

Command #2: **`UNFORMAT N: /U /L /TEST /P`**

Switch	Description
/U	Unformats without using MIRROR files
/L	Lists all file names and directory names found
/TEST	Displays information but does not write changes to disk
/P	Sends messages to LPT1:

Command #3: **`UNFORMAT N: /PARTN /L`**

Switch	Description
/PARTN	Restores disk partition tables
/L	Displays current partition tables when used with /PARTN

Hard disk users are much more likely to survive an accidental formatting if the DOS 5.0 MIRROR program has been run recently. See the topic MIRROR (91) for more information about that program.

Exercise

If you know that you'll never accidentally reformat a disk containing data, you don't need to worry about practicing the recovery of lost data. If, however, you might accidentally reformat a disk with some critical files, spend a few minutes on this exercise.

Exercise 1 of 1

In this exercise, you need a used disk that contains noncritical data. If you are not sure how critical the data is (or if all of your data is critical), use DISKCOPY to make a second copy of a disk.

TRY	NOTE
`C:\>FORMAT A:`	This format goes quickly because FORMAT just copies the FAT, erases the FAT, and checks the disk.
`C:\>UNFORMAT A: /J`	This switch checks the status of the hidden FAT against the current FAT. Notice all the warning messages.
`C:\>UNFORMAT A:`	Go ahead and unformat the disk.
`C:\>DIR`	Then look to see if the files are back.

`C:\>COPY *.* A:`
Wait a few seconds.
`<Ctrl>C`
	Let at least 10 files be copied to the floppy and then press Ctrl-C to interrupt the process.

`C:\>DIR`	Now that you have some new files on the disk, try UNFORMAT.
`C:\>UNFORMAT A:`	Answer *yes* to the prompt and then view the contents of the disk.

The original files on the disk have survived this process. How about the new files copied from the hard disk? Now imagine trying this process to unformat a hard disk.

References

Utility Software (50), FAT — Fat Allocation Table (89), MIRROR (91)

NEXT TOPIC: TREE — Directory Map (87)

Unformatted disk

See FORMAT — Disks (12)
See also UNFORMAT (86)

Unintentionally deleting files

See Wild Cards * and ? (11)

Unknown changes made to AUTOEXEC.BAT and CONFIG.SYS files

See Installing Programs (60)

Unknown compression format

See Compressed Files (80)

Unmatched communications parameters

See Modems (56)

Unrecoverable read/write error

See Floppy Drive Failure (32)

Unregistered software

See No One to Help (59)

Unsupported printer

See Word Processing (43)

Unusual program

See No One to Help (59)

Upgrade copies

See Copyright (51)
See also Product Registration (54)
See also Upgrading Your Software (65)

Upgrading to newer software versions

See Upgrading Your Software (65)

Upgrading Your Software (65)

VERSIONS	
All	●
Some	○
5.0	○
Command	○
Program	○
Concept	●
Problem	○

Developers are constantly changing software programs to fix *bugs* (errors) in the program and to add features. Registered users are usually offered the newer version (upgrade) at a discount. Upgrading to that version is not always necessary, however.

Before You Begin

Software (18)
Application Software (46)
Program Versions (47)

Problems

Deciding to upgrade to a newer software version. Each new version number represents "new and improved" software. This means that more menu choices provide more options. In some cases, the menu and program choices change completely, especially the uses of the function keys. If the new features provide the enhancements you need for your tasks, the time you spend learning the new commands will be worthwhile. But before you purchase and convert to the latest and greatest version of the software, evaluate your needs in relation to those new, and potentially confusing, features.

Determining file compatibility. In redesigning a new version of software, the developers may discover that a new file format is necessary. The newer version usually reads the old files but may convert and save those files to the new format. The older version of the program will then be unable to read the newer version's file.

> Always make backup copies of the older, critical data files before using the newer version of the software.

You will not be able to return to the older version of the program if you have only the newly converted data files.

Finding new bugs. When improving the software, developers are likely to make extensive changes to the program code. With new code comes the chance of new errors. Because most software upgrades are thoroughly tested before they are offered to the users, bugs are not as likely to appear. Still, you may find some new bugs. For example, if you had no trouble printing headers in the older version but you have trouble with the newer version, the new header format may have new options—and new bugs. You'll have to spend time determining whether you have found a new feature or a new bug.

Explanation

In addition to eliminating bugs, developers of new versions of software are always taking advantage of the power provided by newer hardware. For instance, more systems now include a mouse. Almost all new programs can support (use) a mouse as a pointing device, even if using a mouse with the program makes little sense.

As suggested in the "Problems" section, think of an upgrade from the older version as a new software purchase instead of an automatic expense. Because the cost of upgrading is much less than the original purchase price, a $75 upgrade may seem to be a bargain. But if the upgrade contains features you will never use, you'll just be wasting $75. When deciding whether to pay for an upgrade to your current program, consider some of these points:

- Exactly what new features do you need right now? Have you been frustrated that you cannot do certain tasks, or are you just curious about those new features?

- Can your current hardware handle the demands of the newer version? As programs add more features, they require more processing speed or memory to work well. Check the system requirements on the package. If you spend $75 on the upgrade, you may need to spend an additional $1,000 in hardware improvements to use the upgrade effectively.

- Have the menus and commands changed much? Some upgrades just add menu choices. Other upgrades completely change the menu and command structures. Do you really want to learn the program all over again?
- Do you need to remain compatible with other users in your company? If many users who have advanced features trade data files back and forth, you may need to upgrade so that you can read the new and advanced file formats.
- Do you just love to get your hands on new software? Do you buy software just to rip open the cellophane and see what's inside? If you do, upgrades are a cheap way to get your thrills.
- If you did not upgrade the last time a version changed, now may be the time to make the change. You are likely to benefit from the new features. If you have not upgraded at the last two opportunities, there is an excellent chance that you can use the new features. Just be sure that the new software will work on your current system.

References

New Programs on Old Computers (71)

NEXT TOPIC: GRAPHICS — Printing Screens (66)

Use of the root backslash (\)

See CD, MD, and RD — Working with Directories (9)

Using ? when * needed

See Wild Cards * and ? (11)

Using different operating system versions

See Operating Systems (75)

Using disk compression or optimization programs

See FASTOPEN — Speeding Up Disks (70)

Using DOSSHELL without a mouse

See DOSSHELL — DOS 5.0 Menu (44)

Using the ¦ character

See Lost Data Files (77)

Utility Software (50)

VERSIONS
All ●
Some ○
5.0 ○

Command ○
Program ○
Concept ●
Problem ○

Utility programs help you maintain the computer system. With utilities, you can do many tasks more efficiently, including organizing files and directories and recovering from damaged disks.

Before You Begin

Files (2)
DIR — Directory (8)
Floppy Disks (19)
Hard Drive Failure (33)
Disk Damaged (36)

Explanation

Utility programs may be defined as helpful tools for system management. There is no easy way to determine whether a utility is an extra or essential tool. Each new version of DOS contains more commands and programs to help you manage the system. Although you once had to purchase a file-undeletion program from another company, DOS 5.0 now includes an UNDELETE program as an "essential" tool for system management. In this topic, a *utility* is a program used for system management.

Several utility programs have become popular over the past few years, including PC Tools and Norton Utilities. The designers of each of these packages looked at ways to make system management easier as well as ways to recover from, or prevent, problems. They wrote a series of programs that can be used from within one menu. Although a DOS user can "get by" without a utility program, the time and frustration saved are immeasurable.

PC Tools by Central Point Software contains many programs that are helpful for system management. Version 6.0 includes DOS shell, data recovery, backup, and desktop tools, and even more. Consider the purpose of each of these programs to see how it can save time, frustration, or both:

- *DOS shell.* This program provides a menu system that enables you to locate files, start programs, copy files, sort directories, and completely rearrange the directory trees. Although you can accomplish most of these tasks with just DOS, this program, especially when you use it with a mouse, makes the process as easy as point and click.
- *Hard disk backup.* The program menu includes settings for specific backup areas and incremental backups. The backup program compresses the data so that more files can fit on fewer disks. This program can even schedule backups to run automatically.
- *Data recovery.* This disk repair program can diagnose problems with hard disks and floppy disks and then repair them. UNFORMAT can recover files from an accidentally formatted disk and can restore accidentally deleted files. (This program is also part of DOS 5.0.)
- *Desktop.* This program is a small word processing program with a spell checker, four different calculators, an appointment scheduler, and telecommunications.
- *Other features.* In addition to the preceding programs, the package includes disk compression and cache (makes the hard disk run faster), as well as a way to scramble files so that others cannot see or use your files.

The disk included with this book contains a number of utility programs that are described in Part III, "Guide to Using the Disk." Although these programs (or programs like PC Tools and Norton Utilities) are not necessary, spending a few minutes to learn how to use the utilities on this disk may save you some time and effort.

Figure 50-1 shows the PC Tools shell program. Notice how many file functions are in PC Shell, including the move and undelete operations. The complete directory tree is in the left window, and the files for the selected subdirectory are shown in the right window.

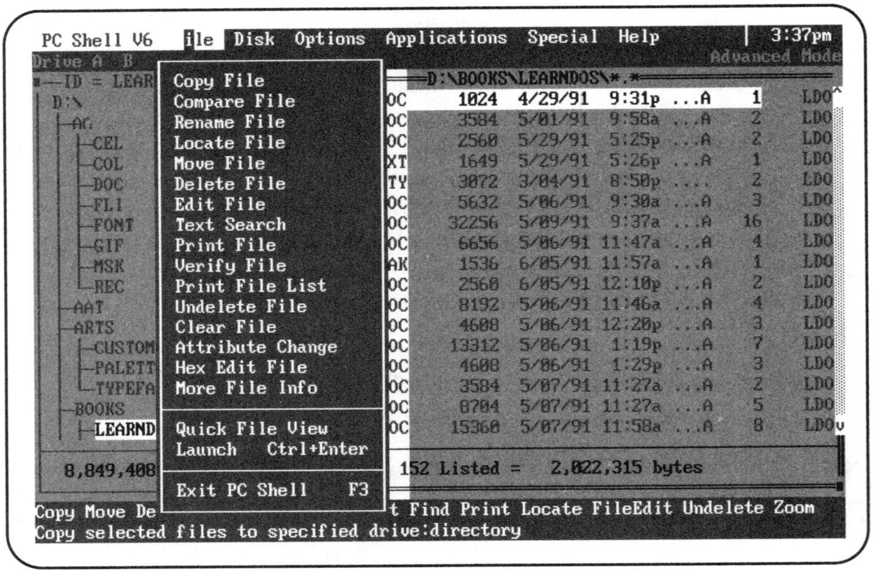

Figure 50-1. The PC Tools shell program.

Exercise

Just as you scout the locations of fire extinguishers and fire alarms in a building, find out which utility programs other users have and how proficient they are with those programs. Better yet, ask which utilities are the most helpful and then buy a copy of each one.

References

Application Software (46), Operating Systems (75), Copyright (51), Security (95)

NEXT TOPIC: Copyright (51)

Vague goals

See Learning More (28)

Versions

See Software (18)

Viewing long ASCII files

See MORE — Pausing Screen Display (84)

Virus (92)

VERSIONS	
All	●
Some	○
5.0	○
Command	○
Program	○
Concept	○
Problem	●

Computer virus programs can duplicate and spread from system to system on floppy disks or through modems. Some virus programs are benign, but many are malicious. All of them constitute a threat to data and program integrity.

Problem

Erratic system behavior. Because some virus programs are designed to cause only occasional problems, the pattern of damage may be hard to detect. Possible symptoms include frequent lost clusters, bad or unreadable parts of files, and slow disk-access times. If you suspect a virus, a special virus-detection program should be used to locate and remove the virus.

Explanation

Computer ***viruses*** are programs intentionally written to disrupt use of the system. The results of a virus may range from a message displayed at random on the screen to the total loss of data on a hard disk or floppy disk. There are several types of viruses, and some systems are more likely to encounter a virus than others. Unfortunately, viruses have become prevalent enough that routine system maintenance should include running a special program for virus detection and repair.

The term ***virus*** describes a specific type of program and program behavior. A virus program is of no value and usually damages the system infected by the virus. Such a program replicates itself and attempts to spread to other systems. Sometimes it does not cause enough problems to be noticed with everyday use, but produces a cumulative damage noticeable only after a period of time.

A *Trojan Horse* is a virus program that appears to do one thing while actually doing something else. Suppose, for example, that you run a program called SMILE. A smiley face appears on the screen for a few moments and then disappears 30 seconds later. What you don't know is that the program was erasing your hard disk as the image appeared on the screen. This program is not a true virus because it destroys itself in the process of creating the damage. But that is small consolation for the user just discovering the massive amount of data lost.

A *worm* program is common on networks. This program uses the connection between computers to transmit itself. In the process of searching for systems, it takes up system resources and may cause a complete shutdown of the entire network. Unless your computer is hooked to a network, this type of virus is not a threat.

The virus *bomb* is a program that runs every time the system is booted. The bomb checks the system date. At a predetermined date, such as Friday the 13th, the program activates and damages the system or just announces its presence. This program may also attempt to spread itself through networks and on floppy disks.

Several commercial programs are available to search for and destroy viruses found on floppy disks and hard disks. Currently there are over 250 known virus-detection programs. These commercial programs must be kept updated constantly to keep up with the viruses being created by malicious programmers.

Virus programs, like diseases, are spread by contact with other virus-infected systems. A virus can infect your system in one of several ways. The most common method of infection occurs when you accept a floppy from someone and run a program from that floppy on your system. If that program contains a virus, the virus program copies itself to your system and begins doing damage. If you copy that same program to a floppy and give it to someone else, that person's system will then be infected.

Sharing programs of unknown origin increases the risk of spreading a virus. Exchanging data files on disk is not likely to spread a virus, however. A virus can be spread only when a program containing the virus is run. A spreadsheet or database file is not likely to carry a virus.

Programs that contain viruses can be downloaded from bulletin board systems. Thousands of files are available on a BBS and can be easily exchanged. One user can send the file to the BBS, and within days, dozens of callers can copy that file to their systems, run the program, and be infected by the virus. Many system operators (SYSOPs) now certify that their files are virus-free by running virus-detection programs on the files before releasing them to be copied by other callers.

Virus transmission is also possible over a network. The more users access the network, the higher the probability that a virus can invade the system. As noted with the worm virus, some of these programs are designed to seek out and transmit themselves over networks. A virus can even attach itself to network software and infect all users attached to the host. The network system administrator should perform a virus check as part of routine maintenance.

How likely is a virus to be on a particular system? The following list suggests several levels of risk:

- *Very unlikely.* The system is the only one in an office, runs commercial programs only, and just copies data files to floppy disks for backup.

- *Possible.* The system is one of several in an office. Some users have public domain programs. Program files are copied both to and from other systems.
- *Probable.* The system is on a network with several dozen users. Programs can be copied to areas available for group access. Anti-virus programs are not run on new programs.
- *Very likely.* Most of the systems have a mix of public domain, shareware, and commercial programs. Users frequently pass programs around within minutes of receiving the programs in the mail or by modem.
- *Highly likely.* Program files are frequently copied from BBS and commercial services and are run without being checked for viruses.

As is usually true with computers, prevention and detection are the best ways to keep your system virus-free. Here are some suggestions:

- Never use a program of unknown origin. Never copy programs to your hard disk without knowing the source of the program. The more useless the program appears, the better the chance that a virus is attached to it.
- Be careful when using **`COPY *.*`** to copy files from a floppy disk to your hard disk. An unwanted file (such as a virus) can be copied along with the data files you expect.
- Use a hard disk protection program to prevent unexpected access to the disk. Such a program may prevent all hard disk access or provide a warning when a program writes to the disk. You should use the protection program only when you run an unknown program; otherwise, you may not get anything done.
- Run CHKDSK weekly. If CHKDSK gives `Lost cluster` messages, a virus may be eating parts of your files.
- If possible, reserve one system to try all new and untested software. Run the software for at least several days and check with virus-detection software before distributing the new software.
- Advise employees of the potential for virus transmission. Establish guidelines for the use and exchange of external software.

Central Point Software has released Central Point Anti-Virus (CPAV). Even before installing itself on the hard disk, the software checks for over 400 viruses. If it finds any, CPAV removes them before going any further in the installation.

Once installed, CPAV automatically checks memory when the system is booted and then watches in the background for any viruses that may be attempting to enter your system. If you don't care to give up the 40K of memory that CPAV uses when running in the background, you can run this program from the DOS command line occasionally to check for any viruses. It then scans the entire disk just as it did when first installed.

Because the people who write virus programs will continue to change them, Central Point operates a 24-hour hot line, provides quarterly mailings, and has a forum on CompuServe for downloading new virus detection files. Registered users are automatically provided with one free upgrade of the CPAV program.

References

Backing Up Data (13), Solving Problems (14), Disk Damaged (36)

NEXT TOPIC: Sharing Devices (93)

Warm boot

See Boot/Startup (1)

What directories are on the hard disk?

See TREE — Directory Map (87)

What does a spreadsheet do?

See Spreadsheets (48)

What software should you buy or use?

See Application Software (46)

What version of DOS do you have?

See Operating Systems (75)

What's a RAM drive?

See Memory (73)

When should you get the latest version?

See Program Versions (47)

Which key should you press?

See `Strike a key when ready...` (16)

Which keys should you *not* press?

See `Strike a key when ready...` (16)

Wild Cards * and ? (11)

VERSIONS	
All	●
Some	○
5.0	○
Command	○
Program	○
Concept	●
Problem	○

The wild cards * (asterisk) and ? (question mark) can be used in a number of DOS commands. These wild cards enable a command to affect more than one file at a time.

Before You Begin

File Names (4)
DIR — Directory (8)
COPY — Files (10)

Syntax

* (asterisk)	Substitutes for the remaining file name or extension
? (question mark)	Substitutes for only one character

Problems

Misunderstanding the asterisk. When reading the * in a command, DOS skips to the period that signifies the beginning of the extension. The command **DIR LDO*OR.DOC** is read the same as **DIR LDO*.DOC**.

Using ? when * is needed. The command **COPY LDO?.DOC** finds only those files that begin with LDO and have one character in the fourth position. Any file name longer than four characters will not be copied. To copy files that begin with LDO, use **LDO*.DOC**.

Unintentionally deleting files. Wild cards can save you time, but they also invite disaster. Although most users are familiar with the `Are you sure (Y/N)?` response to **DEL *.***, no such warning is provided with **DEL *.EXE.** All files—in this case, program files—will be deleted without warning! Always use the intended file name and wild card pattern before any use of DEL. Use **DIR *.BAK** before **DEL *.BAK** to see exactly which files will be deleted.

Explanation

Wild cards are designed to save time by representing multiple files in the same command. You can use * and ? in many DOS commands, including DIR, COPY, DEL, and REName. Wild cards can be used even more effectively if you follow consistent file naming. More information on file names can be found in the topic File Names (4).

Table 11-1 shows examples of the * wild card used in several DOS commands. Valid examples of the ? wild card are in Table 11-2.

Table 11-1. Valid and invalid uses of the * wild card.

Valid Uses	Results
DIR *.EXE	FILE.EXE FILENAME.EXE
COPY LDO*.DOC	LDO001OR.DOC LDO-ORG.DOC
DEL *.*	All files deleted
Invalid Uses	**Results**
DIR *TR.EXE	None
COPY LDO.*C	None
DEL *4Q.*	None

Table 11-2. Valid uses of the ? wild card.

Valid Uses	Results
`DIR LD000?.DOC`	LD0001.DOC LD0003.DOC
`COPY LDO???OR.DOC`	LD0001OR.DOC LD0003OR.DOC

Many of the exercises throughout this book use wild cards. Review the topics DIR — Directory (8), COPY — Files (10), and DEL — DELete Files (30) for effective uses of * and ?.

References

File Organization (17), Command and Program Parameters (34)

NEXT TOPIC: FORMAT — Disks (12)

Windows

See Interfaces (27)

Word Processing (43)

VERSIONS: All ●, Some ○, 5.0 ○
Command ○, Program ○, Concept ●, Problem ○

Word processing is the term used to describe the typing, correcting, saving, and printing of documents with a computer system.

Problems

Incompatible file formats. Of the hundreds of word processing programs, nearly every one uses a unique format for the document files saved to disk. These formats include not only the text itself but also the code for headers and footers, typefaces, and other stylistic features. To use a file created by one word processing program in another program, you'll need to "convert" the first file into the new format. Some programs do this automatically, but others require a conversion program. Even the best conversion programs lose or miss some of the formatting in the conversion process.

Unsupported printer. Printers vary greatly in the quality and range of their output. To maximize printer quality, most word processing programs include special instructions for the different types of printers. Some programs list over 100 printers in the printer setup. If your printer is not listed, consult the word processing manual for the closest substitution. Your printer manual may also list equivalent printers. If, after you select the printer and print a test document, the output is not satisfactory, you may have to call the word processing software company. The software may have additional setup instructions for your printer.

Overwhelming complexity. The trend in word processing software, as with most software, is increased complexity. Like new model cars, new versions of software contain more features. What used to be basic, get-the-letter-typed software now allows you to create a table of contents and print graphics. These new features mean more menu selections. Furthermore, newer programs may require more powerful computers and more hard disk space. Before automatically upgrading to the latest version of a word processing program (or any software), evaluate the new features as though you were buying the program for the first time. If you see features that can help you perform your word processing tasks, consider purchasing the latest version.

Explanation

Word processing might be more accurately described as "thought processing" because the goal is to communicate thoughts with the aid of a computer. Although writing by hand or with a typewriter requires that the words be rewritten or retyped with each effort to clarify your thoughts, the computer enables you to write just one version, make as many changes as you want, and print as many copies as you need.

Newer versions of word processing software can be even more helpful. They can check spelling, provide alternative words with a thesaurus, and suggest grammatical improvements. The printed output can be enhanced with additional typefaces and graphics, depending on the printer. But as helpful as these features may be, they can only clarify the thoughts conveyed. (Of course, you must remember to run the spelling checker.)

Making instant corrections, rearranging paragraphs, saving the results, and printing at any time are capabilities that make word processing an incredibly powerful tool. Because the results are fairly straightforward, word processing is a good way to begin learning about the computer. Making corrections requires learning how to move the cursor. Rearranging paragraphs includes moving the cursor and typing special commands. Saving and recalling a document file familiarizes the new user with the critical concepts of data storage and retrieval. Producing a perfectly printed document provides immediate confirmation that the task has been completed and looks great.

Word processors usually provide most of the space on the screen for the work you are doing. Figure 43-1 shows Microsoft Word 5.0, with the text in the top portion of the screen and a menu at the bottom.

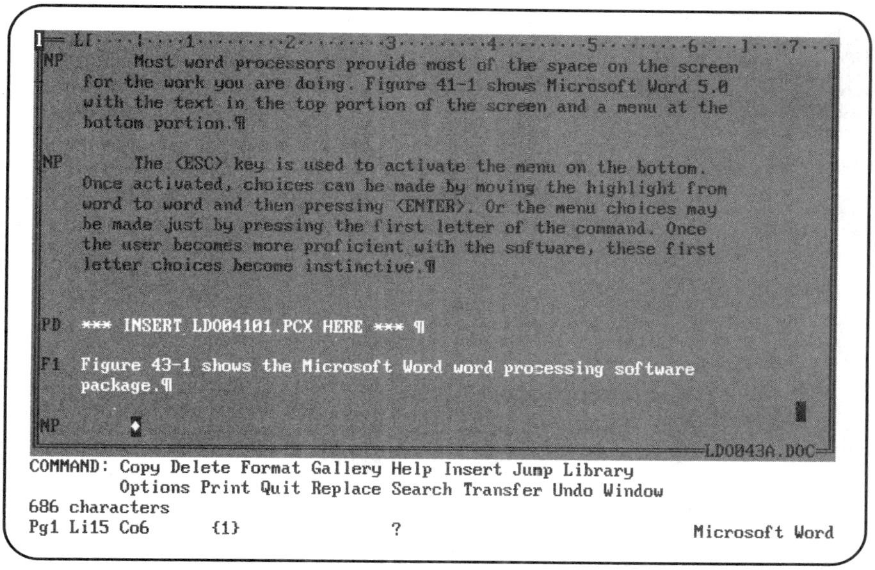

Figure 43-1. The Microsoft Word software package.

You use the Esc key to activate the menu at the bottom. Once you activate the menu, you can make choices by moving the highlight from word to word and pressing Enter. Or you can make menu choices just by pressing the first letter of the command you want to use. When you are more proficient with the software, making a choice by pressing the first letter becomes almost instinctive.

References

Application Software (46), Manuals and Documentation (53), Product Registration (54)

NEXT TOPIC: DOSSHELL — DOS 5.0 Menu (44)

Workspace — User Comfort (85)

VERSIONS
All ●
Some ○
5.0 ○

Command ○
Program ○
Concept ●
Problem ○

A complete computer system includes hardware, software, and the user. Although the computer needs only a stable location and the software needs just enough RAM, *user comfort* depends on a number of important considerations.

Problems

Frequent headaches and muscle tension. Placing the computer screen and keyboard in an improper location can cause discomfort for frequent computer users. The physical arrangement of your system can greatly affect your performance and level of fatigue.

Dry eyes, or "pseudomyopia." Staring at the computer screen tends to slow down the blinking and keeps the eyes focused at the same distance. The eyes dry out and can develop "pseudomyopia" from long sessions in front of the screen. Remember to look up from the screen and focus on something at least 20 feet away. This rewets the eyes and exercises the eye muscles.

Explanation

The most important element of a computer system is you, the user. If using the computer causes physical pain, you will not be working at your full potential. (And you'll like using the computer even less.) Choosing a proper location for the monitor and keyboard is essential for your comfort. In fact, your total environment contributes signficantly to how well you concentrate. Here are some ideas to help make your workspace more comfortable:

- Arrange the screen directly in front of you with the top of the screen just level with your eyes. If the monitor is on top of the system box on a regular desk, the monitor is likely to be too high.
- Avoid direct light on the screen. Bright windows behind you and ceiling lights frequently cause glare. Look at the monitor before turning it on. If there are noticeable reflections, you are likely to develop eye strain. Monitor hoods wrap around the screen to block light. Try turning the monitor slightly up or down to avoid the light in the middle of the screen.
- Always avoid placing the monitor against a window or bright light. This can cause eye strain as your eyes adjust from the monitor to the light.
- If the monitor image seems fuzzy and hard to read, that kind of monitor may not be appropriate for your work. The topic Monitor (61) explains how different monitors can affect you and your work.

- Keyboard height is critical for comfortable typing. Standard desks are too high for most users. Use a computer table or get a keyboard extension that attaches to the desk and lowers the keyboard. If your chair is the proper height, the keyboard can be pulled onto your lap. In this position, your arms are parallel with the keyboard and can rest on your legs. The only movement required is your fingers.
- You spend hundreds of hours sitting in your chair, so you need good back support and a proper seat. Invest in a good chair. As long as the computer table is sturdy, the computer does not care what it sits on.
- You can easily become so intent on the screen that you forget to blink. Remember to look away from the screen for a moment or two every 10 or 15 minutes to change the focus point for your eyes. Position your work so that it is easy to see and does not require moving your head or holding it at an angle to view the screen.
- When you look at paper on the desk, your field of view is restricted to the desk and floor. There is little movement to distract your eyes. Looking at a computer monitor, because it is located at eye level, expands your field of view into the rest of the workspace. If your monitor has no screen behind it, you can be easily distracted by movements across the room. If possible, position the monitor against a wall or divider to minimize distractions in the room.
- External sounds are also distracting. Computer systems do not provide much sound worth hearing. Depending on your job requirements or restrictions, you may be able to use headphones while you work at the computer. If you keep the volume at a reasonable level, you can still hear someone up close and talk with that person, but sounds in the distance may not be noticeable.

Exercises

OK. Stand up (right now!) and do 10 jumping jacks. Then drop and do 5 push-ups. Do at least 10 sit-ups. Then finish with 20 alternate toe touches. For a cool-down, sit quietly in your chair and breath slowly 20 times.
Now those were exercises!

References

Learning More (28), No One to Help (59)

NEXT TOPIC: UNFORMAT (86)

Writing and printing a quick note

See EDIT — DOS 5.0 Text Editor (98)

Wrong directory for the batch file

See Batch Files — Write Your Own (100)

Wrong monitor type

See Monitor (61)

Wrong print type

See Printers (15)

Wrong size of disks

See Floppy Disks (19)

Wrong system date

See DATE (23)

Wrong system time

See TIME (24)

XCOPY — Files (37)

VERSIONS	
All	○
Some	●
5.0	○
Command	○
Program	●
Concept	○
Problem	○

This DOS program provides additional functions to the DOS COPY command, including copying files in subdirectories and copying files selectively.

Before You Begin

Default Drive (3)
COPY — Files (10)

Syntax

`C:\>`**`XCOPY SOURCE.EXT A:`**	Copies SOURCE.EXT to the disk in A:
`C:\WORD>`**`XCOPY *.DOC A: /S`**	Copies to the disk in drive A: all files with the DOC extension in the current directory and all of its subdirectories
`C:\>`**`XCOPY *.* A: /D:08-26-91`**	Copies to the disk in drive A: all files created on or after 08-26-91 in the current directory

Problem

`Bad command or file name.` Because XCOPY is a DOS program and not a command like COPY, the path setting must include the subdirectory that contains XCOPY. If it is not included or if you are not sure, try using **`C:\DOS\XCOPY`** (assuming that the subdirectory with your DOS files is called DOS). Remember that if you have an older version of DOS, you might not have the XCOPY program.

Explanation

The DOS XCOPY program is a much more powerful version of the internal COPY command. Source and destination files can be provided, just as you can include wild cards with COPY. The usefulness of XCOPY comes from switches you can add at the end of the command. These switches enable you to copy subdirectories and files, as well as do selective copying based on the file date, an archive attribute, or user approval.

If a directory contains additional subdirectories and you want to copy all the files in the current directory and in any subdirectories, the /S switch does it all in one step. Suppose, for example, that you have in your directory tree the branch shown in Figure 37-1.

To copy all the files in all the subdirectories shown in the figure, use the /S switch:

```
C:\DOCS>XCOPY *.* A: /S
```

Figure 37-2 illustrates the results of the copy to a floppy in drive A:.

```
DOCS─────────────┬──MEMOS
  RULES.DOC      │     JANE.DOC
                 │     JOE.DOC
                 ├──LETTERS
                 │     FRANK.DOC
                 └──MOTHER
                       (no files)
```

Figure 37-1. A branch in a sample directory tree.

```
DOCS─────────────┬──MEMOS
  RULES.DOC      │     JANE.DOC
                 │     JOE.DOC
                 └──LETTERS
                       FRANK.DOC
```

Figure 37-2. The directory and its subdirectories copied to A:.

What happened to the MOTHER subdirectory? XCOPY creates a destination subdirectory only if there are files in it. To create the destination subdirectory even if it has no files, you add the /E switch:

```
C:\DOCS>XCOPY *.* A: /S/E
```

XCOPY can be used effectively to perform incremental file backups. The file date, the archive attribute (bit), or a prompt (Y/N) for each file can help determine whether to copy a file. The /D switch works with dates. The /M and /A switches use the archive bit. And the /P switch allows you to select each individual file to be copied.

When you create or change a file, a *date stamp* is added to that file. As long as you keep the system date accurate, you can use this stamp to copy files selectively. The command

```
C:\DOCS>XCOPY *.DOC A: /D:03-28-91
```

copies all the files in the DOCS subdirectory with the date stamp of 3-28-91 or later and the DOC extension. If you use this command with the /S command at the end of each day, all files changed during the day will automatically be copied to the disk. The following command might be a good one to use:

```
C:\>XCOPY C:\*.* A: /S/D:03-28-91
```

One problem with XCOPY is that it copies files only until the floppy disk is full. Then it quits. Another problem is that XCOPY cannot copy a file larger than the capacity of the floppy. For these problems, you'll need to use the DOS BACKUP program or a commercial backup program. See the topic Backing Up Data (13) for more ideas.

XCOPY can use the archive bit on a file to determine whether the file should be copied. The archive bit is turned on when a file is created or modified. (You may want to imagine that the file is holding its hand up, waiting to be copied to a floppy disk.) Many backup programs other than XCOPY can use the status of this bit to determine if a file has been changed since the time of the last backup. Most backup programs turn this bit off after backing up. Unless the file is then changed, the bit stays off, and the file will not be backed up the next time the program is run. For more about the archive bit, see the topic ATTRIB — Protecting Files (62).

If you want to use XCOPY for backing up files, you can use the /M switch to copy only those files with their archive bits turned on. After each file is copied, the bit is turned off. (The file can put its hand down, no longer waiting to be copied.) The next time the file is changed, the archive bit is turned on, and XCOPY then copies the file.

With the command

```
C:\DOCS>XCOPY *.* A: /M
```

all files in the DOCS directory that have their archive bits on (hands up) are copied to the disk in drive A:. XCOPY then turns the archive bits of those files off (hands down) after making the copy.

Suppose that you work on two of those files and you create a third file. These three files have their hands up (archive bits on), but the rest of the files still have their hands down (archive bits off). Now the XCOPY command with the /M switch will copy only the two changed files and the third new file. If you want to include all the subdirectories under DOCS, you must include the /S switch:

```
C:\DOCS>XCOPY *.* A: /M/S
```

If you want to copy only those files with their archive bits on and you don't want their bits turned off, you use the /A switch:

```
C:\DOCS>XCOPY *.* A: /A
```

If you used the /A switch instead of the /M switch for those three files, the files would be copied, and their archive bits would remain on. They would be copied the next time even if they weren't changed in the meantime.

Selective copying of a long list of files can be time-consuming. If you have a directory of 60 files and you want to copy only 20 of the files, the /P switch is the one to use. The command

```
C:\DOCS>XCOPY *.TXT A: /P
```

results in the following exchange:

```
DOSKEY.TXT (Y/N)?Y
PROMPT.TXT (Y/N)?N

        1 File(s) copied
```

Two additional switches, /V and /W, can be used with XCOPY to verify that the destination file matches the source file exactly. You can use the /V switch with COPY also, but this switch is rarely needed with either of these commands. The /W switch causes XCOPY to wait until you press a key before it continues. /W is useful when you are working from floppy disks. Table 37-1 lists all the XCOPY switches.

Table 37-1. The XCOPY switches.

Switch	Description
/A	Copies files with their archive bits set on and doesn't change the attributes
/M	Copies files with their archive bits set on and turns the archive bits off
/D:*mm-dd-yy*	Copies files changed on or after the specified date
/P	Prompts you (Y/N) before copying the file
/S	Copies directories and subdirectories except empty ones
/E	Copies all subdirectories, even empty ones
/V	Verifies each new file after making the copy
/W	Prompts you to press a key before copying

A problem with XCOPY is that it can't deal with a full floppy disk. A utility program called FILL, which is included on the accompanying disk, copies files to floppy disks, selecting files as needed from the list to fill the disk. More information about FILL is provided in Part III, "Guide to Using the Disk."

Exercises

The first exercise on XCOPY covers several of the switches, including the subdirectory switch /S, the date switch /D, and the prompt switch /P. Because using XCOPY with the archive bit is a good way to back up files, the second exercise focuses on the /A and /M switches. The files located in the EXER37 subdirectory on the accompanying disk are to be used for these exercises.

Exercise 1 of 2

This exercise requires the disk that comes with this book. A temporary work area on drive C: receives the files. Create a subdirectory called TEMP on the hard drive and change into that subdirectory. Everything you XCOPY from A: will go into that directory.

TRY	NOTE
A:\>**CD EXER37** A:\EXER37>**DIR**	All the files you will XCOPY to C: are in this sample subdirectory and in another subdirectory below this one.
A:\EXER37>**XCOPY *.* C: /S**	This copies to C:\TEMP all the files in EXER37, as well as SUB37 below it. If XCOPY does not work, make sure that you have a copy of it in your C:\DOS directory. (Older versions of DOS don't include XCOPY.)
A:\EXER37>**C:** C:\TEMP>**DIR**	Notice the files and subdirectory.
C:\TEMP>**CD SUB37** C:\TEMP\SUB37>**DIR**	XCOPY also copied the files in this directory.

Use of the /S switch is handy when you have a directory with several subdirectories under it. There may not be many files in each subdirectory, but you may want to copy them all to a floppy disk yet keep them in their own subdirectories. XCOPY can do that for you. The limitation is that all the files must be able to fit on one floppy disk. Use this switch in addition to the /D or /M switch.

TRY	NOTE
C:\TEMP\SUB37>**CD ..** C:\TEMP>**DEL SUB37** Are you sure (Y/N)? **Y** C:\TEMP>**DEL *.*** Are you sure (Y/N)? **Y** C:\TEMP>**A:** A:\EXER37>	You just deleted all the files you copied in the preceding steps. You did it to observe the next XCOPY switch.
A:\EXER37>**XCOPY *.* C: /D:08-26-91** A:\EXER37>**DIR C:*.***	Only the files with a date of 8/26/91 or later are copied to C:. You could add an /S to look in SUB37 as well.
A:\EXER37>**XCOPY *.DOC C: /P**	Each file name and a (Y/N) prompt will be displayed. You can press Ctrl-C to interrupt XCOPY.

Each one of these switches with XCOPY is useful. Together, they provide a convenient way to copy files changed in a work session. The command

```
C:\>XCOPY *.* A: /S/P/D:dd-mm-yy
```

(where *dd-mm-yy* is today's date) searches the hard disk for all files with today's date and asks whether you want to copy the file to the floppy disk. Again, trouble occurs if the disk fills up in this process.

Exercise 2 of 2

When you use XCOPY with the /A or /M switch, the archive bit determines whether a file is to be copied. With the /A switch, XCOPY copies each file with its archive bit set on (changed since last backup) and does not change the bit for that file. With the /M switch, XCOPY copies the file and also sets the bit off.

If you use a backup program regularly that relies on the archive bit for incremental backups, you don't want to use the /M switch. The next example uses both switches to demonstrate how this bit is changed. Usually you use one switch or the other in your regularly scheduled system for backups.

TRY	NOTE
A:\EXER37>**ATTRIB**	This is another DOS program that shows the status of all the attributes. In this case, you see that four of the eight files have an A next to the name.
A:\EXER37>**XCOPY *.* C: /A**	XCOPY just copies these files to C:.
A:\EXER37>**ATTRIB**	Notice that the attributes are still on.
A:\EXER37>**XCOPY *.* C: /M**	These same files are copied to C: (over themselves actually).
A:\EXER37>**ATTRIB**	The difference this time is that the A has been removed. These files would not be seen by a backup program looking for the archive bit set on.

As noted in the first exercise, it is the combination of switches that makes the XCOPY program useful. Be careful, however, if you use XCOPY with a commercial backup program.

References

BACKUP — Files (41), ATTRIB — Protecting Files (62)

NEXT TOPIC: Hardware (38)

Part III

Guide to Using the Disk

Part III

Guide to Using the Disk

This part of the book contains information about the accompanying disk. The information is presented in the same topic format used in Part II. The following sections are included:

- *Disk installation.* This section provides step-by-step instructions for making a backup copy of the disk that comes with this book. Instructions for using some of the disk's files on your hard disk are also included.
- *Disk contents.* A complete directory tree of all the files on the disk, along with comments about the files, is provided.
- *Learning Guide.* This section contains information on the Learning Guide program and how to use it.
- *Utility programs.* Each of the utility programs on the accompanying disk is discussed. Additional information about these programs is also on the disk.
- *Utility author pages.* Some of the authors of the utility programs have provided additional information about other programs that may be of interest.

Disk Installation

Although the disk included with this book can be used immediately, you should first make a backup copy of the disk. You can then use that copy for the exercises and other activities.

Before You Begin

Get a disk of the same capacity and size as the one provided with this book. If you do not have a 5 1/4-inch 360K disk, you'll need to use the procedure described in Exercise 2 of the "Exercises" section to make a backup disk.

Syntax

`C:\>`**`DISKCOPY A: A:`**	You use this syntax if you have a 5 1/4-inch disk drive. See Exercise 1 in the "Exercises" section.
`C:\>`**`XCOPY A:*.* B: /S`**	You use this syntax if you have two drives and will be copying from one drive to the other. See Exercise 2 in the "Exercises" section.

Problem

`Bad command or file name.` If you try to use the DOS program DISKCOPY or XCOPY and you get this message, your PATH does not include the DOS directory. Type **`CD\DOS <Enter>`** and then try the command again. If this fails, you'll have to find the directory with the DOS files, use the CD (Change Directory) command to move into that directory, and try again. You may need to read the first few topics in Part II to learn how to locate the DOS directory.

Explanation

When you use the accompanying disk to complete the exercises or run the Learning Guide, you make changes to that disk. If you want to go back and reuse the original files, or loan the book and disk to a friend, the files will not work properly. For this reason, you should make a second copy of the disk, put away the original disk, and use that backup copy while you read the topics. Then, if you want to start over or loan the book, you can make another copy (from the original disk).

> If you make changes to the original disk, you'll be able to do the exercises only *once* because many of the exercises *change* the contents of the disk.

There are no files on the disk that need to be "installed" in the sense that they need to be configured to work with your system. You can copy any of the programs and files to your hard disk and use them as you would any program or file. Copying the utility programs to your hard disk is highly recommended (see Exercise 3 in the next section).

You can use the exercise materials more easily from the floppy disk, though. None of the exercises requires speedy access to the files, so you won't be kept waiting long for DOS to finish the commands you've entered. Each exercise provides the exact files you need, and all the files are included in the appropriate subdirectories on the accompanying disk. If you copied the exercise files to your hard disk, you would have to create the same subdirectories from the root drive. It's much easier just to use the exercise materials from the disk included with this book.

Exercises

Three exercises are provided here. The first two exercises take you through the process of making a second copy of the disk that comes with this book. You'll use either Exercise 1 or Exercise 2, depending on the capacity of your target disk. Use the first exercise if you have one disk drive and a 5 1/4-inch 360K disk. Use the second exercise if you have two disk drives and a disk with a different capacity.

Exercise 3 provides steps for copying the utility programs to a specific directory on your hard disk. To make these programs available from anywhere in your system, you'll need to modify your PATH to include that directory. At the end of the third exercise is an alternative method that copies the files to your DOS subdirectory but does not require making changes to the PATH.

Exercise 1 of 3

If you have a 5 1/4-inch 360K disk, you can use the DOS DISKCOPY program to make a second, working copy of the accompanying disk. You can use a new, blank disk or an old disk. Remember that any files on the old disk will be erased by the new files from the disk that comes with this book.

Before you begin, cover the write-protect notch on the accompanying disk so that it cannot be written to. Then insert the disk in drive A:.

TRY	NOTE

`C:\>`**`DISKCOPY A: A: <Enter>`**
`Insert SOURCE disk in drive A:`
`Press any key to continue`
	Because the SOURCE (accompanying) disk is in drive A:, just press the Enter key to begin the process.

You may have to exchange the source (original) and target (second) disks several times before the program is finished. When you are asked whether you want to copy another disk, just press N and then Enter. Put the original disk away in a safe place. Label the second disk and use it for the topic exercises.

Exercise 2 of 3

To copy the 360K disk that comes with this book, you may need to use a disk with a different capacity. You cannot use DISKCOPY to copy the contents of the 360K disk to a 1.2M or 1.44M disk. You'll need to use XCOPY with the /S switch to include all the files in all the subdirectories.

For this exercise, it is assumed that you want to use a 1.44M (high-density) 3 1/2-inch disk for your working copy. The 3 1/2-inch drive is B:, and the 5 1/4-inch drive is A:.

TRY	NOTE
`C:\>`**`XCOPY A:*.* B: /S`**	This copies all the files on the disk in A:, including the subdirectories (with the /S switch), to the disk in B:.

Put the original disk away in a safe place. Label the second disk and use it for the topic exercises.

Exercise 3 of 3

Utility programs are useful only when they are as accessible as DOS commands and programs. If, after reading about the utilities included on the accompanying disk, you want to use some of them, you should copy those files to your hard disk so that you can access them easily. This exercise provides the steps for copying the utility programs to the hard disk.

In this exercise, it is assumed that you want to keep only DOS programs in your DOS directory. Therefore, you'll make a new directory on the hard disk for the utility programs. You must add that new directory to the current path by changing a line in the AUTOEXEC.BAT file. If you are fairly new to DOS, you may want to make a note of this exercise and return to it after covering the first 30 topics in the book, including AUTOEXEC.BAT (21) and PATH — Program Search (29).

TRY	NOTE
C:\>**MD LDUTIL** C:\>**CD LDUTIL** C:\LDUTIL>	The name of the directory is not critical. You can use another name if you like.
C:\LDUTIL>**A:\UTILS\UTILS** C:\LDUTIL>**A:\UTILS\DOCS**	This installs all the files in the UTILS subdirectory on the accompanying disk into the current directory (LDUTIL) on C:.

You can now use any of the utility programs from this directory. But to use them from anywhere within the system, you need to add the LDUTIL directory to the current path. Because the path is usually set in the AUTOEXEC.BAT file, you must edit that file.

The following steps use EDLIN because all DOS systems have that line editor program. If you've never used EDLIN before, these steps show you what keystrokes to use.

TRY	NOTE
C:\>**EDLIN AUTOEXEC.BAT** End of input file *	This starts EDLIN and loads AUTOEXEC.BAT. Notice that you must be in the root directory to do this step.
***L**	The L lists the file. Look for the number of the line that starts with PATH.
***3**	Type that line number now and press the Enter key. This step and the next steps use the number 3 as an example.
*3 3: PATH C:\;C:\DOS 3:	EDLIN shows that line—in this case, a short path. Your path is likely to look different.
3:**<F3>** 3: PATH C:\;C:\DOS_	Press the F3 key to move to the end of the line. Then add the next line to this line.
;C:\LDUTILS <Enter>	Don't forget to press the Enter key.
*E	This exits and saves the file.
C:\>**AUTOEXEC**	Run AUTOEXEC to set the new path.
C:\>**PATH** PATH=C:\;C:\DOS;C:\LDUTILS	You should see the path with your latest addition.

TRY	NOTE
`C:\>`**`FD LDU`**	This tests the path to see whether the FD (Find Directory) utility program works.
`C:\LDUTILS>`	If it works, DOS will locate and change directories (from the root to the LDUTILS subdirectory).

Make sure that you at least glance at all the discussions of the utility programs. You are likely to find several that can save you time and effort when working with DOS.

> Remember that the DOCS.EXE and UTILS.EXE programs are compressed programs that include all the documentation and utility programs. The files were compressed with LHA's SFX version 2.11s © Yoshi, 1991. If you want to read the DOC file for information on one of these programs, use the LOOK utility program to examine each DOC file.

Disk Contents

The directory tree in Figure III-1 shows all the subdirectories on the accompanying disk. The disk has four main parts: the GUIDE subdirectory, the EXER (exercise) subdirectories, the UTILS subdirectory, and the BATCH and PROGTEST subdirectories.

```
A:.
├───BATCH
├───EXER30
├───EXER37
│   └───SUB37
├───EXER45
├───EXER76
├───EXER81
├───EXER98
├───GUIDE
├───PROGTEST
└───UTILS
```

Figure III-1. The directory structure of the disk included with this book.

The GUIDE subdirectory contains the Learning Guide program and data files. If you copy the program to your hard disk, make sure that you include all the files in that directory. The program will not run without all of these files.

The UTILS subdirectory contains all the utility programs. If you want to use these programs, follow the installation instructions in the earlier section "Exercises."

The EXER (exercise) subdirectories contain files for the topic exercises. The file EXER.TXT in the root directory shows the names of the topics that have exercises, as well as the contents of each subdirectory. For example, the exercises for topic 30 on deleting files are found in the EXER30 subdirectory.

The subdirectories BATCH and PROGTEST are used with the topic Batch Files — Write Your Own (100).

Learning Guide

This program, provided on the accompanying disk, assesses your DOS skill level and suggests topics you should cover in the book.

Syntax

A:\>**GUIDE**	This starts the Learning Guide program.
A:\>**REPORT**	This provides a report based on the results of the Learning Guide program.

Problem

Won't run. Do you have 640K of memory? Are you using the program with all the necessary files? You should receive error messages if your answer to both of these questions is "No." Although the Learning Guide program has been tested, if you are unable to get the program to run, please write with a description of the problem, a phone number where you can be reached, and your address. Write to *Learning DOS*, Macmillan Computer Publishing, 11711 N. College Ave., Carmel IN 46032.

Explanation

The Learning Guide program helps you discover what you know and don't know about DOS. You answer a series of multiple-choice questions, and based on your responses, the program recommends several topics you should read in Part II of this book. The program keeps all your answers. After you read the suggested topics and run the Learning Guide program again, it returns to your incorrect responses.

The program contains 100 DOS and 6 demographic (about you) questions. Once you have missed several questions, the program ends. From your incorrect answers, the program prints a list of recommended topics.

To start the program, you can type

```
A:\>CD GUIDE
A:\GUIDE>GUIDE
```

or

```
A:\>GUIDE
```

This starts a batch file that moves you into the GUIDE subdirectory and runs the program.

Once you have responded to the Learning Guide questions, the program provides the option to print the results. You can also regenerate those results at any time by typing **REPORT** in the GUIDE subdirectory.

The Learning Guide program screen is divided into four parts (see Figure III-2). The first section on the left provides general information. The upper right part of the screen contains the question to be answered. The lower right portion contains several choices for the answer. Any messages specific to the current screen are displayed across the bottom of the screen.

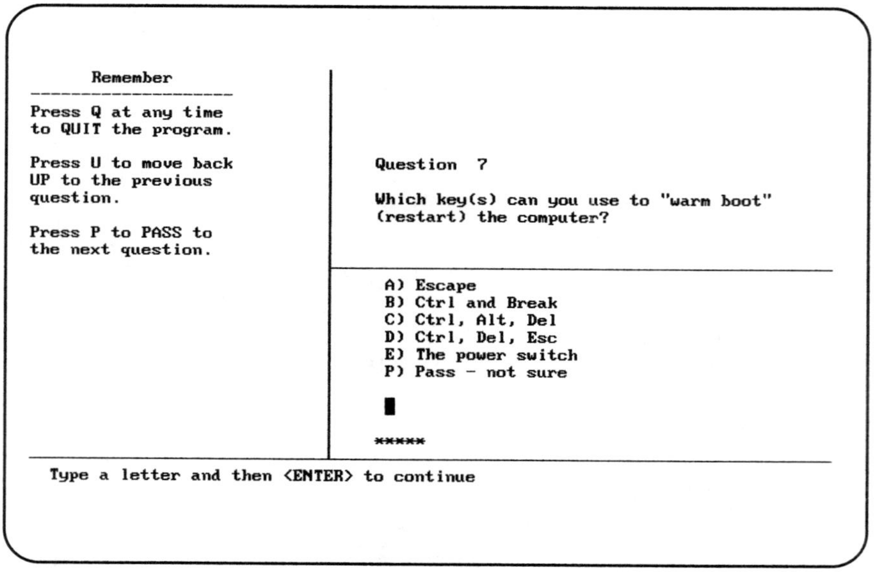

Figure III-2. A sample screen from the Learning Guide program.

When you start the program the first time, the Learning Guide asks for your name and displays some preliminary information about the program. If you or someone else has used the Learning Guide program before, it shows the names of those users. If you are not on the list, the program treats you as a new user and provides the initial information screens.

The first time you use the Learning Guide, it asks six questions, including how long you have used a computer and what you use the computer for. You won't have to answer these questions the next time you use the program.

When you answer each question, just type the letter for your answer and press the Enter key. At any time, you can press P to *p*ass on a question. This means that you do not know the answer, but pressing P will not be counted as wrong. (Wouldn't that have been nice in school?) The final report will suggest that you read all topics covering questions you answered with P.

For any of the responses, you can also press U for *u*p. This allows you to return to the preceding question. You can also use Q for *q*uit. This option terminates the Learning Guide session with incomplete results. Table III-1 shows the active keys for the questions.

Table III-1. The keys used for the Learning Guide program.

Key	Description
A	Possible answer
B	Possible answer
C	Possible answer
D	Possible answer
E	Possible answer
P	Passes on an answer
U	Moves up to the preceding question
Q	Quits the program

If you press a key other than those listed in the table, the program prompts you to use a valid key. If you type a letter and then change your mind before pressing Enter, just type the new letter. It replaces the letter currently showing. You can still change an answer after you press Enter; just press U to move up to the preceding question.

You'll notice a string of asterisks below the answer prompt. Each time you miss an answer, that string is shorter by one. Once you have missed five answers, the program ends and provides a report on your responses. If you are somewhat experienced with DOS, you may answer quite a few questions the first time you use the Learning Guide.

The report will run immediately after you finish using the Learning Guide program *unless* you respond to the final question. You can also run the REPORT program at any time by typing

```
A:\GUIDE>REPORT
```

in the GUIDE subdirectory. REPORT prompts for your name just as the Learning Guide program does. You may choose to display the information on the screen or send it to the printer. And you can choose the short or long version of the report. The short version just shows the questions you missed or passed (didn't know). The long version includes all the questions you answered correctly.

The report includes a suggested list of topics for you to cover in *Learning DOS*. As with any recommendation, you can ignore this list, or you can begin exploring the topics in the list. Remember that the purpose of the report is to guide you to areas of DOS you may know little about.

If you want to continue to use the Learning Guide as you progress through the *Learning DOS* material, the program keeps track of your earlier sessions and asks only those questions you have previously missed. Once you answer the questions correctly, they will no longer appear on the question list.

The Learning Guide program is available for you to use as you like. If you are interested in providing baseline information on the program, you can send a copy of your disk to Dan Derrick, c/o Macmillan Computer Publishing, 11711 N. College Ave., Carmel IN 46032.

Utility Programs

The disk accompanying this book contains programs written by a number of authors. All the authors have agreed to have their programs provided with this book. The actual files are contained in a compressed file called UTILS.EXE. The documentation for each file is contained in a file called DOCS.EXE. You must run these programs to extract each file before you can use it. The files must be extracted to a hard disk or another disk. The steps to accomplish this are covered in Exercise 3 in the "Exercises" section.

The author's statements are from the original documentation supplied with the software. If an author provides support or encourages you to write, please refer to the contact address in the documentation accompanying the program on the disk.

DMD — Disk Meter Deluxe

Author: Ray Johns

Disk Meter Deluxe provides a graphic and numeric representation of remaining disk space. DMD is a good program to insert in AUTOEXEC.BAT.

Before You Begin

AUTOEXEC.BAT (21)
Disk Full (35)

Syntax

`C:\>DMD C: D:`	Shows a graphic and numeric display of the used space and the remaining space on drives C: and D:
`C:\>DMD C: /Q`	Provides a quick display (graphic only) of the remaining space on C:

Problem

Running out of disk space. DMD provides a quick display of the space being used across multiple hard disks. By inserting a command line in the AUTOEXEC.BAT file, you see how much disk space remains every time you boot the system.

Explanation

Disk Meter Deluxe (DMD) provides a graphic display of disk space, both used and remaining. DMD can show the amount of space on any disk. You can add several switches to the command line for more (or less) information. Table III-2 shows the various switches.

Table III-2. The DMD switches.

Switch	Description
/B	Beeps when disk is 95 percent full
/H or /?	Displays help screen
/I	Ignores keyboard input (no pause)
/M	Displays information about memory
/Q	Provides a quick display (bar graph only)

DMD is a helpful program to include in your AUTOEXEC.BAT file. If DMD is installed in a subdirectory named UTILS on the C: drive, you can insert the following lines in AUTOEXEC.BAT:

```
\UTILS\DMD C: /Q /B
PAUSE
```

Every time you reboot the system, DMD runs and provides a graphic display of disk space. If 95 percent of the disk is available, DMD also issues a beep. PAUSE allows you to view the results before the AUTOEXEC.BAT file continues with its tasks.

Additional information about DMD is included in the file DMD.DOC on the accompanying disk.

Author's Notes

DMD Disk Meter Deluxe v. 2.12 © 1991 P.C. Consulting

Disclaimer. P.C. Consulting makes no warranty, express or implied, as to the fitness or condition of this software utility program. It is delivered to you in an AS IS state. In no event shall P.C. Consulting be held liable for loss of data or profits resulting from the use of Disk Meter Deluxe.

Reference

Utility Software (50)

Dupes — Duplicate File Finder

Author: Richard W. Adams

This utility locates duplicate files by name anywhere on the hard disk and lists the file names and directory locations. You can then decide whether to delete one or more files to save disk space.

Before You Begin

Files (2)
File Names (4)
DIR — Directory (8)
CD, MD, and RD — Working with Directories (9)

Syntax

```
C:\>DUPES drive:/M /Odir /Xdir /P /S
```

Parameters can include the following:

drive:	A drive letter, followed by a colon (such as C:)
/M	Checks multiple disks in the indicated drive
/O	Checks only the indicated directory and its subdirectories
/X	Checks all directories except the indicated directory
/P	When showing duplicate files/empty directories, asks whether the user wants to delete each one
/S	Considers two files the same only if the size and date-time stamp match (default: match if the names are the same)
`C:\>DUPES > LPT1:`	Redirects output (list of duplicate files) to the printer

Explanation

Dupes reads files on the disk(s) and produces a report when the /S switch is used (see Listing III-1). The process is fairly fast. The initial check on a hard disk takes only seconds. The report speed depends on how you ask for the output (to the screen, file, printer, and so on).

Listing III-1. A sample listing of the duplicate files located with DUPES. (Portions of the list were removed to save space.)

```
Dupes, version 3.0L,  1991 by Richard W. Adams
Sun Jun 02 08:40:31 1991
Reading file data
C:\
C:\DB3
C:\DB3\BBS
C:\DB3\POC
C:\DB3\SUS
.
.
.
```

continues

Listing III-1. continued

```
C:\DUP
C:\FIL
C:\ELI
C:\PCX

942 files found
Checking - please be patient...

ANSI.SYS
   1647  04/07/88  09:58:29         C:\
   1647  04/07/88  09:58:29         C:\DOS

COMMAND.COM
  25532  10/31/88  14:54:10         C:\DOS
  25532  10/31/88  14:54:10         C:\

2 potential duplicate(s), occupying about 28672 bytes
```

Because the output of Dupes is usually too large for a single screen, you can send the output to the printer or a file. The easiest way is to send it to an ASCII file, such as DUPELIST.TXT. Then use a word processor, the DOS MORE program (**`MORE < DUPELIST.TXT`**), or the LOOK utility to examine the list.

Without the /S switch, Dupes reports any duplicate file names. With the /S switch, Dupes also compares the file size and date, increasing the likelihood that reported files are true duplicates. The /M switch lets you check one or more series of floppy disks for duplicate files.

If you're on a network, you can use the /O switch to have Dupes check only your directory on the file server. If you have a directory that you already know has duplicate files, you can exclude that directory from the search with the /X switch.

If you use the /P switch, Dupes pauses after displaying each potential duplicate file (or empty directory) and asks whether you want to delete it. You can abort Dupes with the Ctrl-C or Ctrl-Break key combination. Dupes ends with the message `Aborted as requested`. Dupes may also finish with a message that there were no duplicates on the disk.

In some cases, if you have many files or limited memory, Dupes won't be able to read all the files. In that case, Dupes reports `Not enough memory`. Additional information about Dupes is located in the file DUPES.DOC.

Author's Notes

Dupes version 3.0L by Richard W. Adams

Disclaimer. Users of Dupes must accept this disclaimer of warranty: "Dupes is supplied as is. The author disclaims all warranties, expressed or implied, including, without limitation, the warranties or merchantability and of fitness for any purpose. The author assumes no liability for damages, direct or consequential, which may result from the use of Dupes." Use of this software constitutes consent to this disclaimer.

Reference

Disk Full (35)

FD — Find Directory

Author: Guy Campbell

This utility locates and changes to a directory based on the directory name or even a partial name. FD searches all drives on the system, starting with C:.

Before You Begin

CD, MD, and RD — Working with Directories (9)

Syntax

`C:\>`**`FD UTIL`** `C:\UTILS>`	Finds a subdirectory based on part of the subdirectory name and changes (CD) to that directory
`C:\>`**`FD COREL`** `E:\COREL>`	Starts searching on drive C: and continues searching through all the available drives

Problem

Lost directories. With FD, you need to remember only part of the subdirectory name for the program to locate and move to that subdirectory.

Explanation

The FD utility program can replace the CD command used with DOS. FD locates a subdirectory, based on a full or partial name, and moves you to that subdirectory. FD can even hop to the drive if necessary.

For example, to move from C: to the COREL directory on E:, you have to type the following lines (assuming that you know exactly where the directory is located):

```
C:\>E:
E:\>CD COREL
E:\COREL>
```

With FD, you simply use

```
C:\>FD COR
E:\COREL>
```

Typing just **FD** results in a small help file. Additional information is available in the file named FD.DOC on the accompanying disk. Also in that subdirectory is a program named FH (for Find Hidden). Running the FH program lists all hidden files on all available disks.

Author's Notes

FD version 1.02 by Guy Campbell

This software is free! Please enjoy using it. It has been tested extensively on a variety of computers without a problem. If you discover anything strange, please let me know. I'd appreciate any feedback you may have. This product is supported.

Reference

Utility Software (50)

FILL

Author: Jean Lalonde

This utility copies a selection of files to floppy disks, choosing files as needed from the list to fill the disk. Files are in standard DOS format and may be used from the floppies to which they are copied.

Before You Begin

COPY — Files (10)
Wild Cards * and ? (11)

Syntax

`C:\SAMPLE>`**`FILL *.* A:`**	Copies files to the disk in A:, prompting for additional disks if needed
`C:\SAMPLE>`**`FILL /?`**	Prompts for all parameters

Problem

Disk full with COPY. If you try to copy files from a subdirectory that require more space than is available on one disk, DOS COPY just quits when the disk gets full. FILL copies the files to make the most use of the disk space and then prompts for additional disks as needed.

Explanation

The FILL program is like a Swiss Army knife when it comes to copying files to floppy disks. Not only will FILL maximize the use of space on the disk, but it also calls DOS FORMAT if the disk is new, erases the contents of the disk (after asking), and can erase the source files after the files are copied to the floppy.

The main purpose of FILL is to copy files, using DOS wild cards, to floppy disks. FILL accomplishes this task by reading all the files to be copied, sorting them by size, and then copying them to the floppy disk. As the disk fills up, FILL looks for the next file that will use the most space in the disk. Once the disk is full, FILL pauses and asks for another disk.

The FILL program can be copied to a directory accessible in your path. The DOS directory usually works well. To work properly, FILL must also have access to the DOS FORMAT, SORT, and LABEL programs. Again, these programs are typically located in the DOS subdirectory and are accessible from any drive or subdirectory through the PATH setting.

FILL can use a number of switches (see Table III-3). The document on the disk named FILL.DOC contains additional information about these and other switches.

Table III-3. Some FILL switches.

Switch	Description
/?	Prompts for all parameters (for novice users)
/E	Requests confirmation for each directory
/F	Requests confirmation for each file
/H	Displays a short help message
/K	Kills (deletes) the source files
/R	Includes subdirectories and keeps directory structure
/V	Verifies integrity of copied files

To examine all the options available with FILL, you type

```
C:\>FILL /?
```

which generates the dialog shown in Listing III-2. For each question, the default answer is enclosed in parentheses. Pressing Enter accepts the default answer to each question.

Listing III-2. The sequence of questions provided when you include the /? switch on the command line.

```
Fill v3.0  Jean Lalonde, Montreal, August 1988
Files to copy ('drives:path\files'), <escape> to end ?
*.*
M(ixed sub-directories,
R(ecreated subdirectories,
S(eparated subdirectories,
N(o sub-directories (N) ? N
Confirm each directory (N) ? N
Confirm each file (N) ? N
Target drive(s) ? A:
Copy only files with Archive attribute (N) ? N
Set Archive attribute OFF (N) ? N
Verify copied files (N) ? N
Erase original files (N) ? N
Discrete scanning (N) ? N
Log files copied (N) ? N
```

```
Building list...
.\.....

Insert disk in 'A:' and press Copy files, Dir target, Erase
target, Format target, List files, Other target or <escape>
to abort  ? C
```

To copy files in the current directory and all subdirectories, use the /R switch at the end of the command line. For example, to copy all the files in the FIRST directory and in the subdirectories FIRSTWO and FIRSTOO, use the command line

```
C:\FIRST>FILL *.* A: /R
```

FILL reads all the files in FIRST and then read the files in FIRSTWO and FIRSTOO. Afterward, FILL provides the prompt that includes L for *l*ist files. This list also shows the total amount of space required to copy all these files.

FILL is useful for archiving files. When you know that you don't need certain files on the hard disk but you want to keep copies on floppies, FILL can copy those files efficiently to floppies and then delete the files from the hard disk. In addition to /K for *k*ill (the source files), the command line can include /V for *v*erify. /V verifies that files have been copied accurately before they are deleted from the hard disk. Note this example:

```
C:\FIRST>FILL *.* /K/V
```

As each file is copied from the FIRST sudirectory, it is verified against the source and then deleted. FILL does not remove or affect the directory in any way.

Author's Notes

FILL version 3.0 © 1988 by Jean Lalonde

From the document FILL.DOC: "You can use or redistribute this program freely as long as it is done at no cost (except floppy's cost), if this documentation file and the copyright remain intact. If you like my program, feel free to send me some money."

Reference

Backing Up Data (13)

FIND — File Finder

Author: Bruce Gavin

This utility searches a disk drive for files specified with the DOS wild cards * and ?.

Before You Begin

File Names (4)
DIR — Directory (8)
CD, MD, and RD — Working with Directories (9)

Syntax

`C:\>FIND *.DOC`	Locates and displays all files with the extension DOC
`C:\>FIND *.DOC > FLIST.TXT`	Sends the list of files to the file named FLIST.TXT

Problem

Locating files on the hard disk. Regardless of how well organized your hard disk is, you'll occasionally lose track of one or more files. The FIND program searches all the drives and directories for the file name, using the DOS wild cards * and ?.

Explanation

The FIND utility program is not at all like the DOS FIND program. The DOS version (see topic 82) searches within one file for a specific string of characters. The FIND utility searches all available drives for specific file names or ones containing wild cards. Before you copy this program to the hard disk, you need to rename your DOS version of FIND to something slightly different, such as FINDX or DOSFIND.

The FIND command line contains the file name or partial file name with wild cards. For example, the command

```
C:\>FIND *.WQ1
```

produces results that scroll off the screen. But the command

```
C:\>FIND *.WQ1 > FLIST
```

creates the file shown in Listing III-3. Each subdirectory is listed, and the matching files are shown below that subdirectory.

Listing III-3. A listing that scrolls off the screen. This list was captured with the redirection character >.

```
D:\QPRO
BMG03     WQ1      2416   5-21-91   9:41a  20h, Archive
TEST09    WQ1      2452  12-08-90   2:45p  20h, Archive
LIBRARY   WQ1      2353  12-08-90   3:00p  20h, Archive
BMG       WQ1      3513  12-09-90   2:19p  20h, Archive
TEST      WQ1      1511  12-11-90   8:08p  20h, Archive
INSTALL   WQ1      8098  10-05-90   2:00a  20h, Archive
SHEET4    WQ1      1651  12-11-90   8:35p  20h, Archive
SHEET3    WQ1      1537  12-11-90   9:22p  20h, Archive
CHAP11    WQ1      3340  12-15-90  10:09a  20h, Archive
DISKS     WQ1      2853   5-09-91   4:17p  20h, Archive
MACPUB    WQ1      5867   4-25-91   4:32p  20h, Archive
FLICS     WQ1     13107   4-29-91   9:07a  20h, Archive
BMG02     WQ1      2355   4-29-91   9:41a  20h, Archive
FTU       WQ1      5588   5-02-91   8:00p  20h, Archive

D:\BOOKS\LEARNDOS\MISC
SCHEDULE WQ1       3191   2-28-91  10:17p  00h, Reset

FIND:     15 matching file(s) out of 2694 files in 98
subdirectories
Time:     00:00:02.36
```

If you use the redirection character > to send the information to a file or the printer, FIND displays the information on the screen and then sends the results to the file or printer.

Author's Notes

FIND version 2.19a by Bruce Gavin, Online Reference

License statement. Online Reference hereby grants you, the user, a nonexclusive license to use FIND in its delivered form. You are encouraged to freely copy and distribute this shareware version of the software as long as it is not modified or missing any of the component files.

Warranty. Online Reference explicitly disclaims all other warranties whether expressed or implied, including, without limitation, the implied warranties of merchantability and fitness for any particular purpose. Online Reference shall have no liability for consequential, incidental, exemplary or special damages, including lost profits.

References

File Organization (17), Lost Data Files (77)

FT — FileType

Author: Cliff Peterson

This utility program makes an educated guess about a file's type, based on over 80 different patterns. It does not rely on the file extension but looks at the first 32 bytes of the file.

Before You Begin

Files (2)
Wild Cards * and ? (11)

Syntax

`C:\UTILS>`**`FT *.*`**	Shows all the file types in the subdirectory and pauses when the screen fills

Problem

What kind of file is this? FT can display a guess by examining the first 32-character "signature" of the file.

Explanation

Every file contains information about itself in the first 32 bytes. FT compares this information with over 80 patterns of file types.

FT supports the standard DOS wild cards and includes the three switches shown in Table III-4. The first two switches display information about FT. The last switch pauses the display if the list of files exceeds the length of the screen.

Table III-4. The FT switches.

Switch	Description
/?	Lists supported file formats
/d	Provides a screen of documentation
-p	Pauses screen when full

Note that switches are placed before wild cards on the command line. For example, the command

```
C:\UTILS>FT -p FT*.*
```

produces this screen:

```
FileType v1.5 - Copyright  1990-91 Cliff Peterson

FT       DOC     7627 03-18-91  3:38p Plain Text
FT       EXE    11268 03-18-91  3:32p Executable Program
```

If the search string had been just *.*, the listing would pause when the screen fills, because so many file names would have been listed. In this case, only files beginning with FT were listed.

Author's Notes

FT — FileType version 1.5 by Cliff Peterson

Although the author has contributed this program to the public domain, he does request that you register it by sending his four-year-old daughter a postcard of your city. Use this address:

Rachel Peterson
c/o Cliff Peterson
P.O. Box 1890
Germantown, MD 20875-1890

Additional information about this utility program is available in the document FT.DOC.

Reference

Data File Formats (52)

HDPARK — Hard Disk Park

Author: Michael Sorensen

The safest way to make sure that the hard disk will not be damaged is to "park" the heads. The HDPARK program moves the heads to a safe location before you turn off the computer.

Before You Begin

Hard Drive Failure (33)

Syntax

`C:\>HDPARK`	The heads are parked and the system can be turned off. Any other key returns you to DOS.

Problem

Head crash. Even when the computer is turned off, the hard drive heads may be "hanging" out over parts of the disk. Even though some hard drives park the heads automatically, if you are not sure, use HDPARK before turning off the system.

Explanation

HDPARK does just one thing. It pulls the hard drive heads back to a safe position, usually the highest cylinder on the disk. This spot is called the "landing zone." If the system is bumped and the heads make contact with the disk, the landing zone has no data.

To use HDPARK, you just type

```
C:\>HDPARK
```

The program responds with the following:

```
Drive 0 is parked at cylinder 0964

All drives are parked.  >>> YOU MAY TURN OFF THE PC <<<
(You may also type any character to return to DOS)
```

At this point, you can turn off the computer. If you change your mind, press any key, and the system returns to DOS. The assembly language listing for this program is contained in the file HDPARK.ASM on the accompanying disk.

Author's Notes

HDPARK version 29 APR 89 by Michael Sorensen

Public Domain. Use at your own risk. If you distribute this program, please distribute it as the source file and the command file: HDPARK.ASM and HDPARK.COM.

Reference

System Maintenance (94)

LOOK — File Viewer

This utility displays on the screen any file you specify and allows you to move up, down, and sideways through the file.

Before You Begin

ASCII — Character Codes (74)

Syntax

`C:\>`**`LOOK AUTOEXEC.BAT`**	Displays this batch file on the screen. You can view longer files with the arrow keys.

Problem

Need to view a file. LOOK quickly displays on the screen any file you specify. Because LOOK just displays the file, you cannot make any changes to the contents of the file.

Explanation

LOOK is a small program (under 1K) that displays on the screen the contents of any file you specify. In some cases, just LOOKing at an ASCII file is safer than using an editor. With any editor, you can inadvertently make changes if you save the file back to disk. Files of any length and width can be viewed.

To use the program, you just type LOOK and the name of the file (including the extension) you want to view. Almost immediately, the contents of the file appear on the screen. Use the arrow keys to move up, down and, if necessary, sideways to see the file. When you are finished, press Esc. Table III-5 shows the keys you can use with LOOK.

Table III-5. The LOOK keys.

Key	Description
Esc	Exits LOOK
Down arrow	Moves down one line
Page Down	Moves down one screen (24 lines)
Up arrow	Moves up one line
Page Up	Moves up one screen
Home	Moves to top of file
End	Moves to end of file
Right arrow	Tabs eight characters to the right
Left arrow	Tabs eight characters to the left

There is no additional documentation for LOOK.COM. Nor are there any switches or parameters for the command line.

Author's Notes

The LOOK utility program was found in the public domain with no author credits.

References

TYPE — Looking at Files (81), MORE — Pausing Screen Display (84), EDIT — DOS 5.0 Text Editor (98)

MV — MoVe Files

Author: Bob Eyer

When rearranging a disk, you frequently need to move files from one directory to another. Using standard DOS commands, you need to COPY and then DEL the files. The MV program performs both steps with one command.

Before You Begin

Files (2)
DIR — Directory (8)
CD, MD, and RD — Working with Directories (9)
COPY — Files (10)
Wild Cards * and ? (11)

Syntax

`C:\FIRST>`**`MV *.* \SECOND`**	Moves all files located in the source directory into the target directory
`C:\SECOND>`**`MV *.* A:`**	Moves all files in the current directory to the disk in A:

Problem

Need to move files across directories. MV saves the extra step of having to DELete files after you have copied them to another location, usually another subdirectory.

Explanation

The MV program works just like DOS COPY, including its use of wild cards and drive designations. MV is an external file and must be located somewhere accessible in the current PATH statement. The easiest way to make sure that MV will work from any location is to copy it into the DOS subdirectory. If your system files are not located in a subdirectory named DOS, use your subdirectory name instead.

Use MV as you would the DOS COPY command. To MoVe all the files from the \FIRST subdirectory to the \SECOND, you type

```
C:\FIRST>MV *.* \SECOND
```

The FIRST subdirectory is now empty, and the SECOND subdirectory has all the files originally contained in FIRST. MV issues a brief message containing the program name, the author's name and CompuServe ID number, and the date of the program. MV then reports the results of the action:

```
MV 2.0  by Bob Eyer [73230,2620]      Feb 22, 1991
File(s) MVd
```

If MV begins the action and finds a duplicate file name in the target subdirectory, the program asks if the file is to be overwritten. This feature is not in DOS COPY. COPY just overwrites the file without checking anything. Note this example with MV:

```
MV 2.0  by Bob Eyer [73230,2620]      Feb 22, 1991
\SECOND\FILENM.NEW   exists.  Overwrite? [Y/N] Y
File(s) MVd
```

Author's Notes

MV version 2.0 February 22, 1991 by Bob Eyer

Disclaimer. This program is circulated as public domain without any guarantee or warranty; and the user, by downloading this program, or any variant thereof or by receiving it or any of its versions in any other form, agrees to accept full responsibility for its use. It is therefore understood that the user accepts this program or any previous version as is.

Reference

Utility Software (50)

PCS — PCStats

Author: Richard M. Rutkowski

This utility program provides a single screen of information about your computer hardware. PCS requires DOS version 3.0 or later.

Syntax

`C:\>`**`PCS`**	Runs the program and displays a screenful of statistics

Problem

What is your system configuration? PCS provides information on 16 different aspects of your system. The most useful items include the amount of memory and the type of disk drives you have.

Explanation

Running PCS provides a screenful of information about your system. Listing III-4 shows the entire screen. Line numbers have been added to the left to help with the explanation that follows. Blank lines have been added to improve readability.

Listing III-4. The screen of information provided by PCS.

```
1) PCStats. R.M.Rutkowski,V2.1System date          08/26/91  10:48:17

2) Current directory       :    C:\
3) DOS Version             :    5.0  BIOS date           :     04/09/90

4) Total main memory       :   640k  Free main memory:             567k
5) Total expanded memory   :     0k
6) Total extended memory   :     0k

7) CPU type                :  80386  Math coprocessor    :         none
8) Parallel ports          :      1  Serial ports        :            2
9) Game adapter            :   none  Mouse driver        :          yes
```

continues

Listing III-4. continued

```
10) CD-ROM drives            :      0
11) Floppy drives            :      2  Fixed disks        :             1
12) Floppy drive A: type     :   --->  1.2Mb, 80 track, 5.25"
13) Floppy drive B: type     :   --->  1.44Mb, 80 track, 3.5"

14) Drive C: information     :  below
15) Number of clusters       :  16318  Total bytes used   :      32514048
16) Sectors per cluster      :      4  Total bytes free   :        905216
17) Bytes per sector         :    512  Percent used       :        97.29%
18) Total bytes on drive     :33419264  Percent free      :         2.71%

19) Video Capabilities       :   below
20) Current video mode       :   CGA 80x25  Color text
21) (EGA) capabilities       :   Available, Color Enhanced Graphics,  256k bytes
22) (VGA) capabilities       :   Available, Video Graphics Array
```

Each of the following items corresponds to the line number indicated in the program and covers the information from left to right:

1. Program name
   Author's name
   Version of PCS
   System date and time

2. Active directory when PCS was run

3. DOS version
   BIOS date from the microprocessor (CPU) chip on the motherboard

   This date can be used to determine whether a system can have certain peripherals attached. For example, older systems cannot support some newer devices, such as CD-ROM drives.

4. Total conventional memory
   Memory available when PCS was run

   If PCS is run from the DOS command line, this shows how much memory is being used by DOS and other programs.

5. Total expanded memory

   This may not be accurate if memory-management programs are controlling this memory.

6. Total extended memory

   This may not be accurate if memory-management programs are controlling this memory.

7. CPU type
   Math coprocessor type

   The CPU can include 8086/8088, 80286 or 80386, or higher. This information is useful for determining whether your system is a PC/XT, an AT, a 386, or higher.

8. Number of parallel ports
   Number of serial ports

9. Game adapter
   Mouse driver

   Some AT systems may not report the game adapter (joystick port). If your mouse is not working, use this line to determine whether the driver or program is installed (MOUSE.SYS or MOUSE.COM).

10. Number of CD-ROM drives installed

11. Number of floppy drives
    Number of hard drives

12. Drive A: type

    This is useful for determining the capacity of the drive. 1.2M is a high-density (HD) drive.

13. Drive B: type

    This is useful for determining the capacity of the drive. 1.44M is a high-density (HD) drive.

14. This line and the next four lines provide information on the current hard drive. Most useful is the percentage of space remaining on the drive in line 18.

15. This line and the next three lines show the current type of video display. This information is useful for determining whether you have a VGA, as well as the amount of VGA memory.

Author's Notes

PCStats Ver. 2.1 by Richard M. Rutkowksi

From the document PCS.DOC: "PCS is in the public domain, so you can distribute it freely to your friends and other users." Additional information on PCStats is available in the PCS.DOC file on the accompanying disk.

References

FORMAT — Disks (12), Floppy Disks (19), Hardware (38), Communications (55), Monitor (61), Memory (73)

ZDIR — Zippy DIR

Author: Ray Johns

This utility program provides an enhanced directory list, including more readable dates, a file-size column, and the total number of bytes for the files listed.

Before You Begin

DIR — Directory (8)
Wild Cards * and ? (11)

Syntax

`C:\>ZDIR *.DOC /P`	Provides an enhanced directory listing of all files with the DOC extension and pauses when the screen is full
`C:\>ZDIR /?`	Lists all the available switches

Problems

Difficult to read file sizes and dates. The ZDIR program displays the file sizes with commas and includes the month with the dates.

Need total bytes for files listed. ZDIR shows total bytes for the selected files and for the remaining files.

Explanation

ZDIR (Zippy DIR) is a utility program you can use in place of the DOS DIR command. The ZDIR display is easier to read, and additional information about each file is provided. The DOS wild cards * and ? are supported as well as additional "string" searches within the file names. For the ZDIR program to be used anywhere in the system, it must be available in a subdirectory within the PATH statement.

Listing III-5 shows the result of the standard DOS 5.0 DIR command. Listing III-6 shows the same result with ZDIR. Notice the file-size column, the attribute column (not shown with DIR), and the date column.

Listing III-5. A directory listing created with DIR.

```
 Volume in drive E is LEARN DOS
 Volume Serial Number is 1681-A996
 Directory of E:\ZDIR

.            <DIR>     05-21-91  12:35p
..           <DIR>     05-21-91  12:35p
READ-ME  1ST        1024 02-14-89   3:24p
ZDIR     COM        5918 02-14-89   3:19p
ZDIR     DOC       39424 02-14-89   3:27p
ZDIR     REG        2560 02-14-89   3:34p
        6 file(s)      48926 bytes
                     3442688 bytes free
```

Listing III-6. The same directory listing created with ZDIR.

```
Zippy DIR 1.02 - Copyright  1989, Ray Johns

Directory path - E:\ZDIR\*.*

.               Directory  ....  May-21-91  12:35 am ...
..              Directory  ....  May-21-91  12:35 am ...
READ-ME  1ST        1,024  .a..  Feb-14-89  03:24 pm ...
ZDIR     COM        5,918  .a..  Feb-14-89  03:19 pm ...
ZDIR     DOC       39,424  .a..  Feb-14-89  03:27 pm ...
ZDIR     REG        2,560  .a..  Feb-14-89  03:34 pm ...

     6 Files       48,926  Bytes used by files
                3,440,640  Bytes free on disk
```

Besides using the standard DIR wild cards and the /P and /W switches, you can use the ZDIR switches /N and /X to list only the *n*onexecutable and e*x*ecutable files, respectively. If you used **`ZDIR /N`** on the directory shown in the preceding listings, ZDIR would list the three files without the COM, EXE, or BAT extensions. **`ZDIR /X`** would list only ZDIR.COM. Table III-6 shows all the switches available in ZDIR.

Table III-6. The ZDIR switches.

Switch	Description
/H or /?	Displays help
/N	Shows only nonexecutable files
/P	Pauses after each screenful
/W	Shows files in wide mode (five columns across)
/X	Shows only executable files

For longer listings, ZDIR can be controlled in a number of ways. For example, once the screen has filled up (using the /P switch), pressing the space bar advances the list just one line at a time. At any time before ZDIR has displayed all the files, you can press the Backspace key to restart the display of file names from the top. Table III-7 shows the keys you can use with ZDIR.

Table III-7. The keys you can use when the directory is being displayed, before you return to the DOS prompt.

Key	Description
Space bar	Single-steps the display
Enter	Resumes display
Tab	Toggles between wide column and normal display
Backspace	Restarts the display from the top
Esc	Terminates ZDIR
A-Z	Begins first-letter file searching

The ASCII document ZDIR.DOC on the accompanying disk contains more information about ZDIR. Additional features include string searches, reverse wild cards, and patchable bytes within the program.

Author's Notes

Disclaimer. Although Zippy DIR Version 1.02 has been extensively tested, you use it at your own risk. I, Ray Johns, shall not be held liable in any way, for any damages which may result from the use, or misuse, of this or any program which I have written. This program is delivered in an "as is" condition.

Note that Zippy DIR does not write to the disk in any way and uses only the most standard DOS function calls. Zippy DIR runs on any IBM or compatible computer using MS-DOS/PC DOS version 2.00 or later.

Reference

Utility Software (50)

Utility Author Pages

The following pages are provided by the authors of the utility programs in exchange for the use of their software. Any arrangement or purchase of additional software is strictly between the author of that software and the purchaser. The publisher and author of this book are not implying or expressing an endorsement of any of this software.

Index

B

C

D

E

G

H

I-J

K

N

O

P-Q

R

S

T

U

V

W-Z

If your computer uses 3 1/2-inch disks . . .

Although most personal computers use 5 1/4-inch disks to store information, some newer computers are switching to 3 1/2-inch disks for information storage. If your computer uses 3 1/2-inch disks, you can return this form to SAMS to obtain a 3 1/2-inch disk to use with this book. Simply fill out the remainder of this form, and mail to:

Learning DOS
Disk Exchange
SAMS
11711 N. College Ave., Suite 140
Carmel, IN 46032

We will then send you, free of charge, the 3 1/2-inch version of the book software.

Name ______________________ Phone ______________

Company ____________________ Title ______________

Address ____

City ______________________ St ________ ZIP ________

Disk Installation

Although you can use the disk included with this book right away, you should first make a backup copy of the disk and use the backup copy for the exercises and other activities.

Get a 360K disk. At the system prompt, type the following to make a copy of the disk:

```
C:\>DISKCOPY A: A:
```

If you try to use the DOS programs DISKCOPY or XCOPY and you get the message `Bad command or file name`, refer to Part III, "Guide to Using the Disk."

Put the original disk away in a safe place. Label the second disk and use it for your exercises and for the Learning Guide.

> **If you make changes to this original disk, you'll be able to do the exercises only *once* because many of the exercises change the contents of the disk.**

The only files on the disk that need to be "installed" before you use them are the utility files. Part III covers the installation process. In short, you need to run the programs DOCS.EXE and UTILS.EXE in the \UTILS subdirectory in order to copy and uncompress the files to your hard disk. You'll learn how to copy and run programs as you read through this book.

Because space is limited on this disk, you may need to delete some files from the disk. After you have installed UTILS and DOCS on your hard disk, you can delete these two files from the accompanying disk to make more room for the Learning Guide data files.